"You're not really doing manga if you're getting enough exercise" goes the saying—which means I'm stiff as a board all the time. I know I should be stretching and doing some self-massage before bed and... Hey, it's kitty! Look at that face! Awww. That's better.

— Yoshiyuki Nishi

Yoshiyuki Nishi was born in Tokyo. Two of his favorite manga series are *Dragon Ball* and the robot-cat comedy *Doraemon*. His latest series, *Muhyo & Roji's Bureau of Supernatural Investigation*, debuted in Japan's *Akamaru Jump* magazine in 2004 and went on to be serialized in *Weekly Shonen Jump*.

MUHYO & ROJI'S

BUREAU OF SUPERNATURAL INVESTIGATION

VOL. 6
The SHONEN JUMP Manga Edition

STORY AND ART BY
YOSHIYUKI NISHI

Translation & Adaptation/Alexander O. Smith
Touch-up Art & Lettering/Brian Bilter
Design/Izumi Hirayama
Editor/Amy Yu

Editor in Chief, Books/Alvin Lu
Editor in Chief, Magazines/Marc Weidenbaum
VP of Publishing Licensing/Rika Inouye
VP of Sales/Gonzalo Ferreyra
Sr. VP of Marketing/Liza Coppola
Publisher/Hyoe Narita

Published by VIZ Media, LLC
P.O. Box 77010
San Francisco, CA 94107

SHONEN JUMP Manga Edition
10 9 8 7 6 5 4 3 2 1
First printing, August 2008

www.viz.com

THE WORLD'S
MOST POPULAR MANGA

www.shonenjump.com

SHONEN JUMP MANGA EDITION

Muhyo & Roji's
Bureau of Supernatural Investigation
BSI

Vol. 6 Awakening

Story & Art by **Yoshiyuki Nishi**

Dramatis Personae

Jiro Kusano (Roji)

Assistant at Muhyo's office and a "Second Clerk," the lowest of the five ranks of practitioners of magic law. Roji cries easily, is meek and gentle, and has been known to freak out in the presence of spirits. Irritated at his own inability to help Muhyo, Roji has devoted himself to studying magic law. Likes: tea and cakes. Dislikes: scary ghosts and scary Muhyo.

Toru Muhyo (Muhyo)

Genius elite practitioner of magic law, one of the youngest to achieve the highest rank of "Executor." Always calm and collected (though sometimes considered cold due to his tendency to make harsh comments), Muhyo possesses a strong sense of justice and has even been known to show kindness at times. Sleeps a lot to recover from the exhaustion caused by his practice. Likes: *Jabin* (a manga). Dislikes: interruptions while sleeping.

Yu Abiko (Biko)

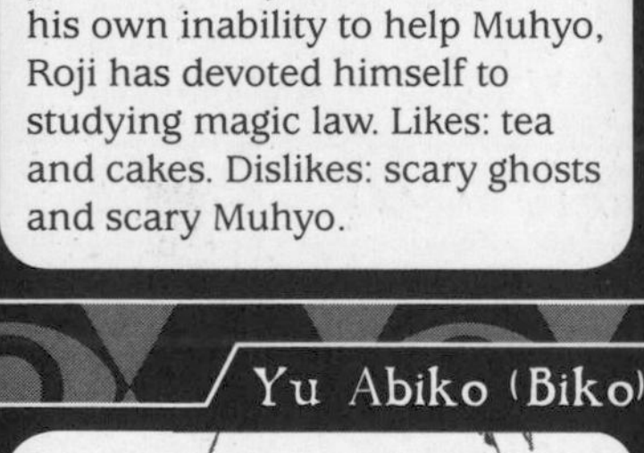

Muhyo's classmate and an Artificer. Makes seals, pens, magic law books, and other accoutrements of magic law.

Yoichi Himukai (Yoichi)

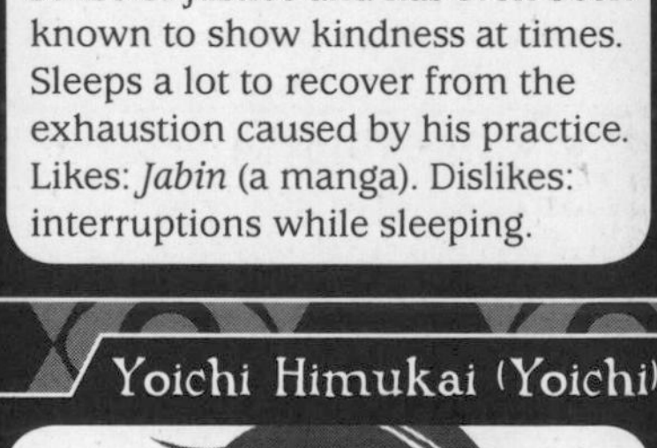

Judge and Muhyo's former classmate. Expert practitioner of all magic law except execution.

Hanao Ebisu (Ebisu)

Judge and Goryo's underling. Fears Goryo's wrath above all else and follows his orders to the letter.

Daranimaru Goryo (Goryo)

An Executor and gifted strategist who considers Muhyo his rival. Head of the centuries-old Goryo Group syndicate.

The Story

Magic law is a newly established practice for judging and punishing the increasing crimes committed by spirits; those who use it are called "practitioners."

The altercations at the prison Arcanum leave Muhyo at death's door with his tempering, or willpower, at rock-bottom. Nemesis Enchu does not deliver the final blow, choosing instead to abscond with fellow traitor Rio and prolong Muhyo's suffering. Meanwhile, events spur the Magic Law Association to begin a cleansing, targeting the practitioners of Forbidden Law… Muhyo and Roji return to their office to find fellow practitioners Goryo and Ebisu planning to take their office away from them. Muhyo accepts a challenge to defeat a pernicious ghost in a haunted apartment complex. The stakes: Muhyo and Roji's business. Muhyo proceeds to vanquish the ghost successfully, but…?!

Nana Takenouchi (Nana)

High school student and aspiring photographer. She's also a spirit medium, which gets her into all sorts of trouble…

Reiko Imai

Brave Judge who joined Muhyo and gang during the fight against Face-Ripper Sophie.

Page Klaus

Chief Investigator for the Magic Law Association. Muhyo and Enchu's old teacher and Yoichi's current supervisor.

Muhyo & Roji's

Bureau of Supernatural Investigation

BSI

CONTENTS

6

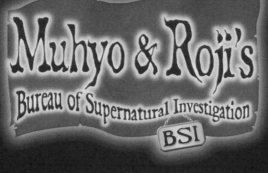

ARTICLE 42
MANUEVER 108

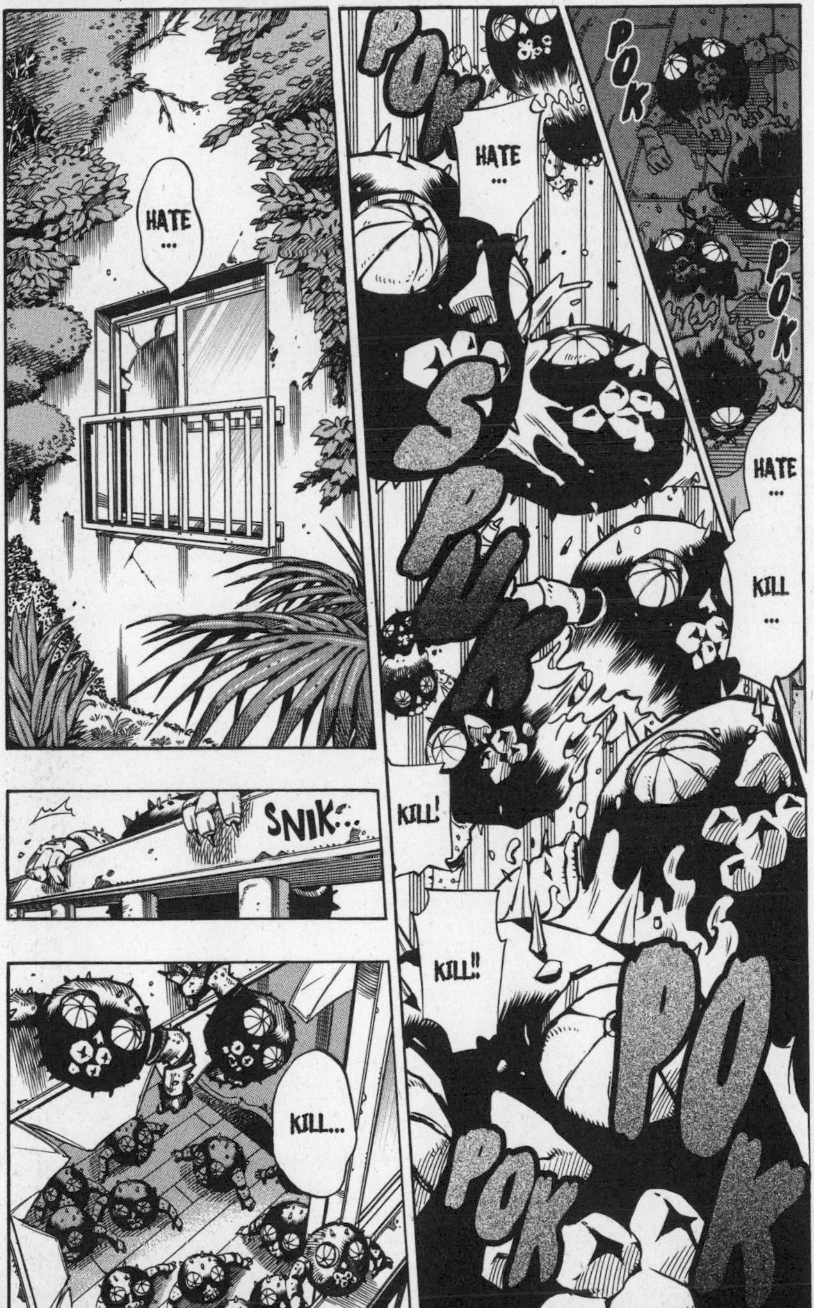
POK
POK
HATE...
KILL...
POK
HATE...
SPLUK
KILL!
KILL!!
POK
POK
HATE...
SNIK...
KILL...

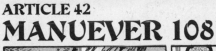

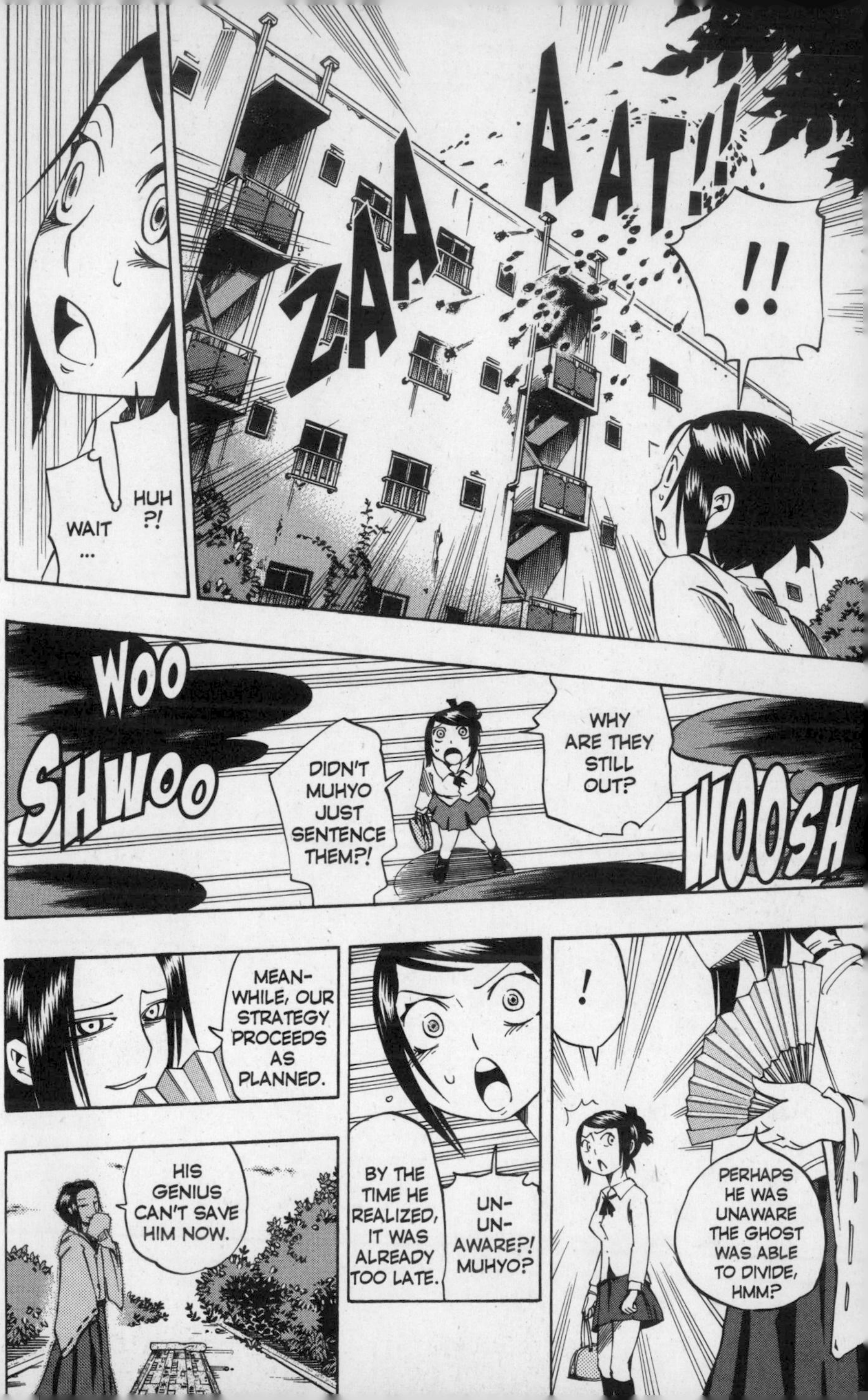
ZAAAAT!!
!!
HUH ?!
WAIT ...
WOOSH
WHY ARE THEY STILL OUT?
DIDN'T MUHYO JUST SENTENCE THEM?!
WOO SHWOO
!
PERHAPS HE WAS UNAWARE THE GHOST WAS ABLE TO DIVIDE, HMM?
UN-UN-AWARE?! MUHYO?
BY THE TIME HE REALIZED, IT WAS ALREADY TOO LATE.
MEAN-WHILE, OUR STRATEGY PROCEEDS AS PLANNED.
HIS GENIUS CAN'T SAVE HIM NOW.

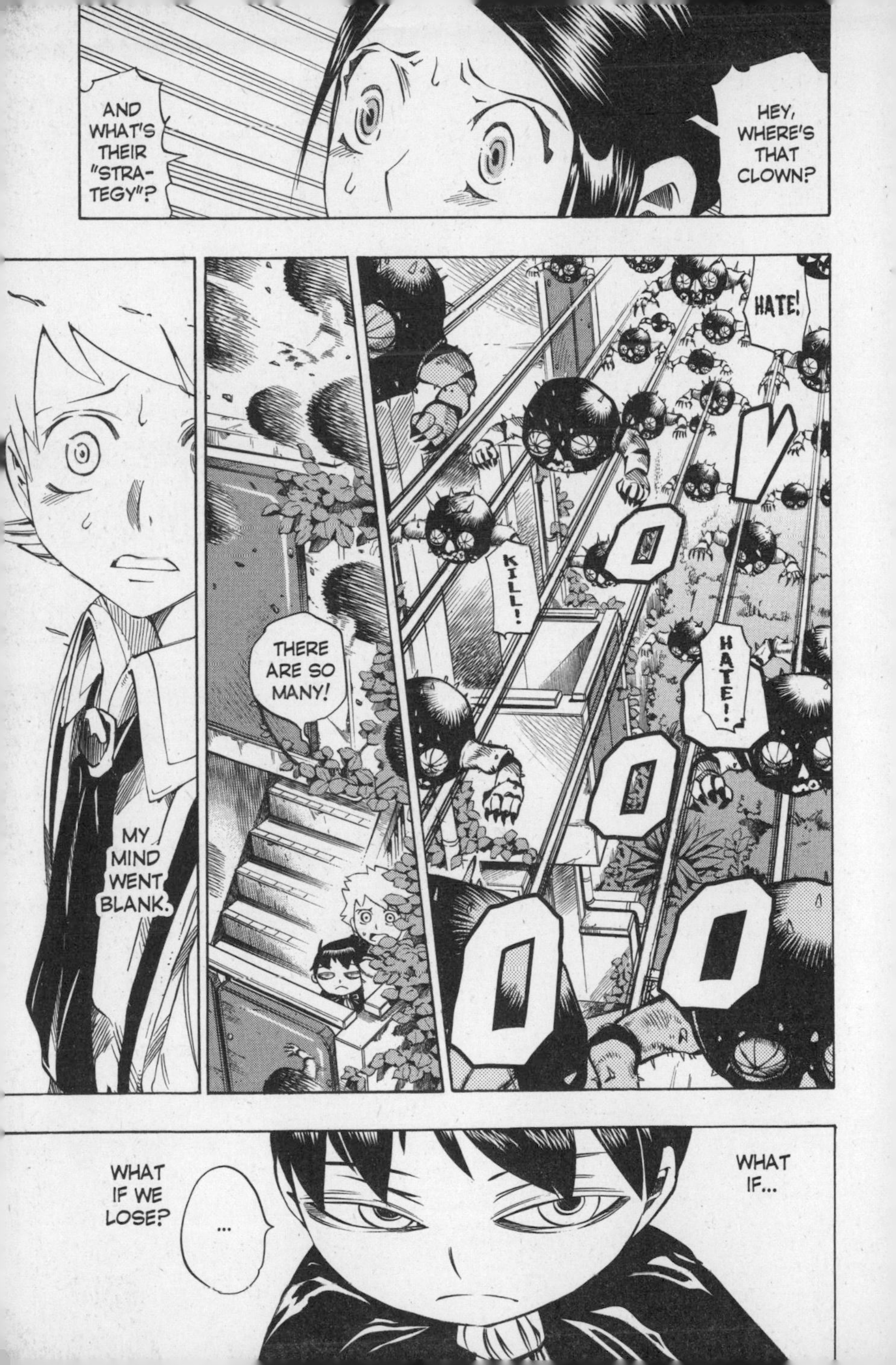
HEY, WHERE'S THAT CLOWN?
AND WHAT'S THEIR "STRATEGY"?
HATE!
VOOOOO
KILL!
HATE!
THERE ARE SO MANY!
MY MIND WENT BLANK.
WHAT IF...
...
WHAT IF WE LOSE?

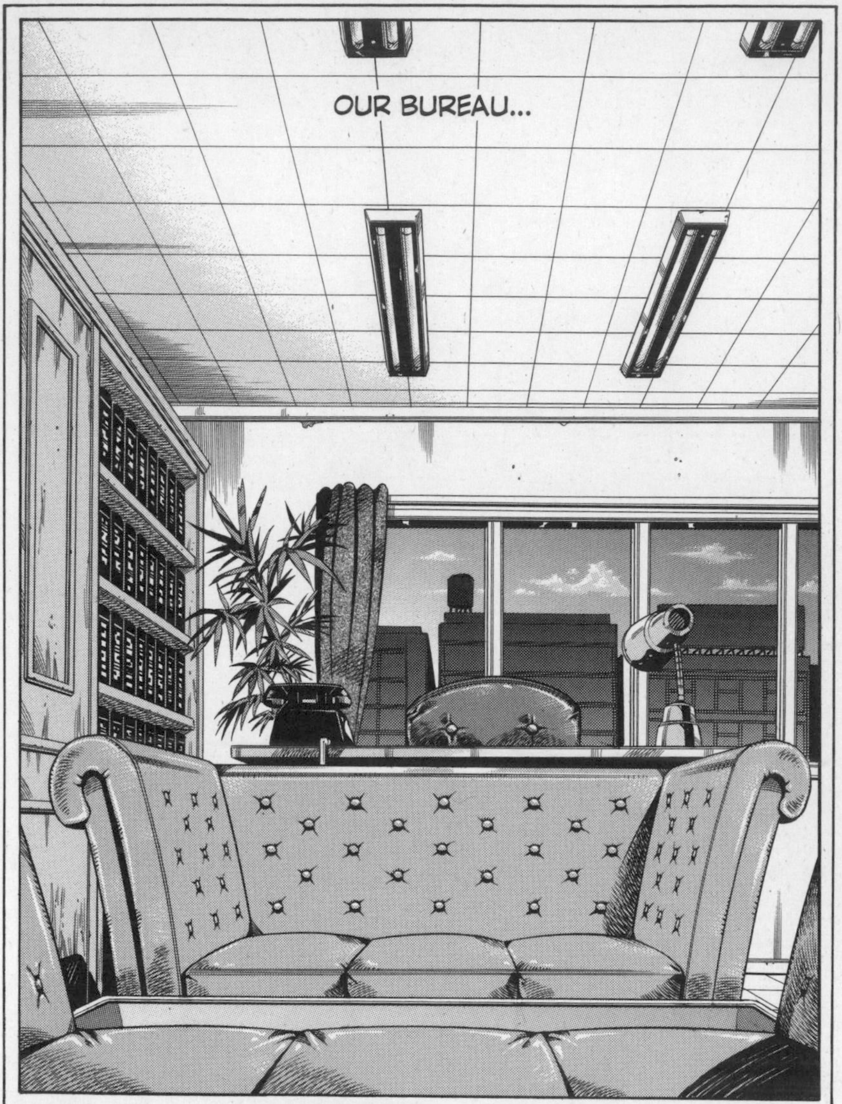
OUR BUREAU...

ARTICLE 42
MANUEVER 108

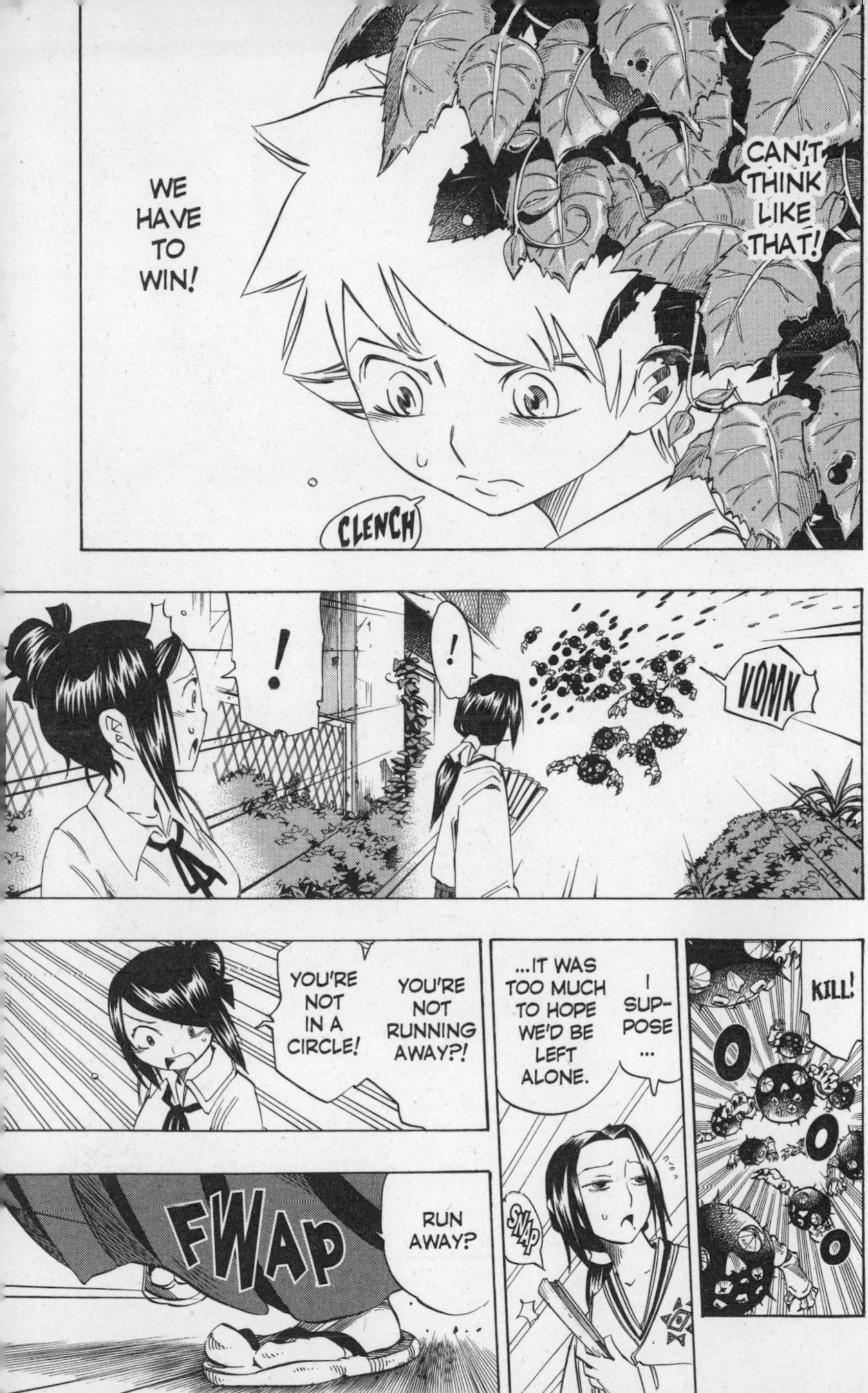
CAN'T THINK LIKE THAT!
WE HAVE TO WIN!
CLENCH
VOMK
!
!
KILL!
I SUPPOSE...
...IT WAS TOO MUCH TO HOPE WE'D BE LEFT ALONE.
SNAP
YOU'RE NOT RUNNING AWAY?!
YOU'RE NOT IN A CIRCLE!
RUN AWAY?
FWAP

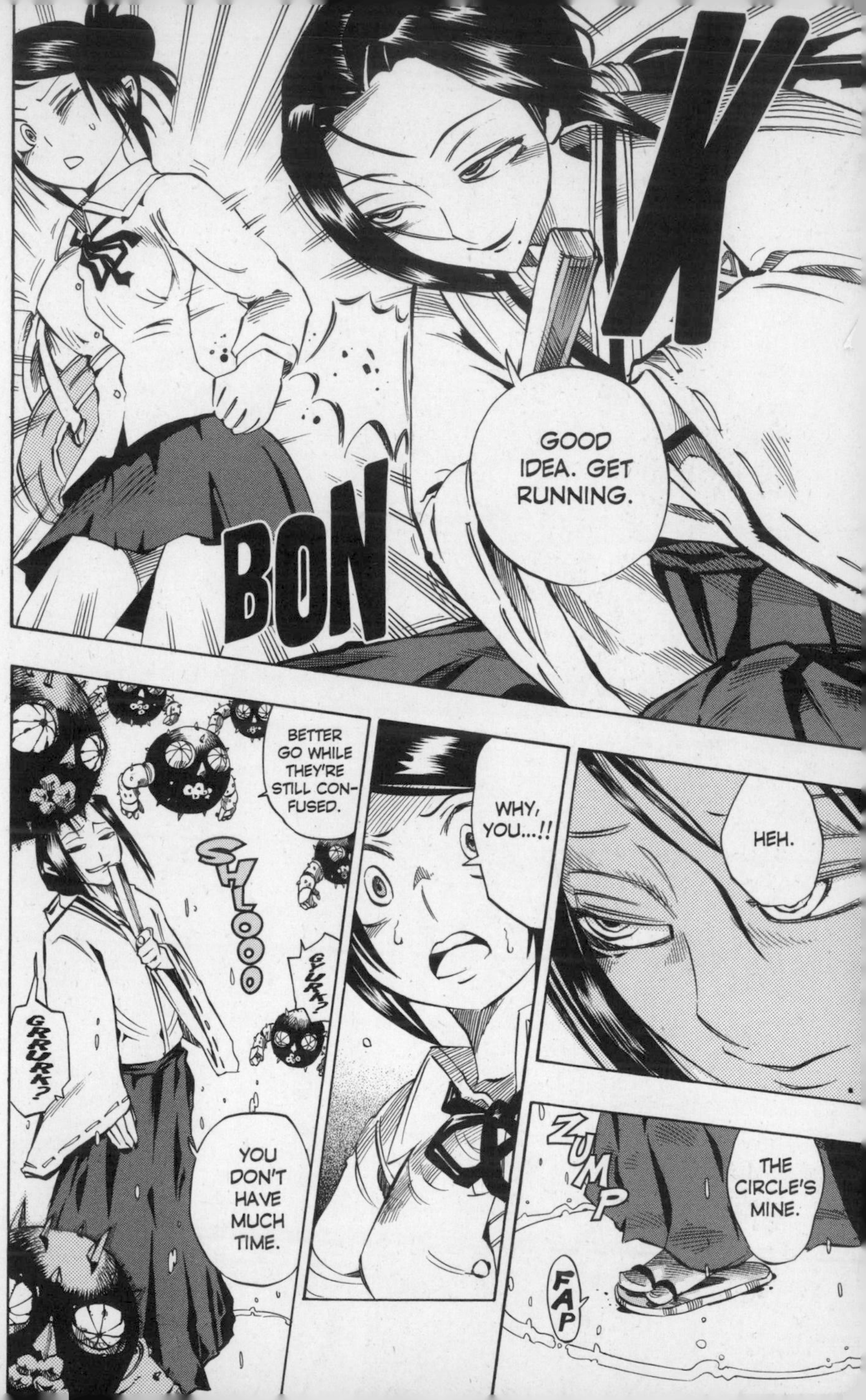
GOOD IDEA. GET RUNNING.
BON
HEH.
THE CIRCLE'S MINE.
ZUMP
FAP
WHY, YOU...!!
BETTER GO WHILE THEY'RE STILL CON-FUSED.
SHLOOO
GLURK?
GRRURK?
YOU DON'T HAVE MUCH TIME.

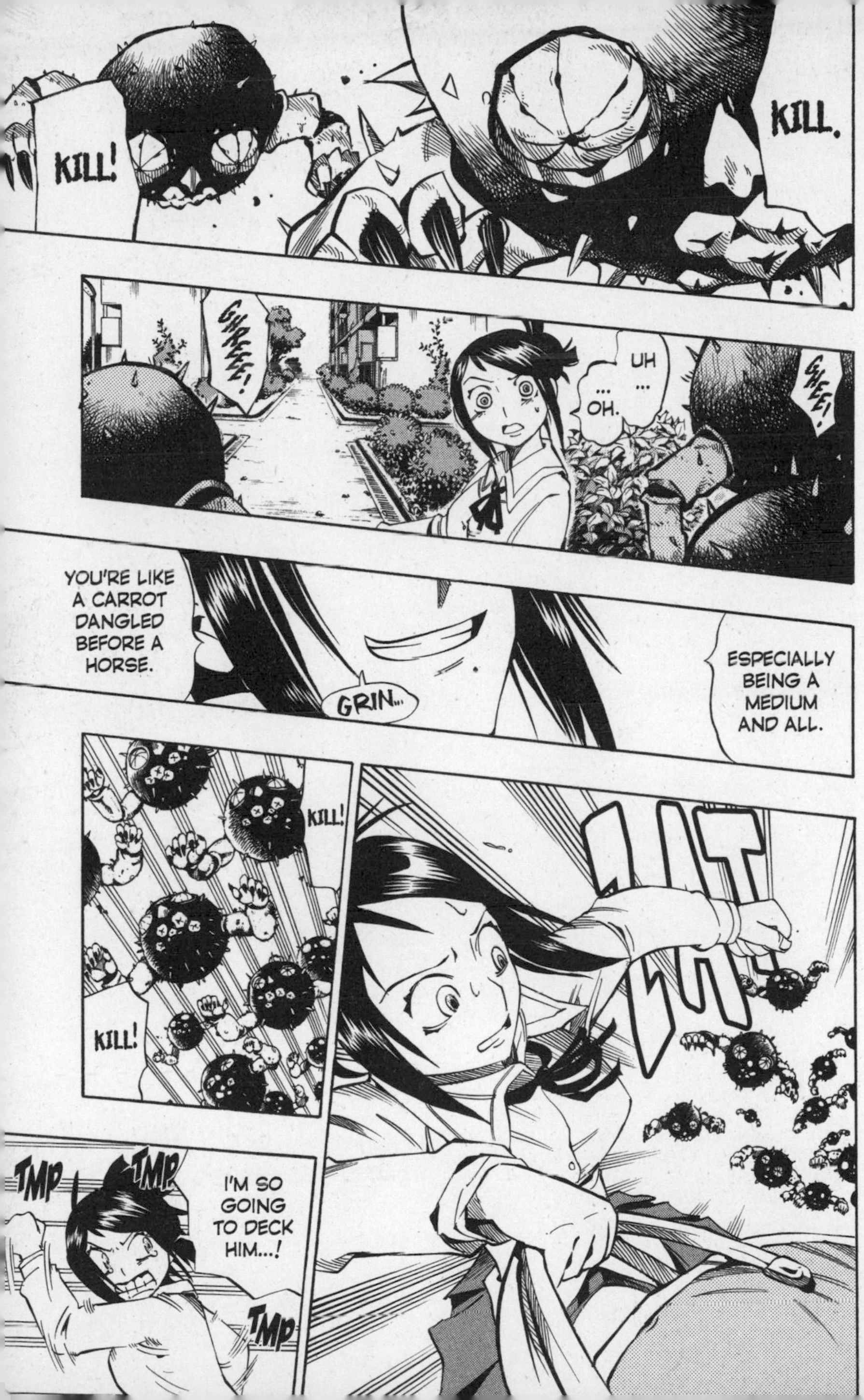
KILL.
KILL!
GHEE!
UH ... ... OH.
GHREEE!
ESPECIALLY BEING A MEDIUM AND ALL.
GRIN...
YOU'RE LIKE A CARROT DANGLED BEFORE A HORSE.
KILL!
KILL!
TMP
TMP
I'M SO GOING TO DECK HIM...!
TMP

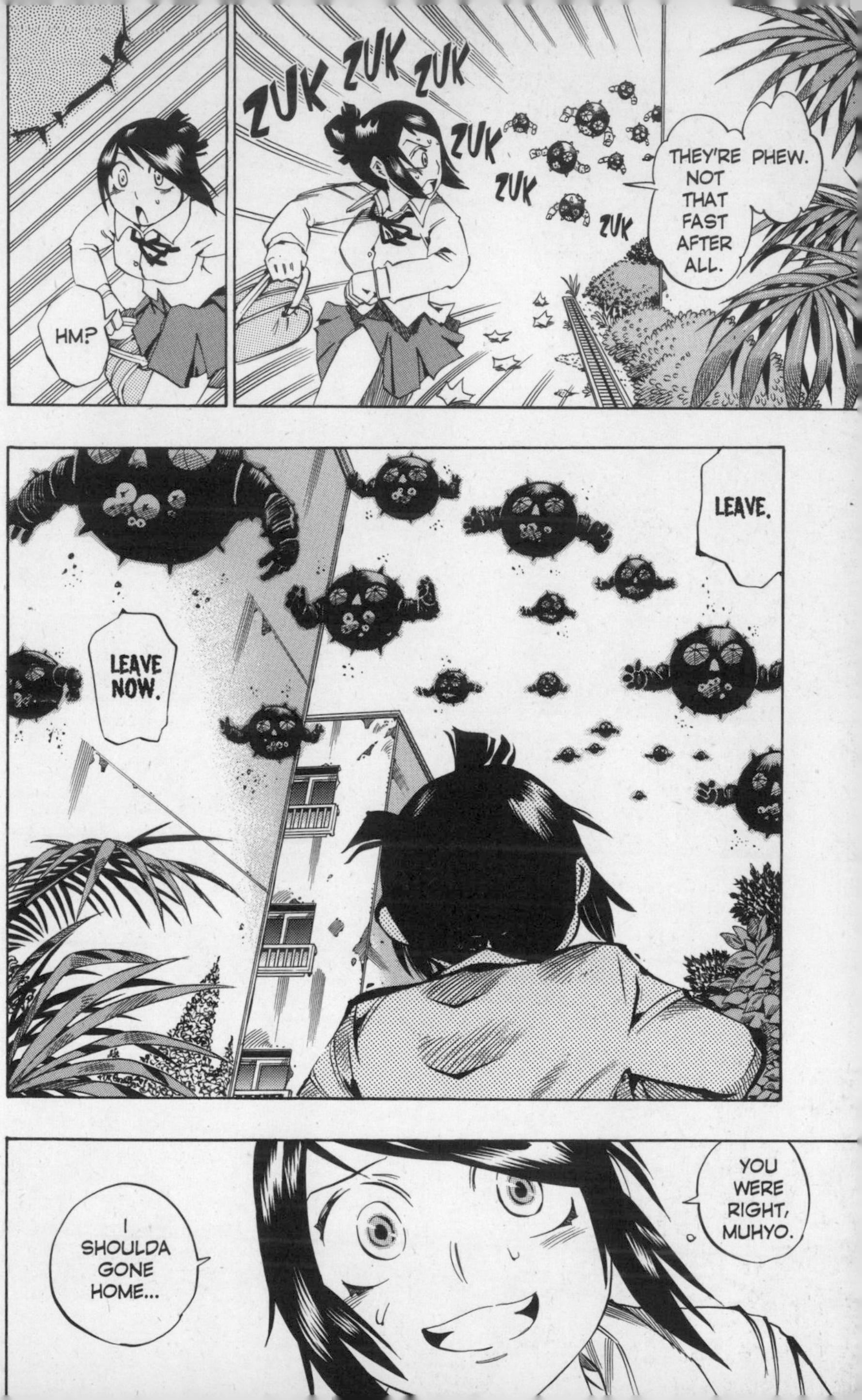
ZUK ZUK ZUK
ZUK
ZUK
ZUK
PHEW.
THEY'RE NOT THAT FAST AFTER ALL.
HM?
LEAVE.
LEAVE NOW.
YOU WERE RIGHT, MUHYO.
I SHOULDA GONE HOME...

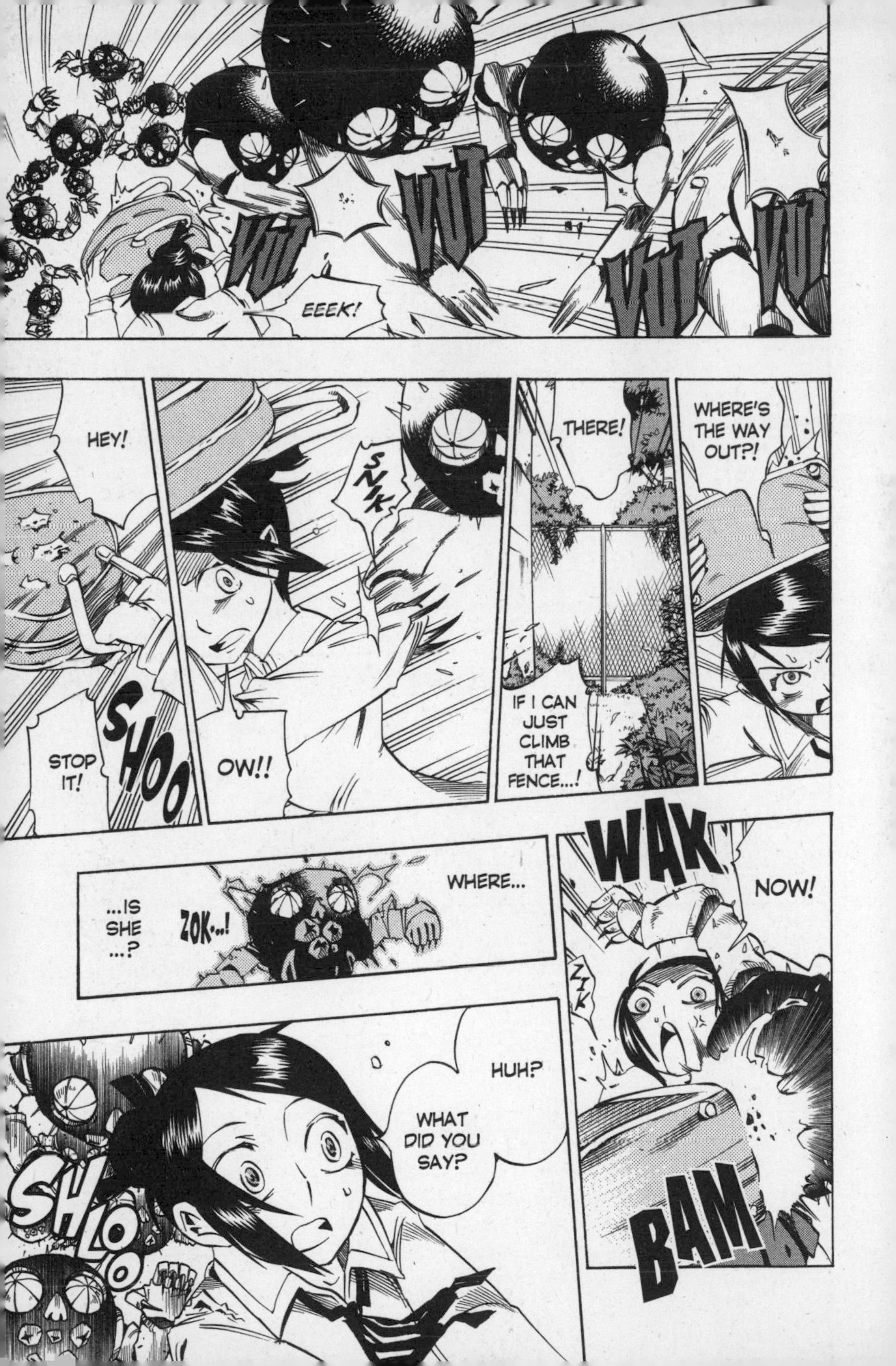
VUT
VUT
VUT
VUT
EEEK!
WHERE'S THE WAY OUT?!
THERE!
IF I CAN JUST CLIMB THAT FENCE...!
SNK
OW!!
HEY!
SHOO
STOP IT!
WAK
NOW!
ZIK
BAM
WHERE...
ZOK...!
...IS SHE ...?
HUH?
WHAT DID YOU SAY?
SHLOO

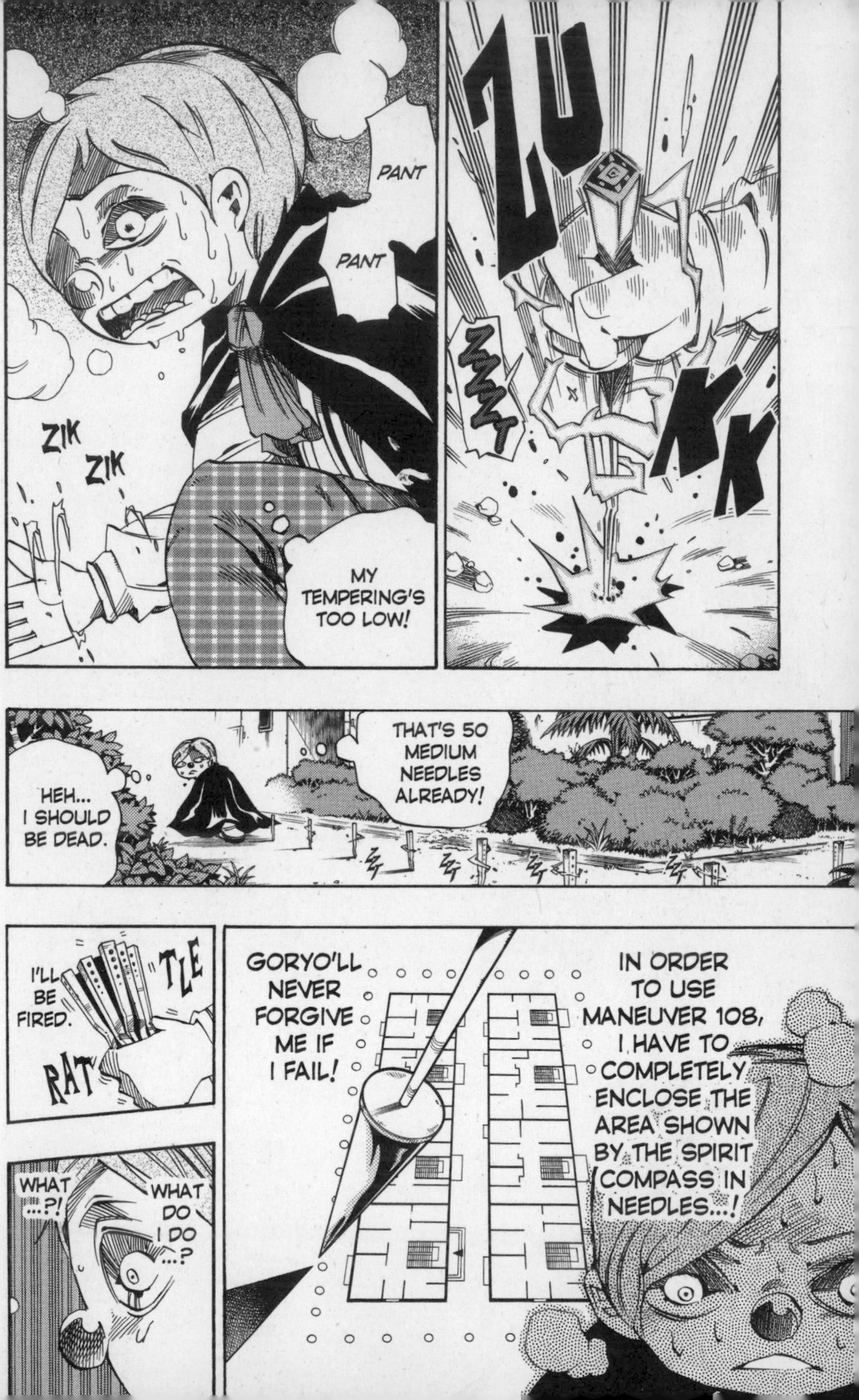

ZU
ZZZZT
KK
PANT
PANT
ZIK
ZIK
MY TEMPERING'S TOO LOW!
THAT'S 50 MEDIUM NEEDLES ALREADY!
HEH... I SHOULD BE DEAD.
IN ORDER TO USE MANEUVER 108, I HAVE TO COMPLETELY ENCLOSE THE AREA SHOWN BY THE SPIRIT COMPASS IN NEEDLES...!
GORYO'LL NEVER FORGIVE ME IF I FAIL!
TLE
I'LL BE FIRED.
RAT
WHAT ...?!
WHAT DO I DO ...?

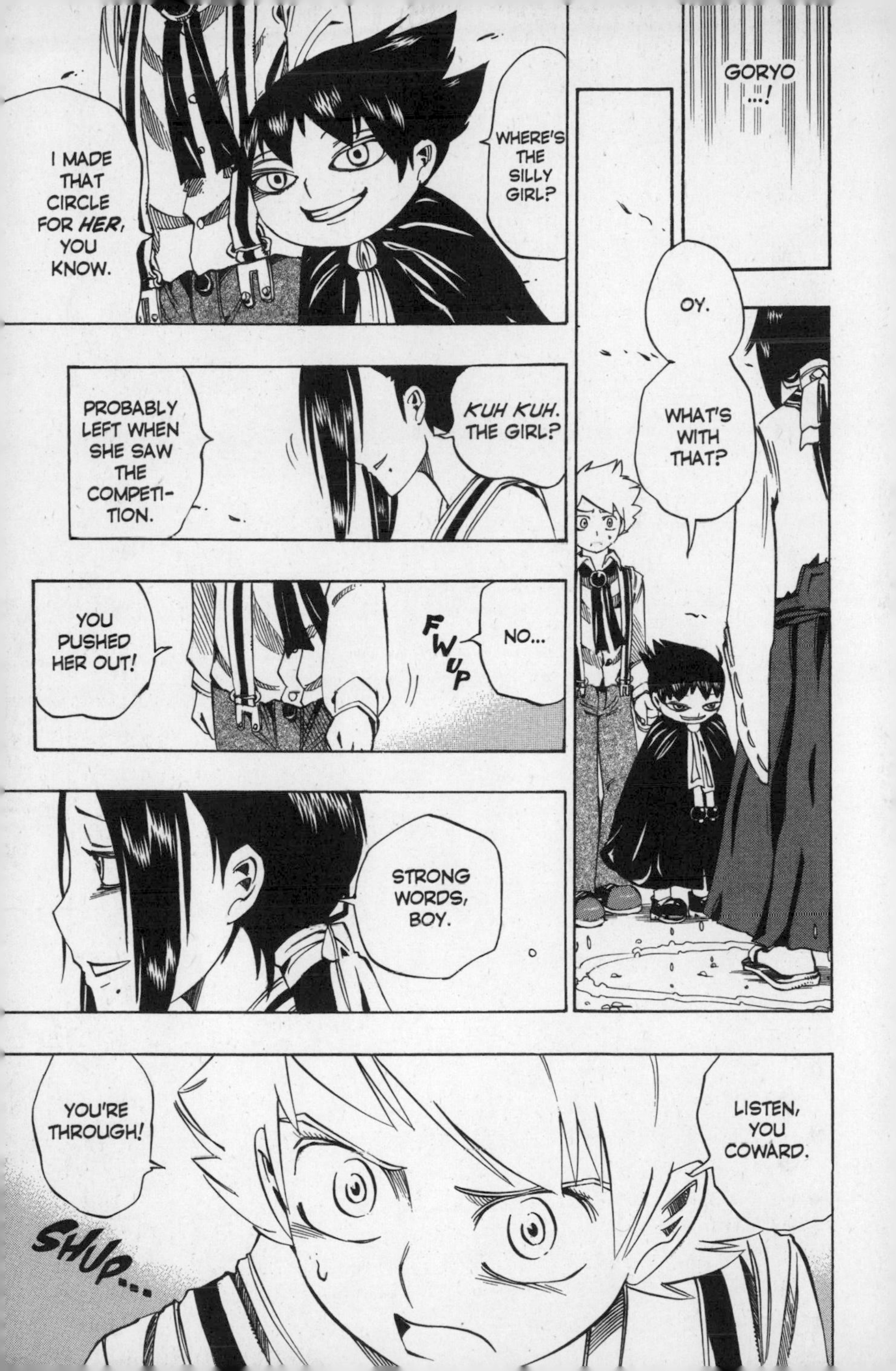
GORYO ...!
OY.
WHAT'S WITH THAT?
WHERE'S THE SILLY GIRL?
I MADE THAT CIRCLE FOR *HER*, YOU KNOW.
KUH KUH. THE GIRL?
PROBABLY LEFT WHEN SHE SAW THE COMPETITION.
NO...
FWUP
YOU PUSHED HER OUT!
STRONG WORDS, BOY.
LISTEN, YOU COWARD.
YOU'RE THROUGH!
SHUP...

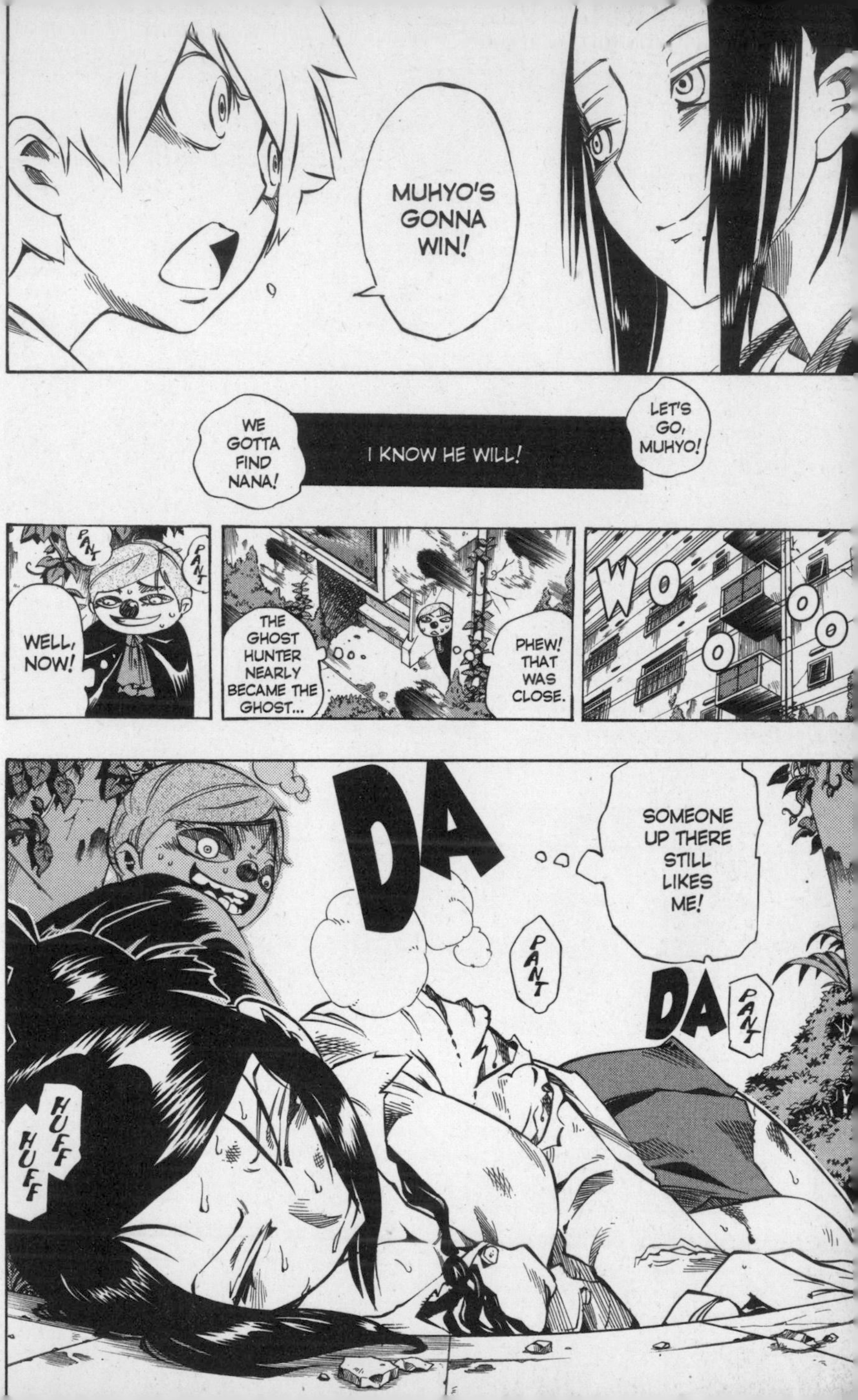
MUHYO'S GONNA WIN!
LET'S GO, MUHYO!
I KNOW HE WILL!
WE GOTTA FIND NANA!
WOOOOO
PHEW! THAT WAS CLOSE.
THE GHOST HUNTER NEARLY BECAME THE GHOST...
PANT
PANT
WELL, NOW!
SOMEONE UP THERE STILL LIKES ME!
DA
DA
PANT
PANT
HUFF
HUFF

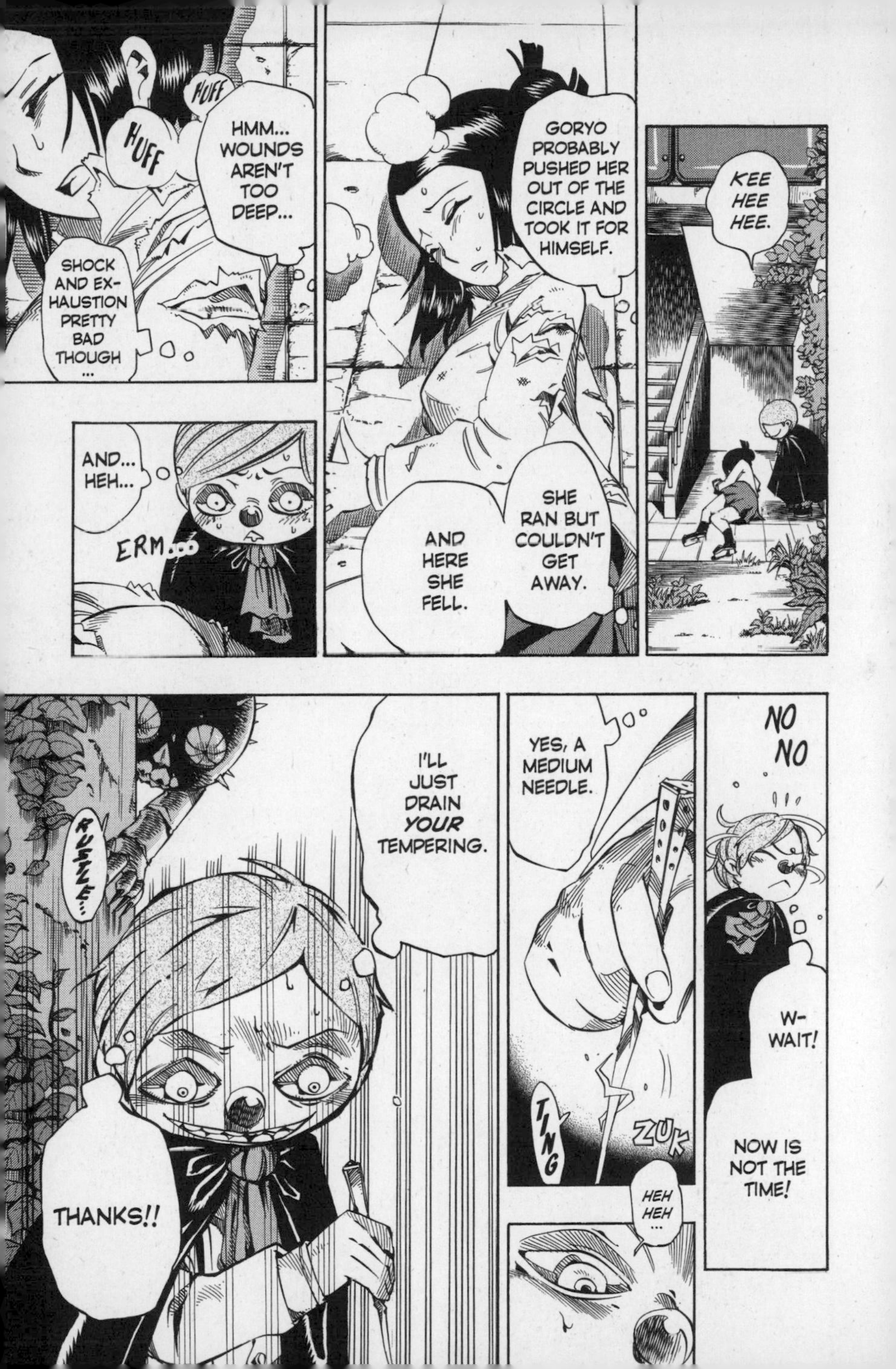
KEE HEE HEE.
GORYO PROBABLY PUSHED HER OUT OF THE CIRCLE AND TOOK IT FOR HIMSELF.
SHE RAN BUT COULDN'T GET AWAY.
AND HERE SHE FELL.
HUFF
HUFF
HMM... WOUNDS AREN'T TOO DEEP...
SHOCK AND EX-HAUSTION PRETTY BAD THOUGH ...
AND... HEH...
ERM...
NO NO
W-WAIT!
NOW IS NOT THE TIME!
YES, A MEDIUM NEEDLE.
TING
ZUK
HEH HEH ...
I'LL JUST DRAIN *YOUR* TEMPERING.
RUSTLE...
THANKS!!

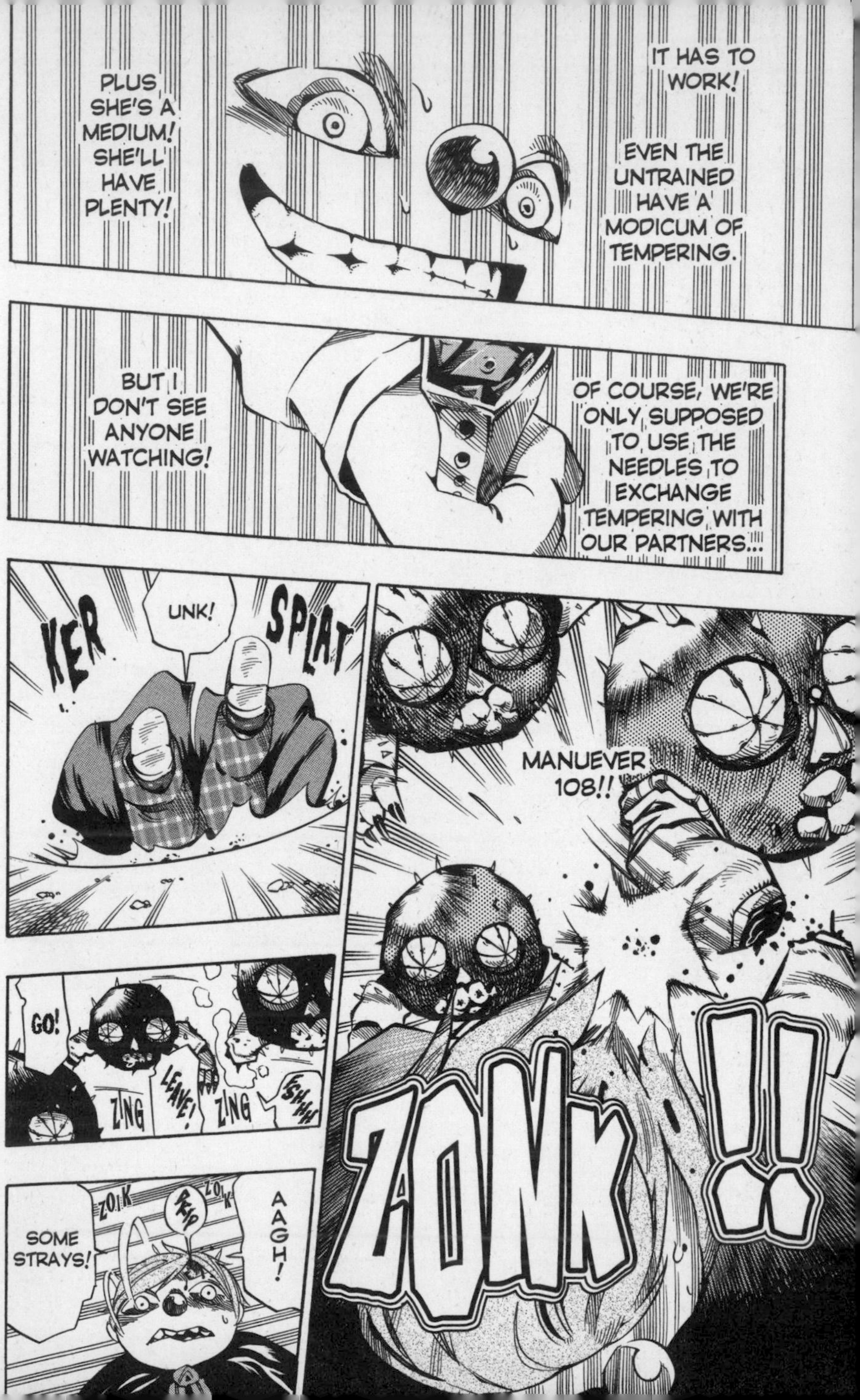

IT HAS TO WORK!
EVEN THE UNTRAINED HAVE A MODICUM OF TEMPERING.
PLUS SHE'S A MEDIUM! SHE'LL HAVE PLENTY!
OF COURSE, WE'RE ONLY SUPPOSED TO USE THE NEEDLES TO EXCHANGE TEMPERING WITH OUR PARTNERS...
BUT I DON'T SEE ANYONE WATCHING!
MANUEVER 108!!
ZONK!!
KER SPLAT
UNK!
FSHHH
ZING
LEAVE!
ZING
GO!
ZOIK ZOIK
DRIP
AAGH!
SOME STRAYS!

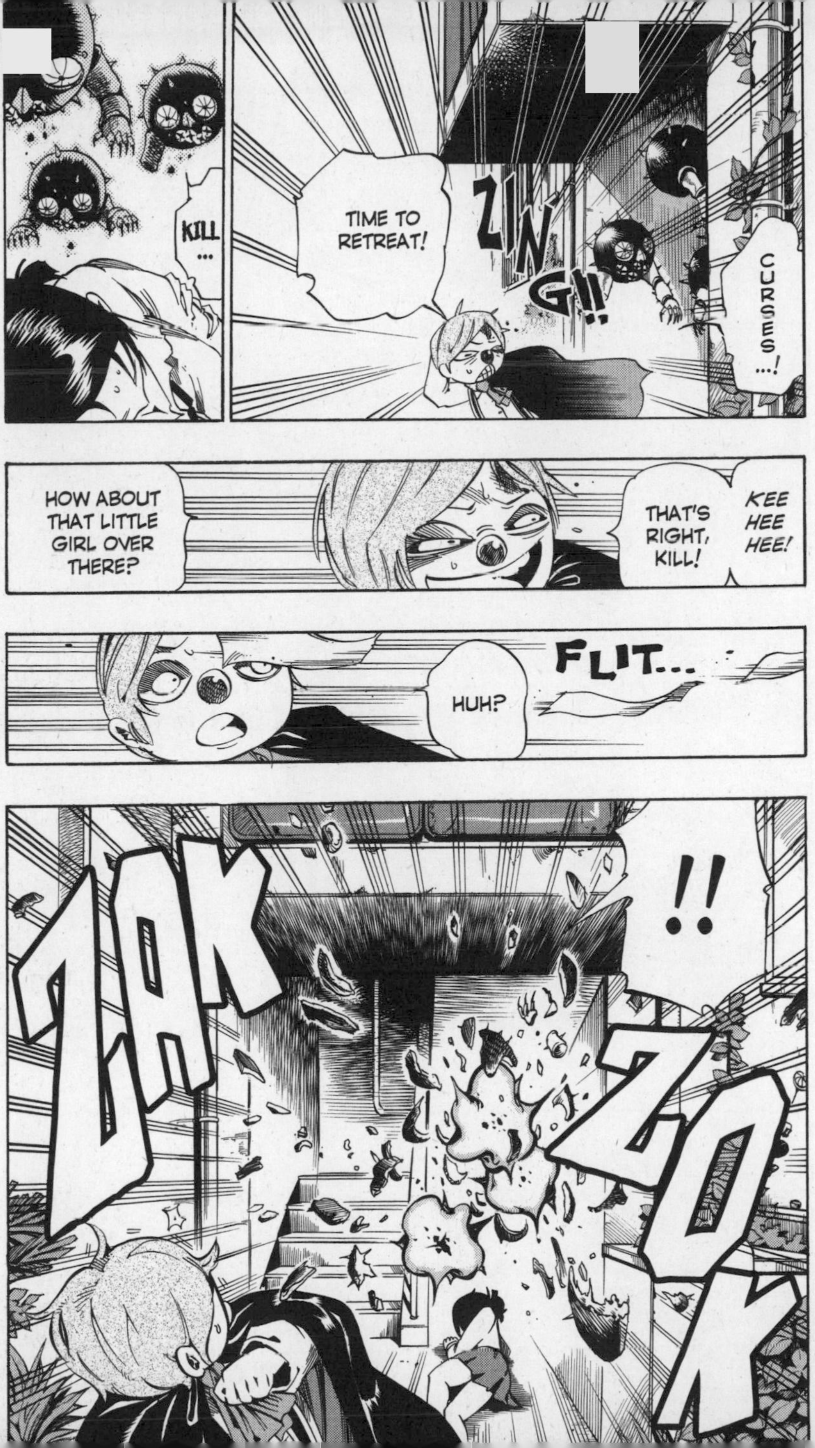
CURSES ...!
ZING!!
TIME TO RETREAT!
KILL ...
KEE HEE HEE!
THAT'S RIGHT, KILL!
HOW ABOUT THAT LITTLE GIRL OVER THERE?
FLIT...
HUH?
!!
ZOK
ZAK

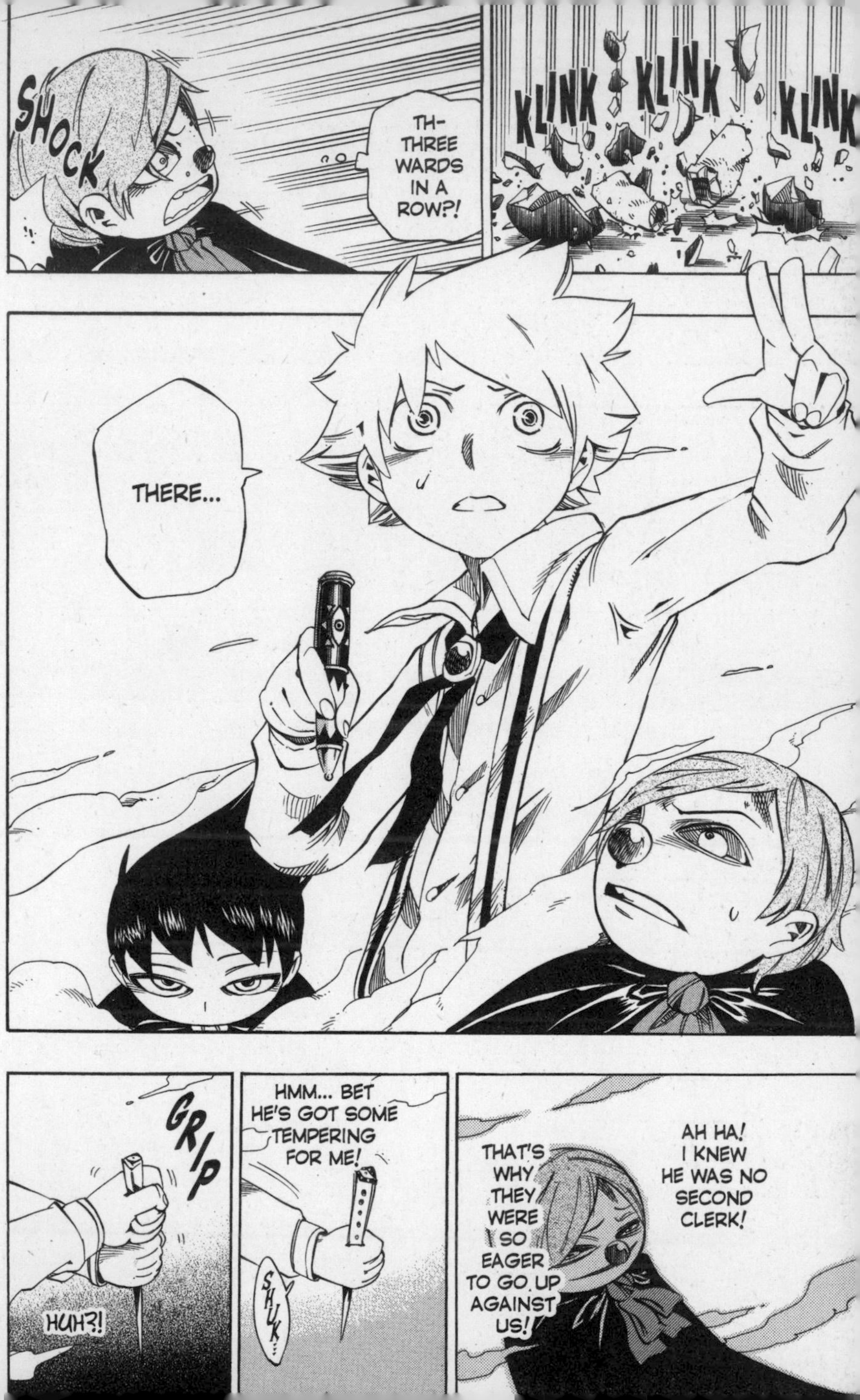
KLINK KLINK KLINK
SHOCK
TH- THREE WARDS IN A ROW?!
THERE...
AH HA! I KNEW HE WAS NO SECOND CLERK!
THAT'S WHY THEY WERE SO EAGER TO GO UP AGAINST US!
HMM... BET HE'S GOT SOME TEMPERING FOR ME!
SHUK...
GRIP
HUH?!

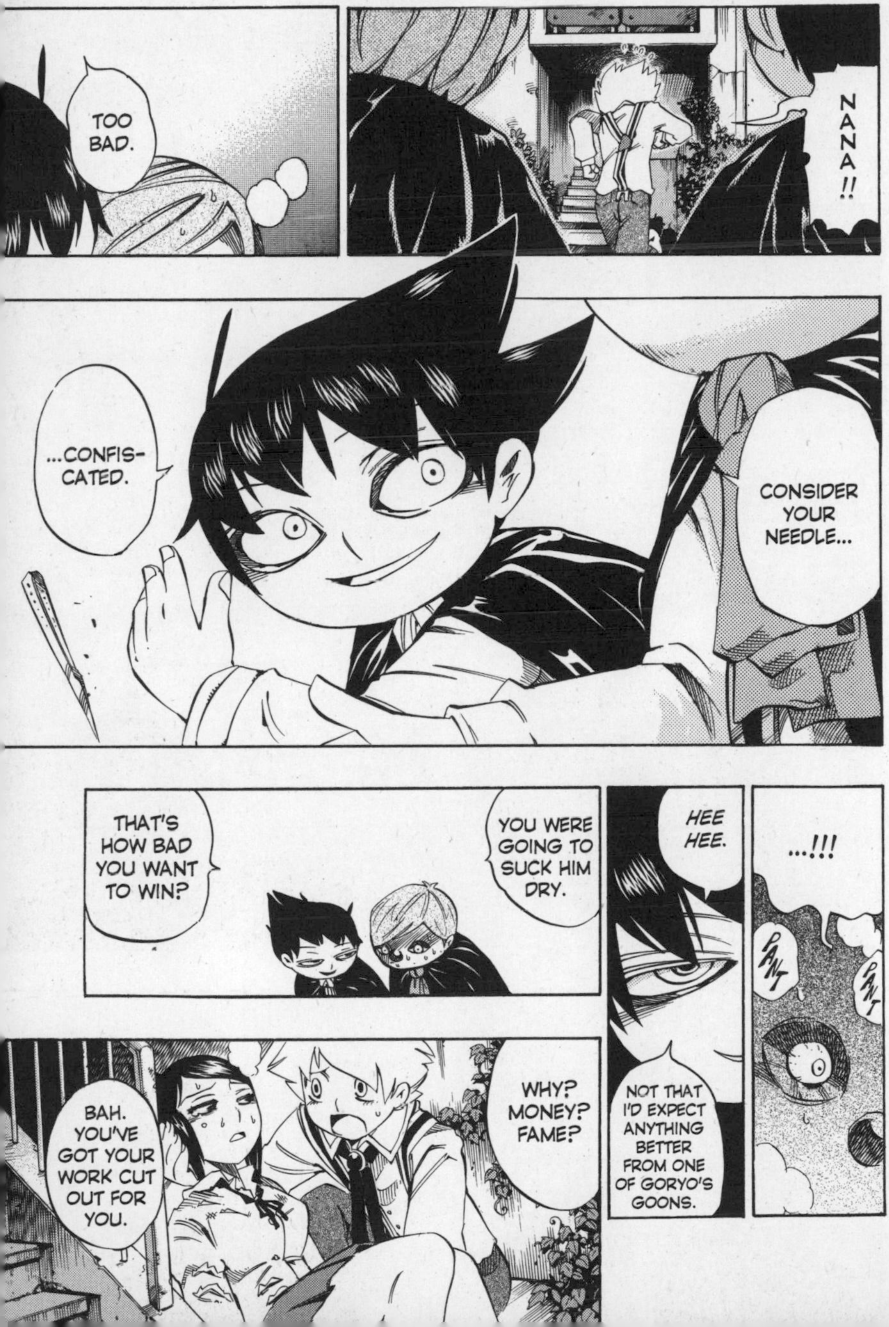
NANA!!
TOO BAD.
CONSIDER YOUR NEEDLE...
...CONFIS-CATED.
...!!!
PANT
PANT
HEE HEE.
NOT THAT I'D EXPECT ANYTHING BETTER FROM ONE OF GORYO'S GOONS.
YOU WERE GOING TO SUCK HIM DRY.
THAT'S HOW BAD YOU WANT TO WIN?
WHY? MONEY? FAME?
BAH. YOU'VE GOT YOUR WORK CUT OUT FOR YOU.

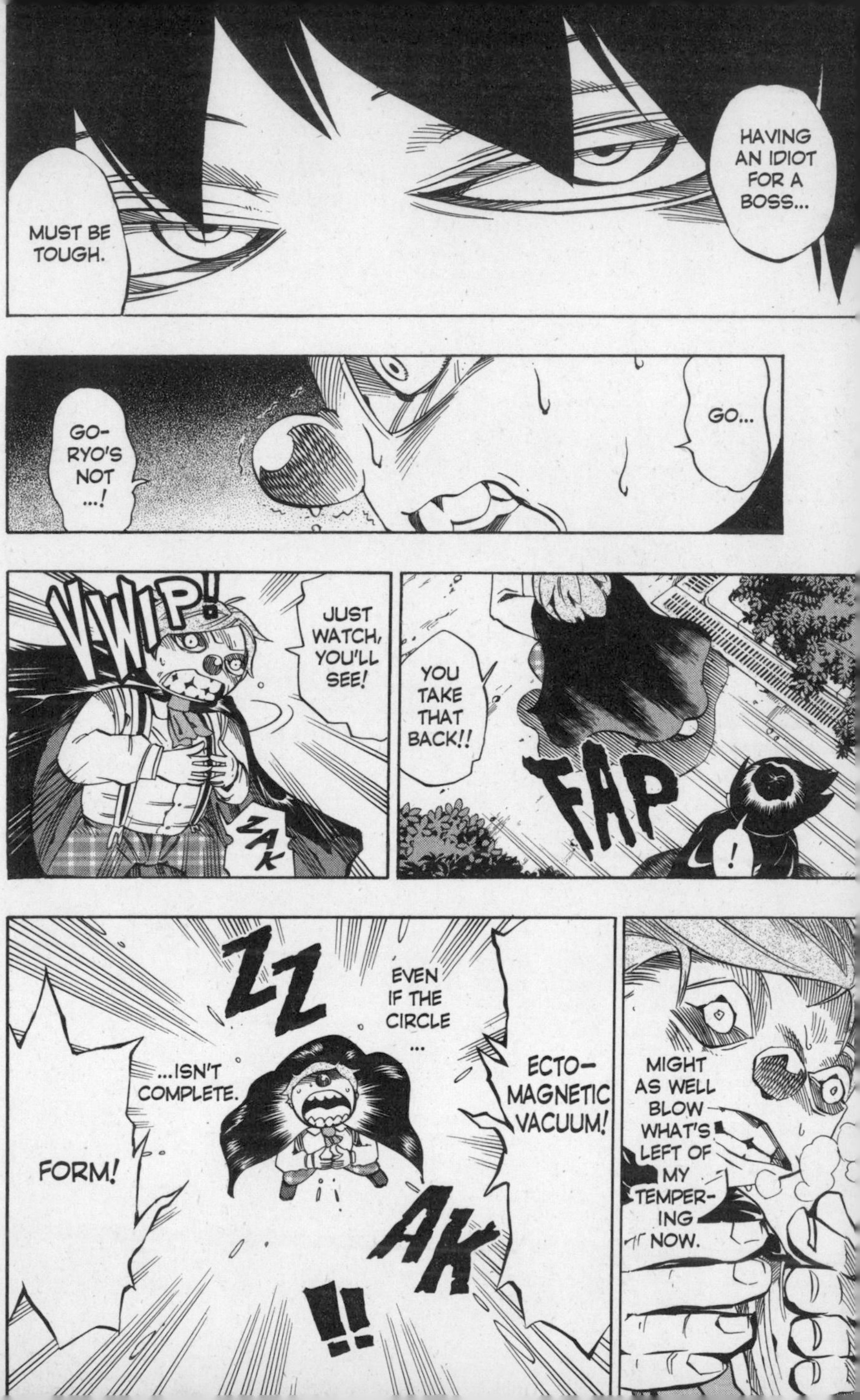
HAVING AN IDIOT FOR A BOSS...
MUST BE TOUGH.
GO...
GO-RYO'S NOT ...!
YOU TAKE THAT BACK!!
FAP
!
VWIP!
JUST WATCH, YOU'LL SEE!
ZAK
MIGHT AS WELL BLOW WHAT'S LEFT OF MY TEMPERING NOW.
ECTO-MAGNETIC VACUUM!
EVEN IF THE CIRCLE ...
...ISN'T COMPLETE.
FORM!
ZZ
AK
!!

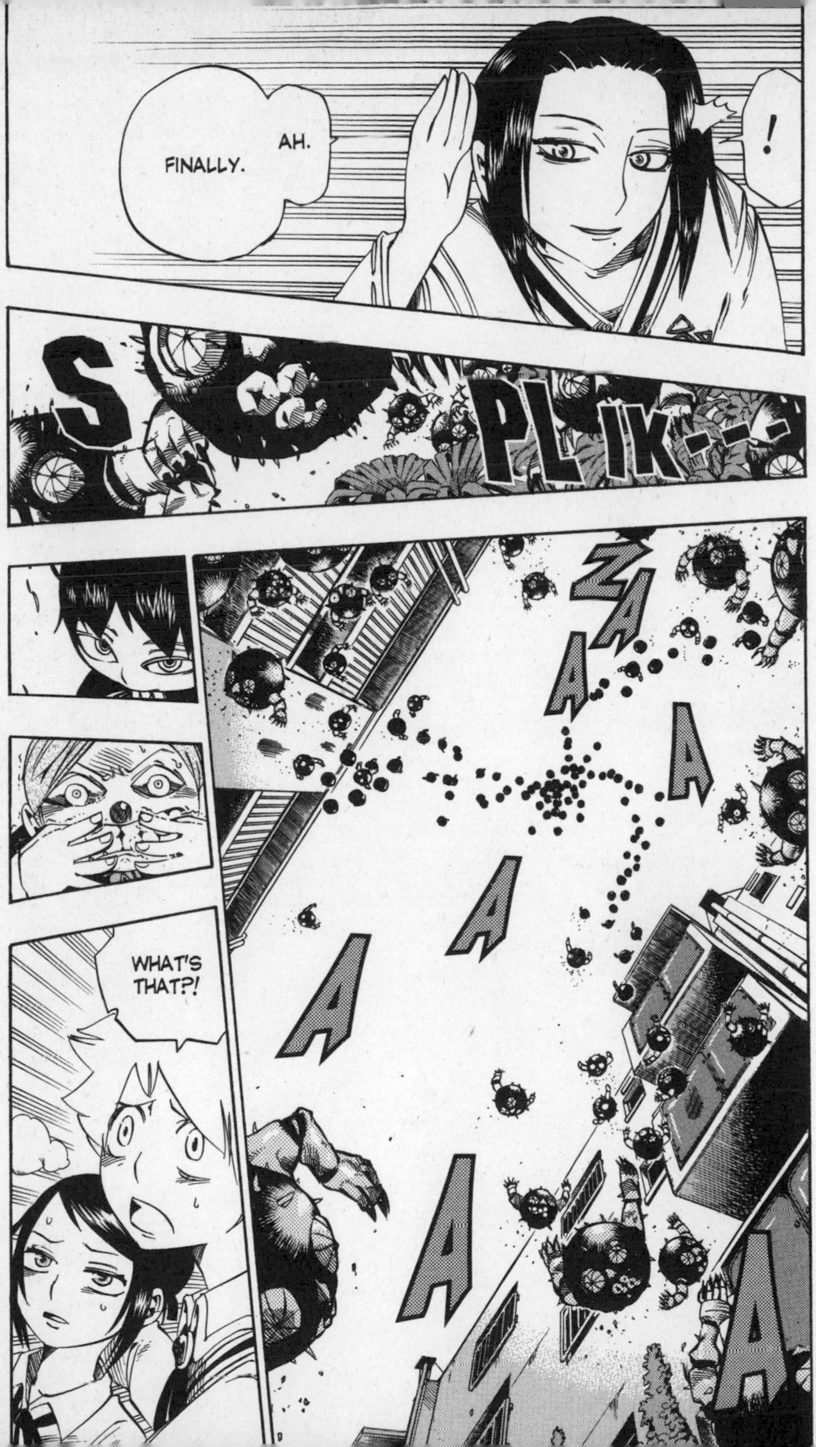
!
AH. FINALLY.
SPLIK...
ZAAAAAAA
WHAT'S THAT?!

I DID A LOT OF SILLY BONUS MANGA IN THE LAST VOLUME, SO THE QUESTIONS HAVE REALLY PILED UP. NOW LET'S GET SOME OF THESE GUYS PROPERLY ANSWERED!!

Q: WHY IS THE MANGA THAT MUHYO AND ROJI READ CALLED *JABIN*? COULDN'T YOU CALL IT *JUMP*?
—M.T., TOKYO

A: HAH! DIDN'T SEE THAT ONE COMING! ACTUALLY, IT USED TO BE *JUMP*. REMEMBER THE ONE THAT SHOWS UP IN ARTICLE 1, PAGE 8? WELL, I HAD IT AS *JUMP* ORIGINALLY, BUT MY EDITOR MR. K DIDN'T THINK HAVING A *JUMP* GETTING RIPPED IN TWO WAS GOOD BUSINESS. "HEY, NISHI! NO! REJECTED! CHANGE IT!" SO I DID, TO *JABIN*. INCIDENTALLY, MR. K LOVES TO SHOUT OUT "NO!" AND MAKE AN "X" IN THE AIR WITH HIS ARMS. IT'S KINDA FUNNY.

ARTICLE 43
HER VOICE

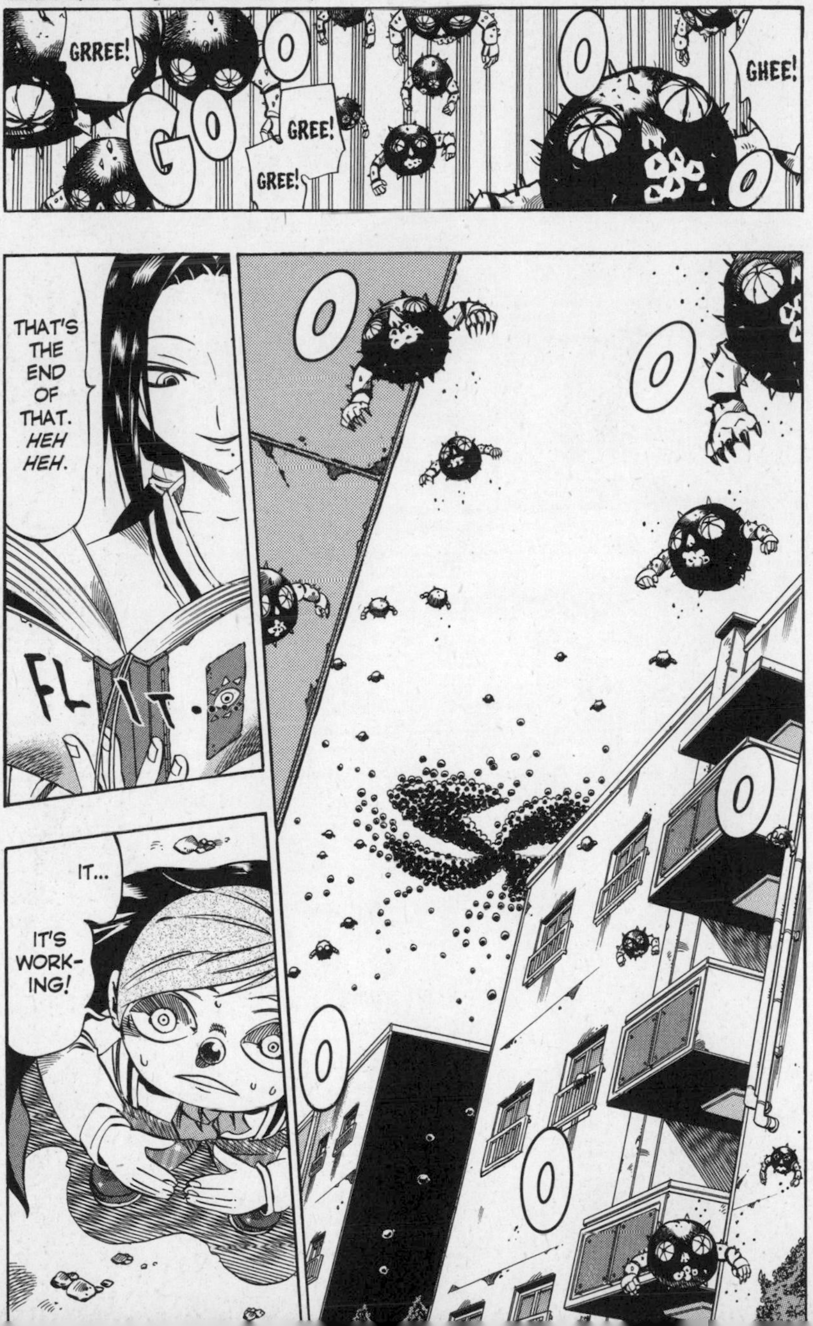

GHEE!
GOOOO
GREE!
GREE!
GRREE!
OOOOOO
THAT'S THE END OF THAT. *HEH HEH.*
FLIT
IT...
IT'S WORKING!

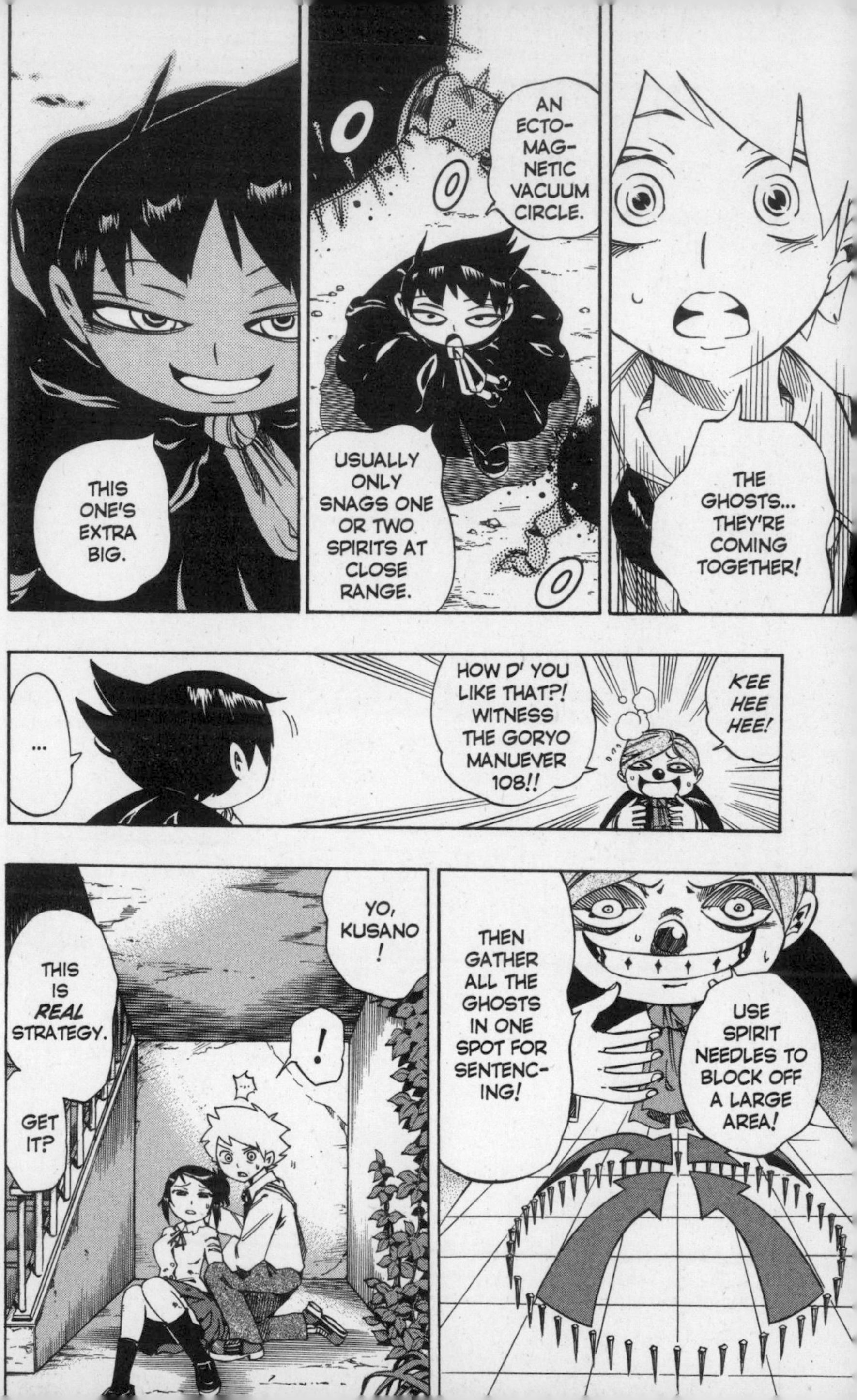
THE GHOSTS... THEY'RE COMING TOGETHER!
AN ECTO-MAGNETIC VACUUM CIRCLE.
USUALLY ONLY SNAGS ONE OR TWO SPIRITS AT CLOSE RANGE.
THIS ONE'S EXTRA BIG.
KEE HEE HEE!
HOW D' YOU LIKE THAT?! WITNESS THE GORYO MANUEVER 108!!
...
USE SPIRIT NEEDLES TO BLOCK OFF A LARGE AREA!
THEN GATHER ALL THE GHOSTS IN ONE SPOT FOR SENTENCING!
YO, KUSANO!
!
THIS IS *REAL* STRATEGY.
GET IT?

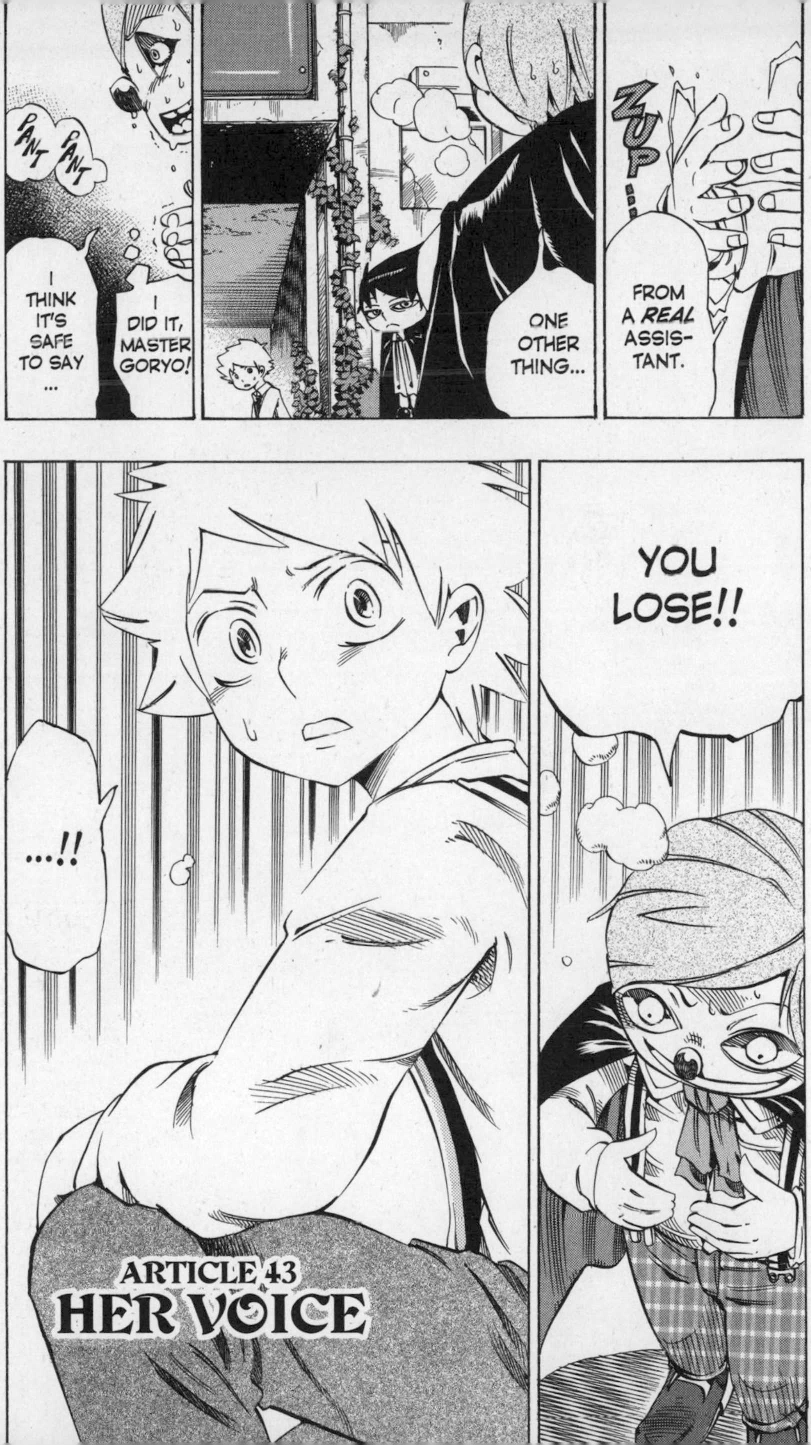
ZUP...
FROM A *REAL* ASSIS-TANT.
ONE OTHER THING...
PANT PANT
I DID IT, MASTER GORYO!
I THINK IT'S SAFE TO SAY ...
YOU LOSE!!
...!!
ARTICLE 43
HER VOICE

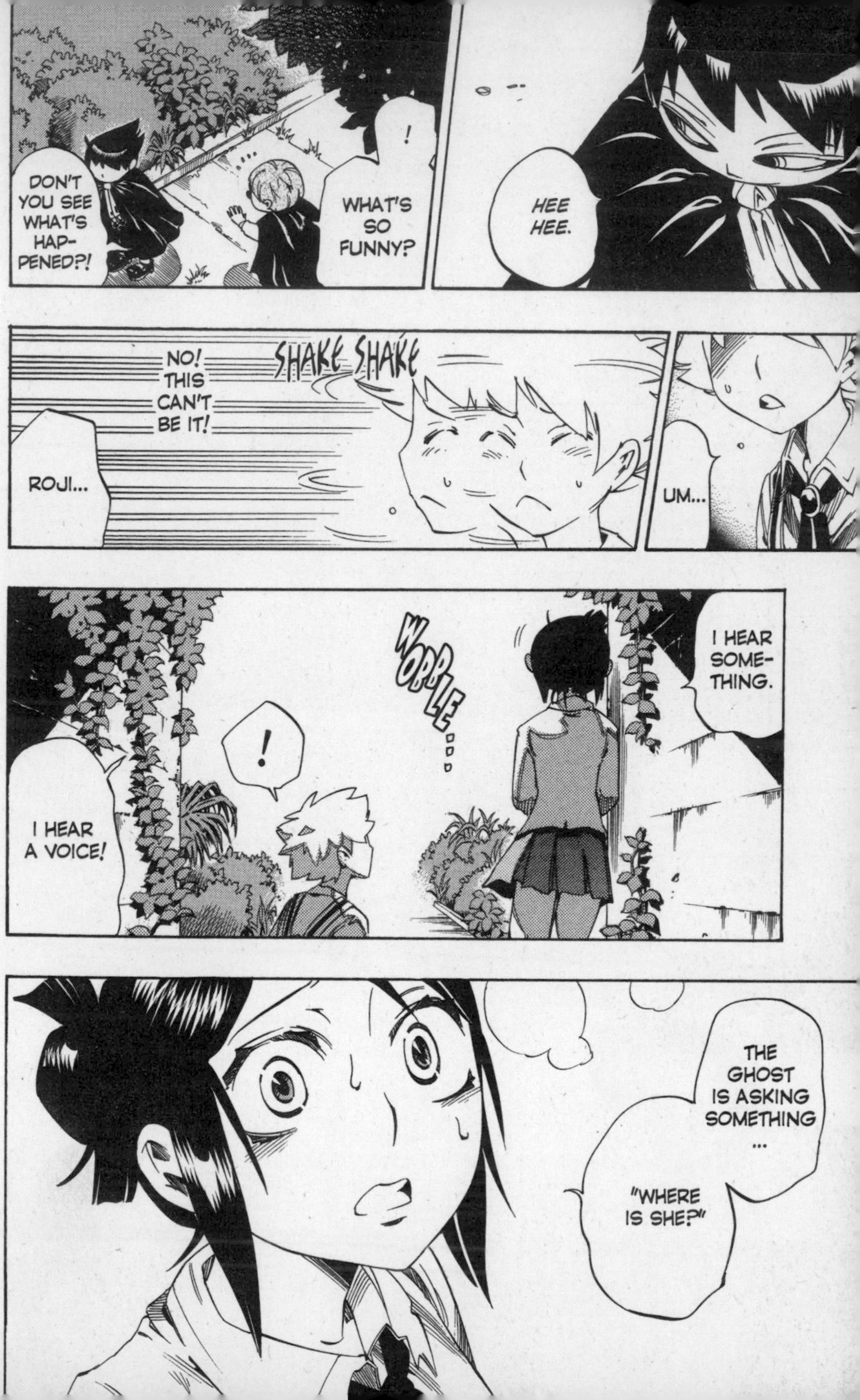
HEE HEE.
!
WHAT'S SO FUNNY?
DON'T YOU SEE WHAT'S HAP-PENED?!
UM...
SHAKE SHAKE
NO! THIS CAN'T BE IT!
ROJI...
I HEAR SOME-THING.
WOBBLE
!
I HEAR A VOICE!
THE GHOST IS ASKING SOMETHING ...
"WHERE IS SHE?"

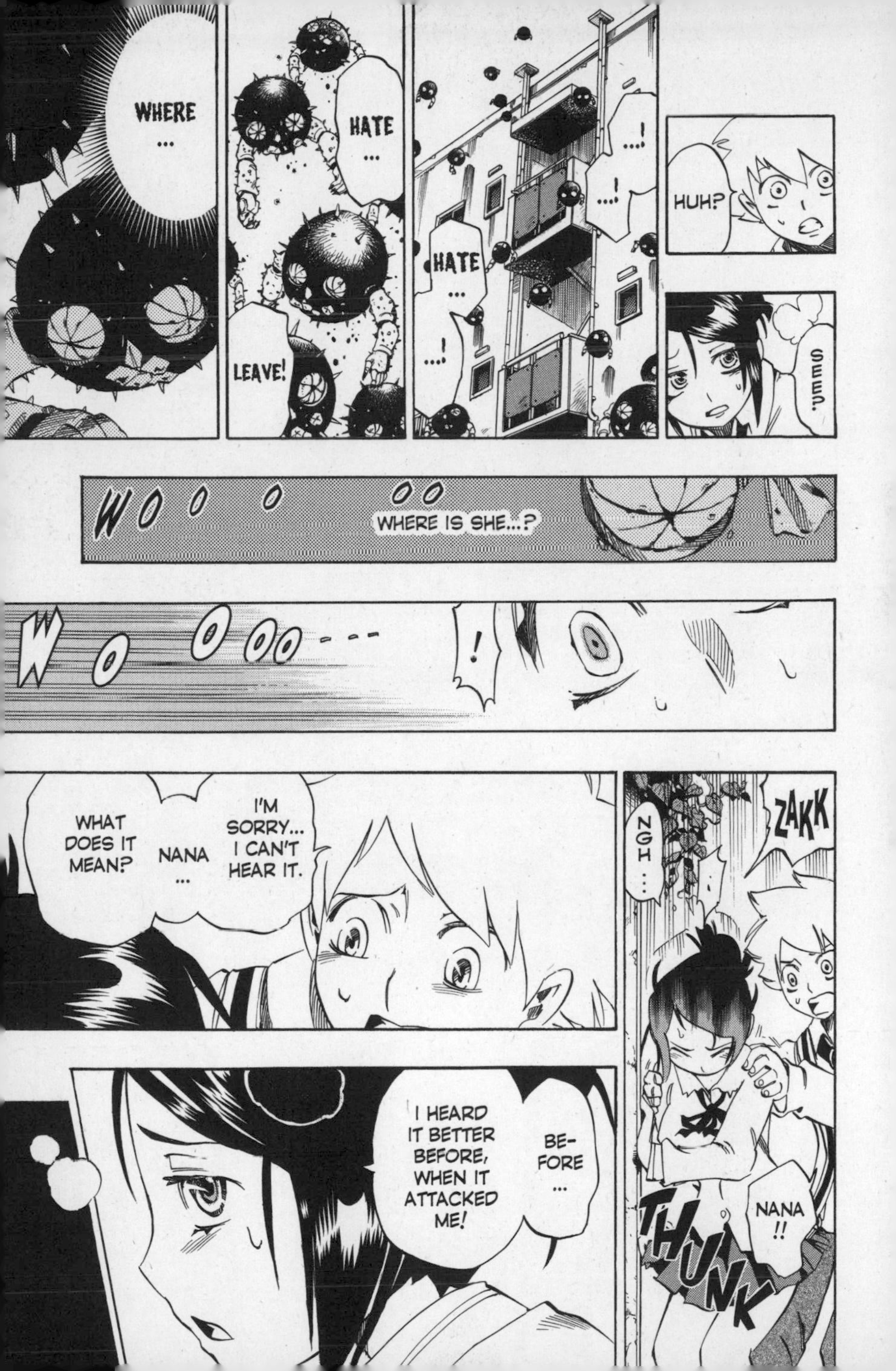
HUH?
SEE?
...!
...!
HATE ...
...!
HATE ...
LEAVE!
WHERE ...
WOOOOO
WHERE IS SHE...?
!
WOOOOO---
ZAKK
NGH ...
NANA !!
THUNK
I'M SORRY... I CAN'T HEAR IT.
NANA ...
WHAT DOES IT MEAN?
BE-FORE ...
I HEARD IT BETTER BEFORE, WHEN IT ATTACKED ME!

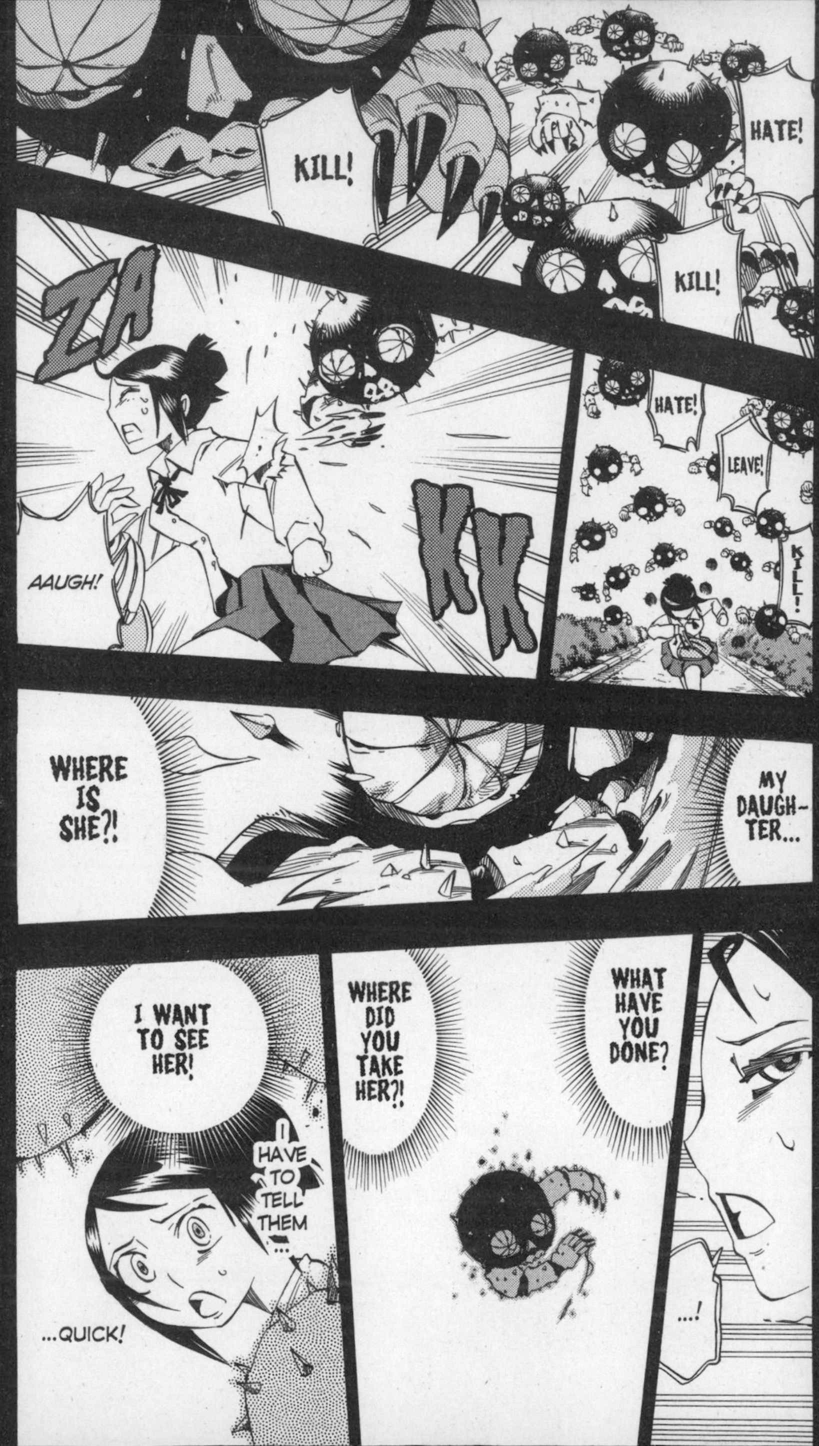
HATE!
KILL!
KILL!
HATE!
LEAVE!
KILL!
ZA
KK
AAUGH!
MY DAUGH-TER...
WHERE IS SHE?!
WHAT HAVE YOU DONE?
...!
WHERE DID YOU TAKE HER?!
I WANT TO SEE HER!
I HAVE TO TELL THEM...
...QUICK!

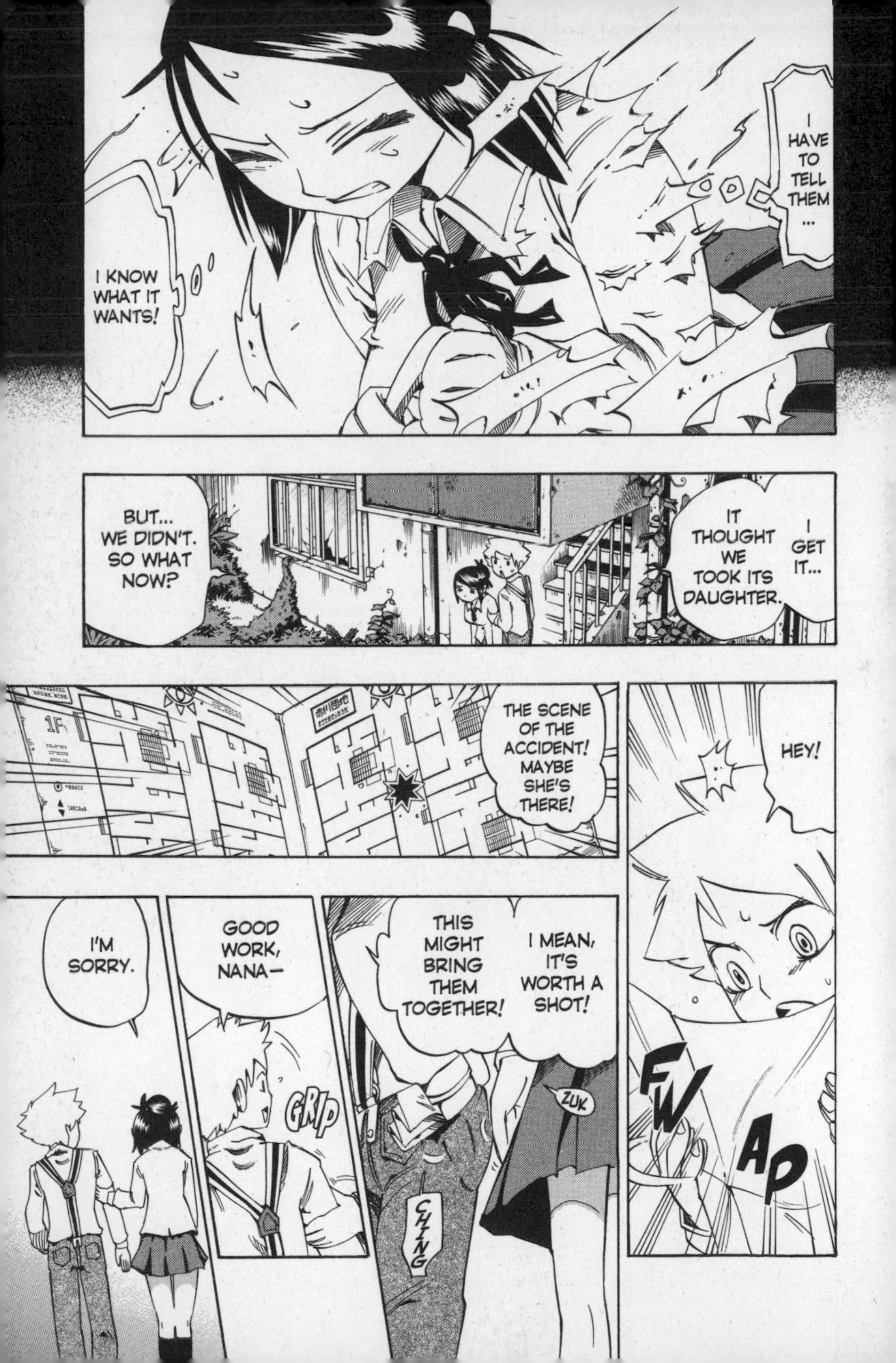
I HAVE TO TELL THEM...
I KNOW WHAT IT WANTS!
I GET IT...
IT THOUGHT WE TOOK ITS DAUGHTER.
BUT... WE DIDN'T. SO WHAT NOW?
HEY!
FWAP
THE SCENE OF THE ACCIDENT! MAYBE SHE'S THERE!
I MEAN, IT'S WORTH A SHOT!
THIS MIGHT BRING THEM TOGETHER!
ZUK
CHING
GRIP
GOOD WORK, NANA—
I'M SORRY.
1F

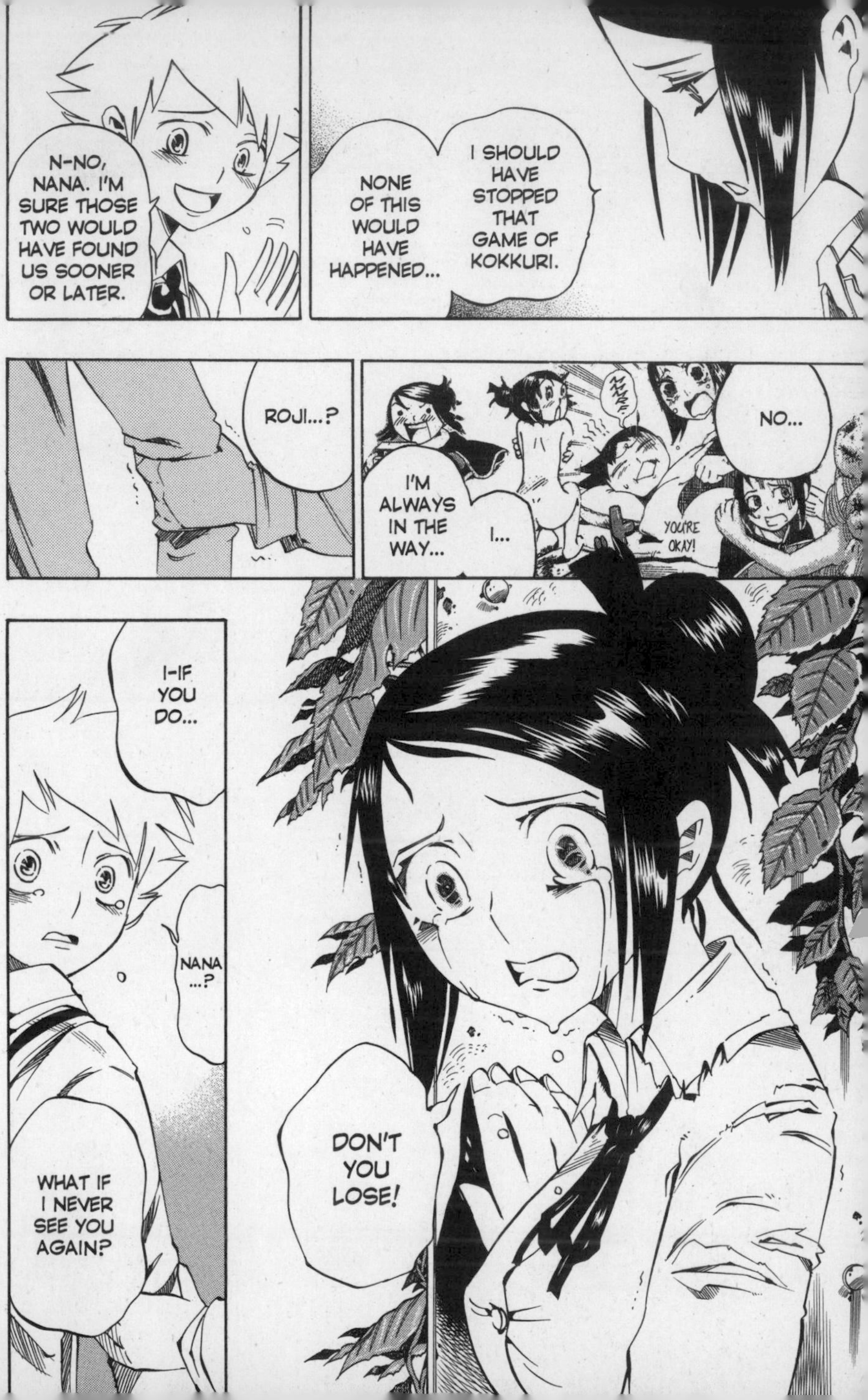
I SHOULD HAVE STOPPED THAT GAME OF KOKKURI.
NONE OF THIS WOULD HAVE HAPPENED...
N-NO, NANA. I'M SURE THOSE TWO WOULD HAVE FOUND US SOONER OR LATER.
NO...
YOU'RE OKAY!
I...
I'M ALWAYS IN THE WAY...
ROJI...?
DON'T YOU LOSE!
I-IF YOU DO...
NANA...?
WHAT IF I NEVER SEE YOU AGAIN?

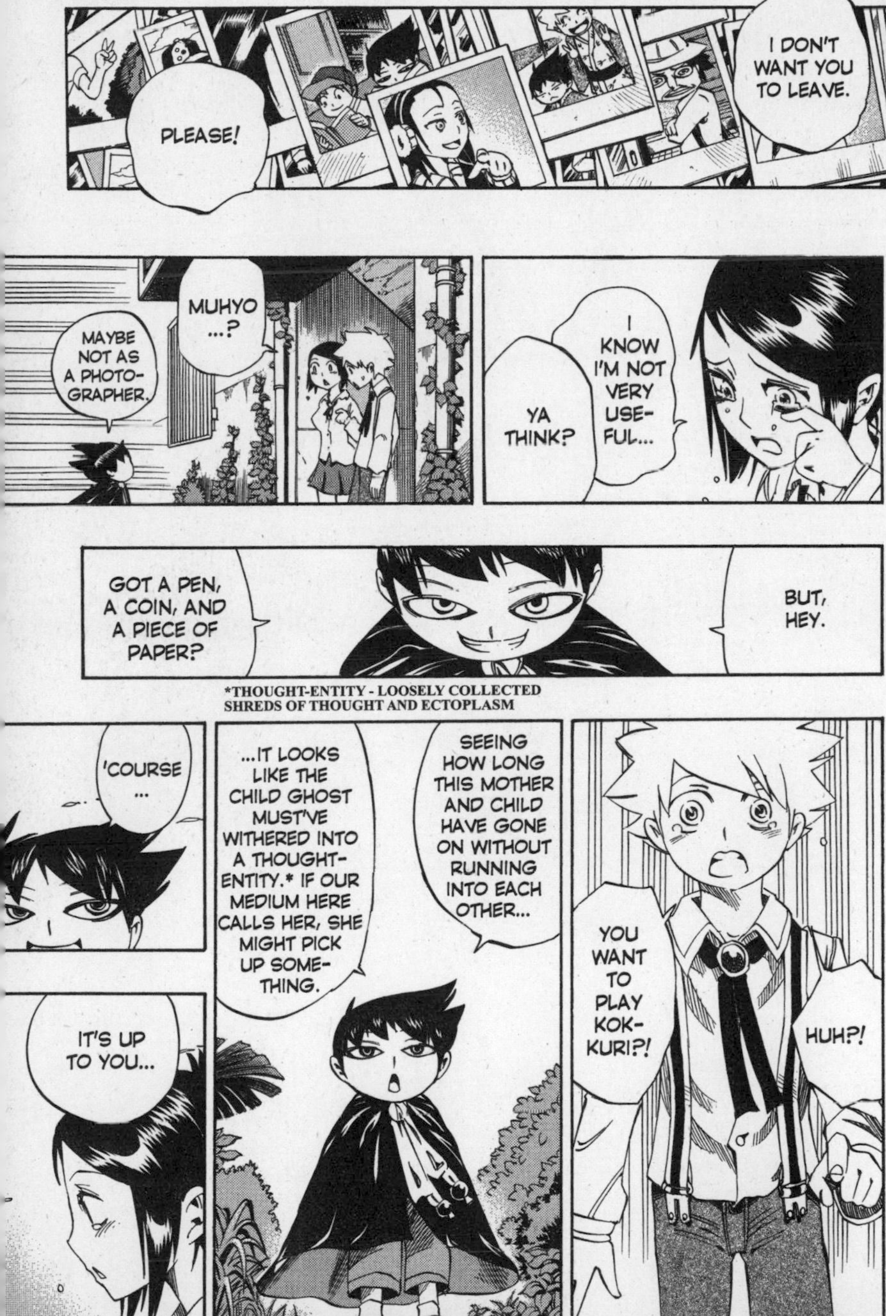
I DON'T WANT YOU TO LEAVE.
PLEASE!
I KNOW I'M NOT VERY USE-FUL...
YA THINK?
MUHYO ...?
MAYBE NOT AS A PHOTO-GRAPHER.
BUT, HEY.
GOT A PEN, A COIN, AND A PIECE OF PAPER?
HUH?!
YOU WANT TO PLAY KOK-KURI?!
SEEING HOW LONG THIS MOTHER AND CHILD HAVE GONE ON WITHOUT RUNNING INTO EACH OTHER...
...IT LOOKS LIKE THE CHILD GHOST MUST'VE WITHERED INTO A THOUGHT-ENTITY.* IF OUR MEDIUM HERE CALLS HER, SHE MIGHT PICK UP SOME-THING.
'COURSE ...
IT'S UP TO YOU...

*THOUGHT-ENTITY - LOOSELY COLLECTED SHREDS OF THOUGHT AND ECTOPLASM

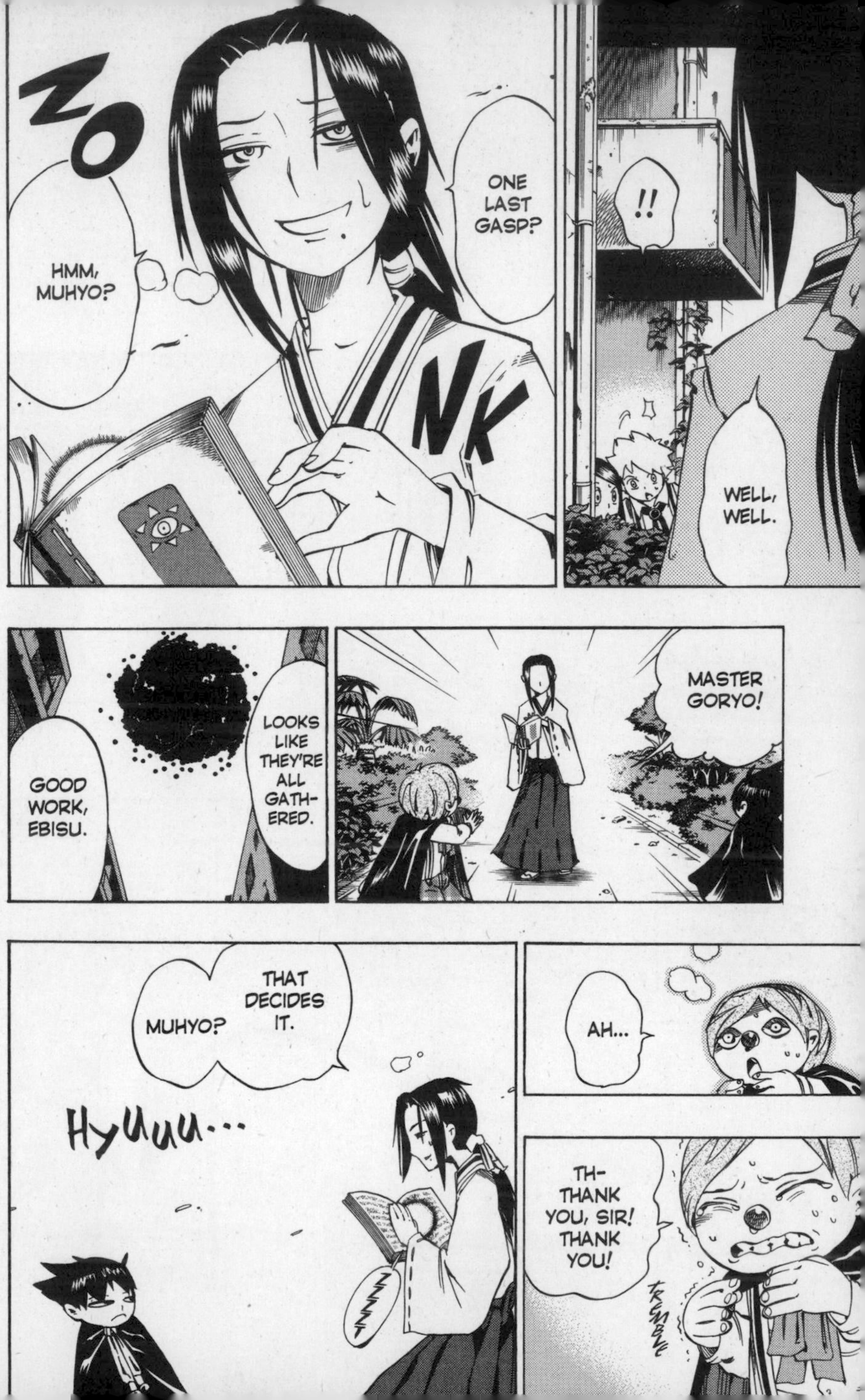
!!
WELL, WELL.
ONE LAST GASP?
ZO
NK
HMM, MUHYO?
MASTER GORYO!
LOOKS LIKE THEY'RE ALL GATH-ERED.
GOOD WORK, EBISU.
AH...
TH- THANK YOU, SIR! THANK YOU!
TREMBLE
THAT DECIDES IT.
MUHYO?
Hyuuu...
ZZZZT

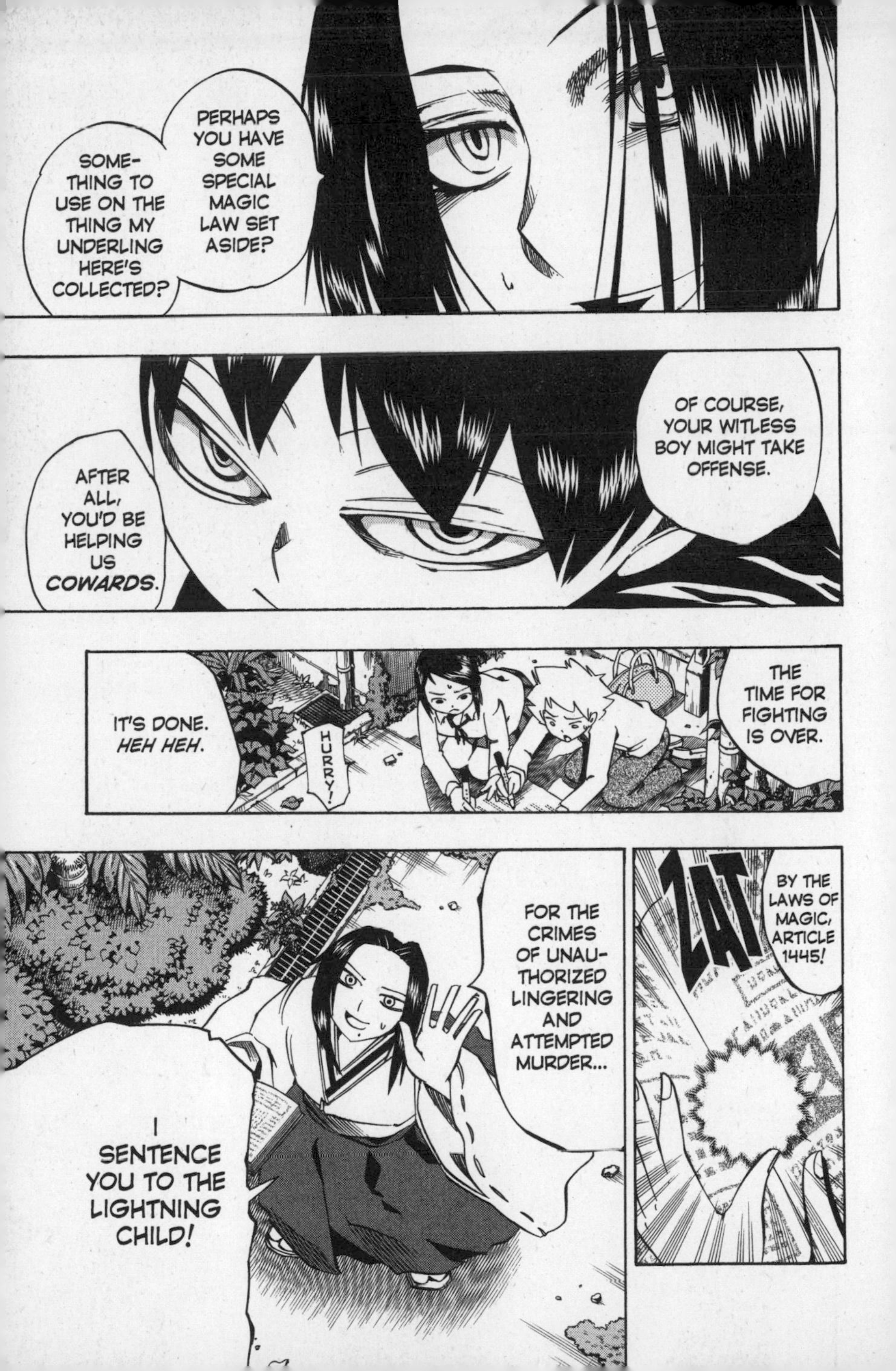
PERHAPS YOU HAVE SOME SPECIAL MAGIC LAW SET ASIDE?
SOME-THING TO USE ON THE THING MY UNDERLING HERE'S COLLECTED?
OF COURSE, YOUR WITLESS BOY MIGHT TAKE OFFENSE.
AFTER ALL, YOU'D BE HELPING US *COWARDS*.
THE TIME FOR FIGHTING IS OVER.
HURRY!
IT'S DONE. *HEH HEH*.
ZAT
BY THE LAWS OF MAGIC, ARTICLE 1445!
FOR THE CRIMES OF UNAU-THORIZED LINGERING AND ATTEMPTED MURDER...
I SENTENCE YOU TO THE LIGHTNING CHILD!

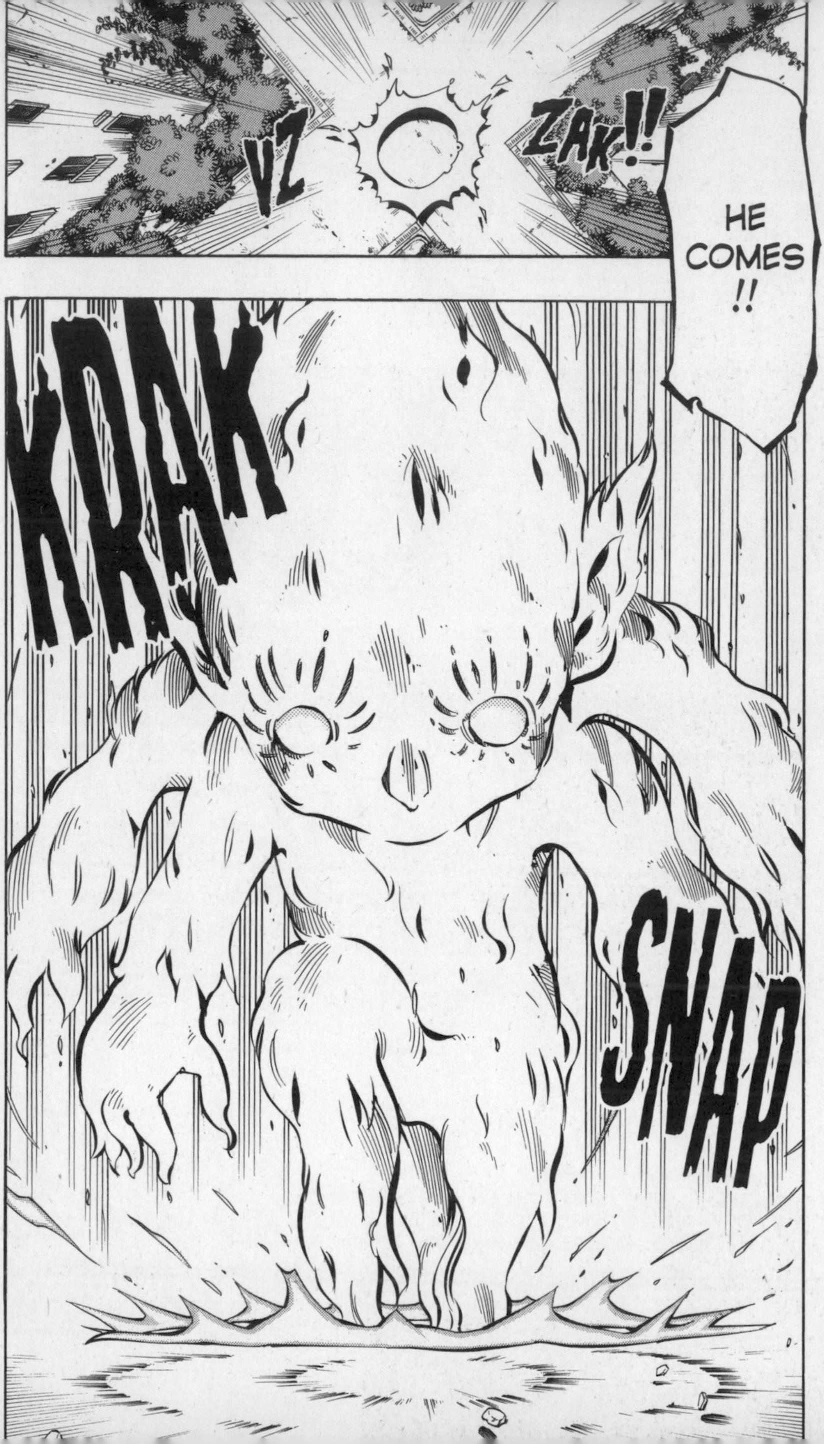
HE COMES !!
ZAK!!
VZ
KRAK
SNAP

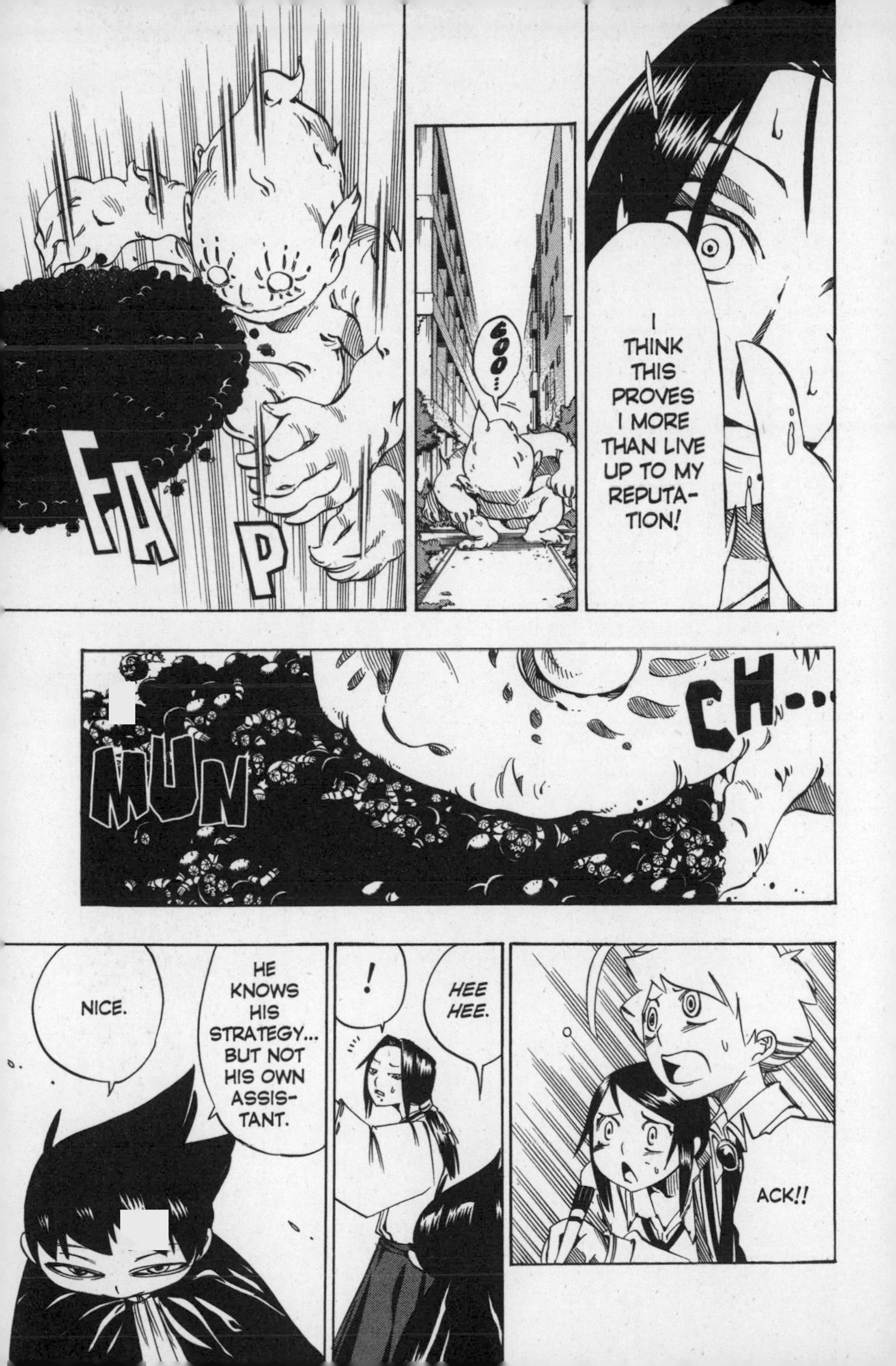
I THINK THIS PROVES I MORE THAN LIVE UP TO MY REPUTATION!
GOO...
FAP
MUNCH...
ACK!!
HEE HEE.
!
HE KNOWS HIS STRATEGY... BUT NOT HIS OWN ASSISTANT.
NICE.

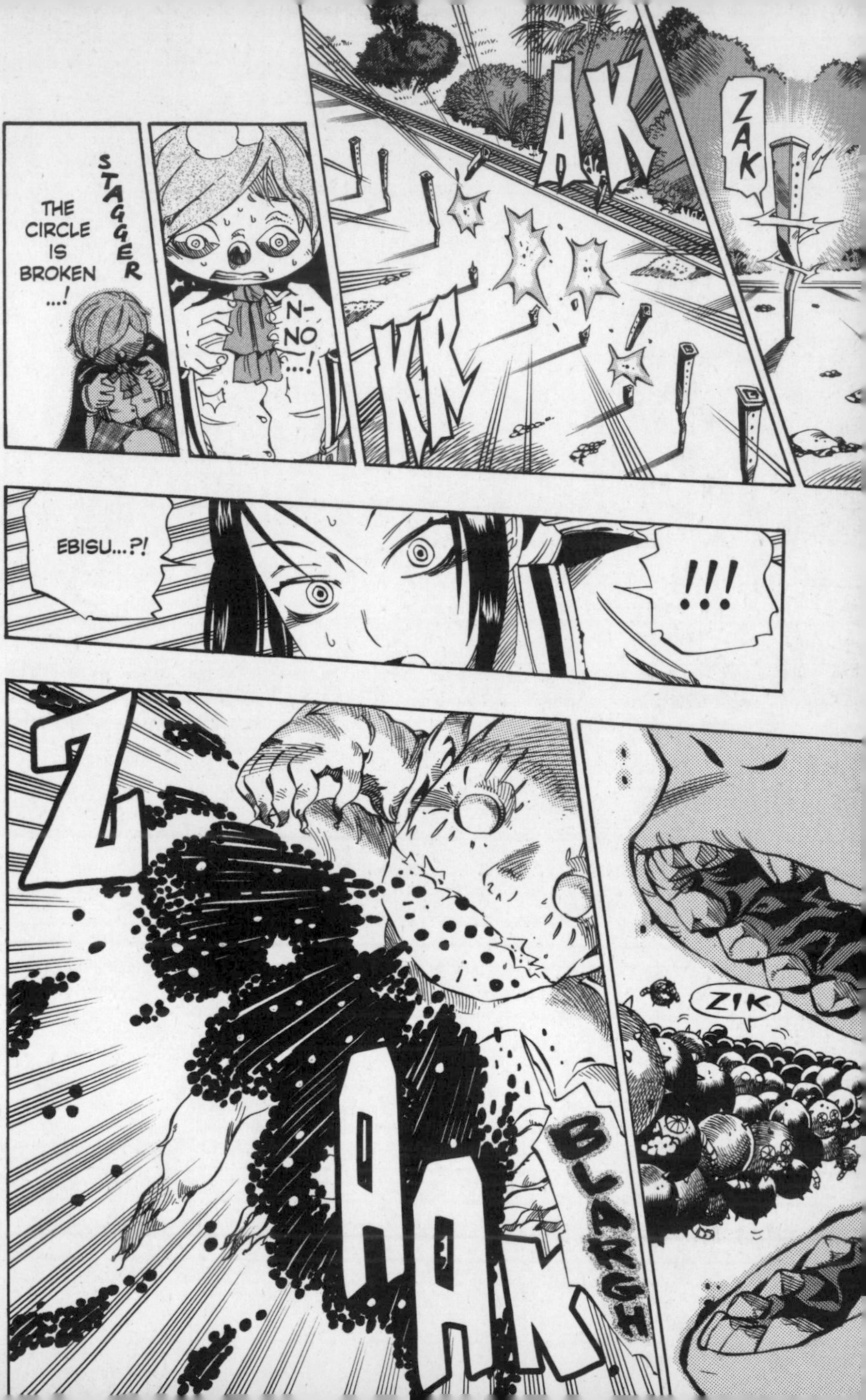
ZAK
KR
AK
N-NO ...!
STAGGER
THE CIRCLE IS BROKEN ...!
!!!
EBISU...?!
ZIK
Z
AAK
BLARGH

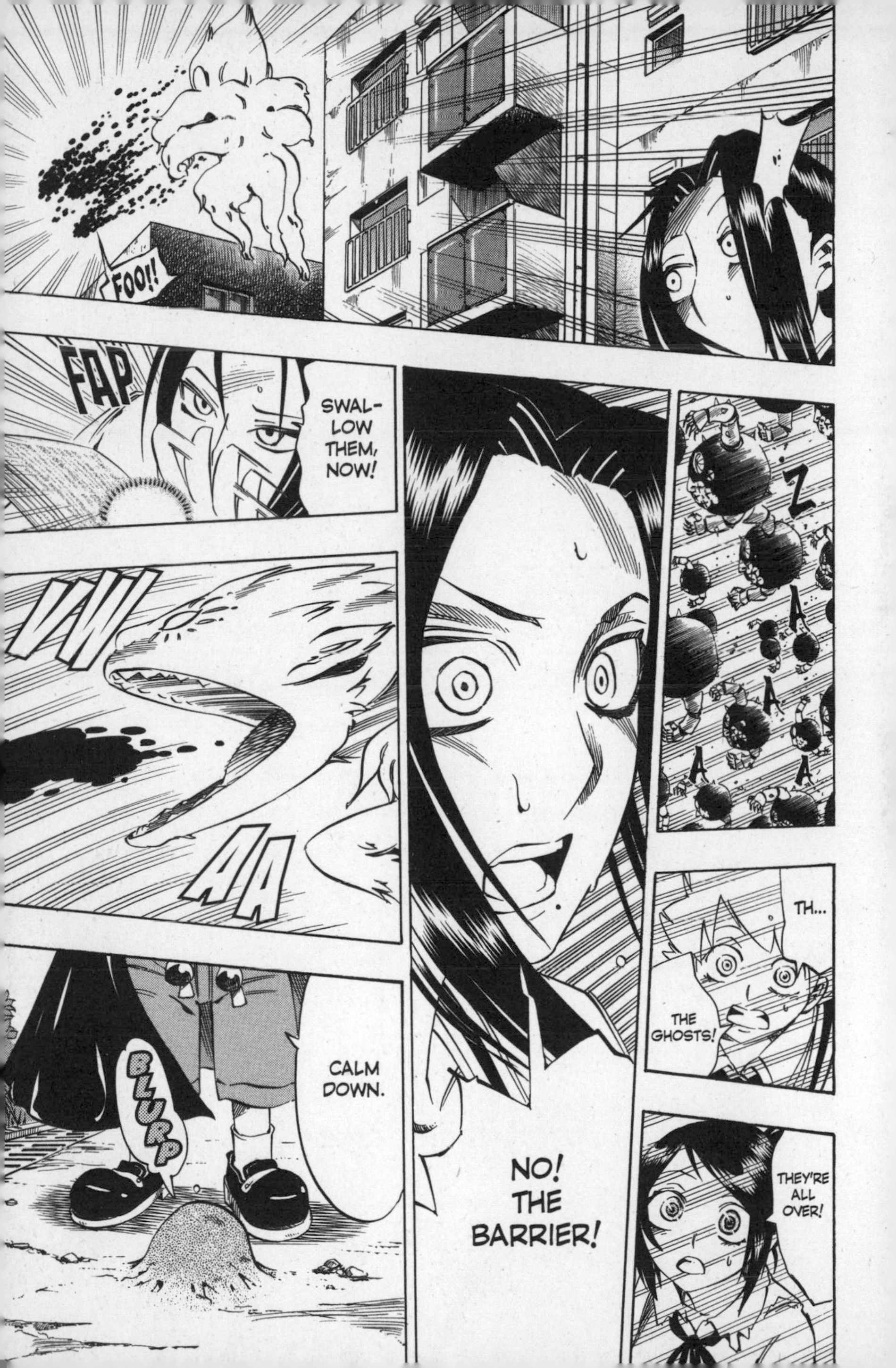
FOO!!
TH...
THE GHOSTS!
THEY'RE ALL OVER!
NO! THE BARRIER!
FAP
SWAL-LOW THEM, NOW!
VNN
AA
CALM DOWN.
BLURP

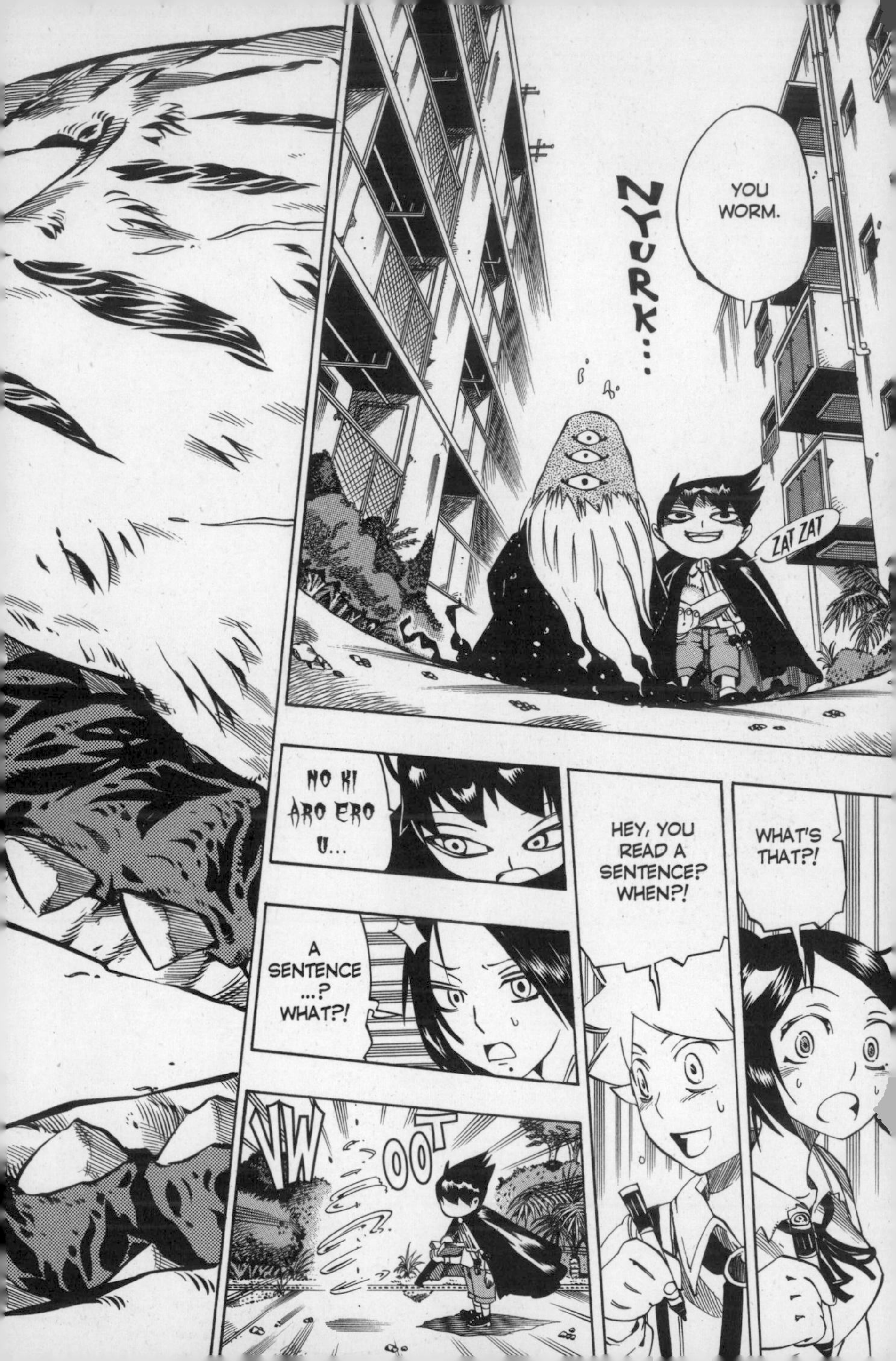
YOU WORM.
NYURK...
ZAT ZAT
WHAT'S THAT?!
HEY, YOU READ A SENTENCE? WHEN?!
NO KI ARO ERO U...
A SENTENCE ...? WHAT?!
VWOOT

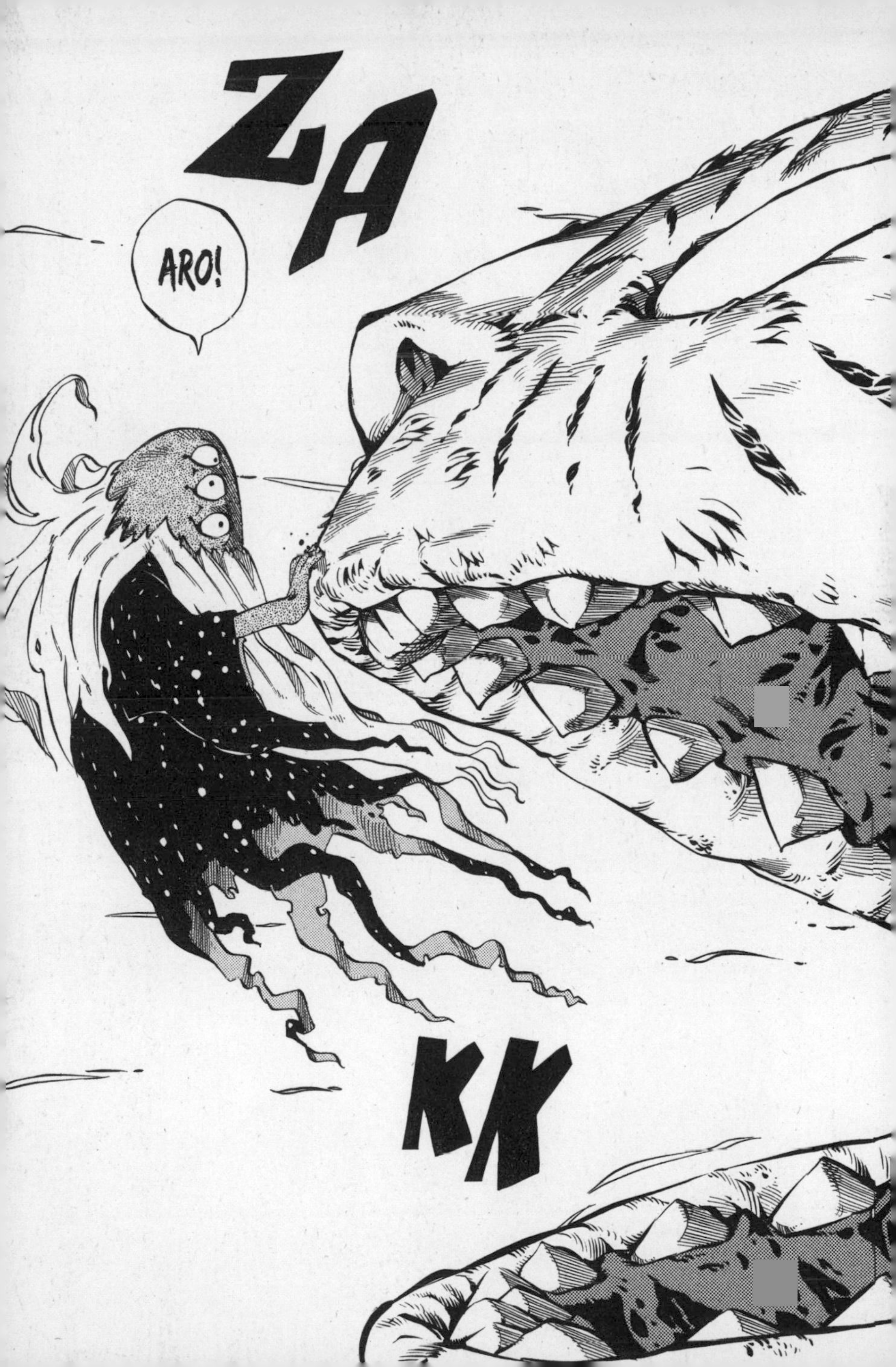
ZA
ARO!
KK

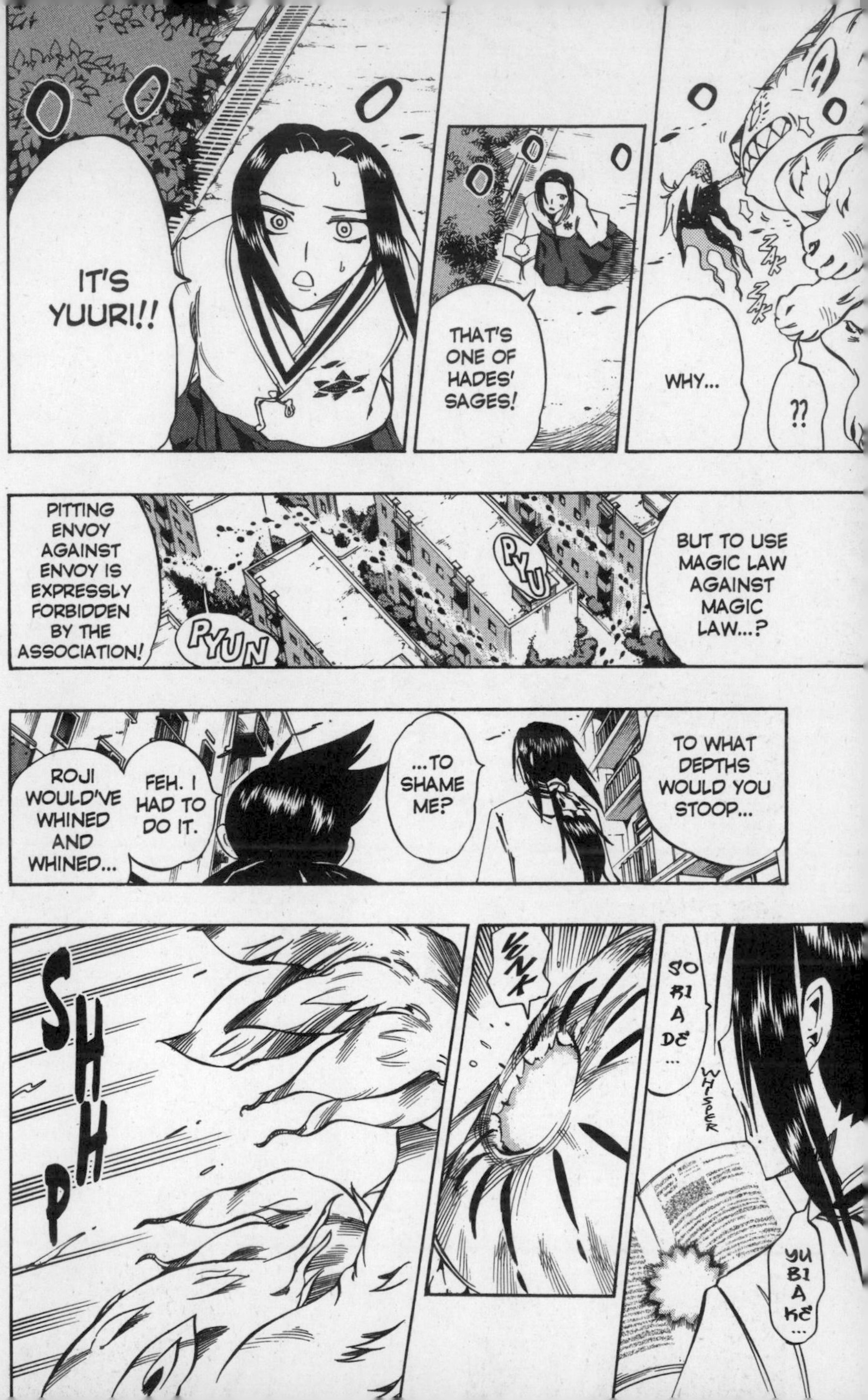
??
WHY...
ZAK
ZAK
THAT'S ONE OF HADES' SAGES!
IT'S YUURI!!
BUT TO USE MAGIC LAW AGAINST MAGIC LAW...?
RYU
PYUN
PITTING ENVOY AGAINST ENVOY IS EXPRESSLY FORBIDDEN BY THE ASSOCIATION!
TO WHAT DEPTHS WOULD YOU STOOP...
...TO SHAME ME?
FEH. I HAD TO DO IT.
ROJI WOULD'VE WHINED AND WHINED...
SO RI A DĚ ...
WHISPER
YU BI A KĚ ...
VENK
SHHHP

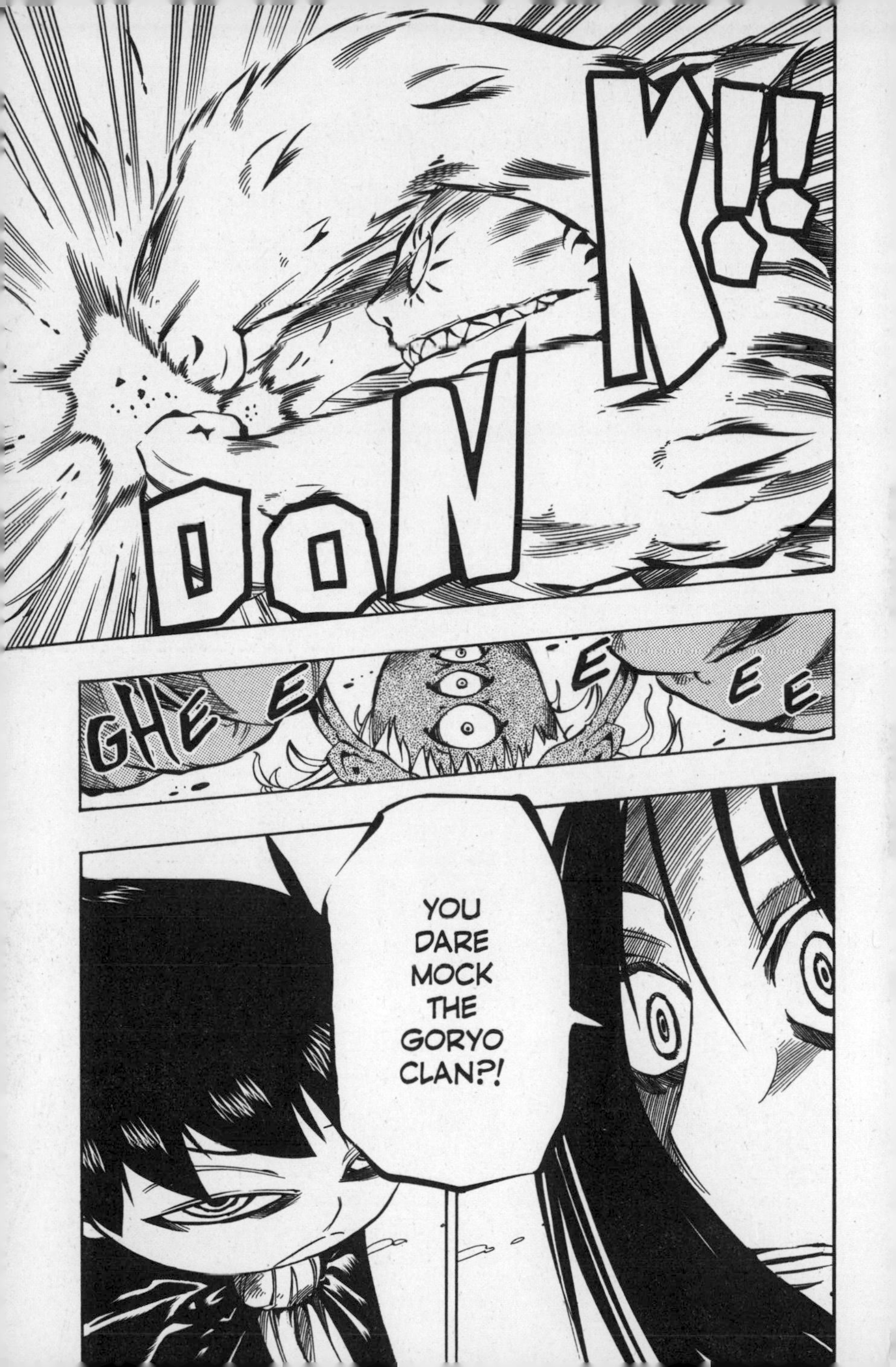
DONK!!
GHEEEEEE
YOU DARE MOCK THE GORYO CLAN?!

Q: IS MUHYO REALLY ONLY 4' 2"? ARE YOU COUNTING HIS SPIKEY HAIR? (OR ONION, WHICHEVER YOU PREFER.)

-T.Y., AOMORI PREFECTURE

A: HMM... I WAS HOPING NO ONE WOULD ASK THAT. THAT IS, I'VE GOTTEN LOTS OF MAIL ASKING THIS QUESTION, AND I CAN RUN AWAY NO LONGER! I HAVE TO FACE IT! I WON'T HIDE IT IN THE BOTTOM DRAWER AND... AHEM. LET'S ASK ROJI, SHALL WE?

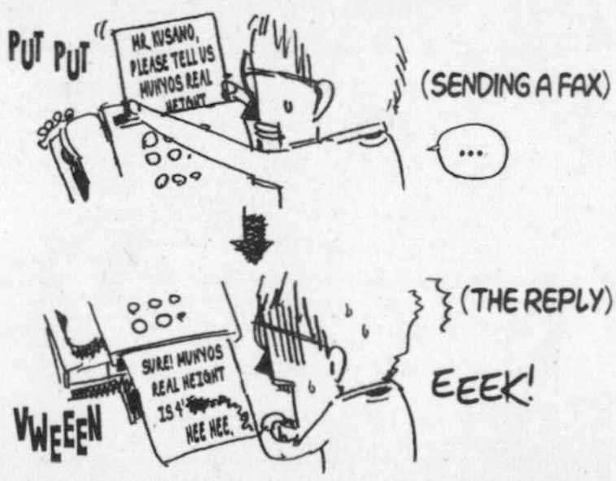
PUT PUT
MR. KUSANO, PLEASE TELL US MUHYOS REAL HEIGHT
(SENDING A FAX)
...
(THE REPLY)
SURE! MUHYOS REAL HEIGHT IS 4'
HEE HEE.
EEEK!
VWEEEN

SO, THERE YOU HAVE IT! HE'S 4 FEET AND...??

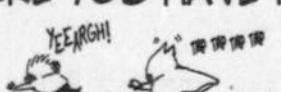
YEEARGH!

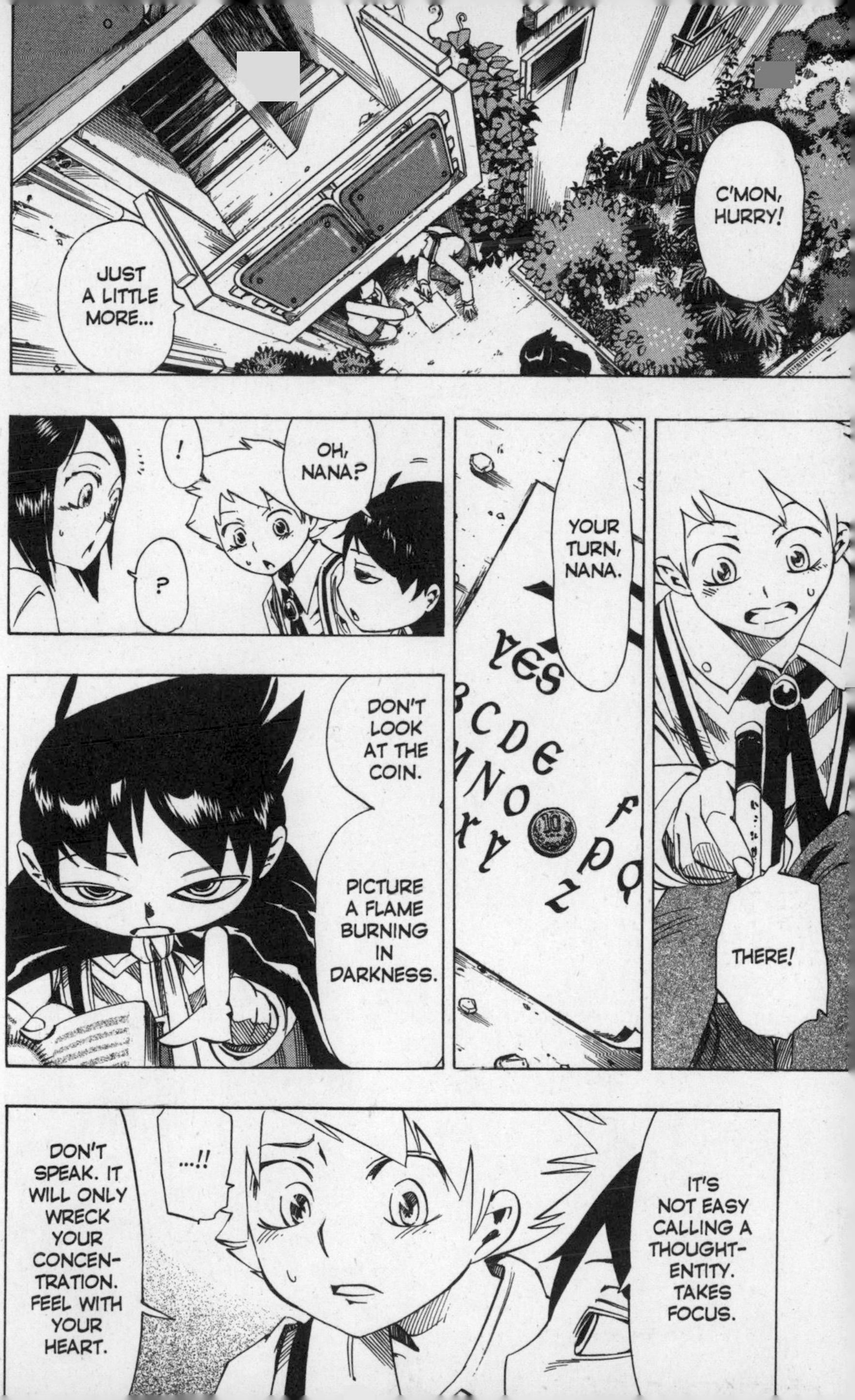
C'MON, HURRY!
JUST A LITTLE MORE...
THERE!
YOUR TURN, NANA.
OH, NANA?
!
?
DON'T LOOK AT THE COIN.
PICTURE A FLAME BURNING IN DARKNESS.
IT'S NOT EASY CALLING A THOUGHT-ENTITY. TAKES FOCUS.
...!!
DON'T SPEAK. IT WILL ONLY WRECK YOUR CONCEN-TRATION. FEEL WITH YOUR HEART.

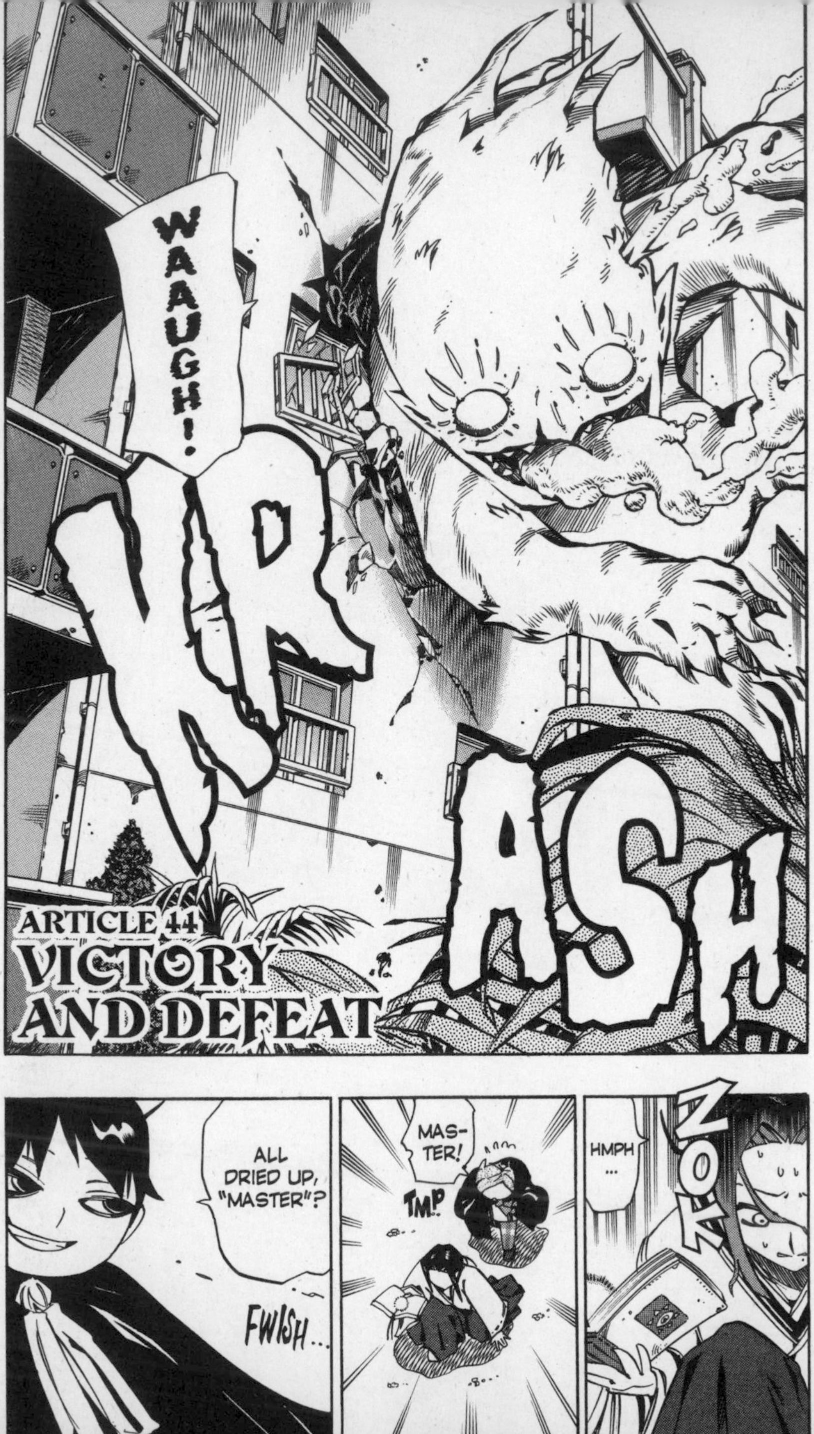
WAAUGH!
ASH
ARTICLE 44
VICTORY AND DEFEAT
ZOK
HMPH ...
MAS-TER!
TMP
ALL DRIED UP, "MASTER"?
FWISH...

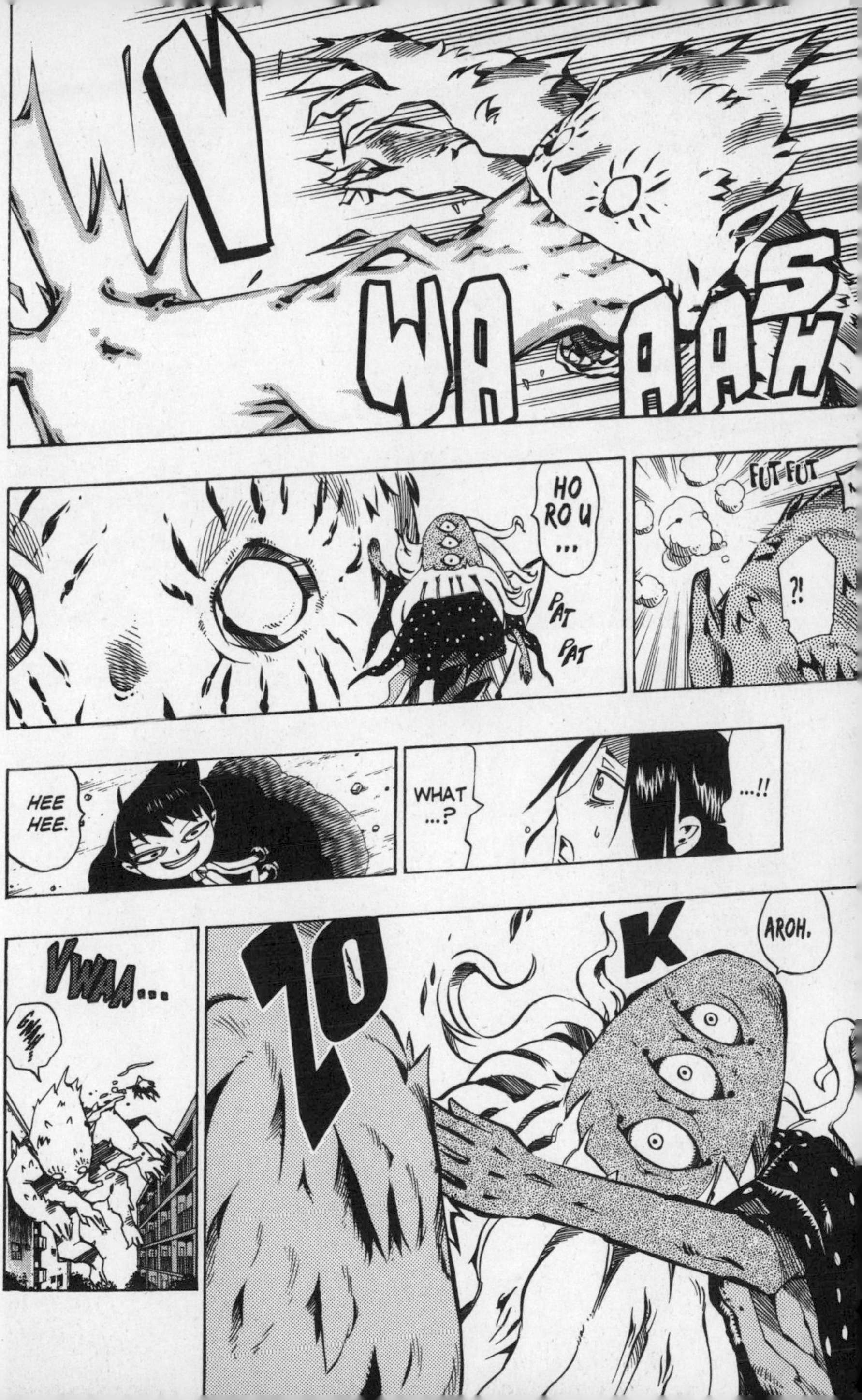
WAAASH
FUT FUT
?!
HO RO U...
PAT PAT
...!!
WHAT ...?
HEE HEE.
ZOK
AROH.
VWAA...
GNAH...

ARTICLE 44
VICTORY AND DEFEAT

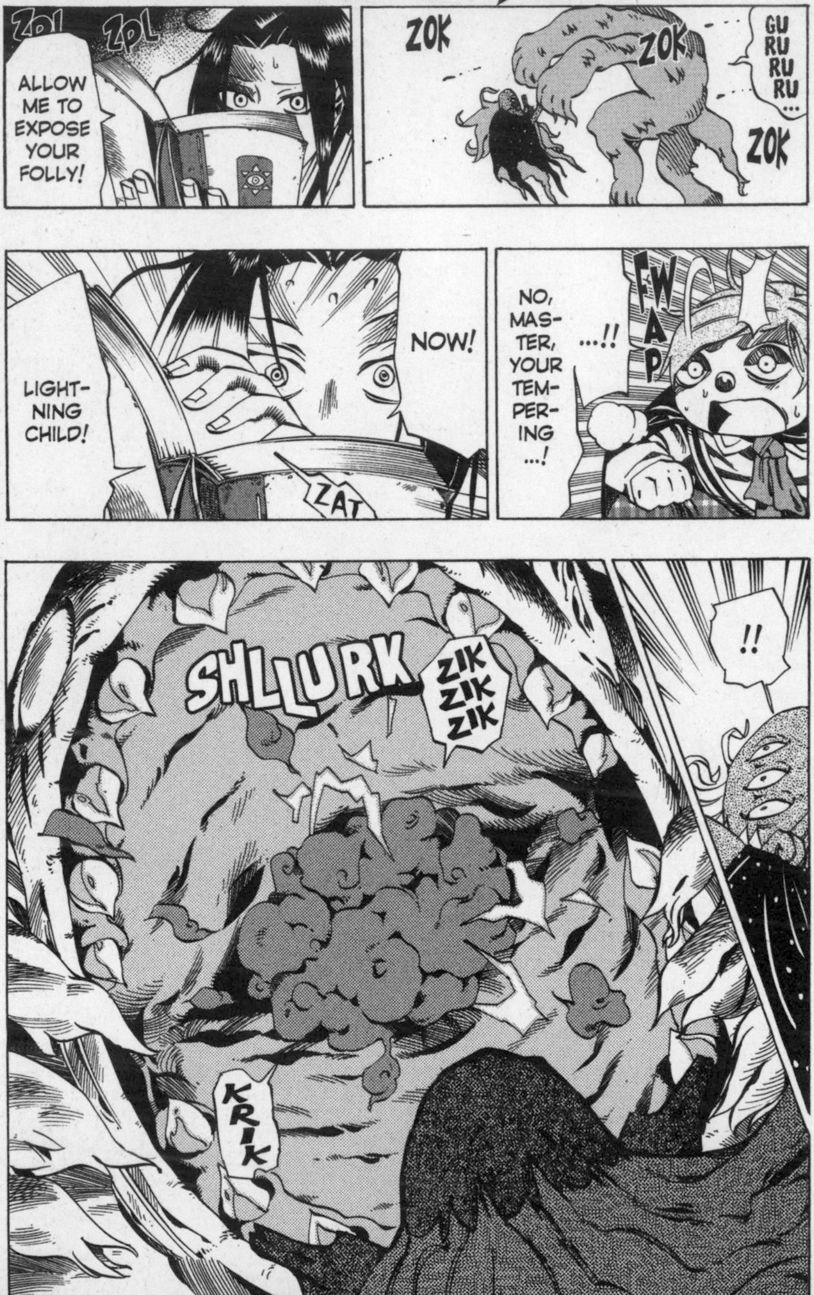
ZOK
ZOK
GURU RU RU RU...
ZOK
ZPL
ZPL
ALLOW ME TO EXPOSE YOUR FOLLY!
FWAP
NO, MASTER, YOUR TEMPERING...!
...!!
NOW!
LIGHTNING CHILD!
ZAT
!!
SHLLURK
ZIK ZIK ZIK
KRIK

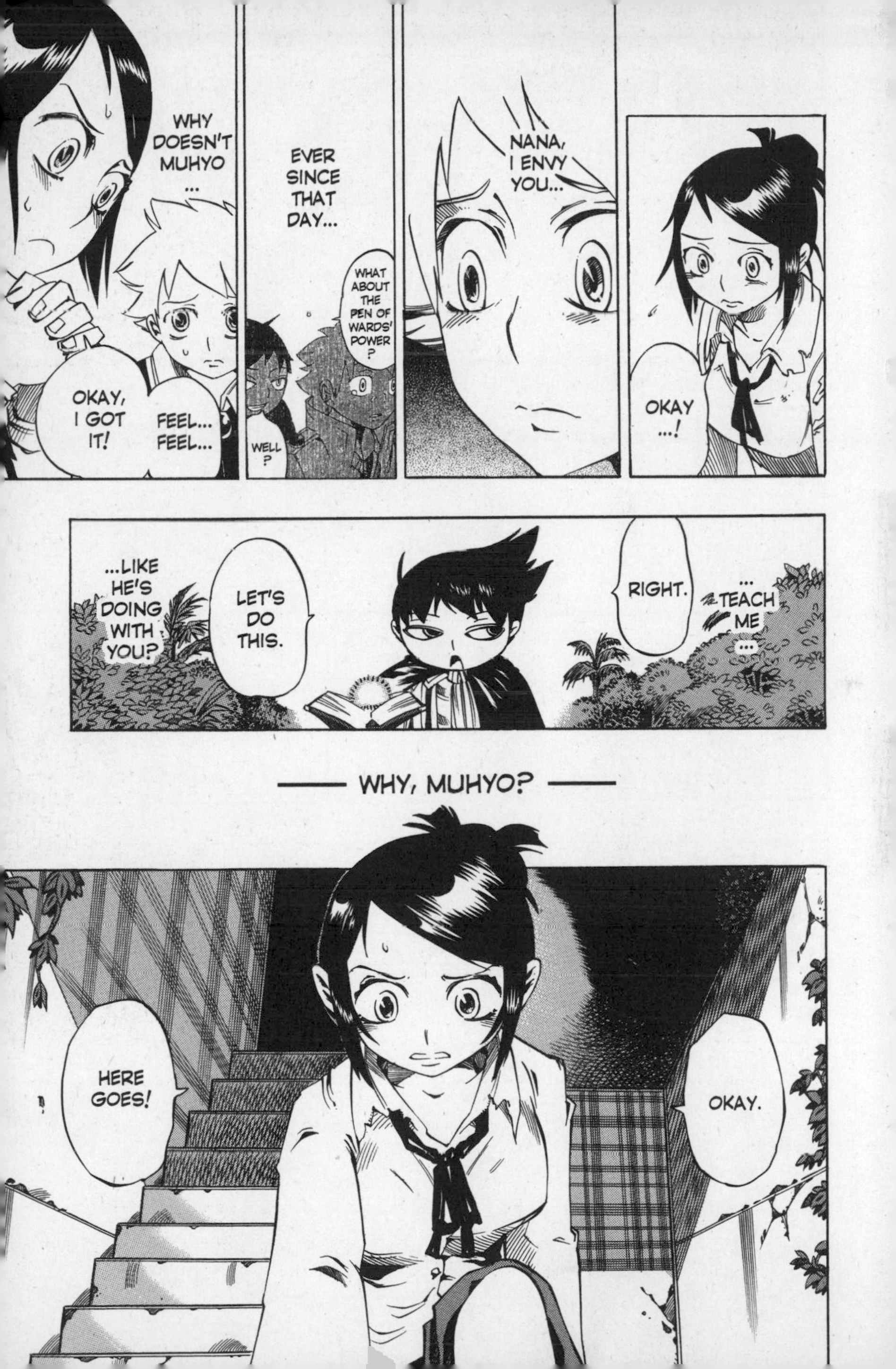
OKAY ...!
NANA, I ENVY YOU...
EVER SINCE THAT DAY...
WHAT ABOUT THE PEN OF WARDS' POWER?
WELL?
WHY DOESN'T MUHYO ...
FEEL... FEEL...
OKAY, I GOT IT!
... TEACH ME ...
RIGHT.
LET'S DO THIS.
...LIKE HE'S DOING WITH YOU?
— WHY, MUHYO? —
OKAY.
HERE GOES!

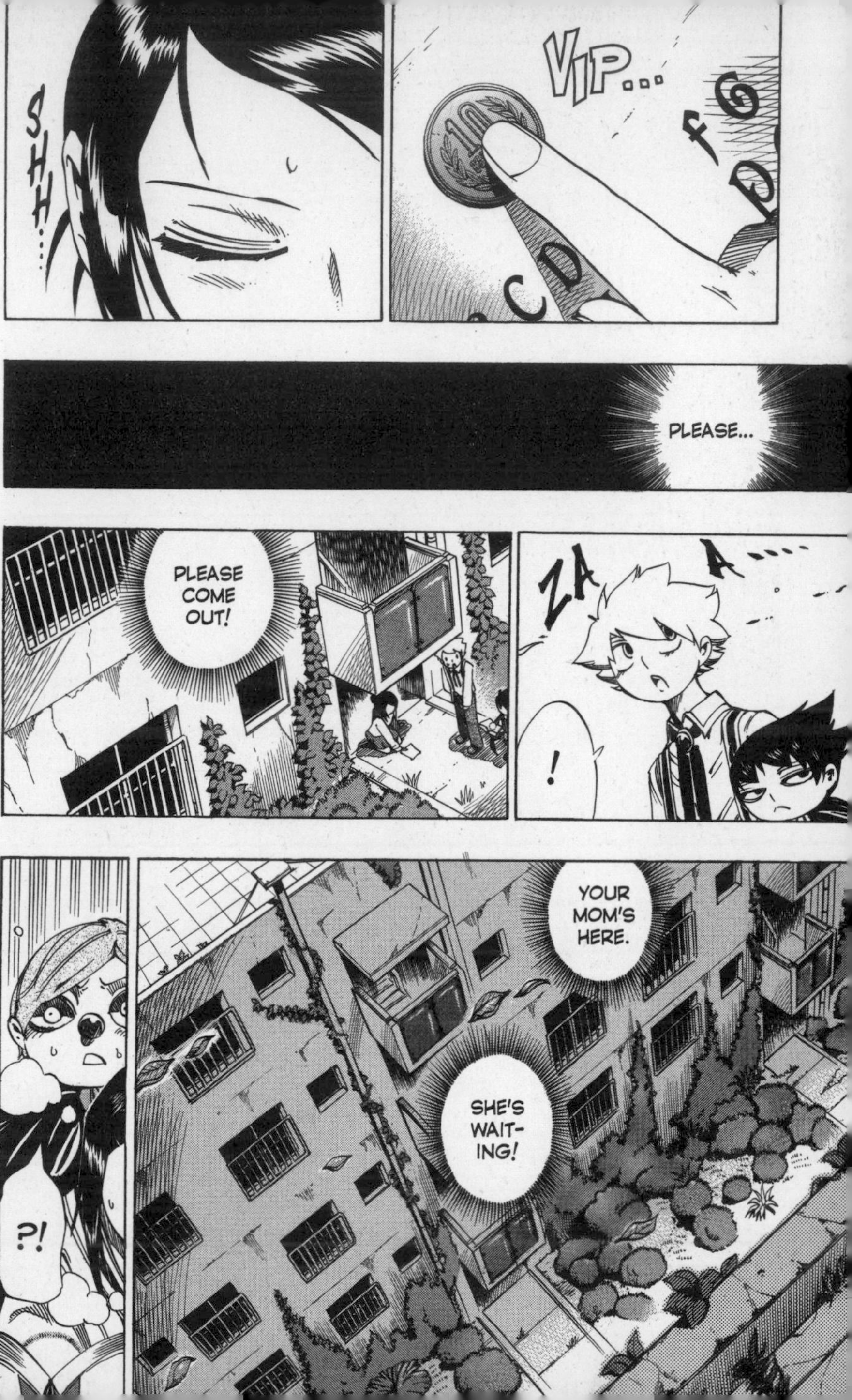
VIP...
SHH...
PLEASE...
ZA
A...
!
PLEASE COME OUT!
YOUR MOM'S HERE.
SHE'S WAIT-ING!
?!

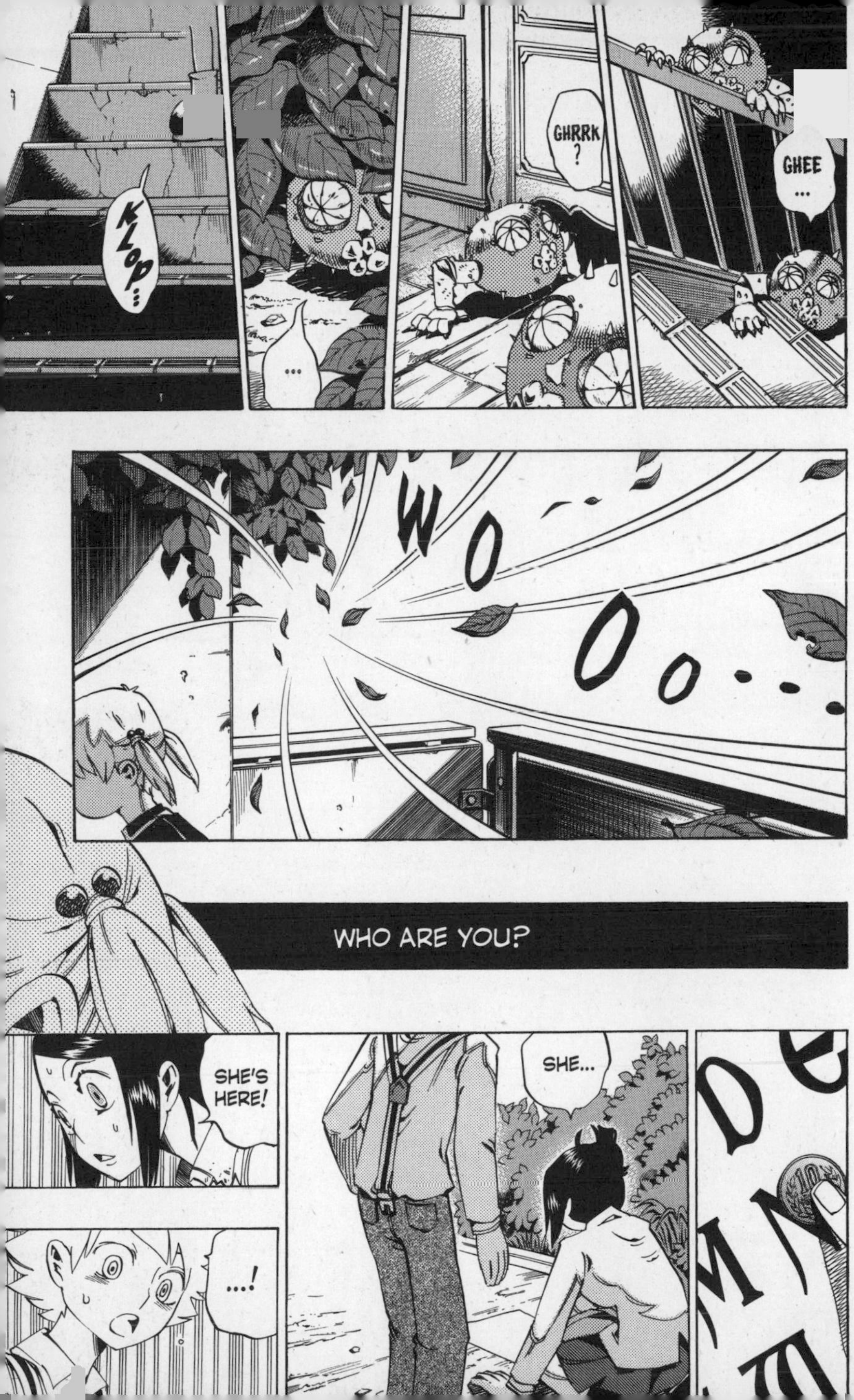
GHEE ...
GHRRK ?
...
KLOP...
WOOOo...
WHO ARE YOU?
SHE...
SHE'S HERE!
...!

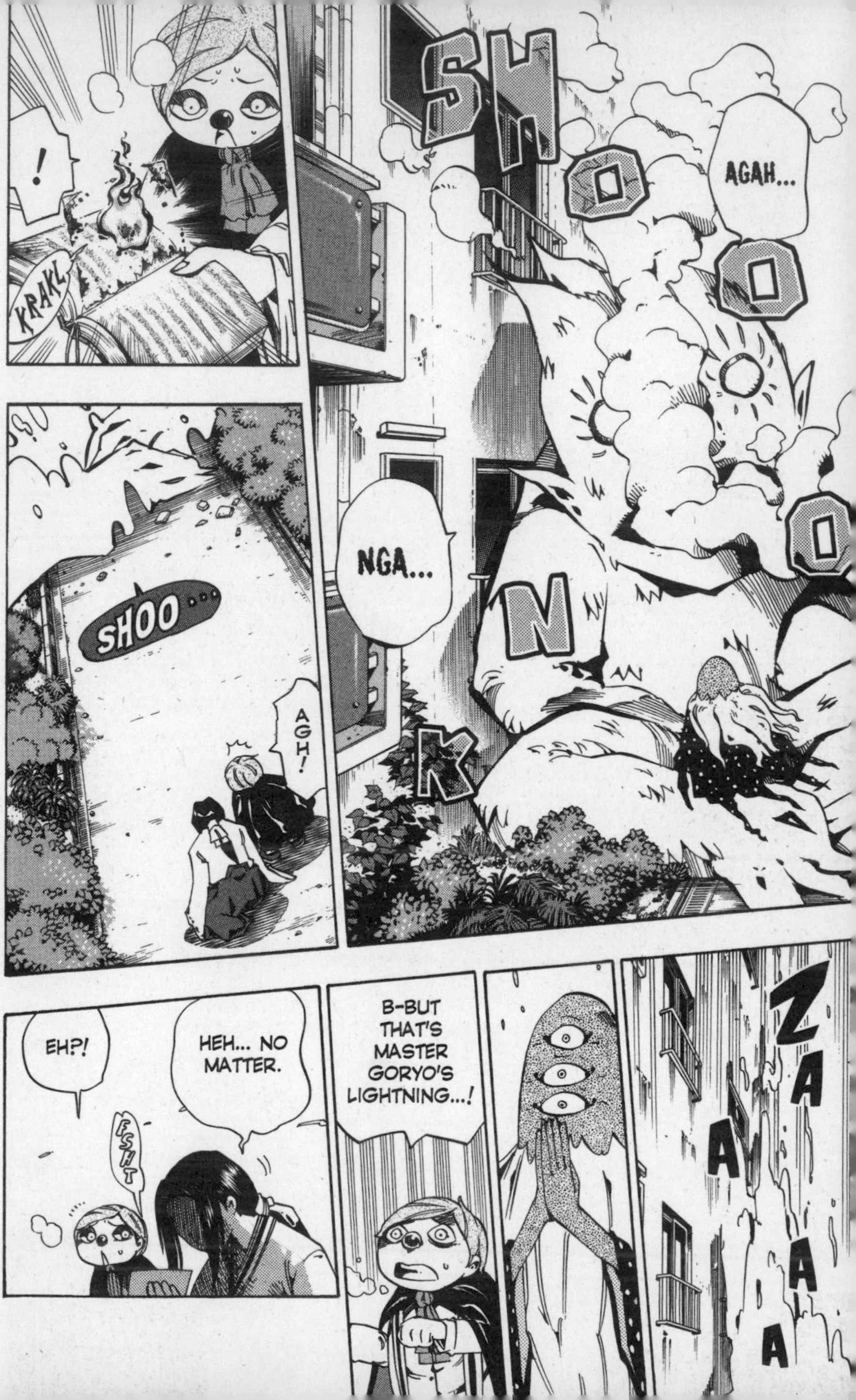
SHOOOOOONK
AGAH...
NGA...
!
KRAKL
SHOO...
AGH!
ZAAAAAA
B-BUT THAT'S MASTER GORYO'S LIGHTNING...!
HEH... NO MATTER.
EH?!
FSHT

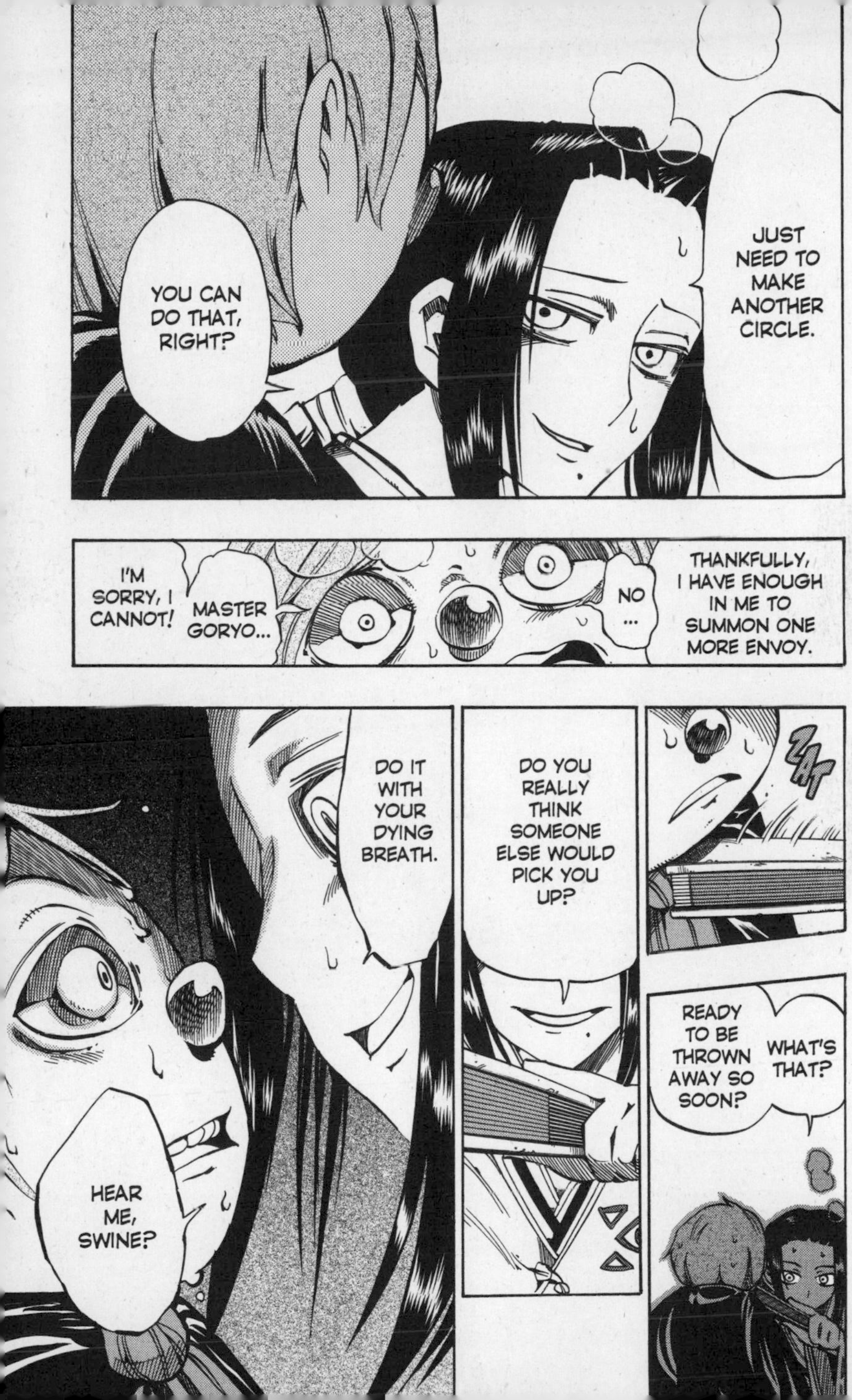
JUST NEED TO MAKE ANOTHER CIRCLE.
YOU CAN DO THAT, RIGHT?
THANKFULLY, I HAVE ENOUGH IN ME TO SUMMON ONE MORE ENVOY.
NO ...
MASTER GORYO...
I'M SORRY, I CANNOT!
ZAT
WHAT'S THAT?
READY TO BE THROWN AWAY SO SOON?
DO YOU REALLY THINK SOMEONE ELSE WOULD PICK YOU UP?
DO IT WITH YOUR DYING BREATH.
HEAR ME, SWINE?

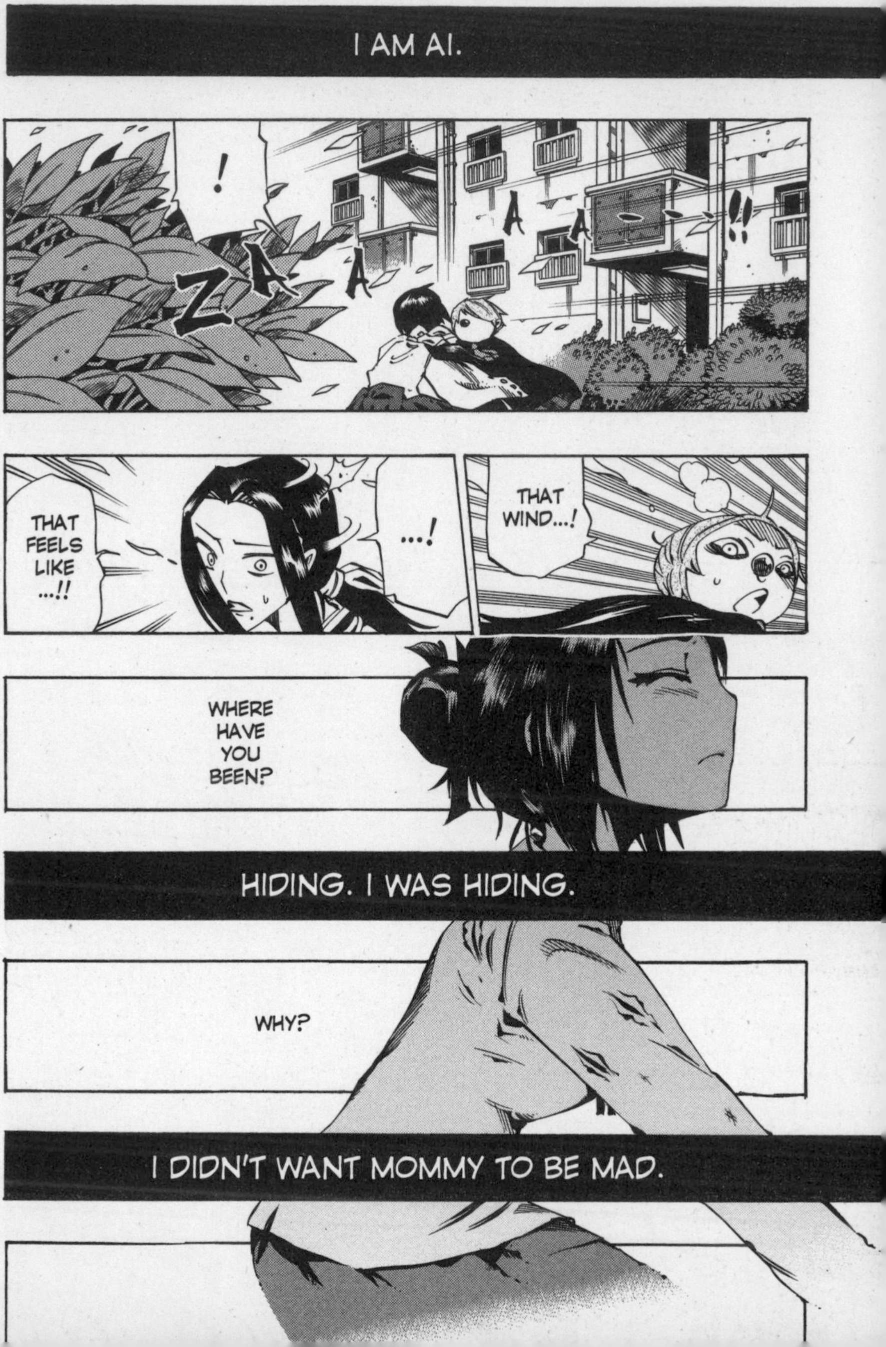
I AM AI.
!
ZA
A
A
A
!!
THAT WIND...!
...!
THAT FEELS LIKE ...!!
WHERE HAVE YOU BEEN?
HIDING. I WAS HIDING.
WHY?
I DIDN'T WANT MOMMY TO BE MAD.

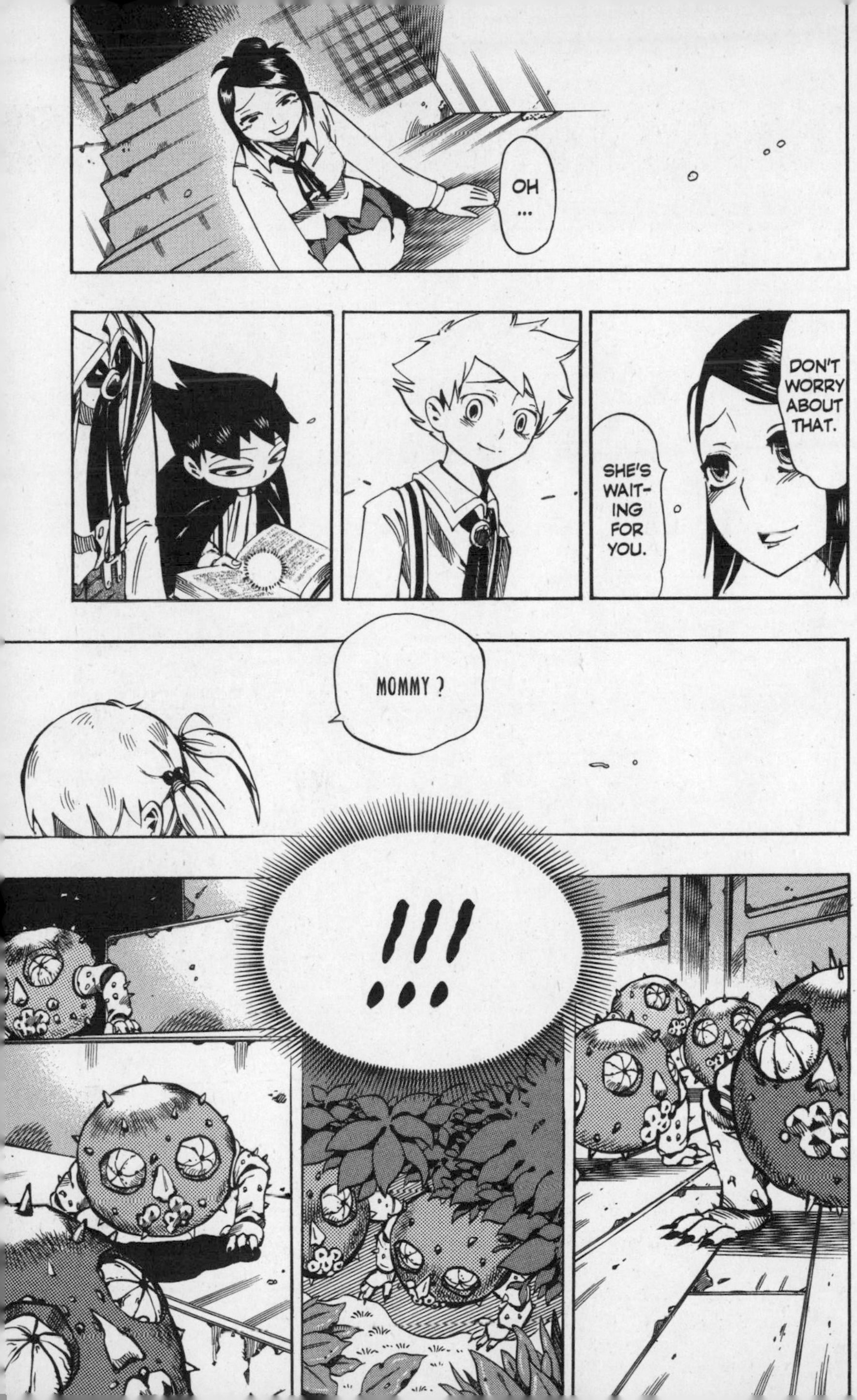
OH ...
DON'T WORRY ABOUT THAT.
SHE'S WAIT-ING FOR YOU.
MOMMY ?
!!! ...

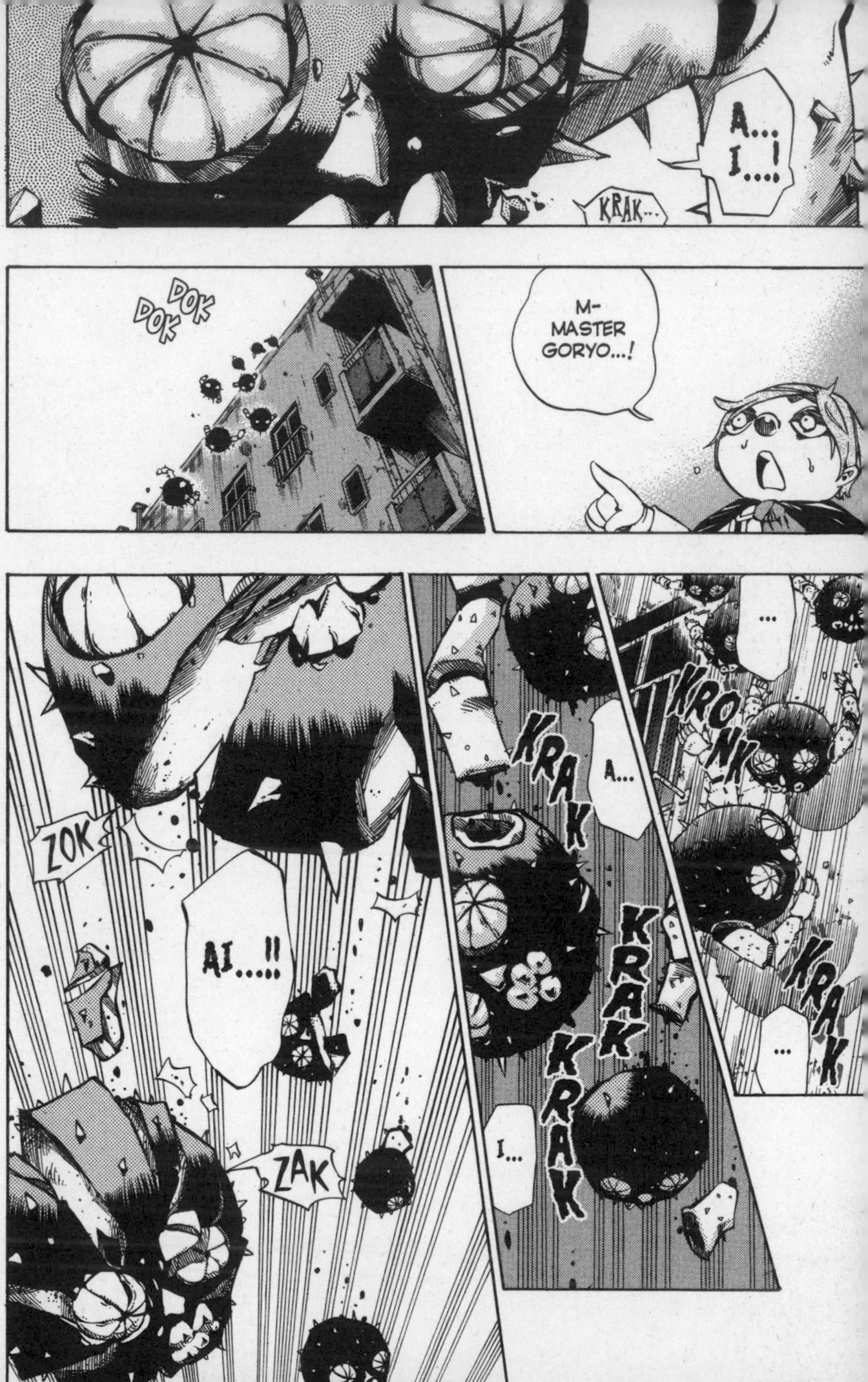
A... I...!
KRAK...
M-MASTER GORYO...!
DOK DOK
...
KRONK
KRAK
...
KRAK
A...
KRAK KRAK
KRAK KRAK
I...
ZOK
AI....!!
ZAK

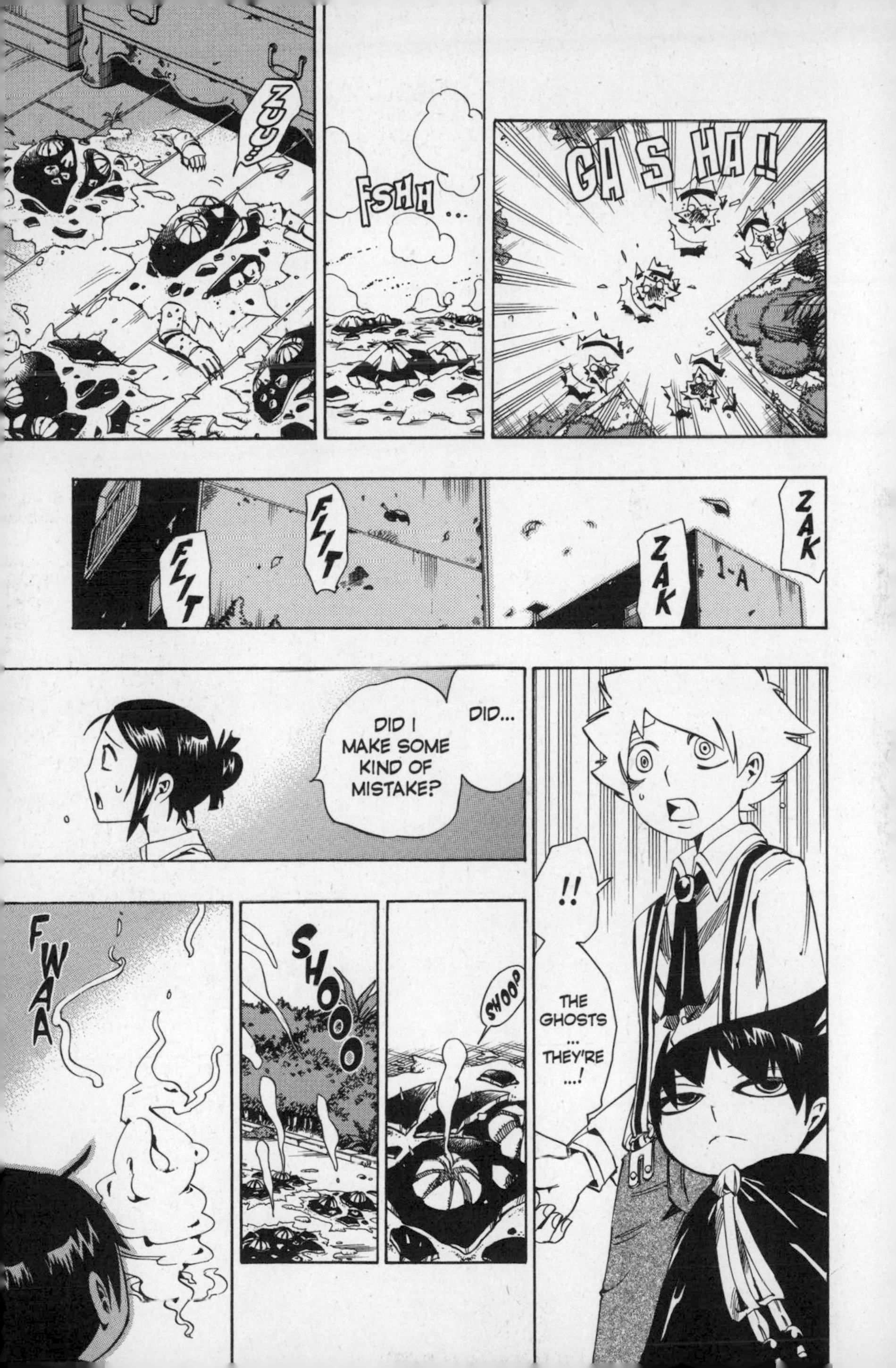
GASHA!!
FSHH...
ZUZU...
ZAK
ZAK
FLIT
FLIT
!!
THE GHOSTS ... THEY'RE ...!
DID...
DID I MAKE SOME KIND OF MISTAKE?
SHOOP
SHOOOO
FWAA

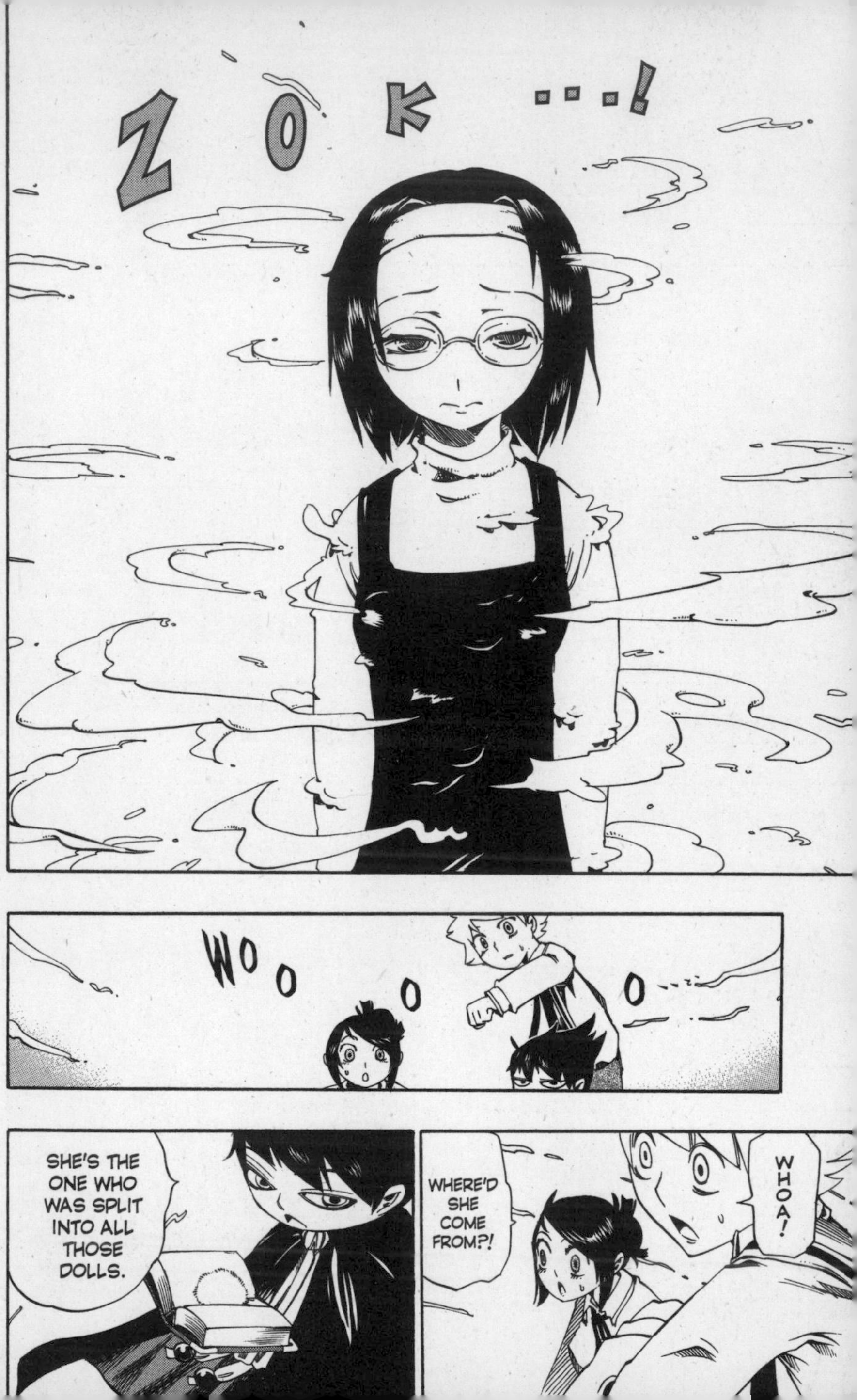
ZOK...!
WOOOO...
WHOA!
WHERE'D SHE COME FROM?!
SHE'S THE ONE WHO WAS SPLIT INTO ALL THOSE DOLLS.

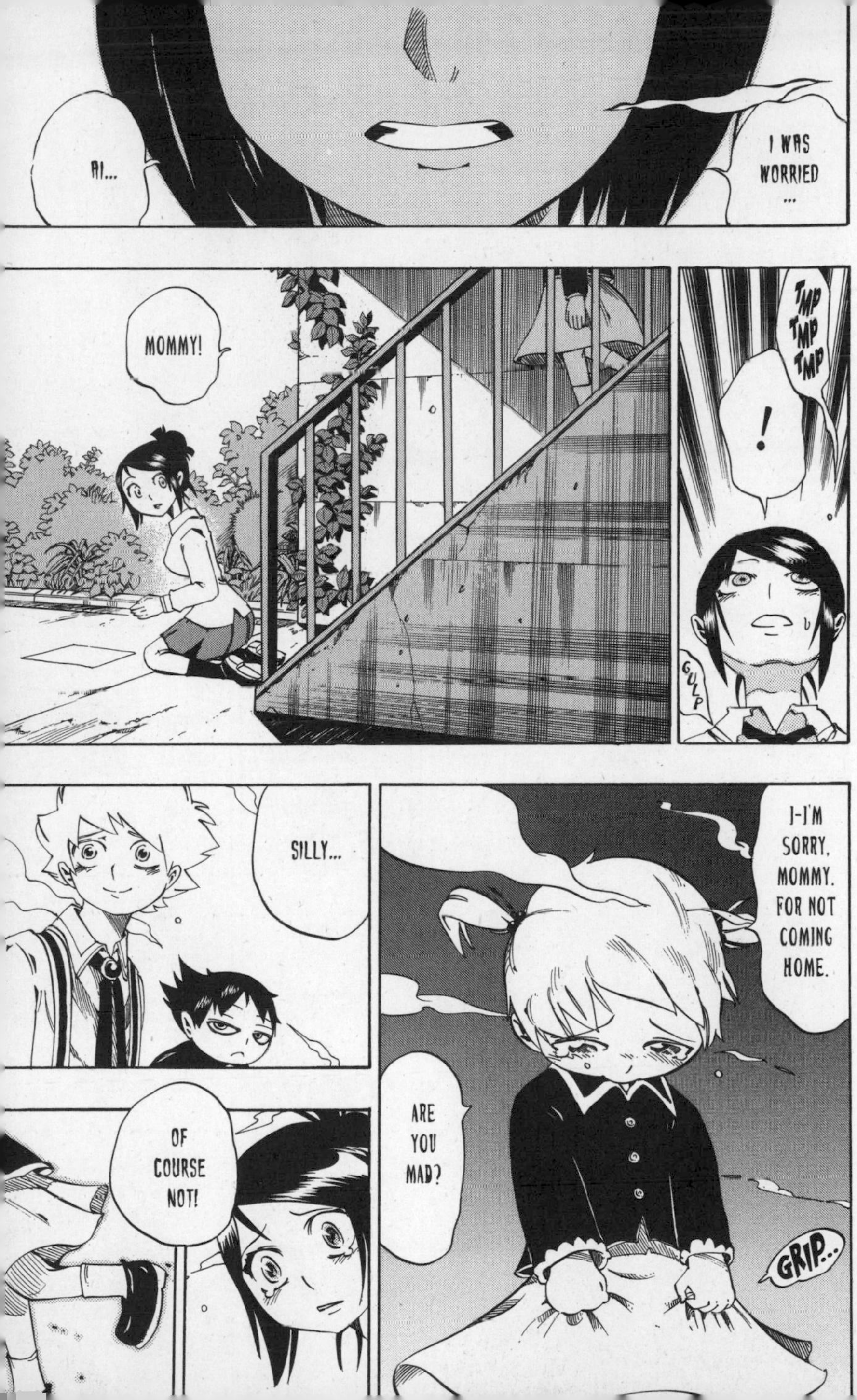

I WAS WORRIED ...
AI...
TMP TMP TMP
!
GULP
MOMMY!
I-I'M SORRY, MOMMY. FOR NOT COMING HOME.
ARE YOU MAD?
GRIP...
SILLY...
OF COURSE NOT!

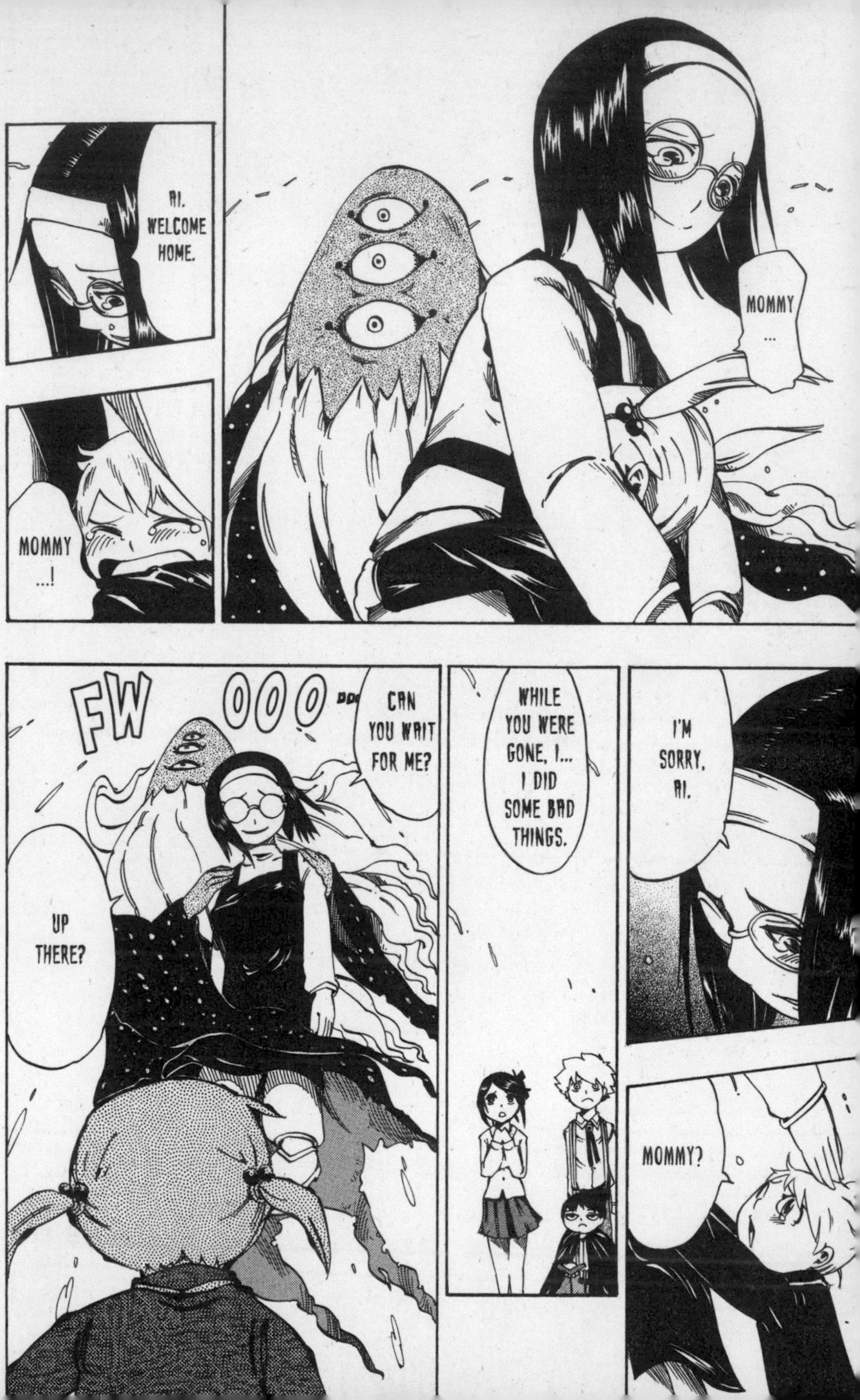
MOMMY ...
AI. WELCOME HOME.
MOMMY ...!
I'M SORRY, AI.
MOMMY?
WHILE YOU WERE GONE, I... I DID SOME BAD THINGS.
CAN YOU WAIT FOR ME?
FWOOO
UP THERE?

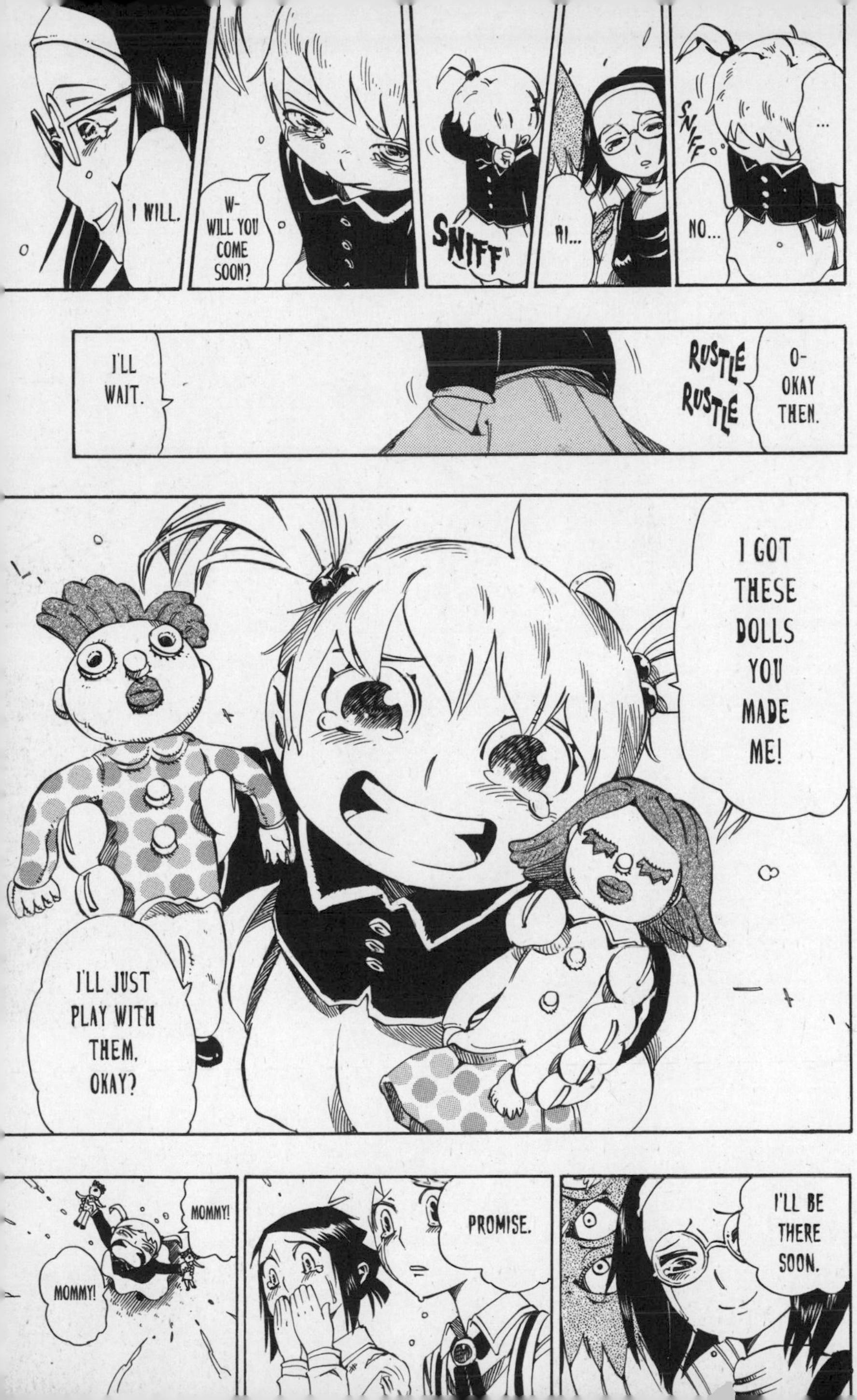
...
SNIFF
NO...
HI...
SNIFF
W-WILL YOU COME SOON?
I WILL.
O-OKAY THEN.
RUSTLE RUSTLE
I'LL WAIT.
I GOT THESE DOLLS YOU MADE ME!
I'LL JUST PLAY WITH THEM, OKAY?
I'LL BE THERE SOON.
PROMISE.
MOMMY!
MOMMY!

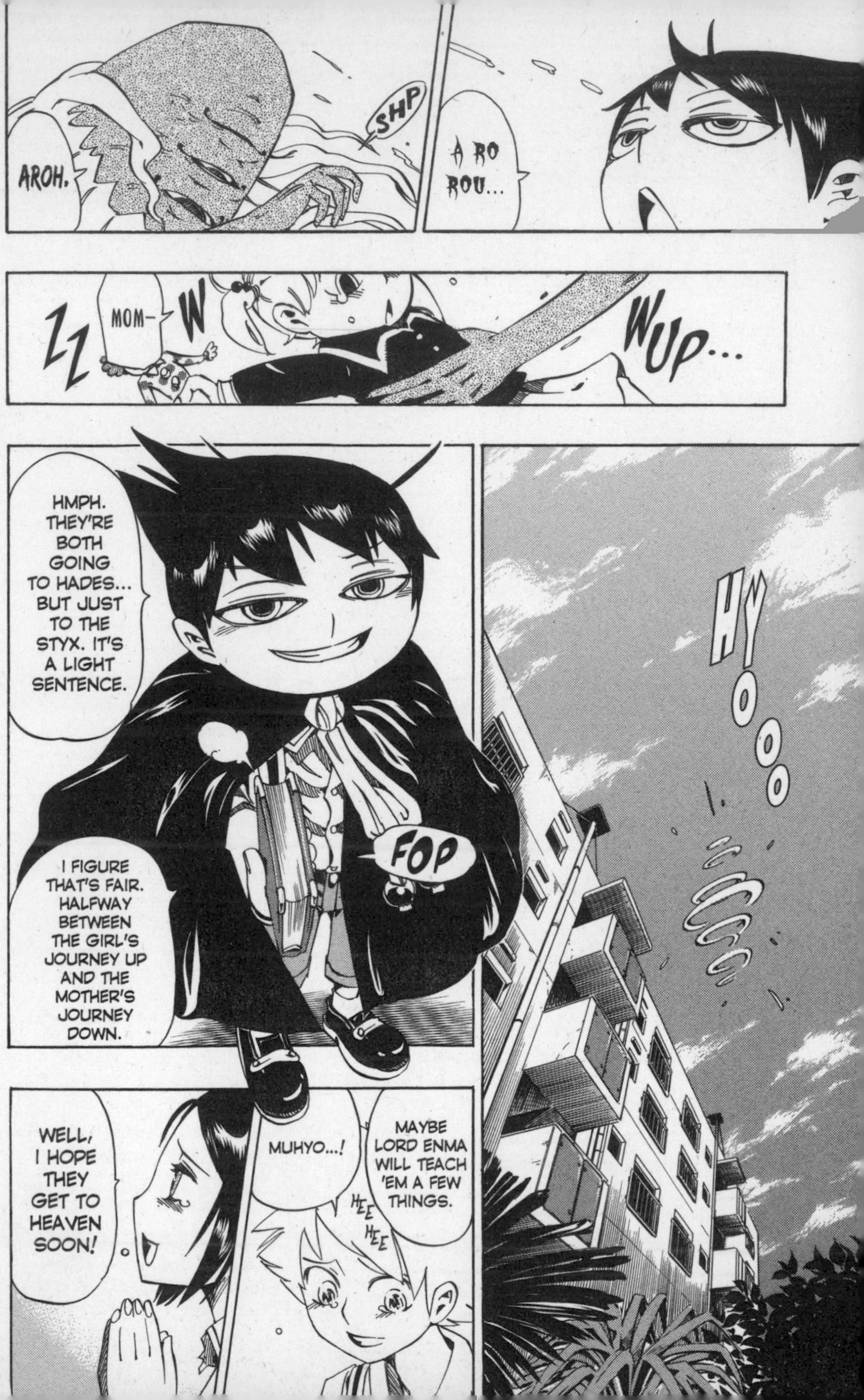
A RO ROU...
SHP
AROH.
WUP...
W
MOM-
ZZ
HYOOO
HMPH. THEY'RE BOTH GOING TO HADES... BUT JUST TO THE STYX. IT'S A LIGHT SENTENCE.
FOP
I FIGURE THAT'S FAIR. HALFWAY BETWEEN THE GIRL'S JOURNEY UP AND THE MOTHER'S JOURNEY DOWN.
MAYBE LORD ENMA WILL TEACH 'EM A FEW THINGS.
HEE HEE
MUHYO...!
WELL, I HOPE THEY GET TO HEAVEN SOON!

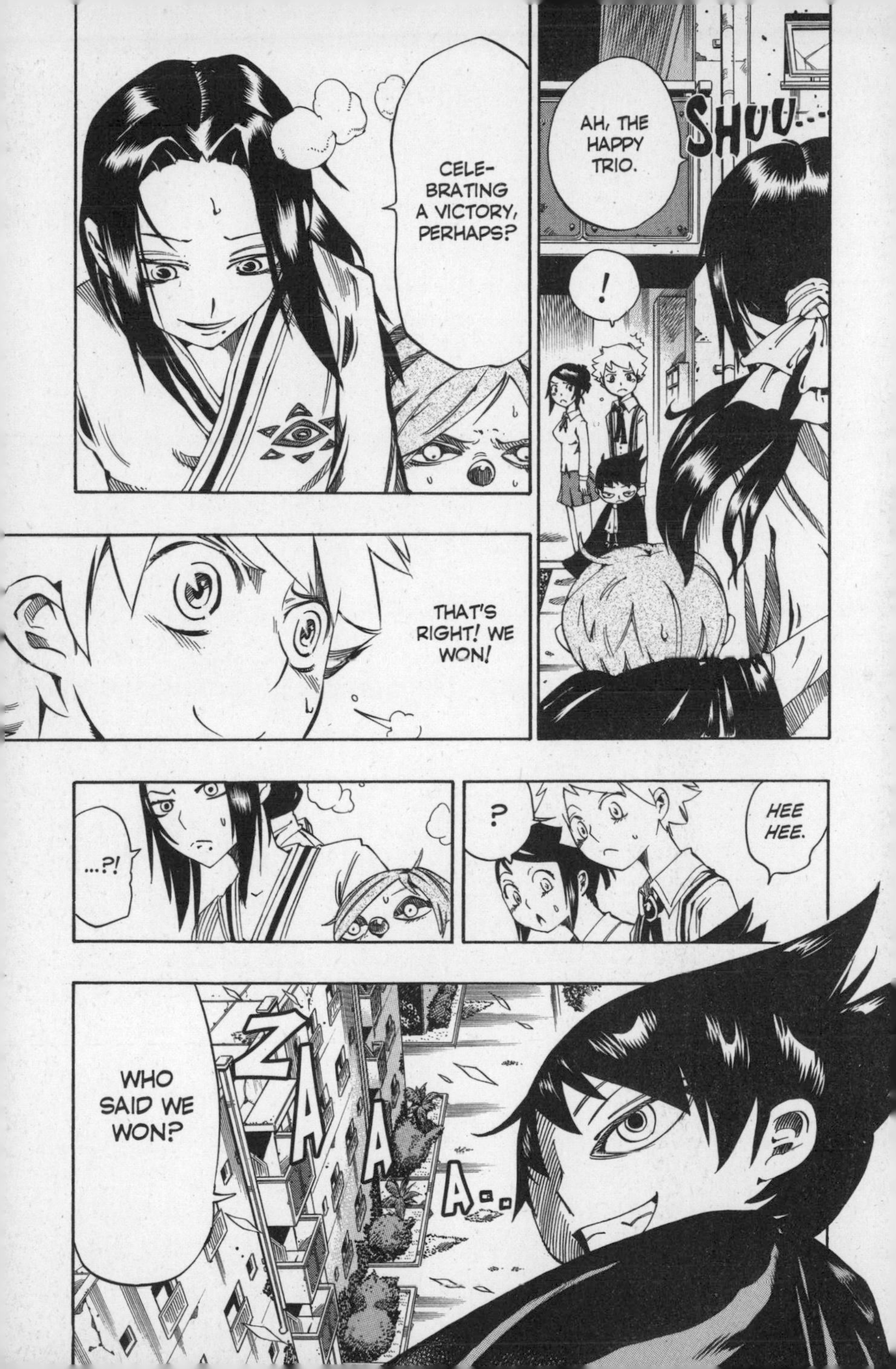
SHUU...
AH, THE HAPPY TRIO.
!
CELE-BRATING A VICTORY, PERHAPS?
THAT'S RIGHT! WE WON!
HEE HEE.
?
...?!
WHO SAID WE WON?
ZAAA..

YUURI, AFTER WORK

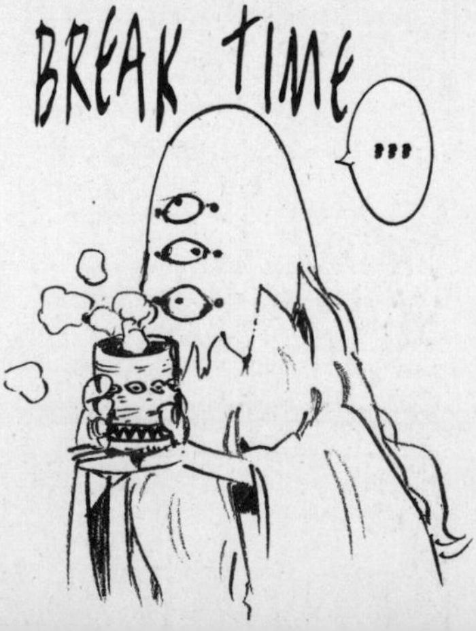
BREAK TIME
...

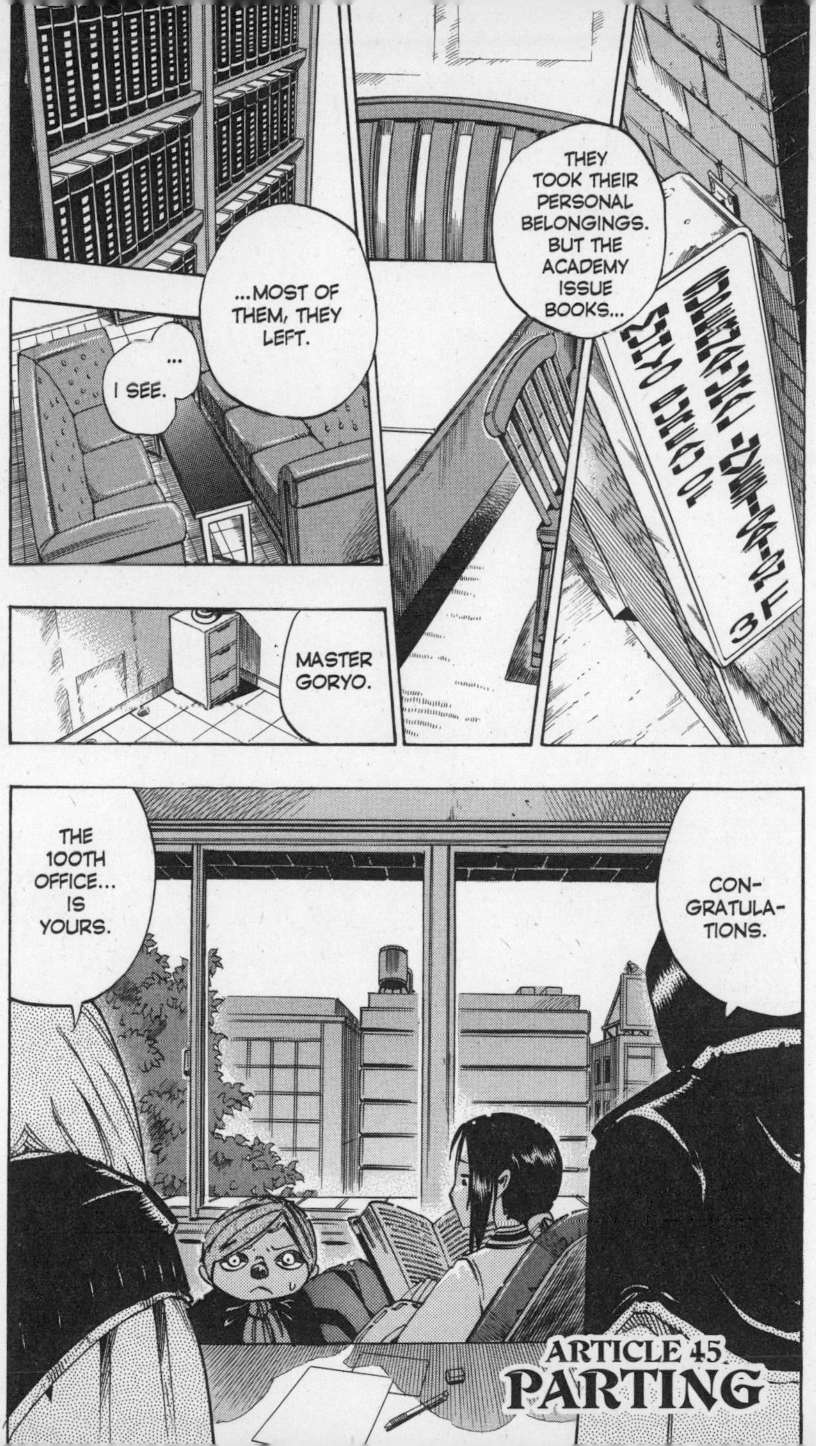
THEY TOOK THEIR PERSONAL BELONGINGS. BUT THE ACADEMY ISSUE BOOKS...
...MOST OF THEM, THEY LEFT.
... I SEE.
MASTER GORYO.
CON-GRATULA-TIONS.
THE 100TH OFFICE... IS YOURS.

ARTICLE 45 PARTING

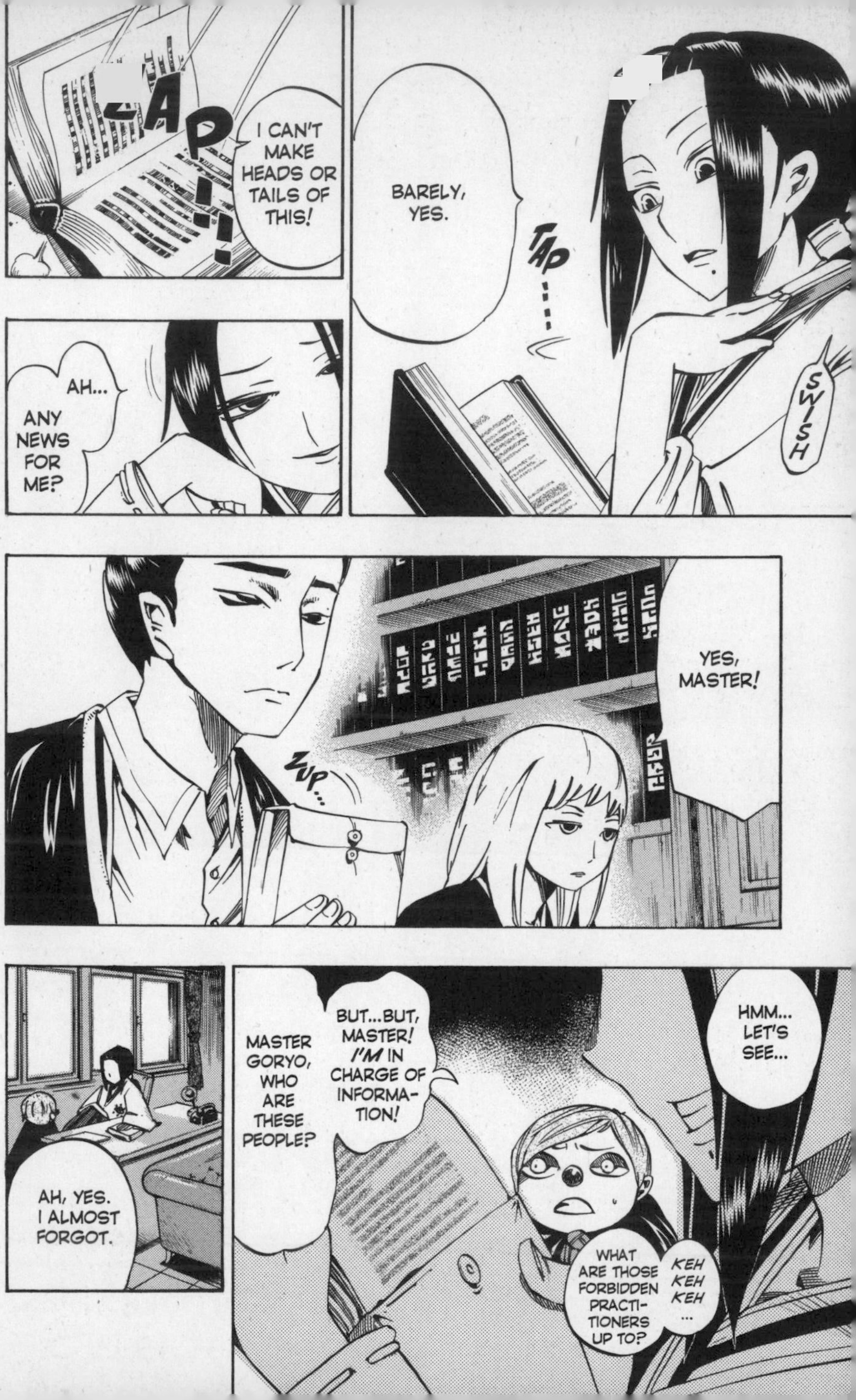
BARELY, YES.
TAP...
SWISH
ZAP!!
I CAN'T MAKE HEADS OR TAILS OF THIS!
AH... ANY NEWS FOR ME?
YES, MASTER!
ZUP...
HMM... LET'S SEE...
BUT...BUT, MASTER! I'M IN CHARGE OF INFORMATION!
MASTER GORYO, WHO ARE THESE PEOPLE?
KEH KEH KEH...
WHAT ARE THOSE FORBIDDEN PRACTITIONERS UP TO?
AH, YES. I ALMOST FORGOT.

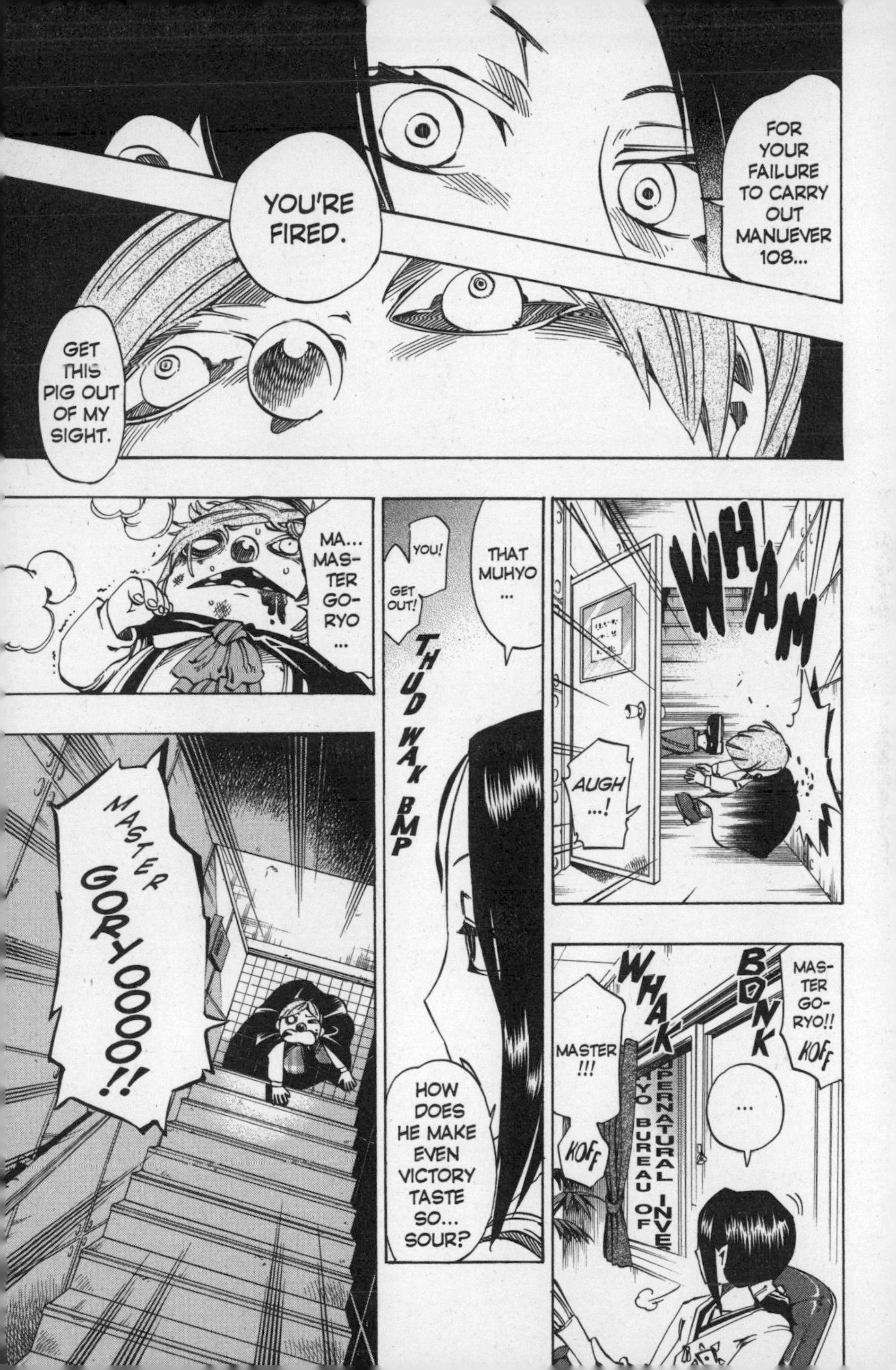

FOR YOUR FAILURE TO CARRY OUT MANUEVER 108...
YOU'RE FIRED.
GET THIS PIG OUT OF MY SIGHT.
WHAM
AUGH ...!
BDNK
WHAK
MASTER GORYO!! KOFF
MASTER !!!
KOFF
...
HYO BUREAU OF SUPERNATURAL INVE
THAT MUHYO ...
YOU! GET OUT!
THUD WAK BMP
HOW DOES HE MAKE EVEN VICTORY TASTE SO... SOUR?
MA... MASTER GORYO ...
MASTER GORYOOOOO!!

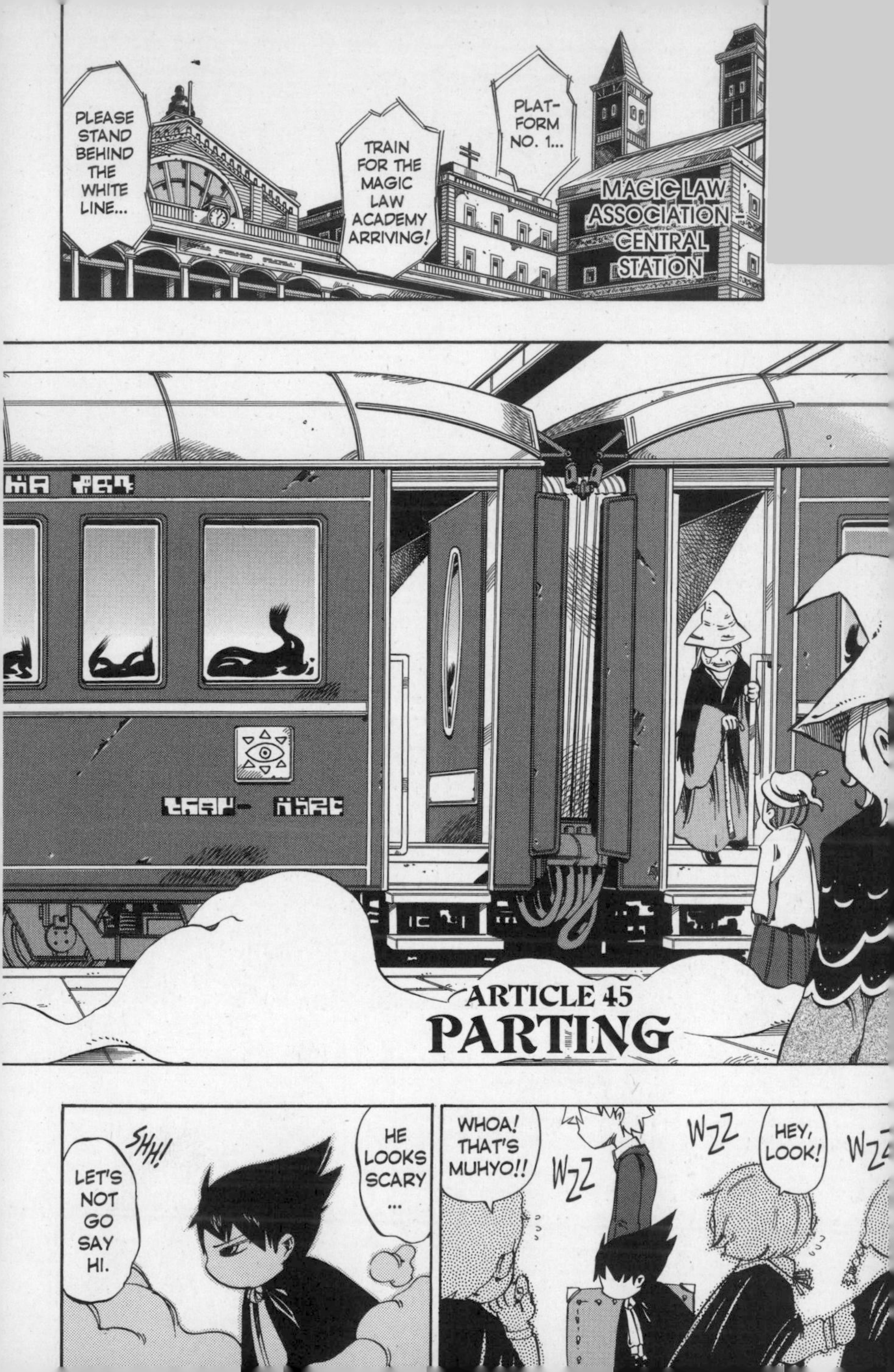
MAGIC LAW ASSOCIATION - CENTRAL STATION
PLATFORM NO. 1...
TRAIN FOR THE MAGIC LAW ACADEMY ARRIVING!
PLEASE STAND BEHIND THE WHITE LINE...
ARTICLE 45
PARTING
WZZ
HEY, LOOK!
WZZ
WHOA! THAT'S MUHYO!!
WZZ
HE LOOKS SCARY ...
SHH!
LET'S NOT GO SAY HI.

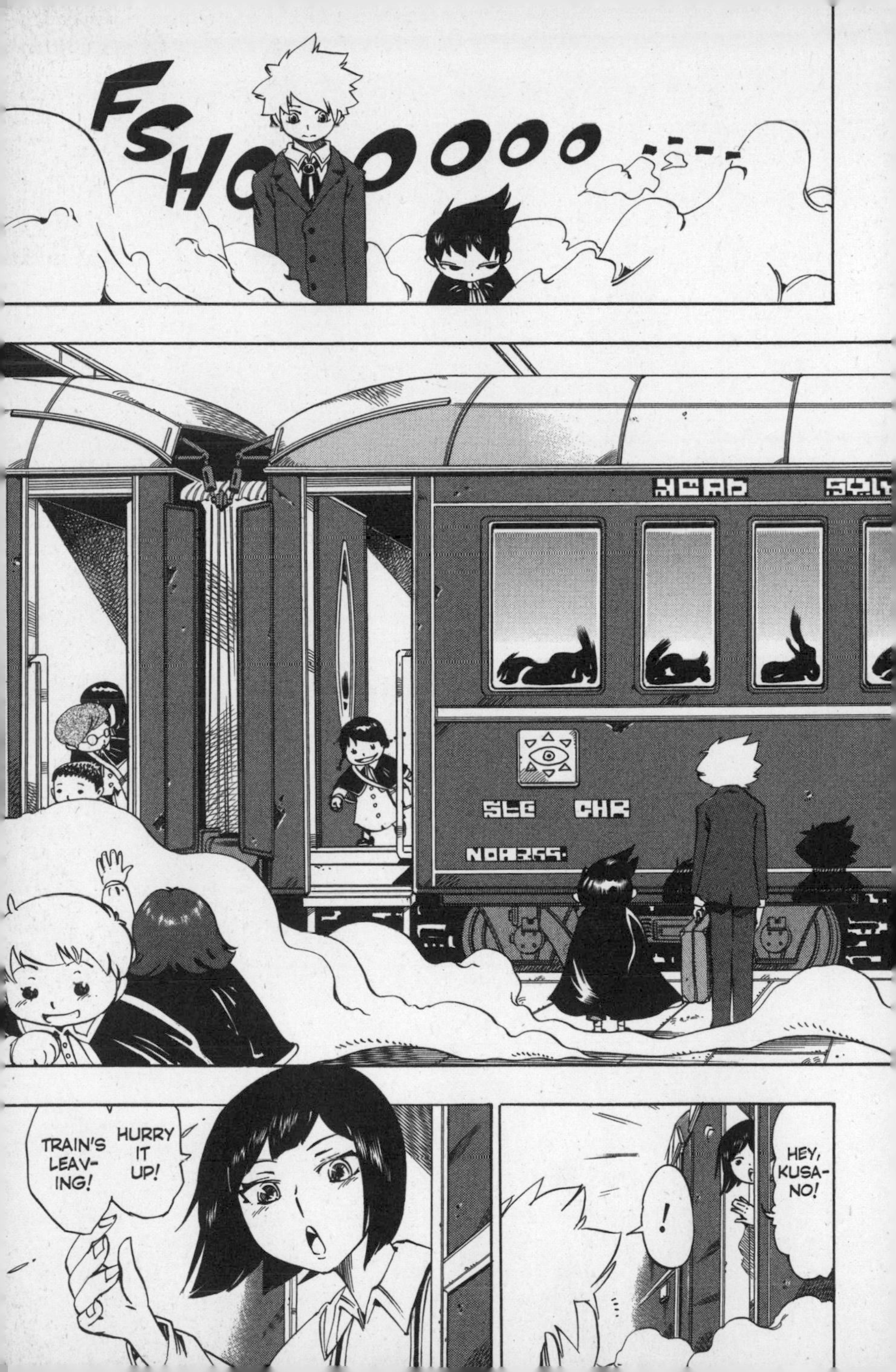
FSHOOOOO
HEY, KUSA-NO!
!
HURRY IT UP!
TRAIN'S LEAV-ING!

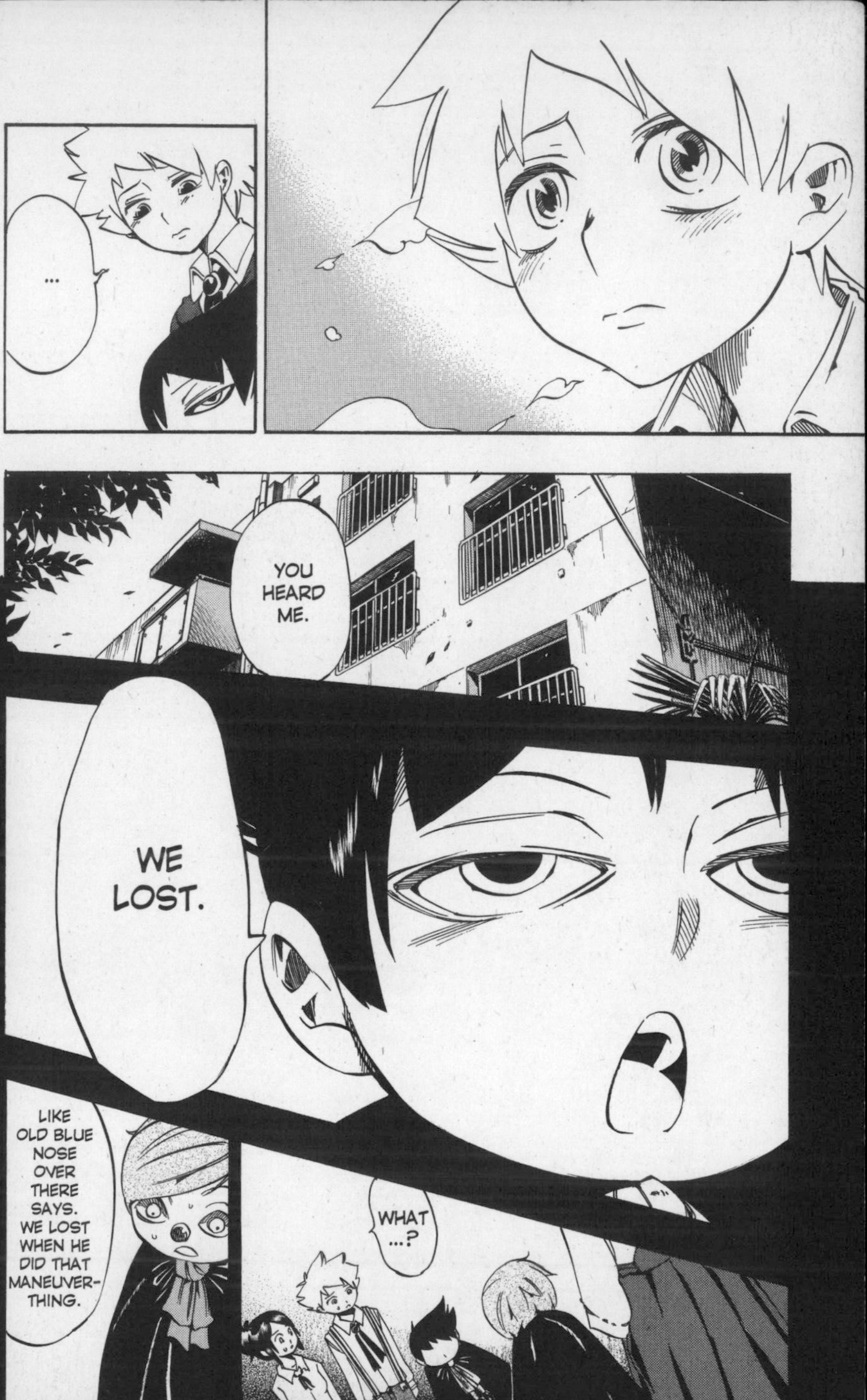
...
YOU HEARD ME.
WE LOST.
WHAT ...?
LIKE OLD BLUE NOSE OVER THERE SAYS. WE LOST WHEN HE DID THAT MANEUVER-THING.

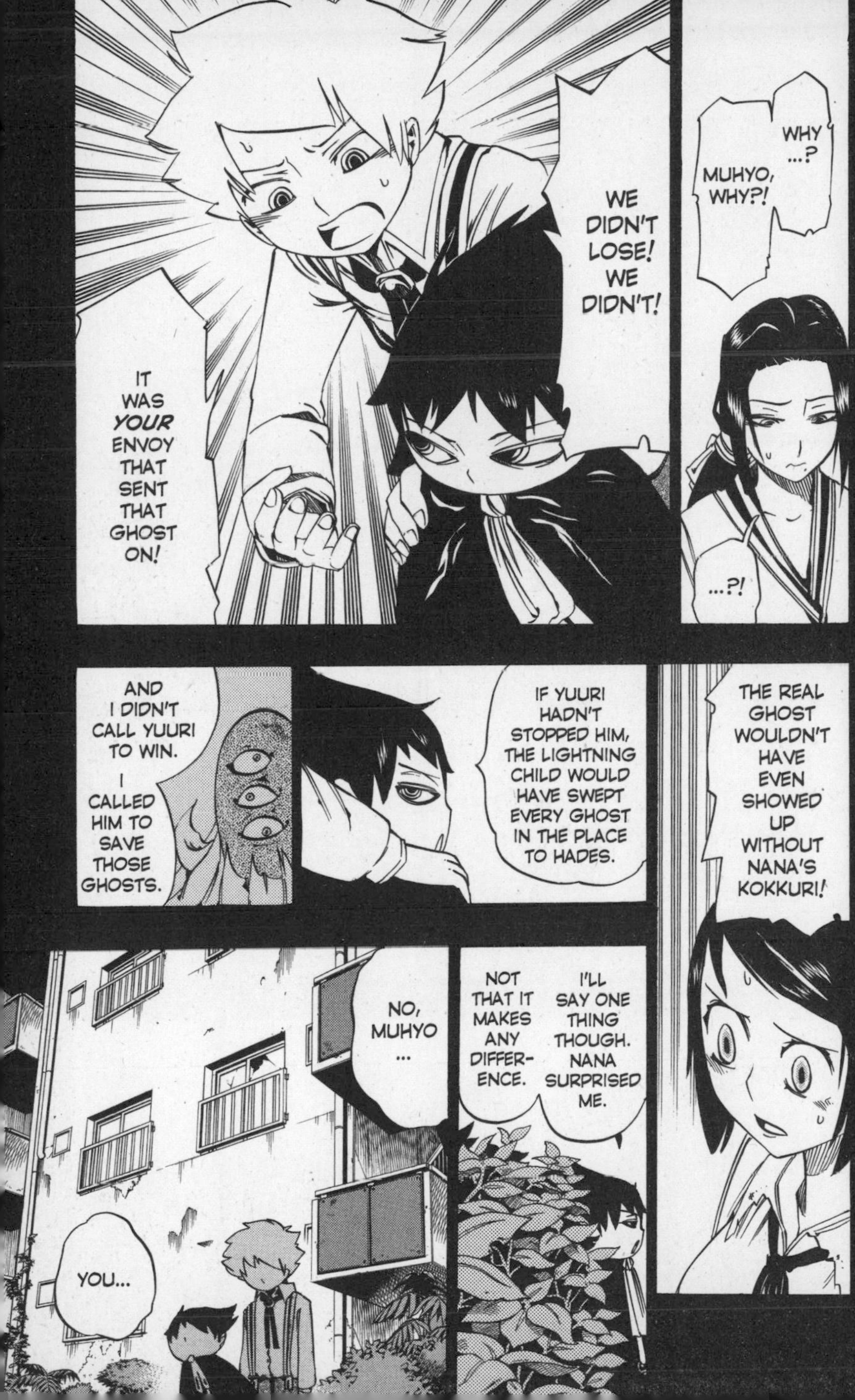
WHY ...?
MUHYO, WHY?!
...?!
WE DIDN'T LOSE! WE DIDN'T!
IT WAS *YOUR* ENVOY THAT SENT THAT GHOST ON!
THE REAL GHOST WOULDN'T HAVE EVEN SHOWED UP WITHOUT NANA'S KOKKURI!
IF YUURI HADN'T STOPPED HIM, THE LIGHTNING CHILD WOULD HAVE SWEPT EVERY GHOST IN THE PLACE TO HADES.
AND I DIDN'T CALL YUURI TO WIN.
I CALLED HIM TO SAVE THOSE GHOSTS.
I'LL SAY ONE THING THOUGH. NANA SURPRISED ME.
NOT THAT IT MAKES ANY DIFFER-ENCE.
NO, MUHYO ...
YOU...

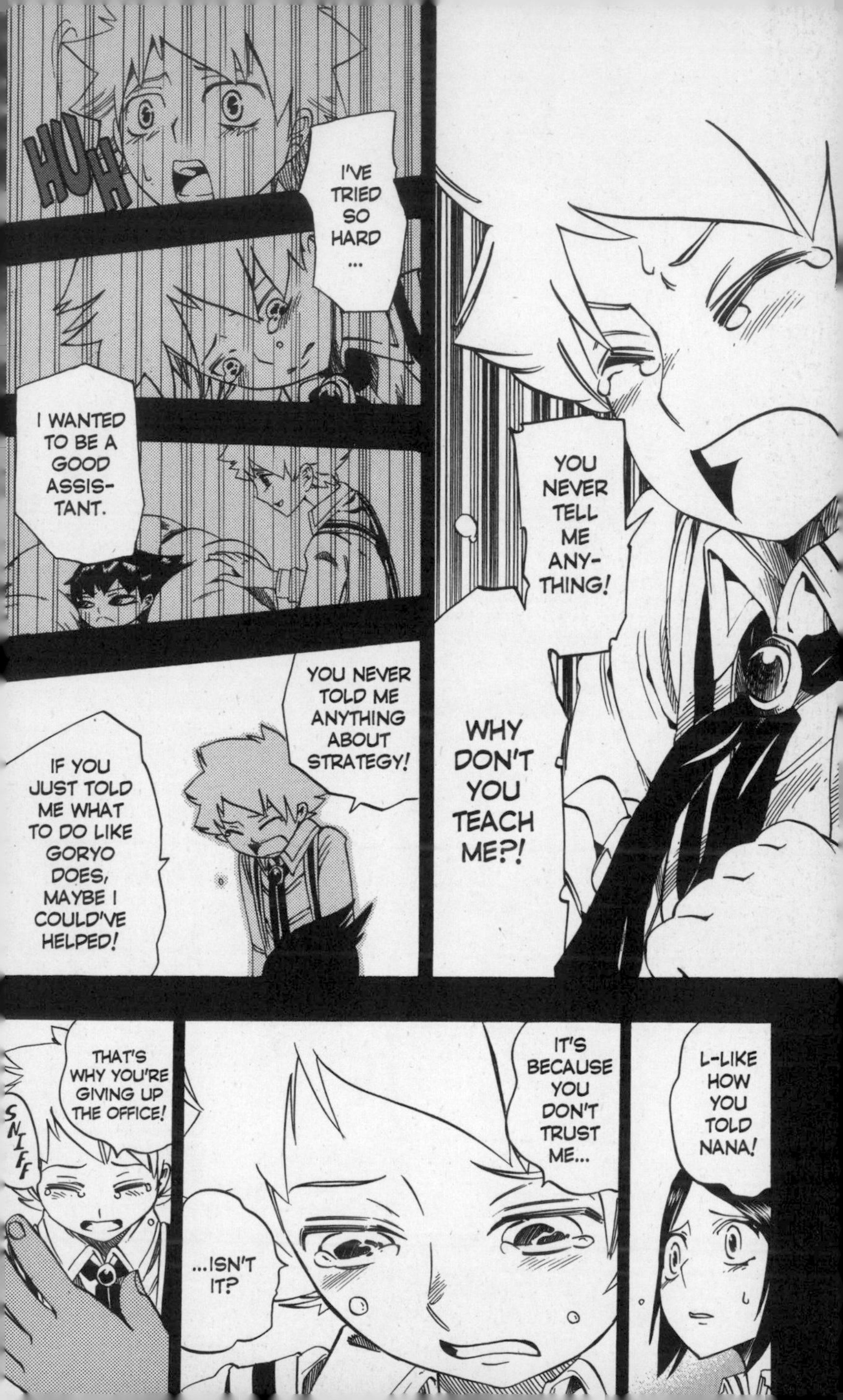
YOU NEVER TELL ME ANY-THING!
WHY DON'T YOU TEACH ME?!
HUH
I'VE TRIED SO HARD ...
I WANTED TO BE A GOOD ASSIS-TANT.
YOU NEVER TOLD ME ANYTHING ABOUT STRATEGY!
IF YOU JUST TOLD ME WHAT TO DO LIKE GORYO DOES, MAYBE I COULD'VE HELPED!
L-LIKE HOW YOU TOLD NANA!
IT'S BECAUSE YOU DON'T TRUST ME...
...ISN'T IT?
THAT'S WHY YOU'RE GIVING UP THE OFFICE!
SNIFF

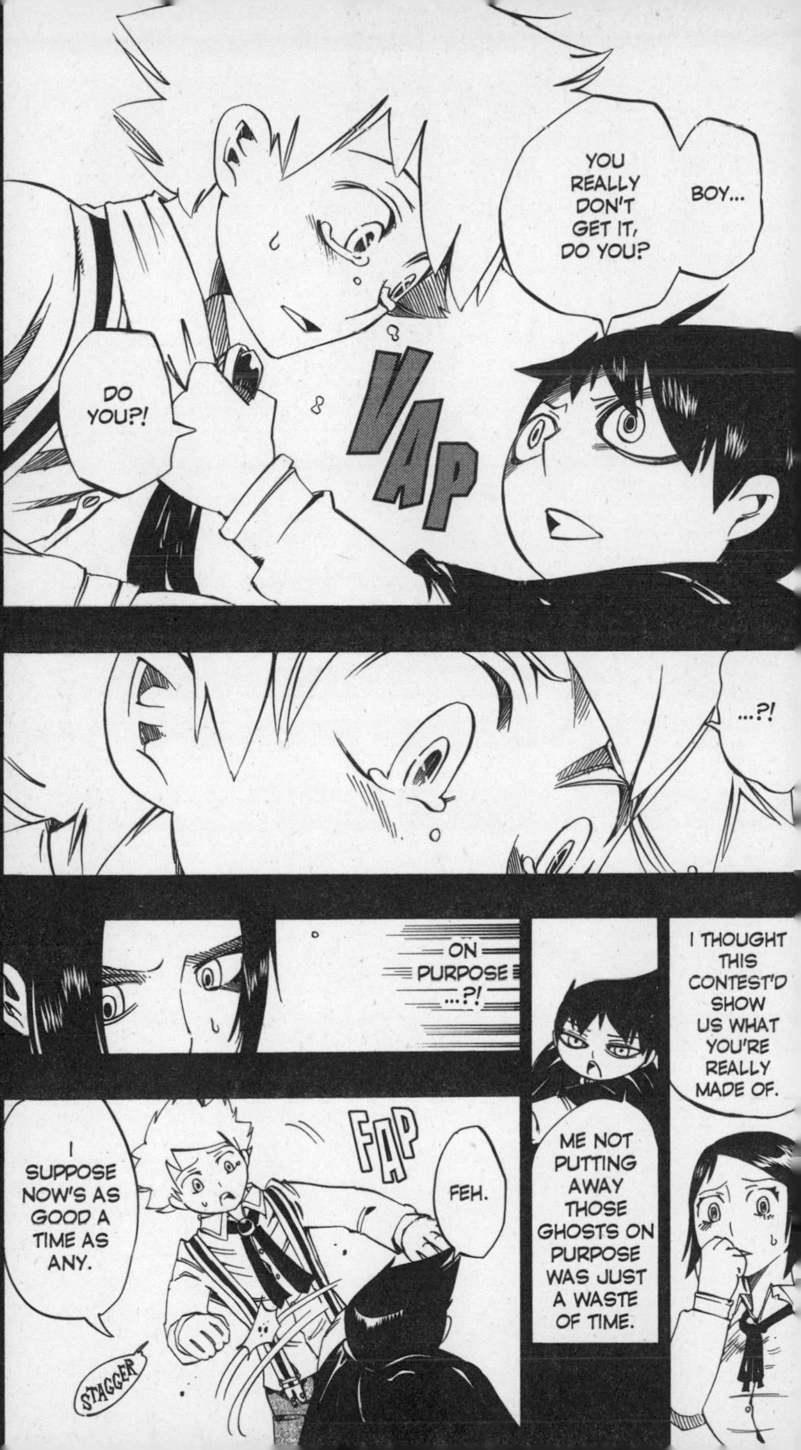
BOY...
YOU REALLY DON'T GET IT, DO YOU?
VAP
DO YOU?!
...?!
I THOUGHT THIS CONTEST'D SHOW US WHAT YOU'RE REALLY MADE OF.
ME NOT PUTTING AWAY THOSE GHOSTS ON PURPOSE WAS JUST A WASTE OF TIME.
ON PURPOSE ...?!
FEH.
FAP
I SUPPOSE NOW'S AS GOOD A TIME AS ANY.
STAGGER

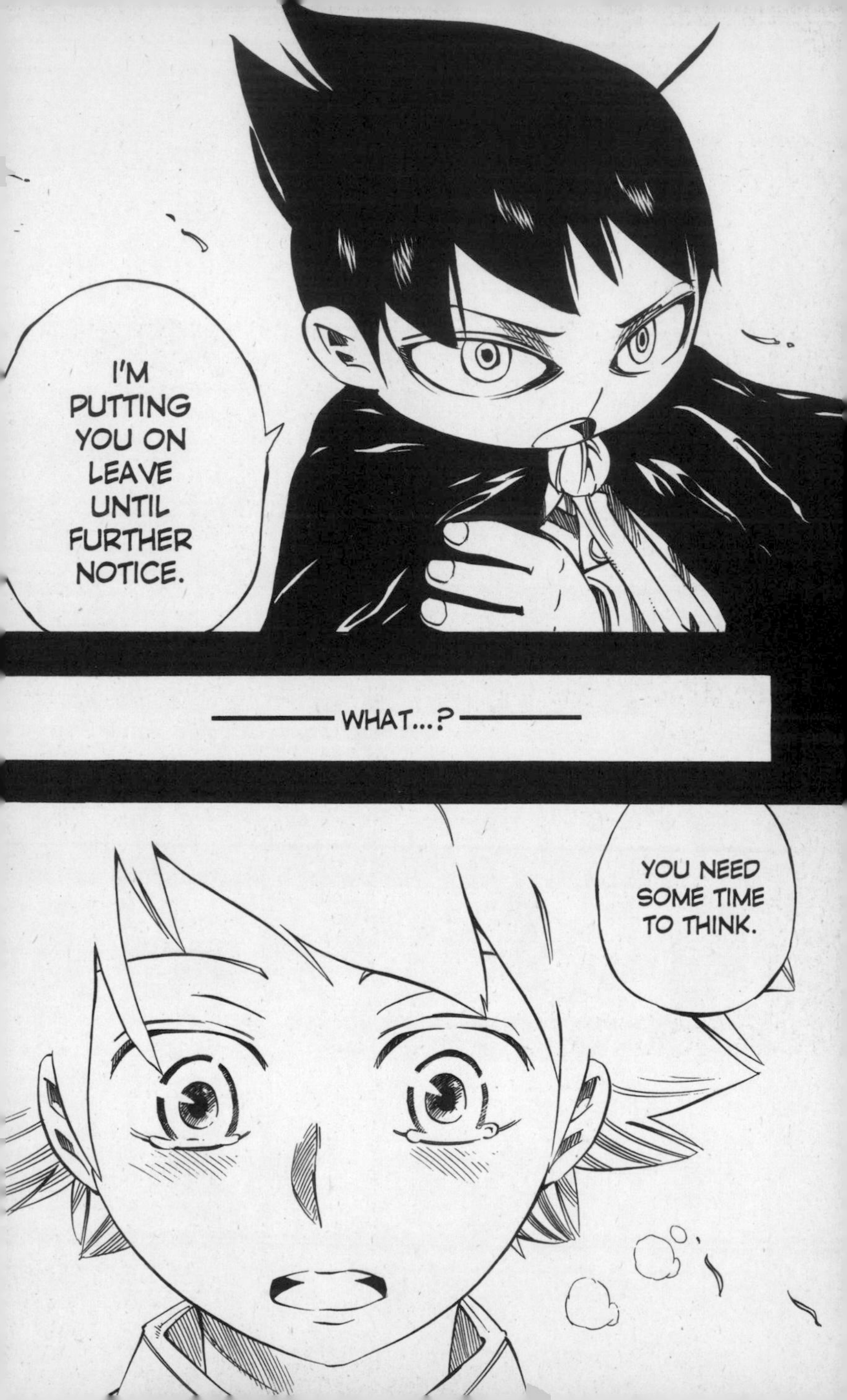
I'M PUTTING YOU ON LEAVE UNTIL FURTHER NOTICE.
—WHAT...?—
YOU NEED SOME TIME TO THINK.

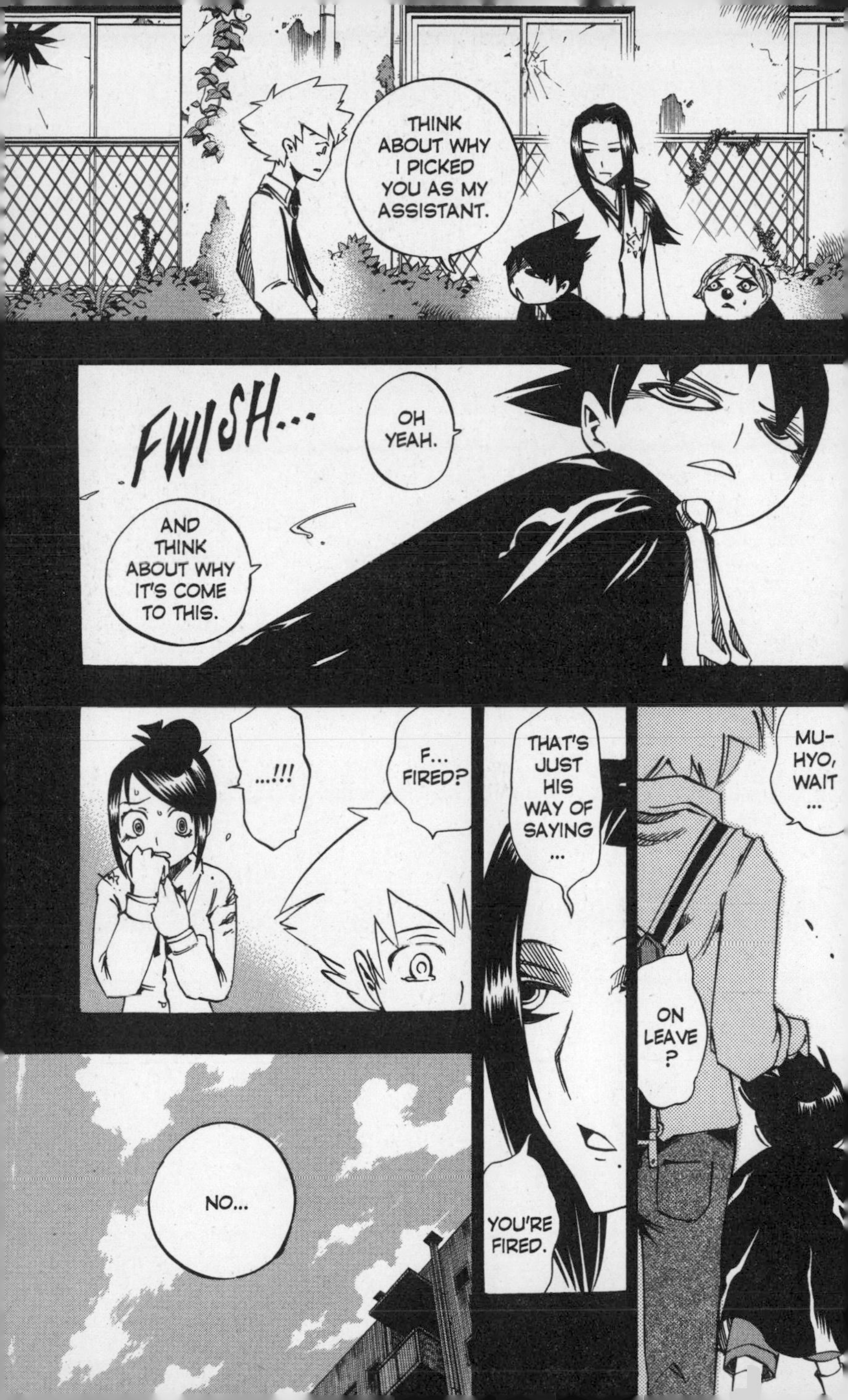
THINK ABOUT WHY I PICKED YOU AS MY ASSISTANT.
OH YEAH.
FWISH...
AND THINK ABOUT WHY IT'S COME TO THIS.
MU-HYO, WAIT ...
ON LEAVE?
THAT'S JUST HIS WAY OF SAYING ...
YOU'RE FIRED.
F... FIRED?
...!!!
NO...

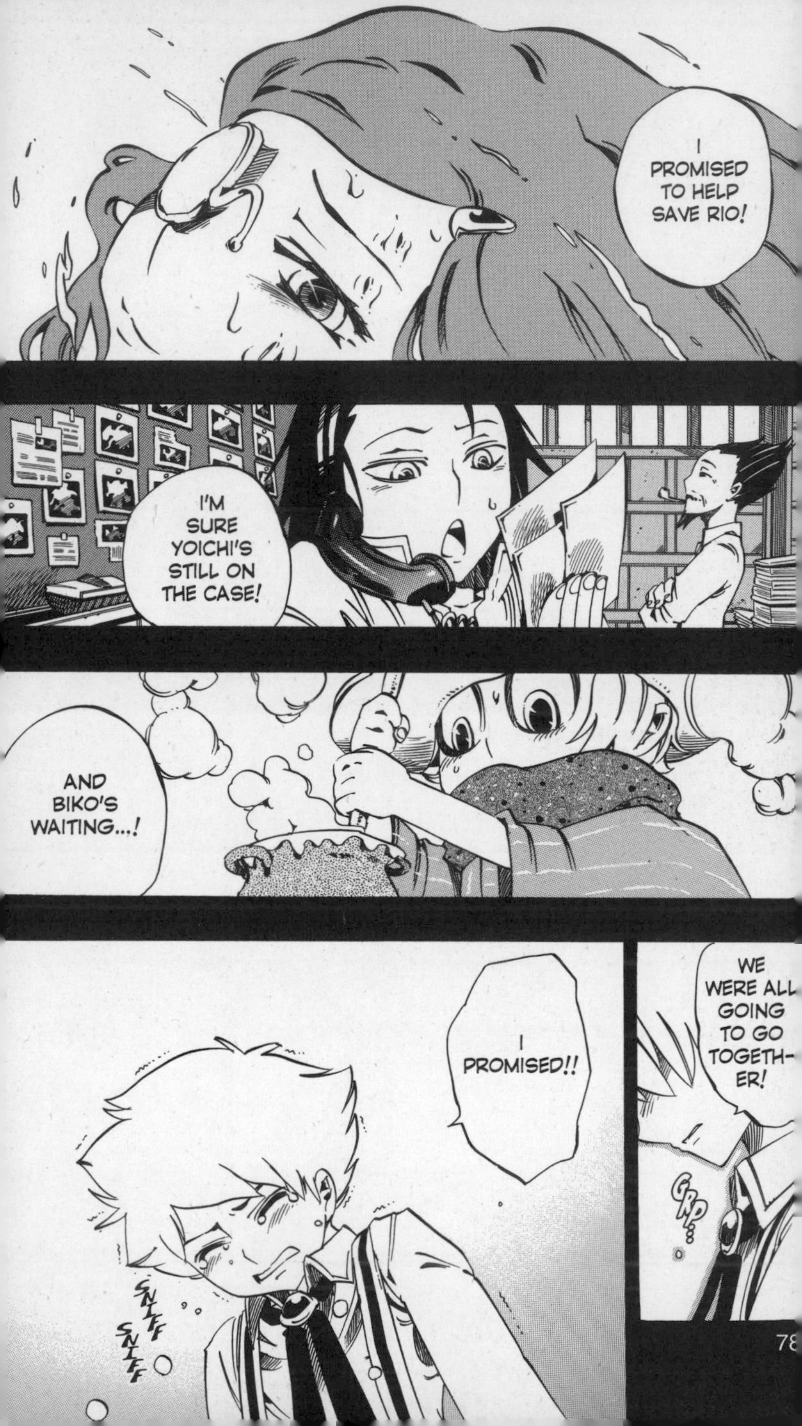
I PROMISED TO HELP SAVE RIO!
I'M SURE YOICHI'S STILL ON THE CASE!
AND BIKO'S WAITING...!
WE WERE ALL GOING TO GO TOGETH-ER!
GRP...
I PROMISED!!
SNIFF
SNIFF

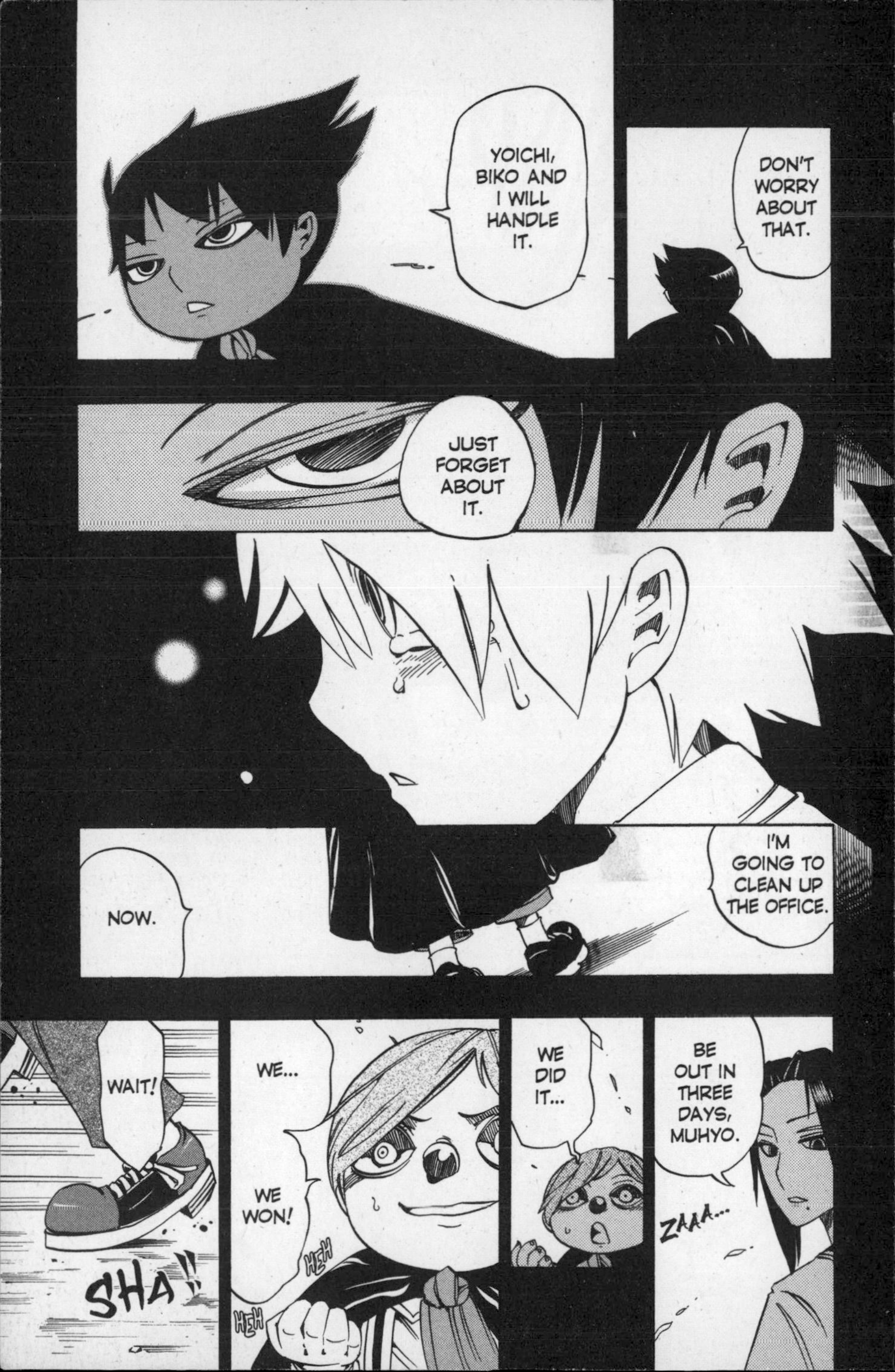
DON'T WORRY ABOUT THAT.
YOICHI, BIKO AND I WILL HANDLE IT.
JUST FORGET ABOUT IT.
I'M GOING TO CLEAN UP THE OFFICE.
NOW.
BE OUT IN THREE DAYS, MUHYO.
ZAAA...
WE DID IT...
WE...
WE WON!
HEH
HEH
WAIT!
SHA!!

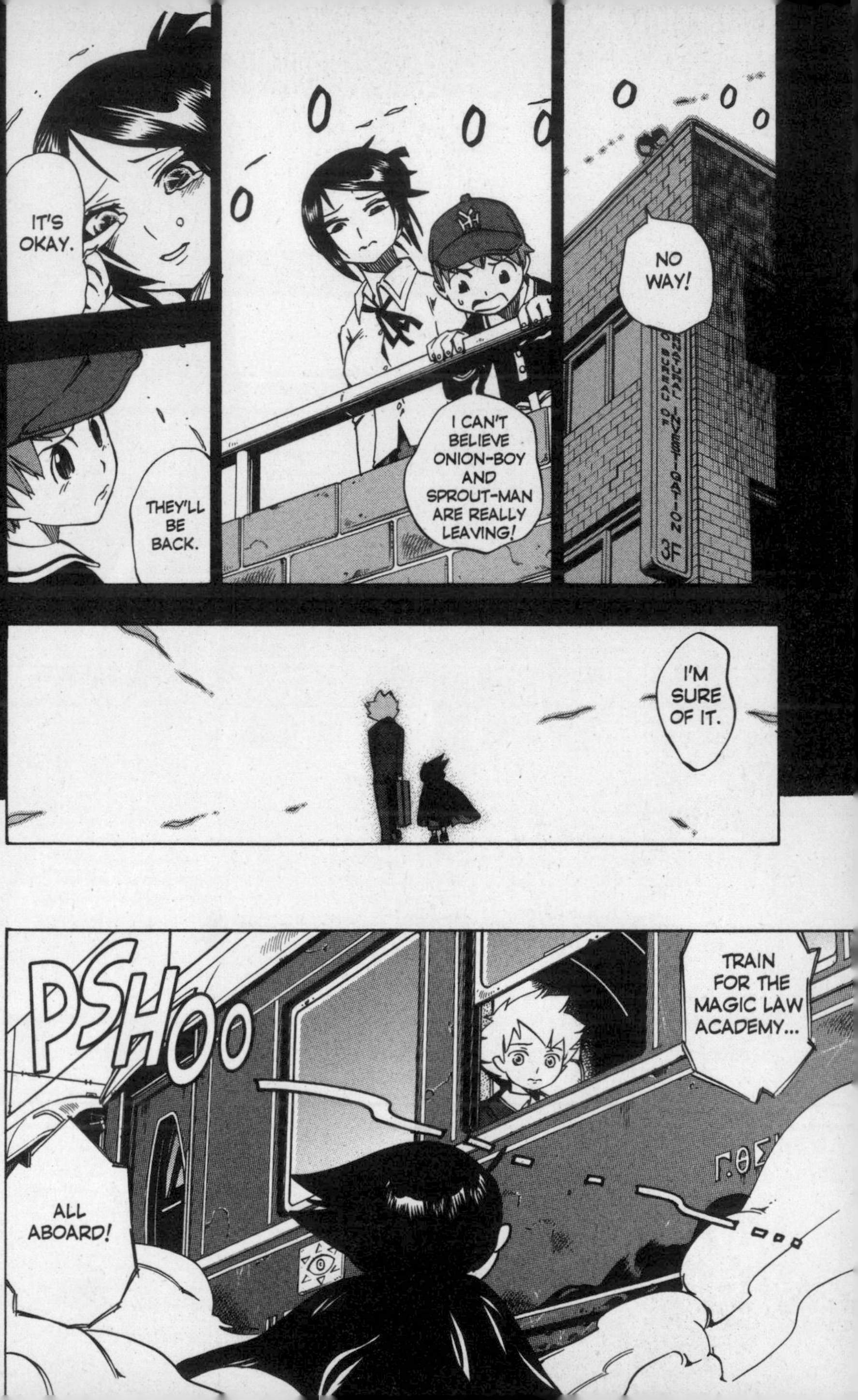
NO WAY!
I CAN'T BELIEVE ONION-BOY AND SPROUT-MAN ARE REALLY LEAVING!
3F
IT'S OKAY.
THEY'LL BE BACK.
I'M SURE OF IT.
TRAIN FOR THE MAGIC LAW ACADEMY...
PSHOO
ALL ABOARD!

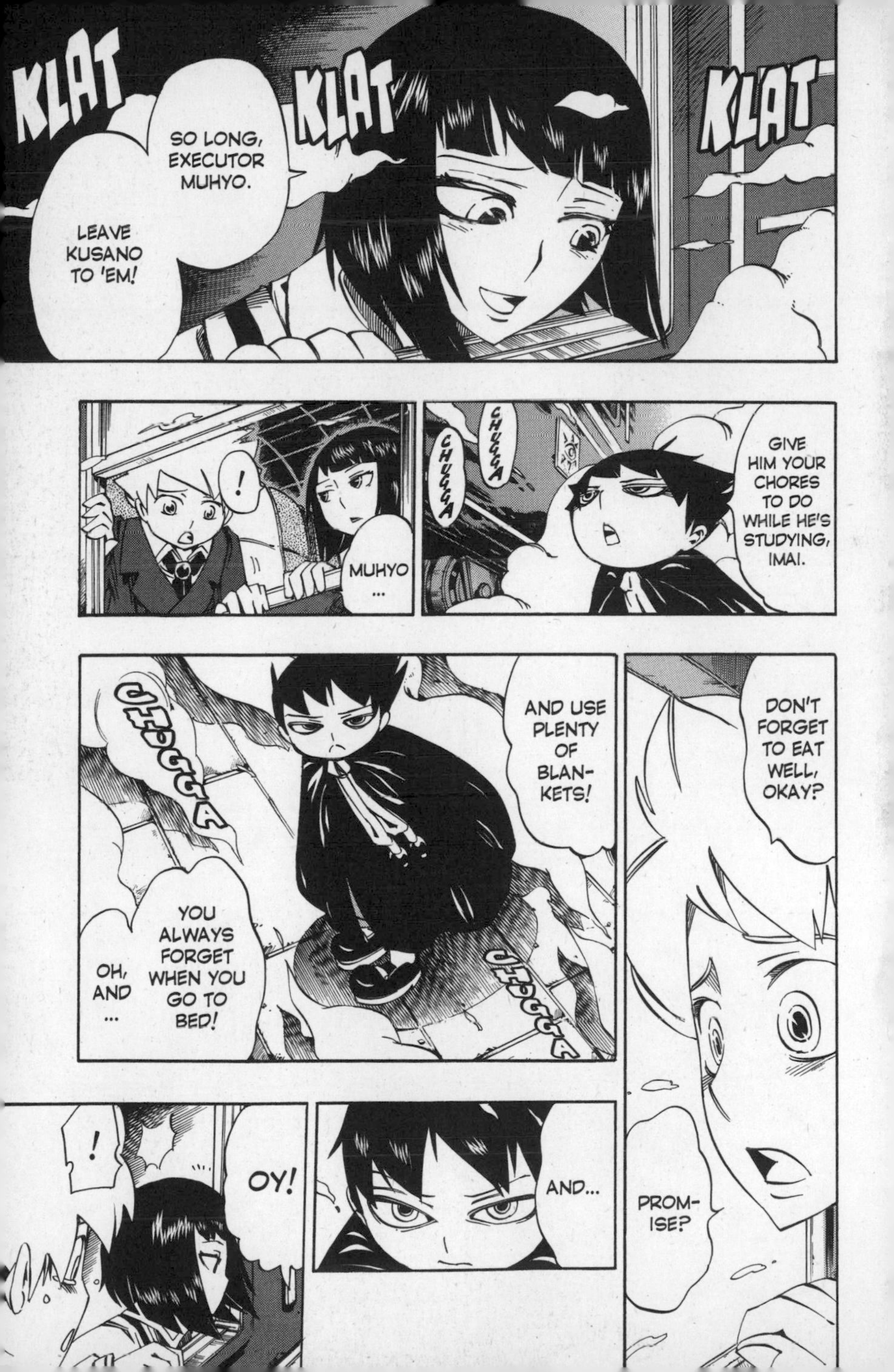
KLAT
KLAT
KLAT
SO LONG, EXECUTOR MUHYO.
LEAVE KUSANO TO 'EM!
CHUGGA CHUGGA
GIVE HIM YOUR CHORES TO DO WHILE HE'S STUDYING, IMAI.
!
MUHYO ...
DON'T FORGET TO EAT WELL, OKAY?
PROM-ISE?
CHUGGA
AND USE PLENTY OF BLAN-KETS!
OH, AND ...
YOU ALWAYS FORGET WHEN YOU GO TO BED!
CHUGGA
AND...
OY!
!

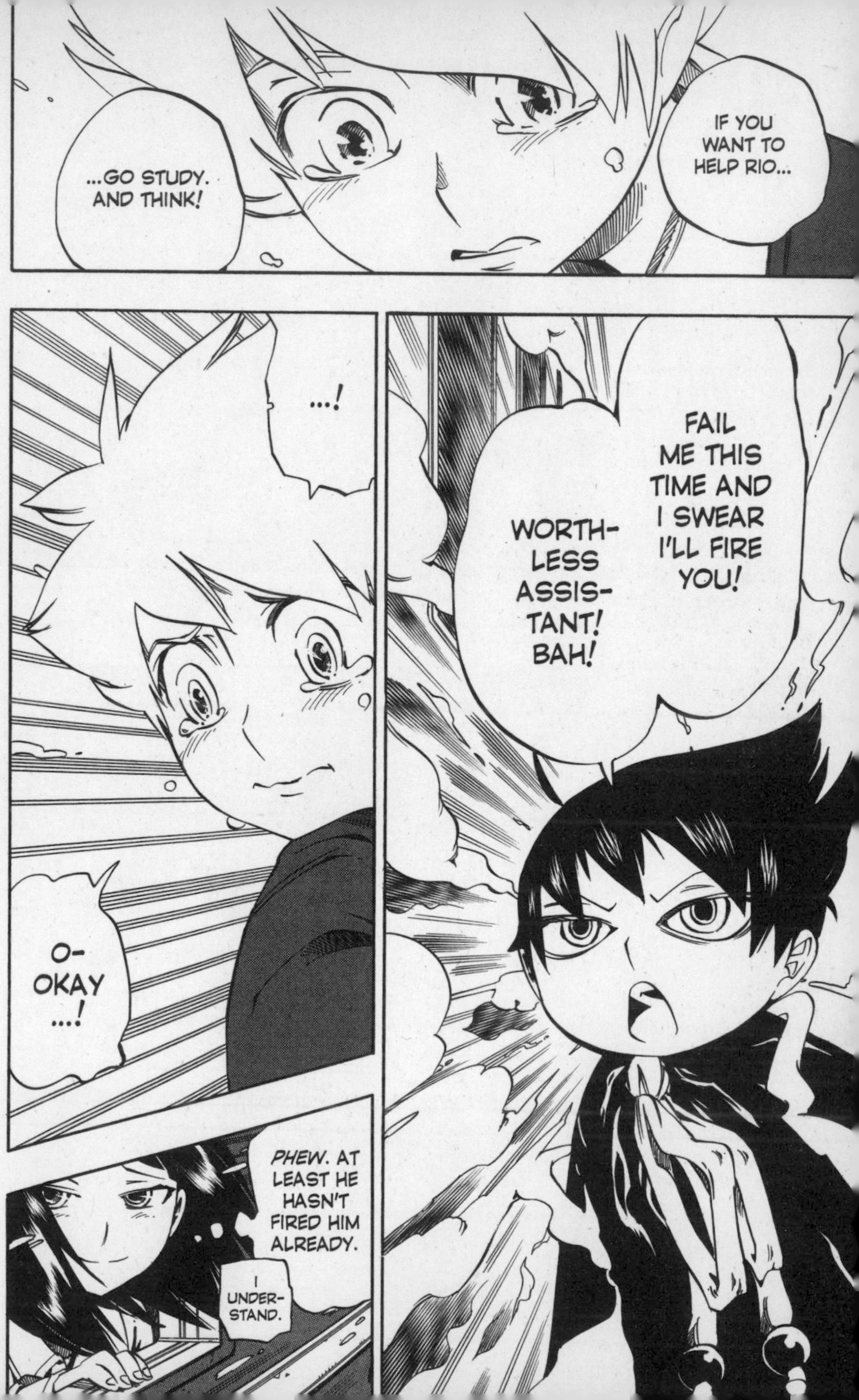
IF YOU WANT TO HELP RIO...
...GO STUDY. AND THINK!
FAIL ME THIS TIME AND I SWEAR I'LL FIRE YOU!
WORTH-LESS ASSIS-TANT! BAH!
...!
O-OKAY ...!
PHEW. AT LEAST HE HASN'T FIRED HIM ALREADY.
I UNDER-STAND.

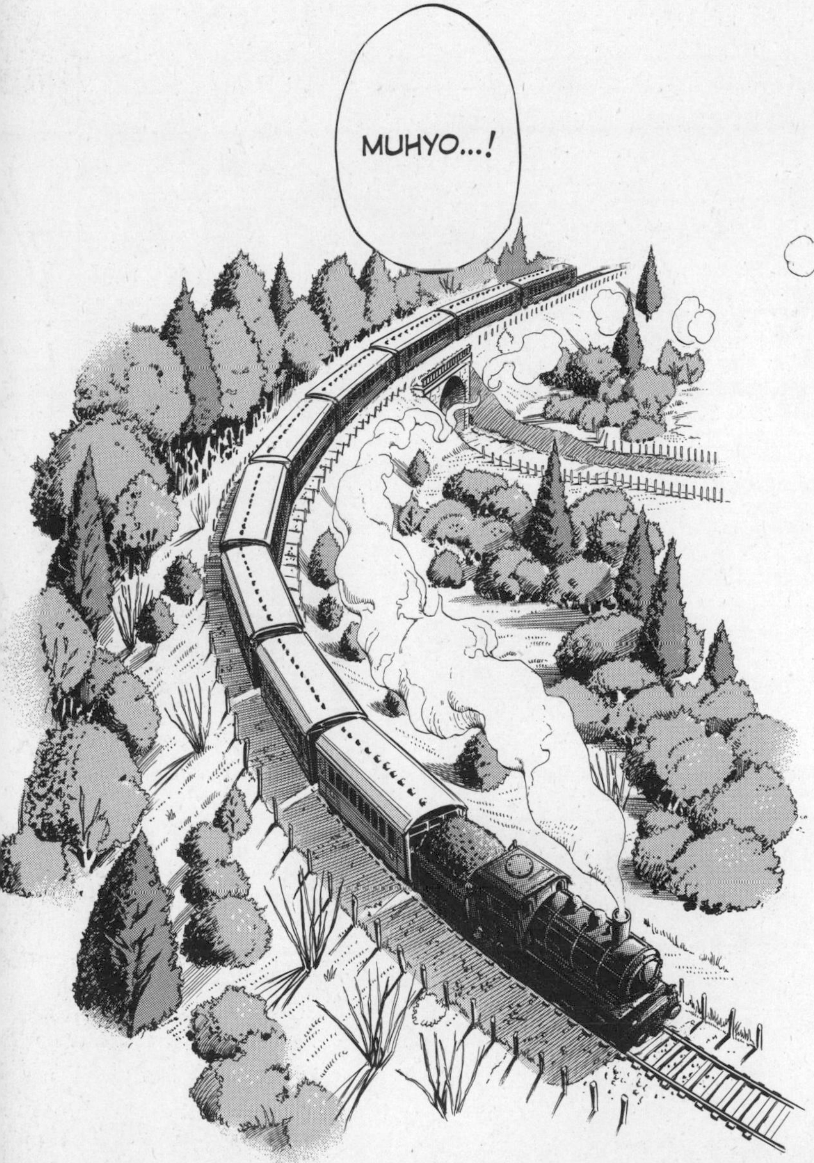
MUHYO...!

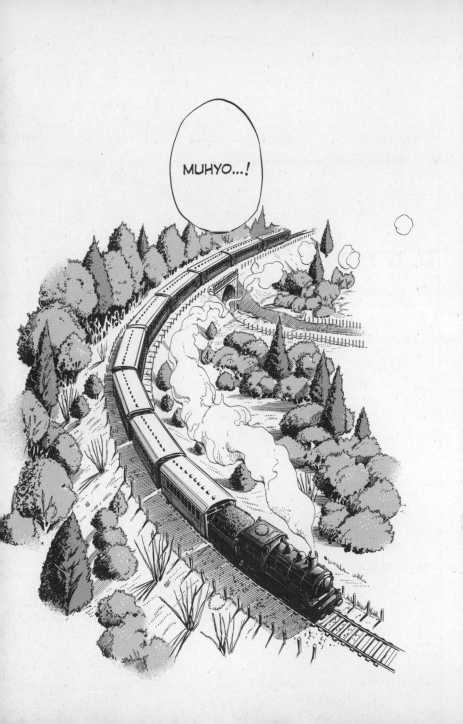

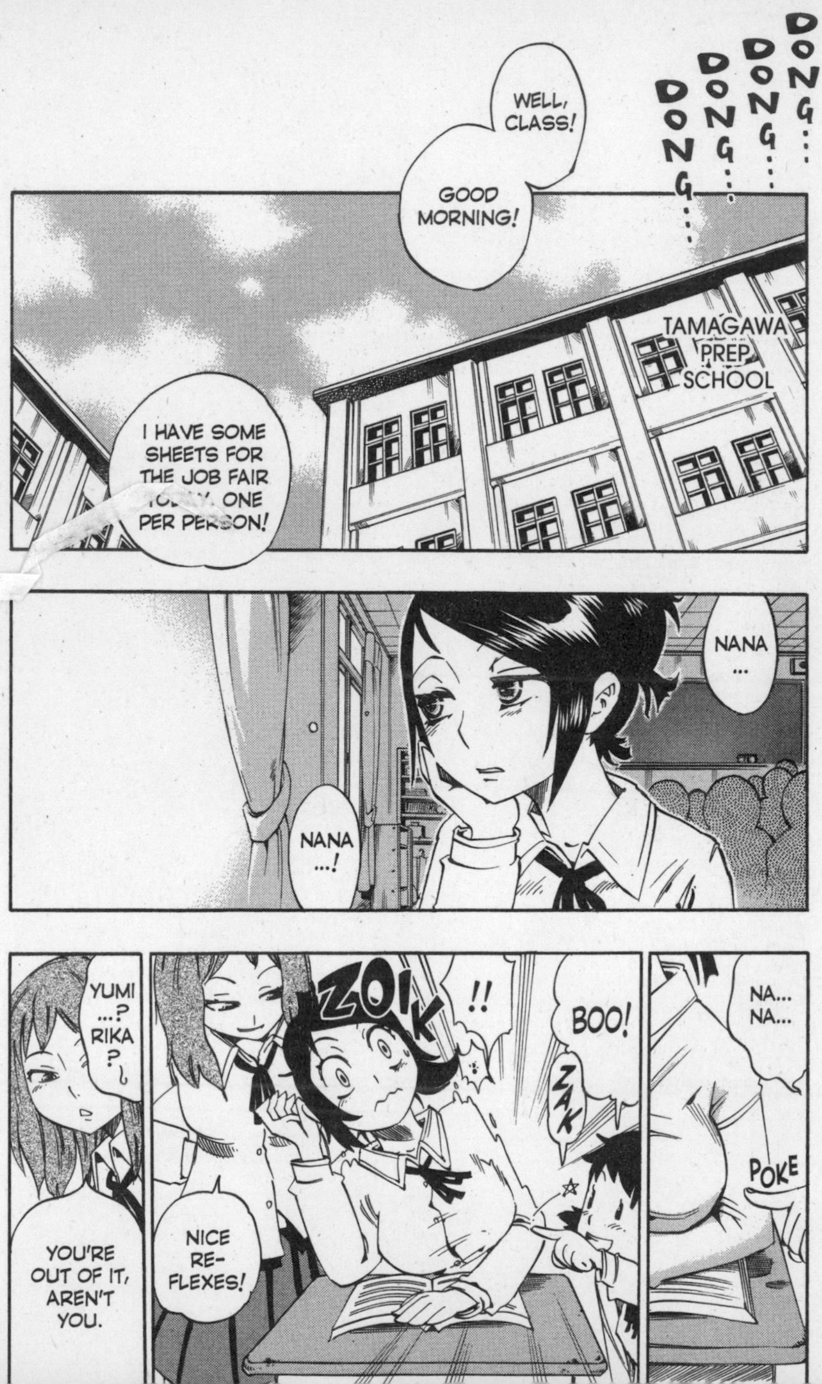
DONG... DONG... DONG... DONG...
WELL, CLASS!
GOOD MORNING!
TAMAGAWA PREP SCHOOL
I HAVE SOME SHEETS FOR THE JOB FAIR TODAY. ONE PER PERSON!
NANA...
NANA...!
NA... NA...
POKE
BOO!
ZAK
ZOIK
!!
NICE RE-FLEXES!
YUMI...? RIKA?
YOU'RE OUT OF IT, AREN'T YOU.

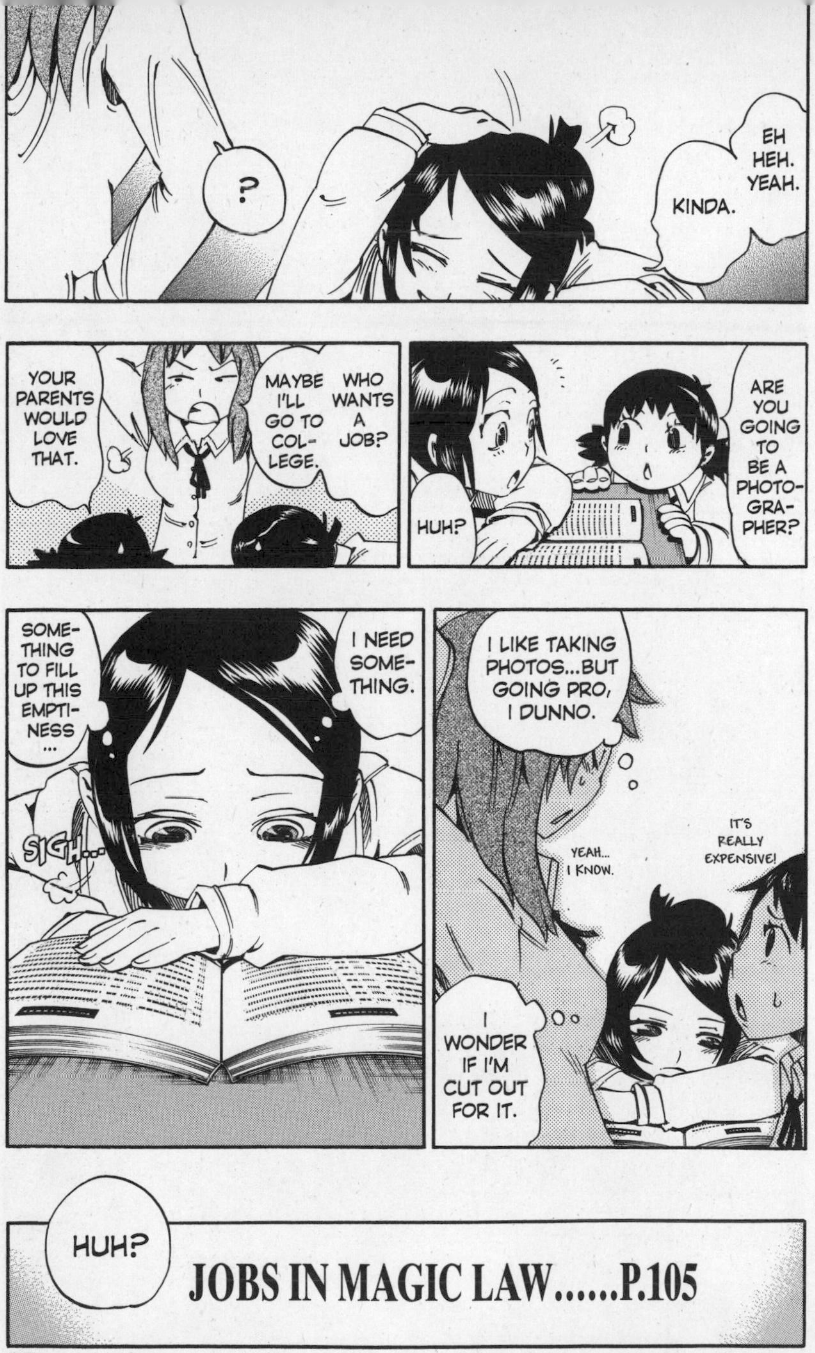
EH HEH. YEAH.
KINDA.
?
ARE YOU GOING TO BE A PHOTOGRAPHER?
HUH?
WHO WANTS A JOB?
MAYBE I'LL GO TO COLLEGE.
YOUR PARENTS WOULD LOVE THAT.
I LIKE TAKING PHOTOS...BUT GOING PRO, I DUNNO.
IT'S REALLY EXPENSIVE!
YEAH... I KNOW.
I WONDER IF I'M CUT OUT FOR IT.
I NEED SOMETHING.
SOMETHING TO FILL UP THIS EMPTINESS...
SIGH...
HUH?
JOBS IN MAGIC LAW......P.105

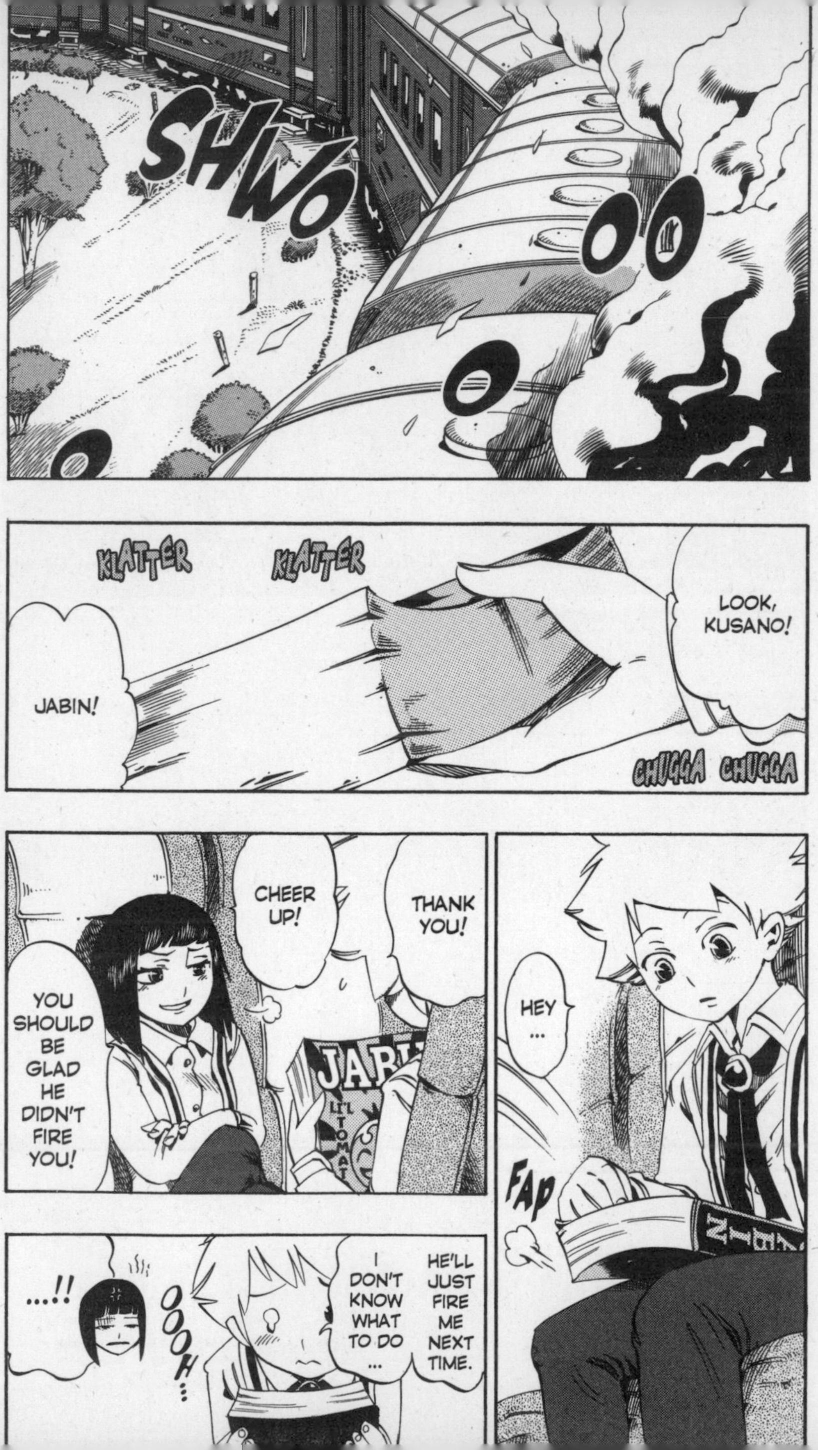
SHWOOOOO
LOOK, KUSANO!
CHUGGA CHUGGA
KLATTER KLATTER
JABIN!
HEY ...
FAP
THANK YOU!
CHEER UP!
YOU SHOULD BE GLAD HE DIDN'T FIRE YOU!
HE'LL JUST FIRE ME NEXT TIME.
I DON'T KNOW WHAT TO DO ...
OOOH...
...!!

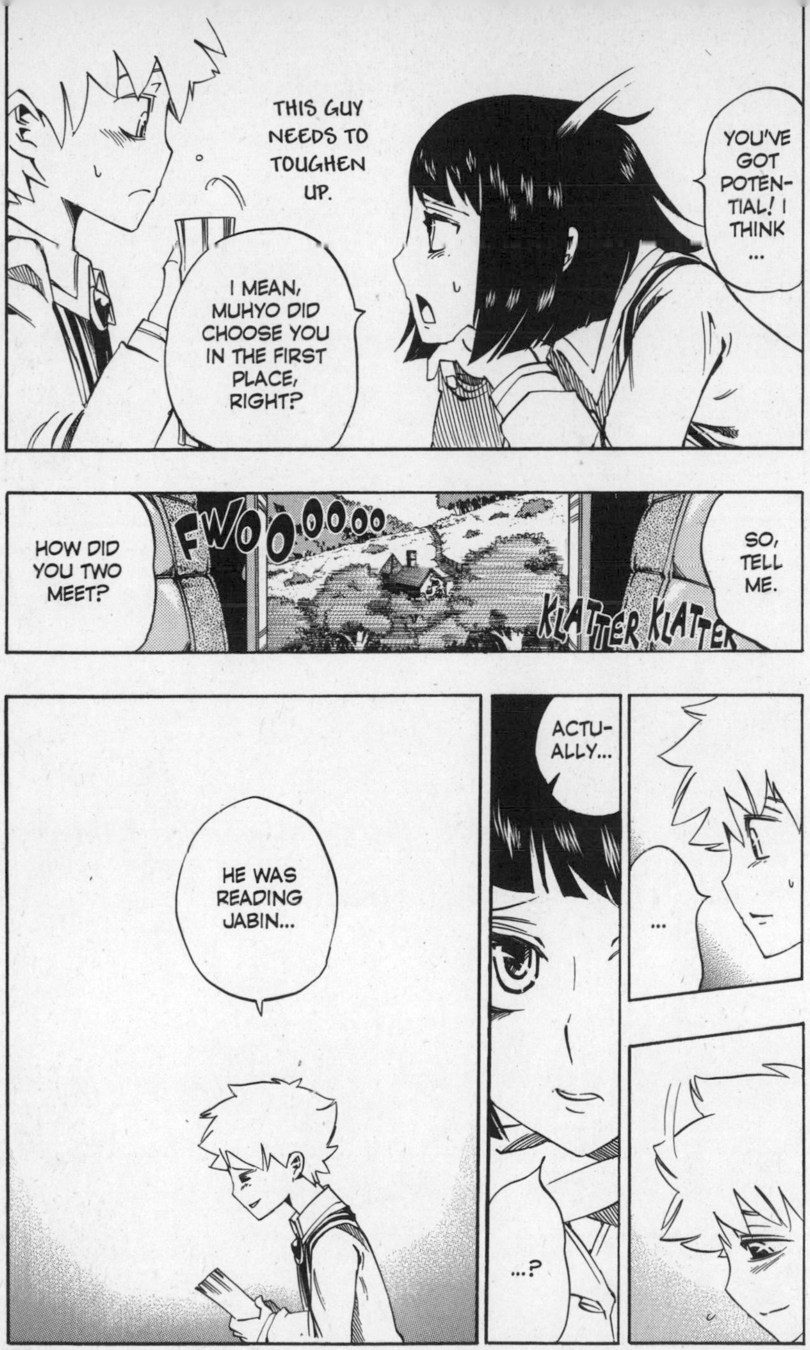
YOU'VE GOT POTEN-TIAL! I THINK ...
THIS GUY NEEDS TO TOUGHEN UP.
I MEAN, MUHYO DID CHOOSE YOU IN THE FIRST PLACE, RIGHT?
SO, TELL ME.
FWOOOOOO
KLATTER KLATTER
HOW DID YOU TWO MEET?
...
ACTU-ALLY...
...?
HE WAS READING JABIN...

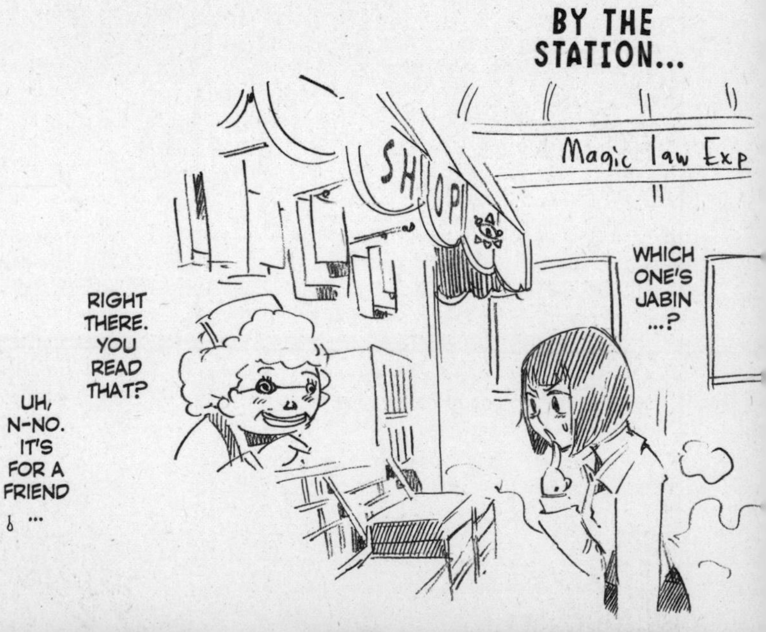
BY THE STATION...
Magic law Exp
SHOP
WHICH ONE'S JABIN ...?
RIGHT THERE. YOU READ THAT?
UH, N-NO. IT'S FOR A FRIEND ...

ARTICLE 46
MEETING

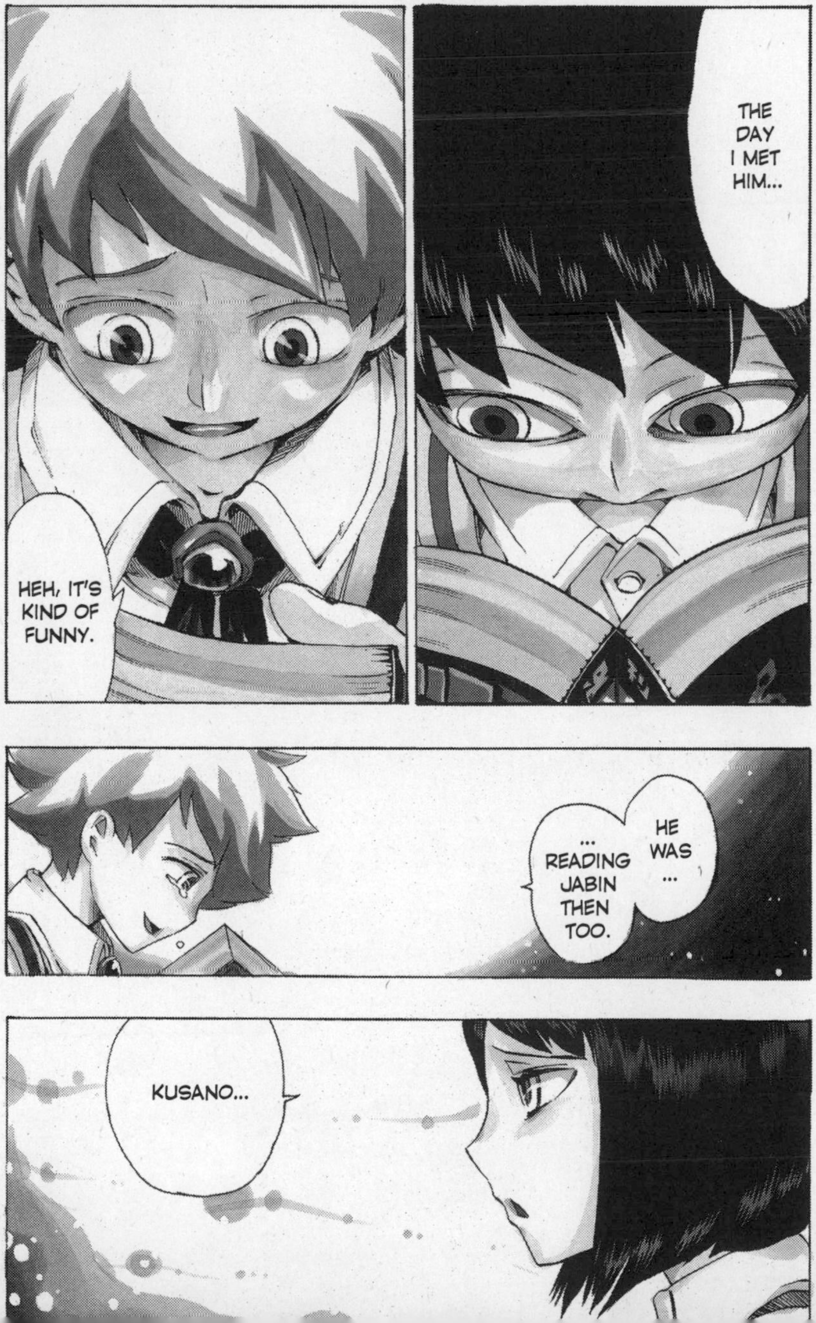

THE DAY I MET HIM...
HEH, IT'S KIND OF FUNNY.
HE WAS ...
... READING JABIN THEN TOO.
KUSANO...

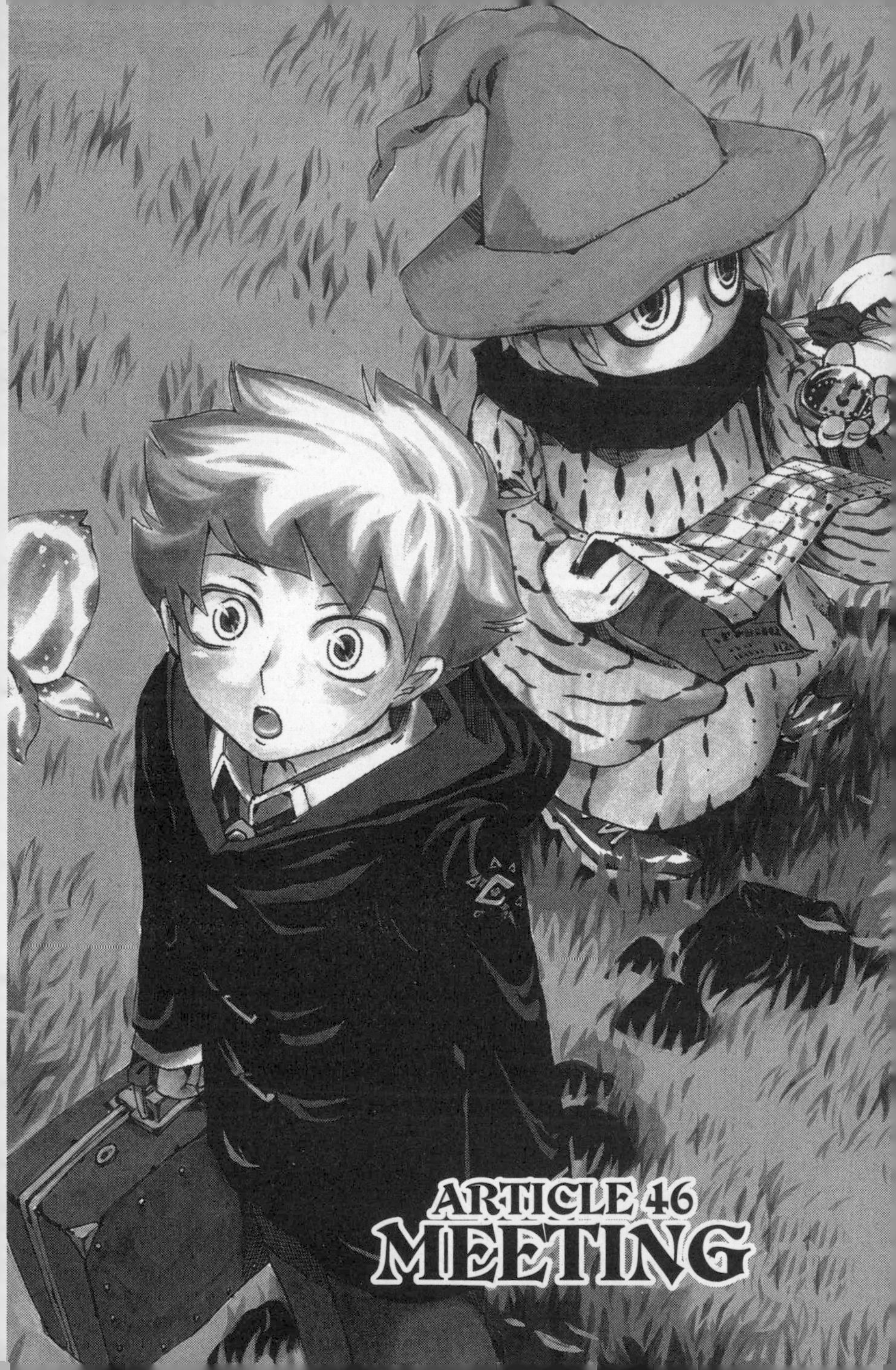
ARTICLE 46
MEETING

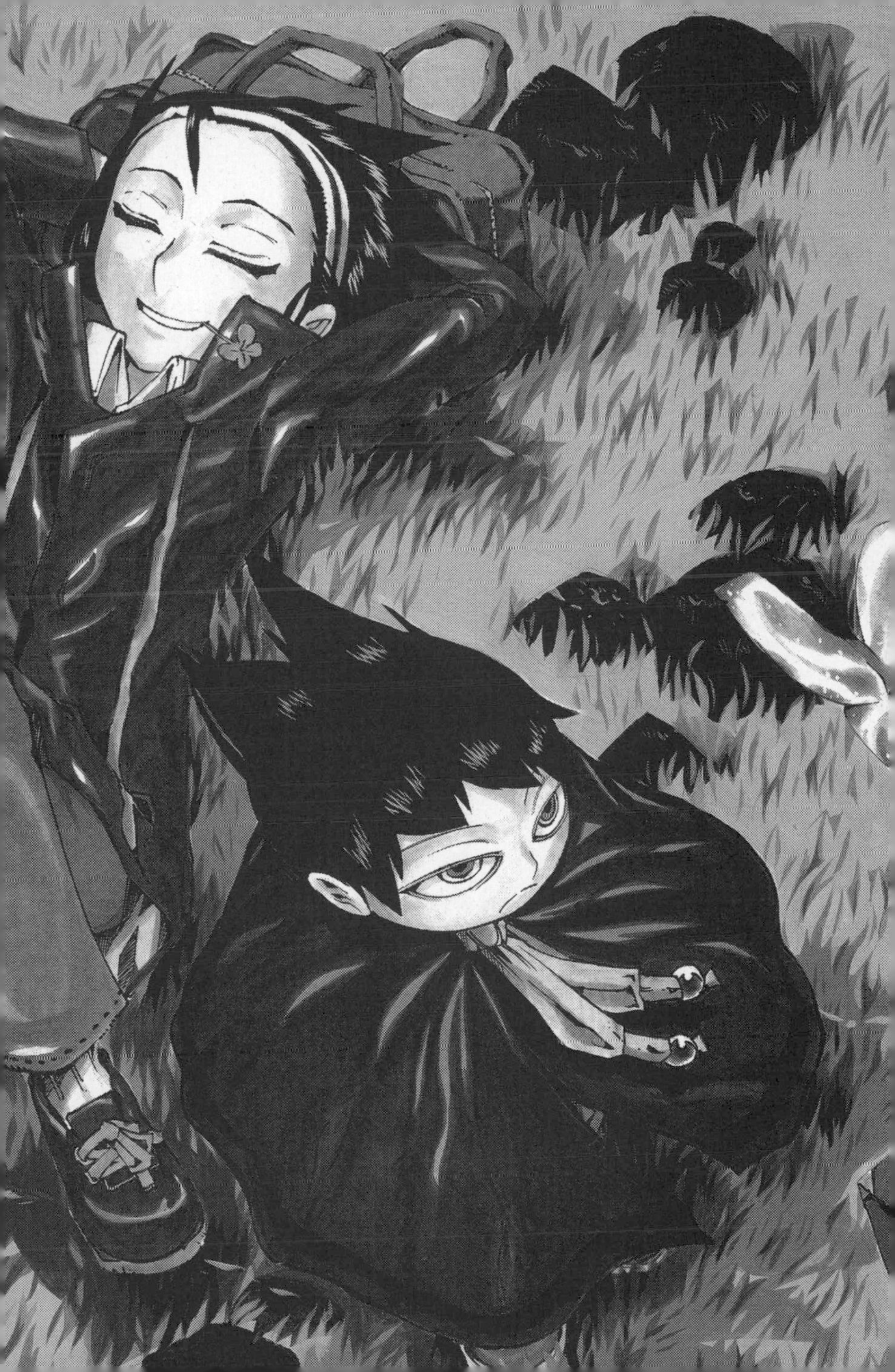

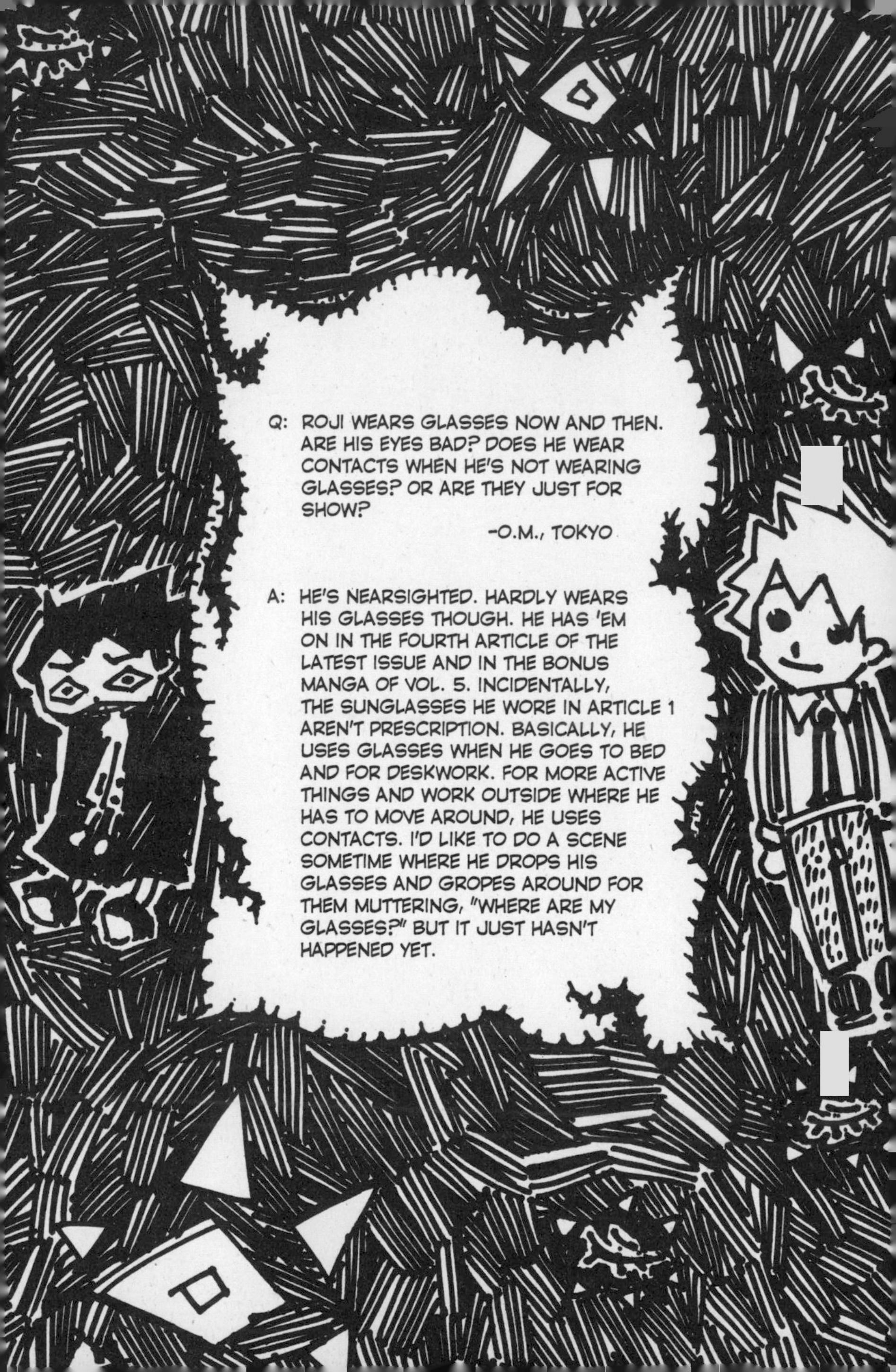

Q: ROJI WEARS GLASSES NOW AND THEN. ARE HIS EYES BAD? DOES HE WEAR CONTACTS WHEN HE'S NOT WEARING GLASSES? OR ARE THEY JUST FOR SHOW?

-O.M., TOKYO

A: HE'S NEARSIGHTED. HARDLY WEARS HIS GLASSES THOUGH. HE HAS 'EM ON IN THE FOURTH ARTICLE OF THE LATEST ISSUE AND IN THE BONUS MANGA OF VOL. 5. INCIDENTALLY, THE SUNGLASSES HE WORE IN ARTICLE 1 AREN'T PRESCRIPTION. BASICALLY, HE USES GLASSES WHEN HE GOES TO BED AND FOR DESKWORK. FOR MORE ACTIVE THINGS AND WORK OUTSIDE WHERE HE HAS TO MOVE AROUND, HE USES CONTACTS. I'D LIKE TO DO A SCENE SOMETIME WHERE HE DROPS HIS GLASSES AND GROPES AROUND FOR THEM MUTTERING, "WHERE ARE MY GLASSES?" BUT IT JUST HASN'T HAPPENED YET.

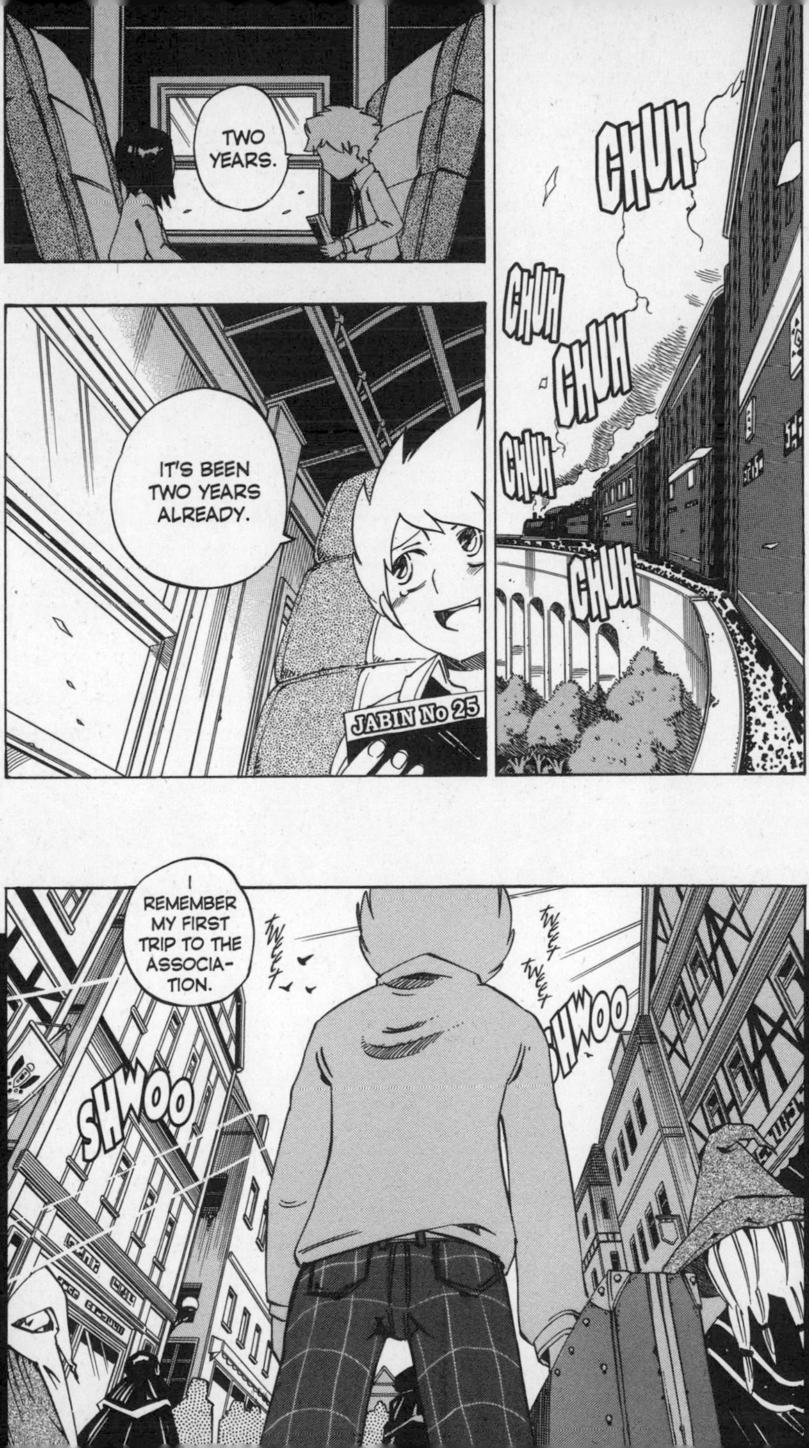
CHUH
CHUH
CHUH
CHUH
CHUH
TWO YEARS.
IT'S BEEN TWO YEARS ALREADY.
JABIN No 25
KNEEK KNEEK
I REMEMBER MY FIRST TRIP TO THE ASSOCIA-TION.
KNEEK
SHWOO
SHWOO

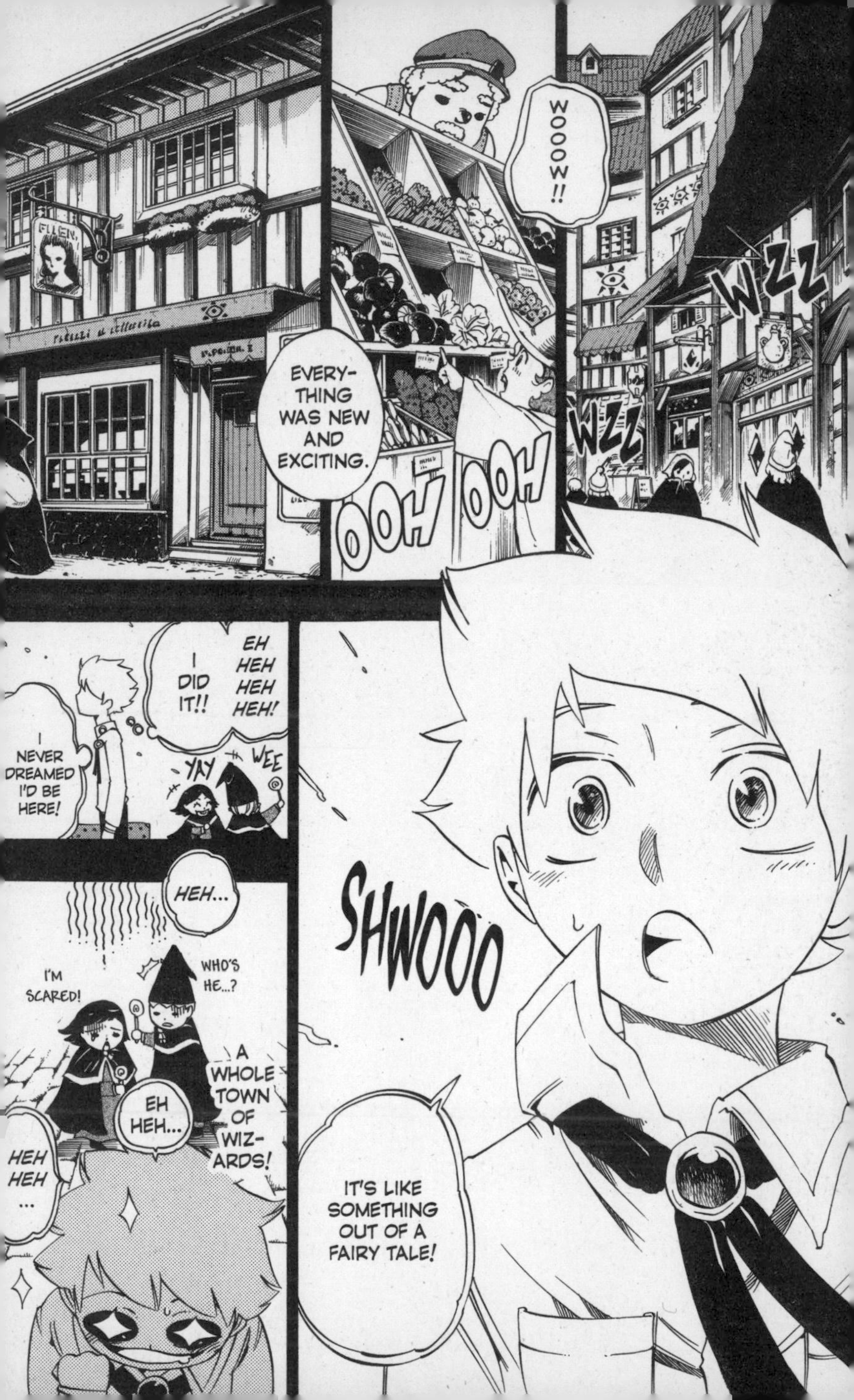
WZZ
WZZ
WOOOW!!
EVERY-THING WAS NEW AND EXCITING.
OOH OOH
SHWOOO
IT'S LIKE SOMETHING OUT OF A FAIRY TALE!
EH HEH HEH HEH!
I DID IT!!
I NEVER DREAMED I'D BE HERE!
WEE
YAY
HEH...
WHO'S HE...?
I'M SCARED!
A WHOLE TOWN OF WIZ-ARDS!
EH HEH...
HEH HEH ...

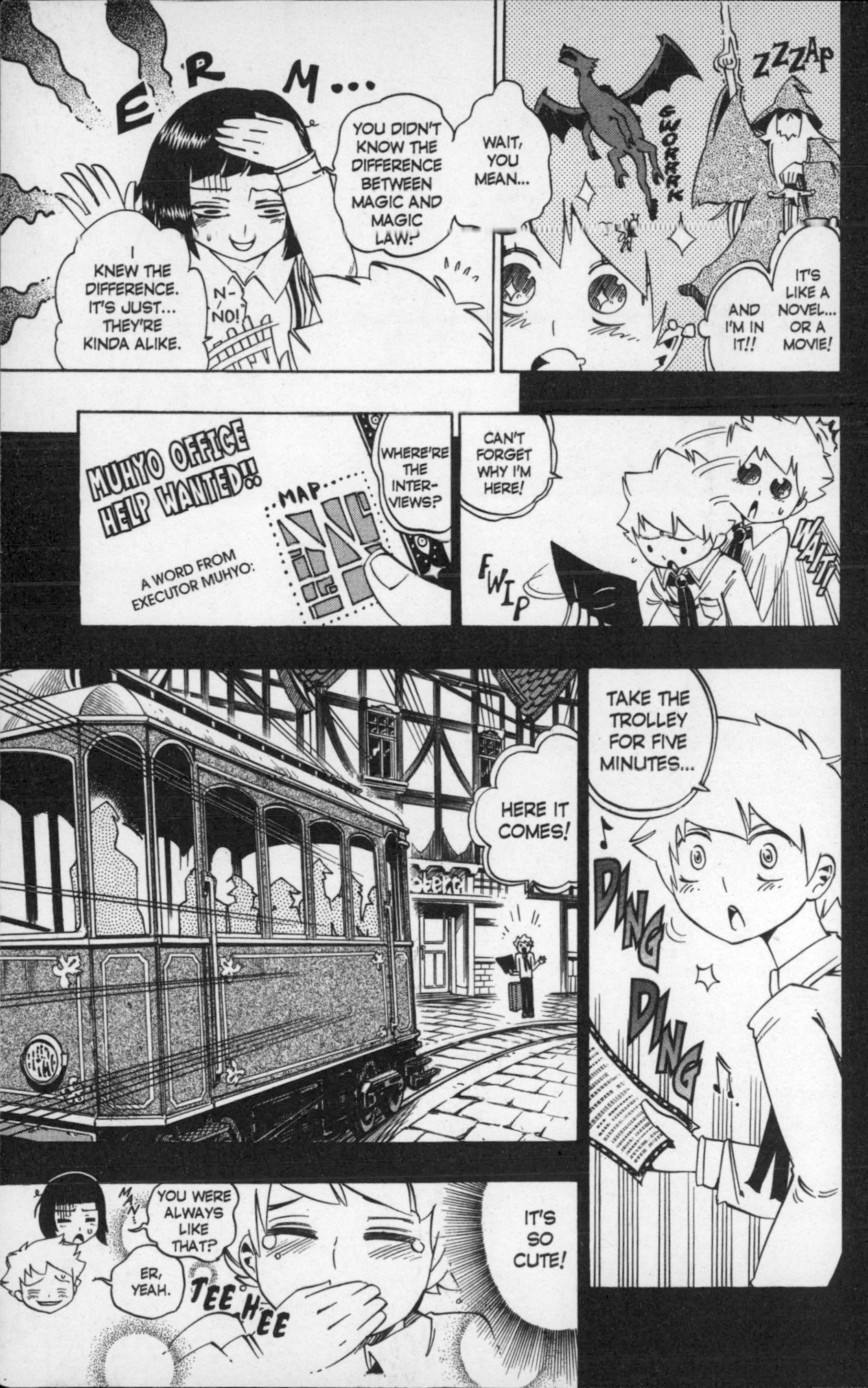
ZZZAP
SWORRRK
IT'S LIKE A NOVEL... OR A MOVIE!
AND I'M IN IT!!
WAIT, YOU MEAN...
YOU DIDN'T KNOW THE DIFFERENCE BETWEEN MAGIC AND MAGIC LAW?
ERM...
N-NO!
I KNEW THE DIFFERENCE. IT'S JUST... THEY'RE KINDA ALIKE.
CAN'T FORGET WHY I'M HERE!
WAIT!
FWIP
WHERE'RE THE INTERVIEWS?
MAP
MUHYO OFFICE HELP WANTED!!
A WORD FROM EXECUTOR MUHYO:
TAKE THE TROLLEY FOR FIVE MINUTES...
DING DING DING
HERE IT COMES!
IT'S SO CUTE!
TEE HEE
YOU WERE ALWAYS LIKE THAT?
MAN...
ER, YEAH.

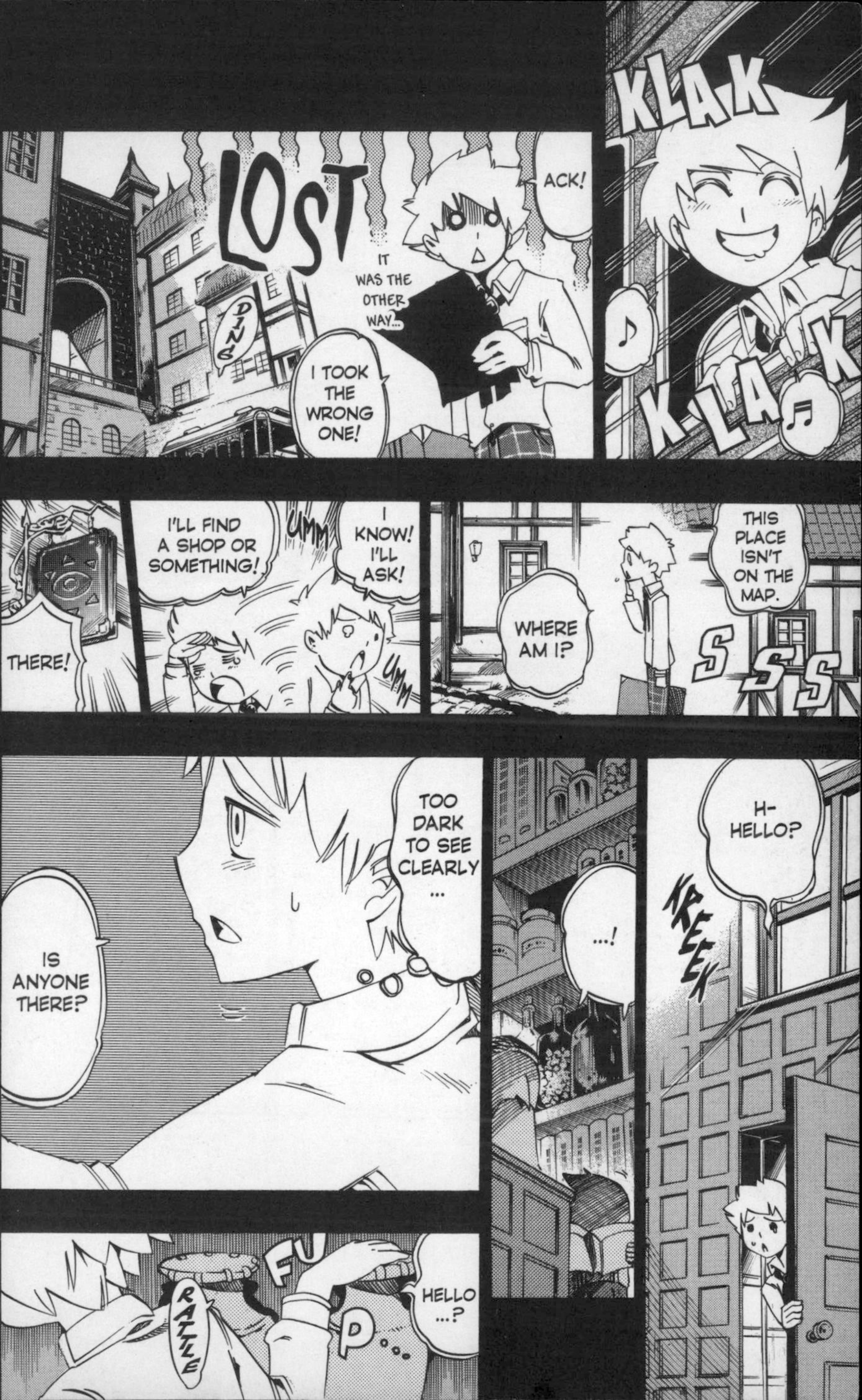
KLAK
♪
KLAK
♪
ACK!
LOST
IT WAS THE OTHER WAY...
I TOOK THE WRONG ONE!
DING
THIS PLACE ISN'T ON THE MAP.
SSS
WHERE AM I?
I KNOW! I'LL ASK!
UMM
I'LL FIND A SHOP OR SOMETHING!
UMM
THERE!
H- HELLO?
KREEK
...!
TOO DARK TO SEE CLEARLY...
IS ANYONE THERE?
HELLO...?
FUP
RATTLE

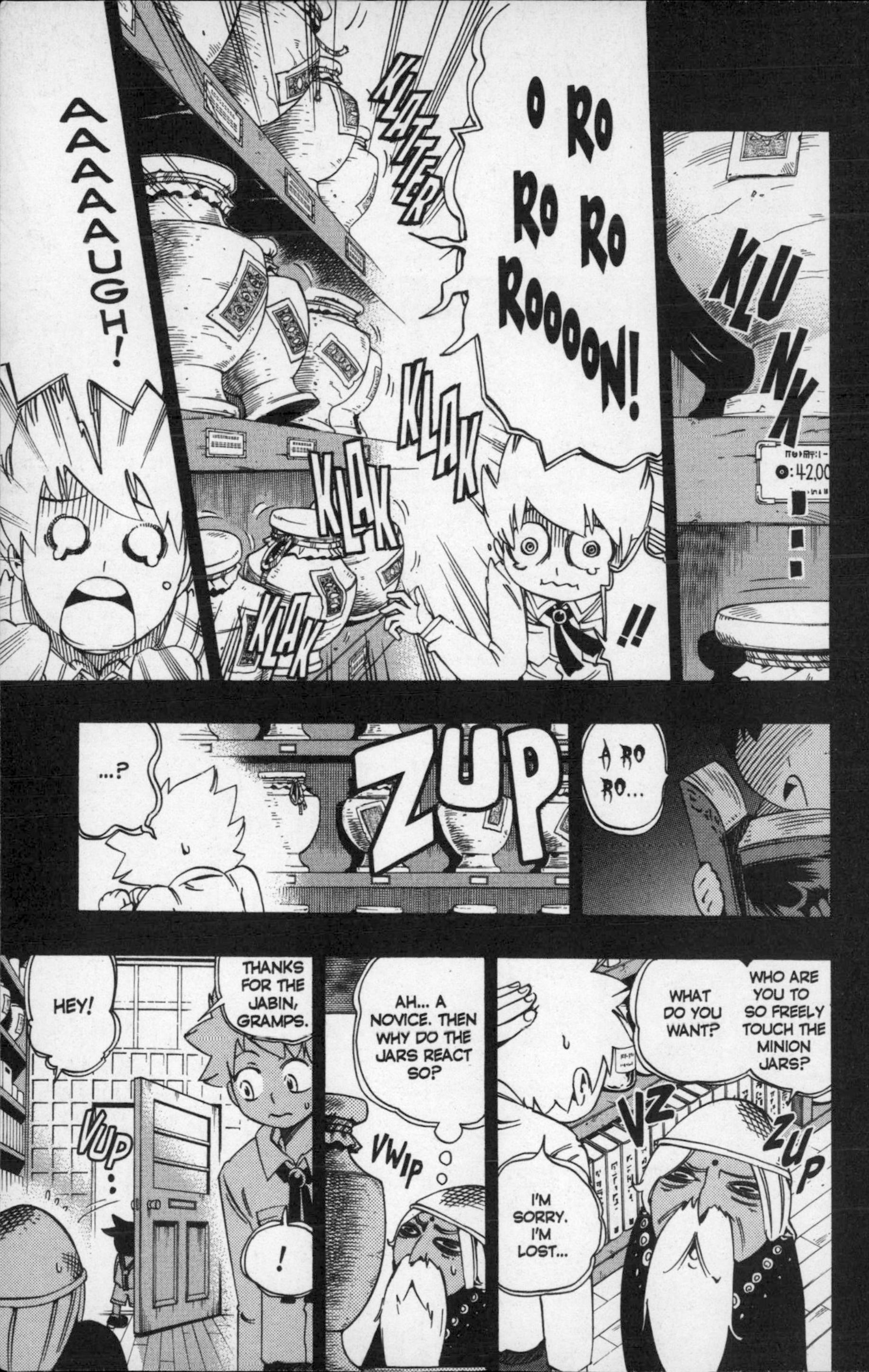
KLUNNK
O RO RO RO ROOOON!
KLATTER
KLAK
KLAK
KLAK
!!
AAAAAUGH!
A RO RO...
ZUP
...?
WHO ARE YOU TO SO FREELY TOUCH THE MINION JARS?
WHAT DO YOU WANT?
VZ
ZUP
I'M SORRY. I'M LOST...
AH... A NOVICE. THEN WHY DO THE JARS REACT SO?
VWIP
THANKS FOR THE JABIN, GRAMPS.
HEY!
VUP
!

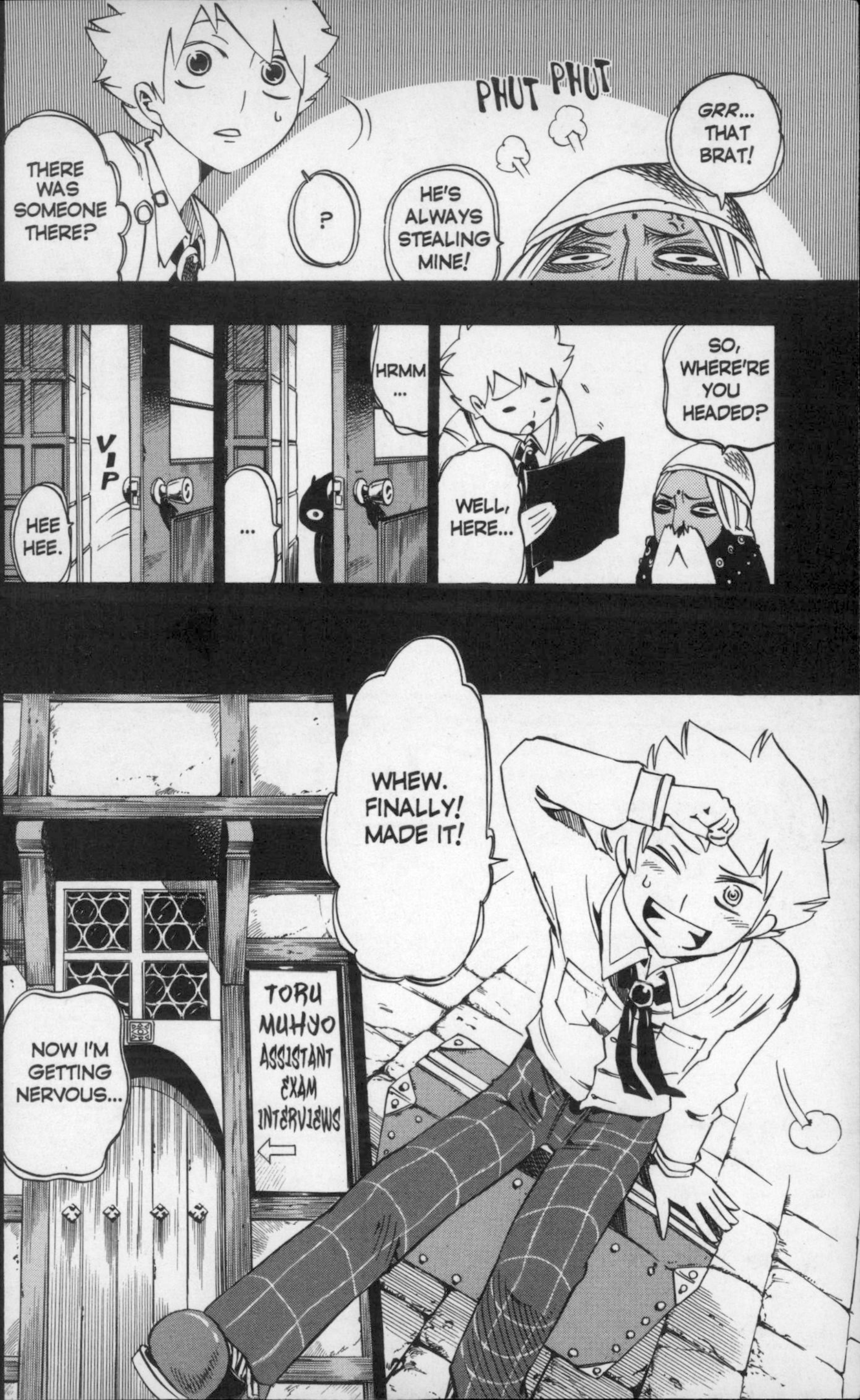
GRR... THAT BRAT!
PHUT PHUT
HE'S ALWAYS STEALING MINE!
?
THERE WAS SOMEONE THERE?
SO, WHERE'RE YOU HEADED?
HRMM...
WELL, HERE...
...
VIP
HEE HEE.
WHEW. FINALLY! MADE IT!
TORU MUHYO ASSISTANT EXAM INTERVIEWS
NOW I'M GETTING NERVOUS...

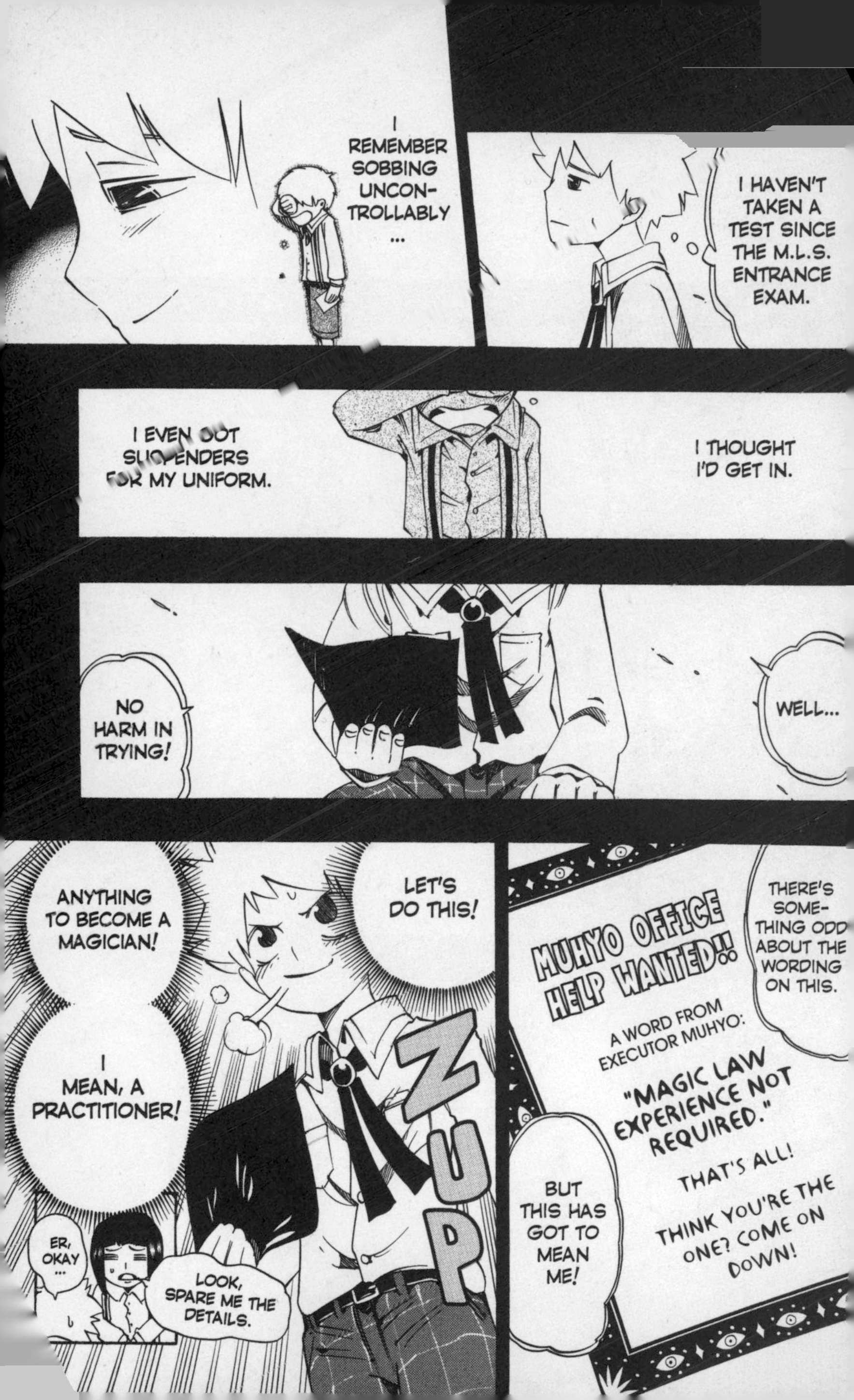
I HAVEN'T TAKEN A TEST SINCE THE M.L.S. ENTRANCE EXAM.
I REMEMBER SOBBING UNCONTROLLABLY...
I THOUGHT I'D GET IN.
I EVEN GOT SUSPENDERS FOR MY UNIFORM.
WELL...
NO HARM IN TRYING!
THERE'S SOMETHING ODD ABOUT THE WORDING ON THIS.
MUHYO OFFICE HELP WANTED!!
A WORD FROM EXECUTOR MUHYO:
"MAGIC LAW EXPERIENCE NOT REQUIRED."
THAT'S ALL!
THINK YOU'RE THE ONE? COME ON DOWN!
BUT THIS HAS GOT TO MEAN ME!
LET'S DO THIS!
ANYTHING TO BECOME A MAGICIAN!
I MEAN, A PRACTITIONER!
ZUP
LOOK, SPARE ME THE DETAILS.
ER, OKAY...

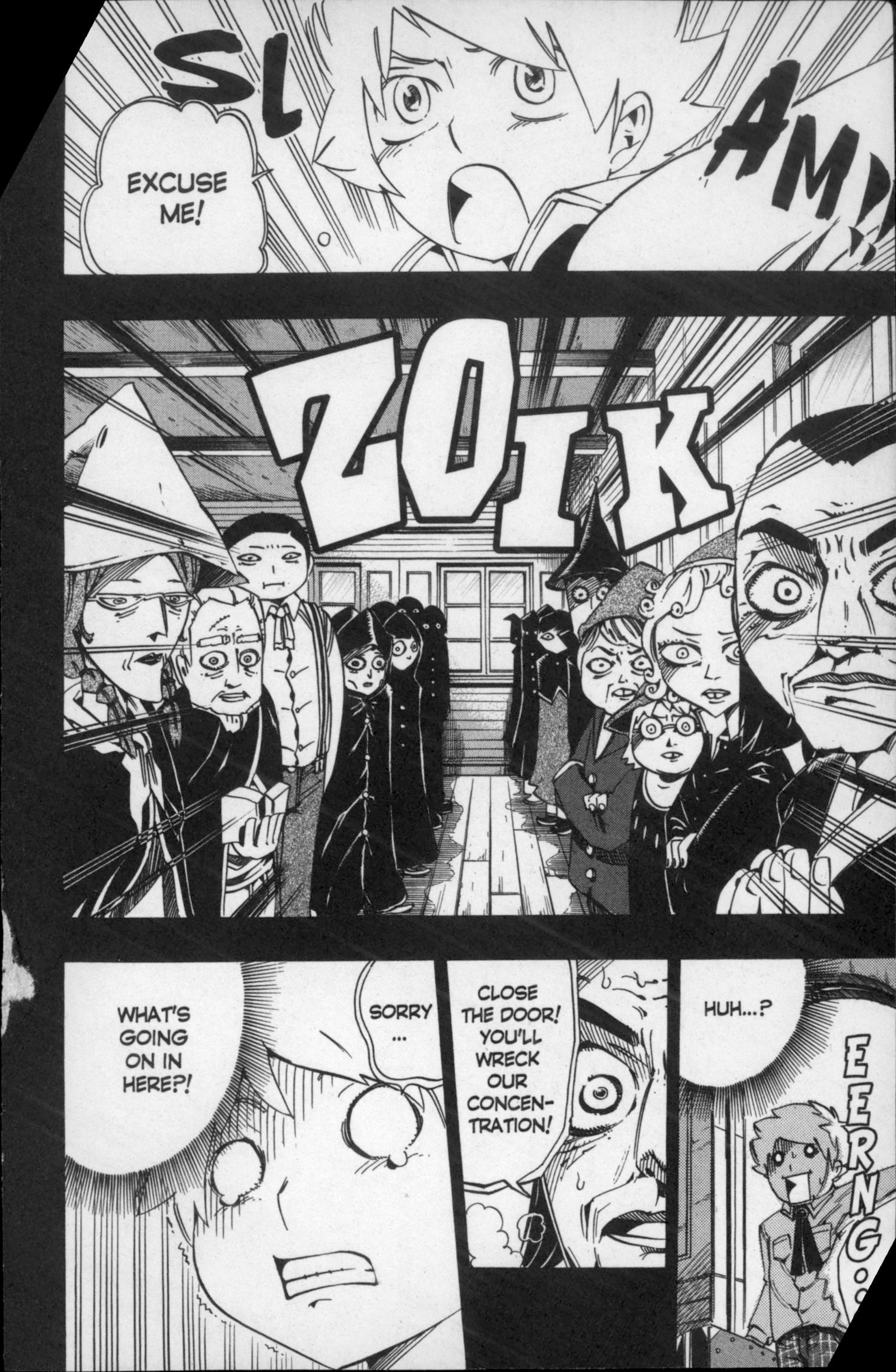

SLAM!!
EXCUSE ME!
ZOIK
HUH...?
EERNG...
CLOSE THE DOOR! YOU'LL WRECK OUR CONCENTRATION!
SORRY...
WHAT'S GOING ON IN HERE?!

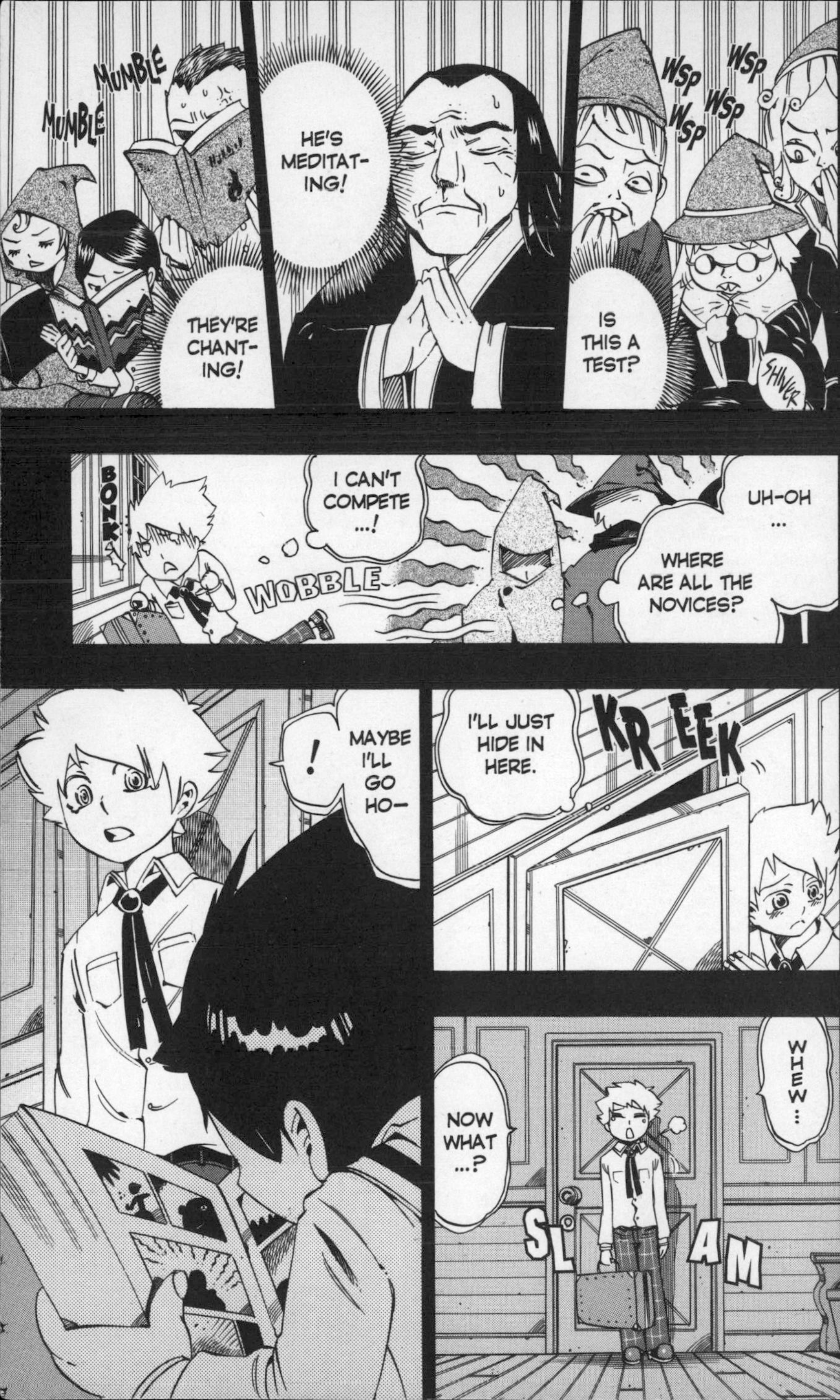
WSP WSP WSP WSP
IS THIS A TEST?
SHIVER
HE'S MEDITATING!
MUMBLE MUMBLE
THEY'RE CHANTING!
UH-OH ... WHERE ARE ALL THE NOVICES?
I CAN'T COMPETE ...!
WOBBLE
BONK
KREEEK
I'LL JUST HIDE IN HERE.
WHEW ...
NOW WHAT ...?
SLAM
MAYBE I'LL GO HO—
!

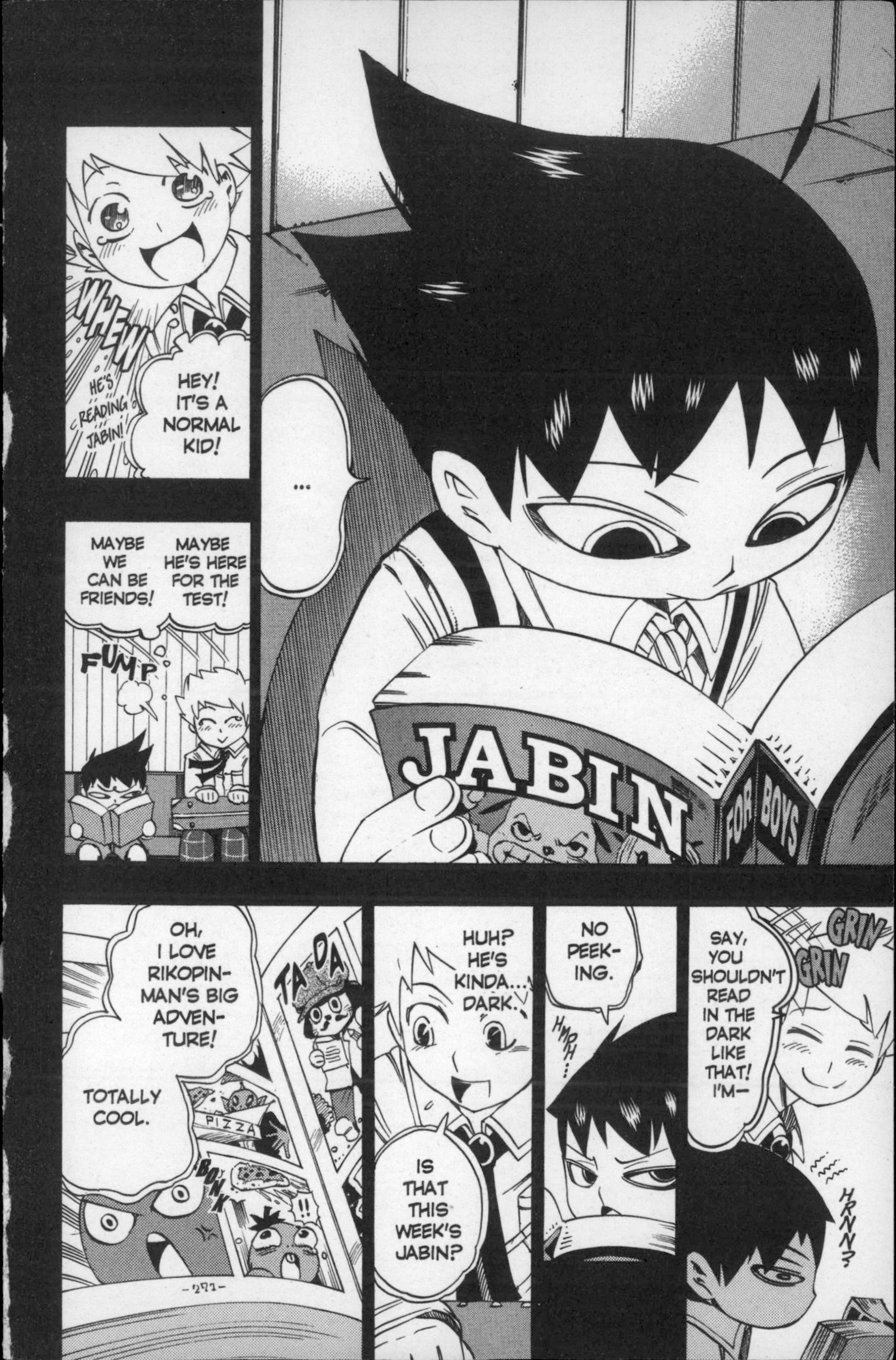
...
JABIN
FOR BOYS
HEY! IT'S A NORMAL KID!
HE'S READING JABIN!
WHEW
MAYBE HE'S HERE FOR THE TEST!
MAYBE WE CAN BE FRIENDS!
FUMP
GRIN
GRIN
SAY, YOU SHOULDN'T READ IN THE DARK LIKE THAT! I'M—
HRNN?
NO PEEK-ING.
HMPH!
HUH? HE'S KINDA... DARK.
IS THAT THIS WEEK'S JABIN?
TA-DA
OH, I LOVE RIKOPIN-MAN'S BIG ADVEN-TURE!
TOTALLY COOL.
PIZZA
BONK
!!

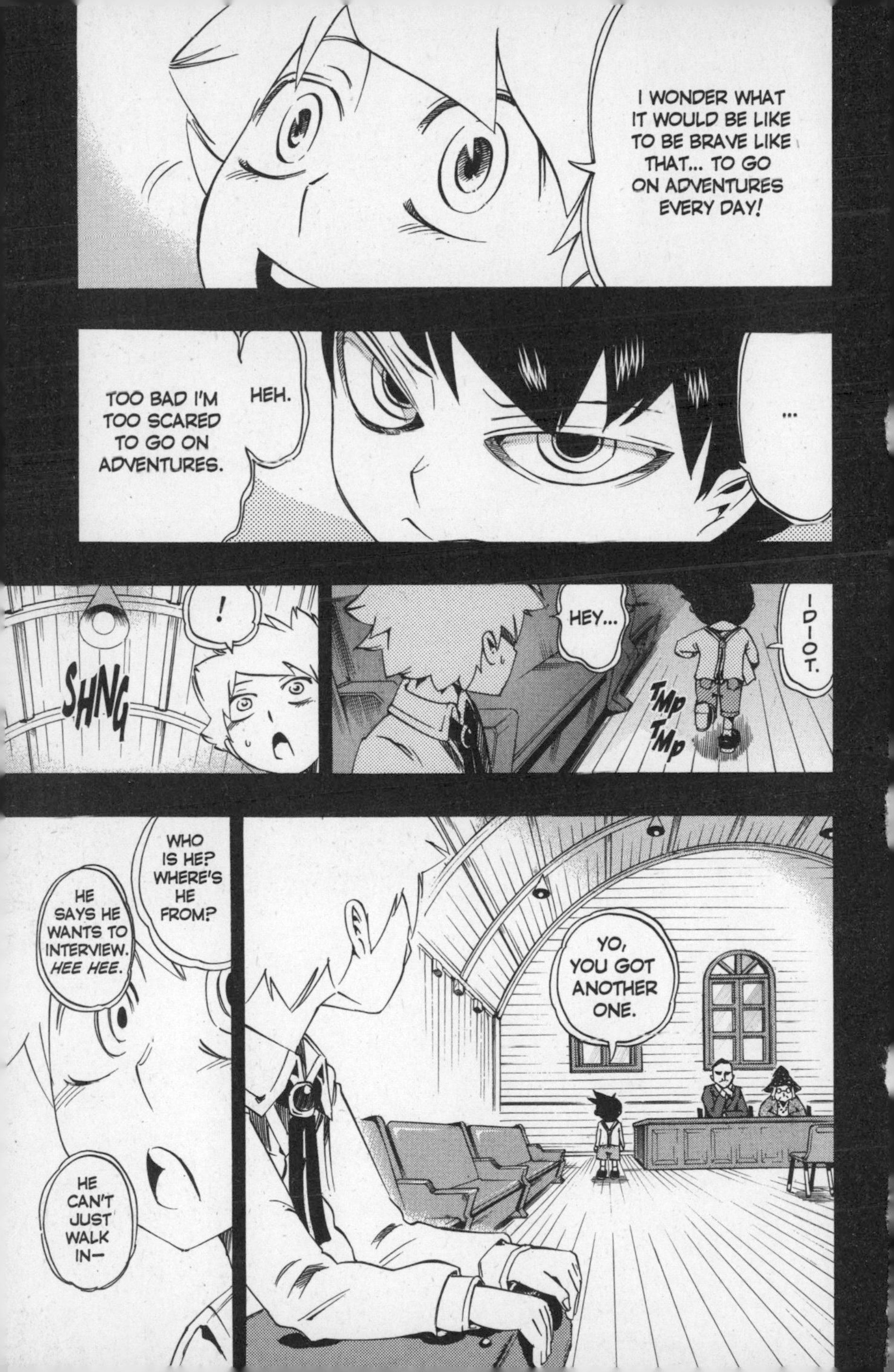
I WONDER WHAT IT WOULD BE LIKE TO BE BRAVE LIKE THAT... TO GO ON ADVENTURES EVERY DAY!
...
HEH.
TOO BAD I'M TOO SCARED TO GO ON ADVENTURES.
IDIOT.
TMP TMP
HEY...
!
SHNG
YO, YOU GOT ANOTHER ONE.
WHO IS HE? WHERE'S HE FROM?
HE SAYS HE WANTS TO INTERVIEW. *HEE HEE*.
HE CAN'T JUST WALK IN—

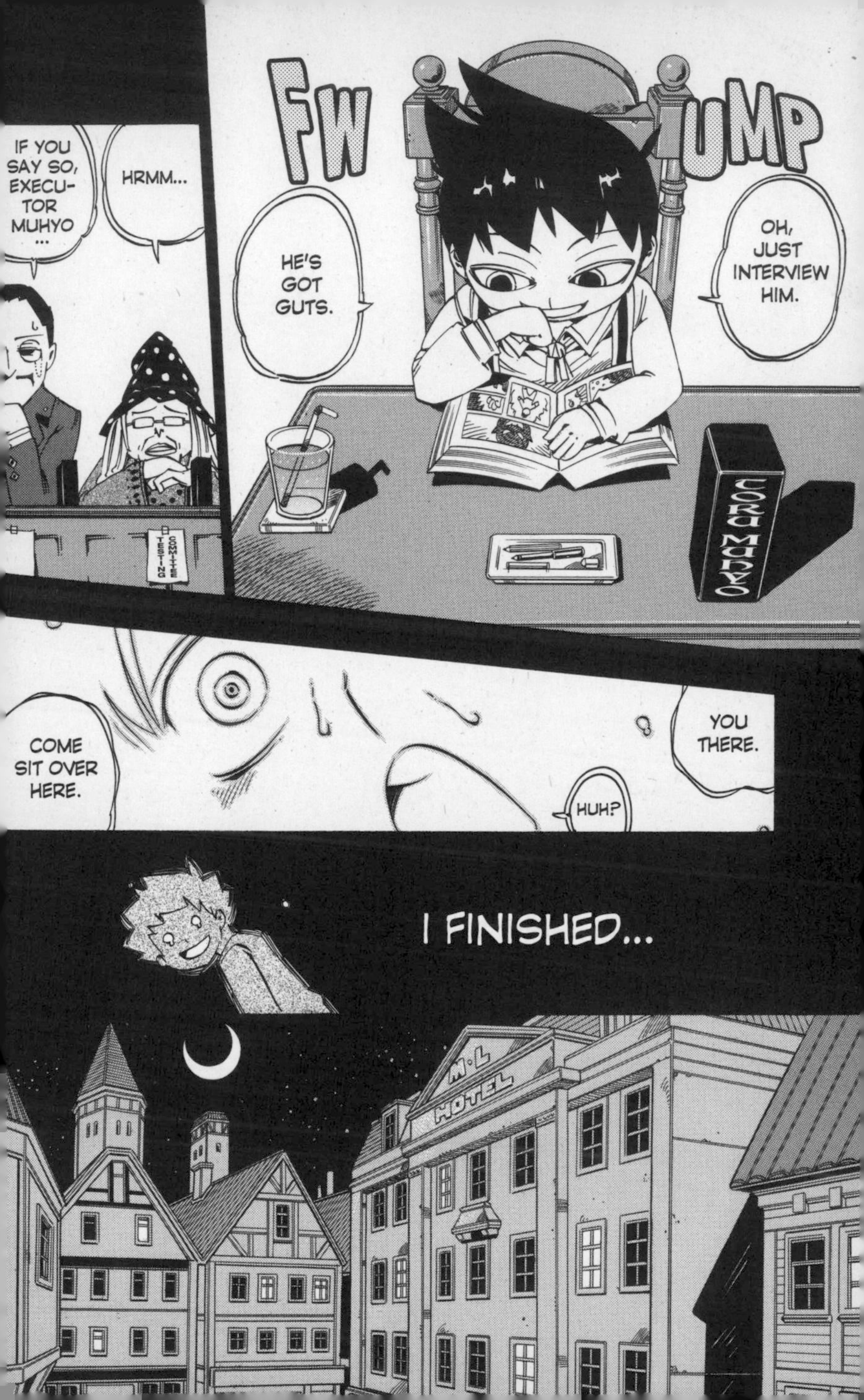
FWUMP
OH, JUST INTERVIEW HIM.
HE'S GOT GUTS.
TORU MUHYO
HRMM...
IF YOU SAY SO, EXECUTOR MUHYO...
TESTING COMMITTEE
YOU THERE.
HUH?
COME SIT OVER HERE.
I FINISHED...
M·L HOTEL

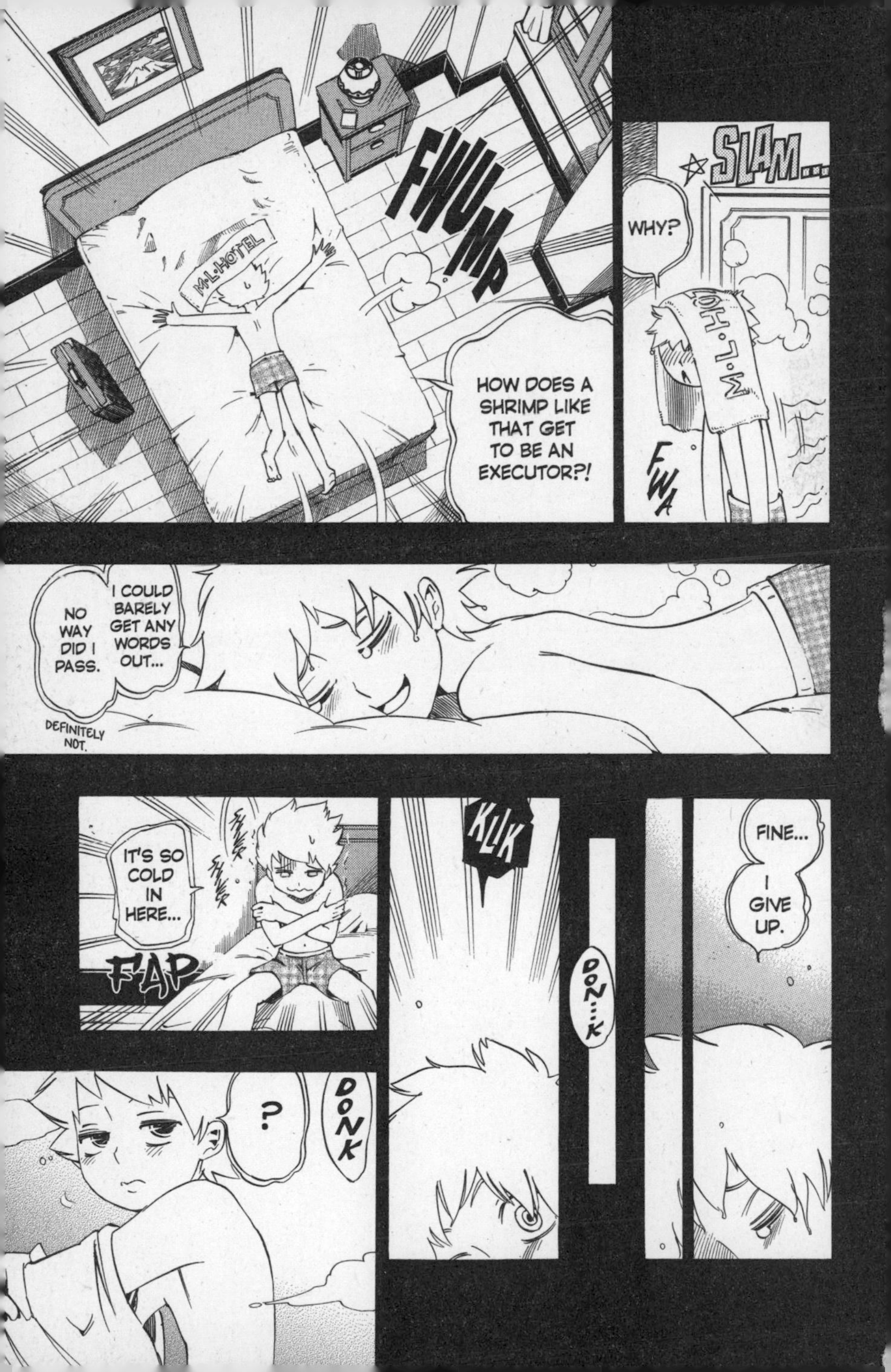
SLAM...
WHY?
FWA
FWUMP
M·L·HOTEL
HOW DOES A SHRIMP LIKE THAT GET TO BE AN EXECUTOR?!
I COULD BARELY GET ANY WORDS OUT...
NO WAY DID I PASS.
DEFINITELY NOT.
FINE... I GIVE UP.
DON...K
KLIK
IT'S SO COLD IN HERE...
SHIVER SHIVER
FAP
?
DONK

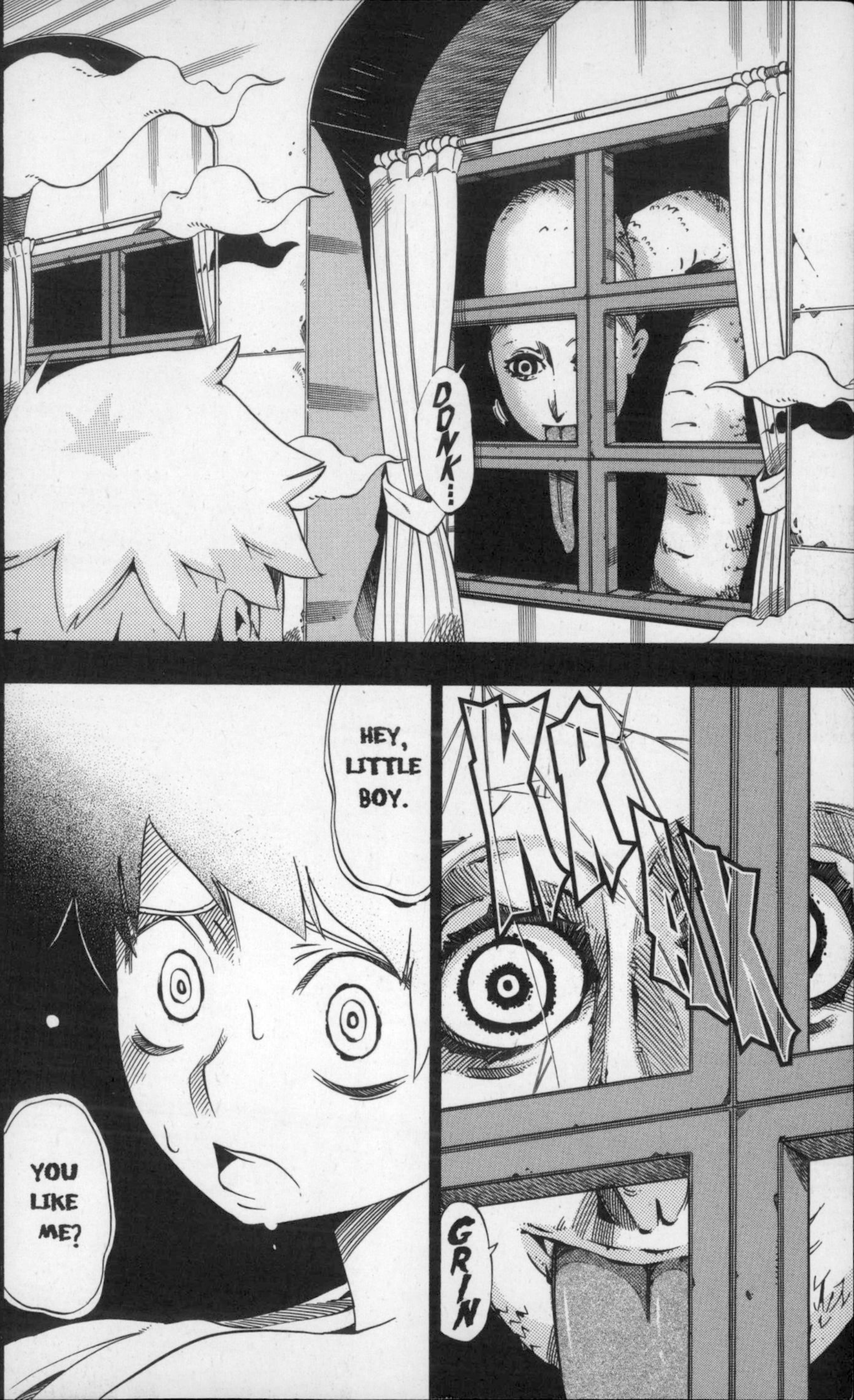
DONK...
GRIN
HEY, LITTLE BOY.
YOU LIKE ME?

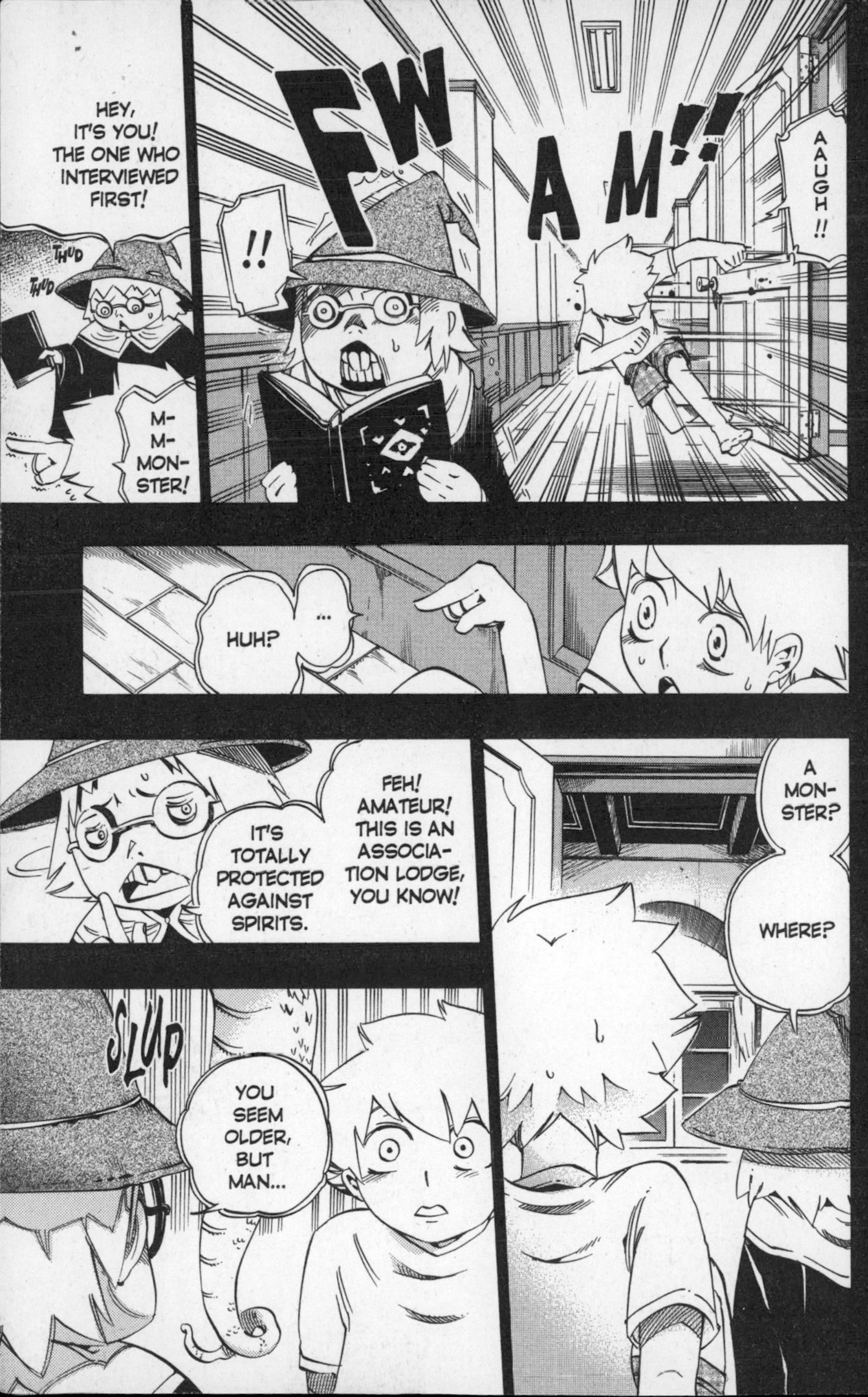
FWAM!!
AAUGH!!
!!
HEY, IT'S YOU! THE ONE WHO INTERVIEWED FIRST!
THUD
THUD
M-M-MONSTER!
...
HUH?
A MONSTER?
WHERE?
FEH! AMATEUR! THIS IS AN ASSOCIATION LODGE, YOU KNOW!
IT'S TOTALLY PROTECTED AGAINST SPIRITS.
SLUP
YOU SEEM OLDER, BUT MAN...

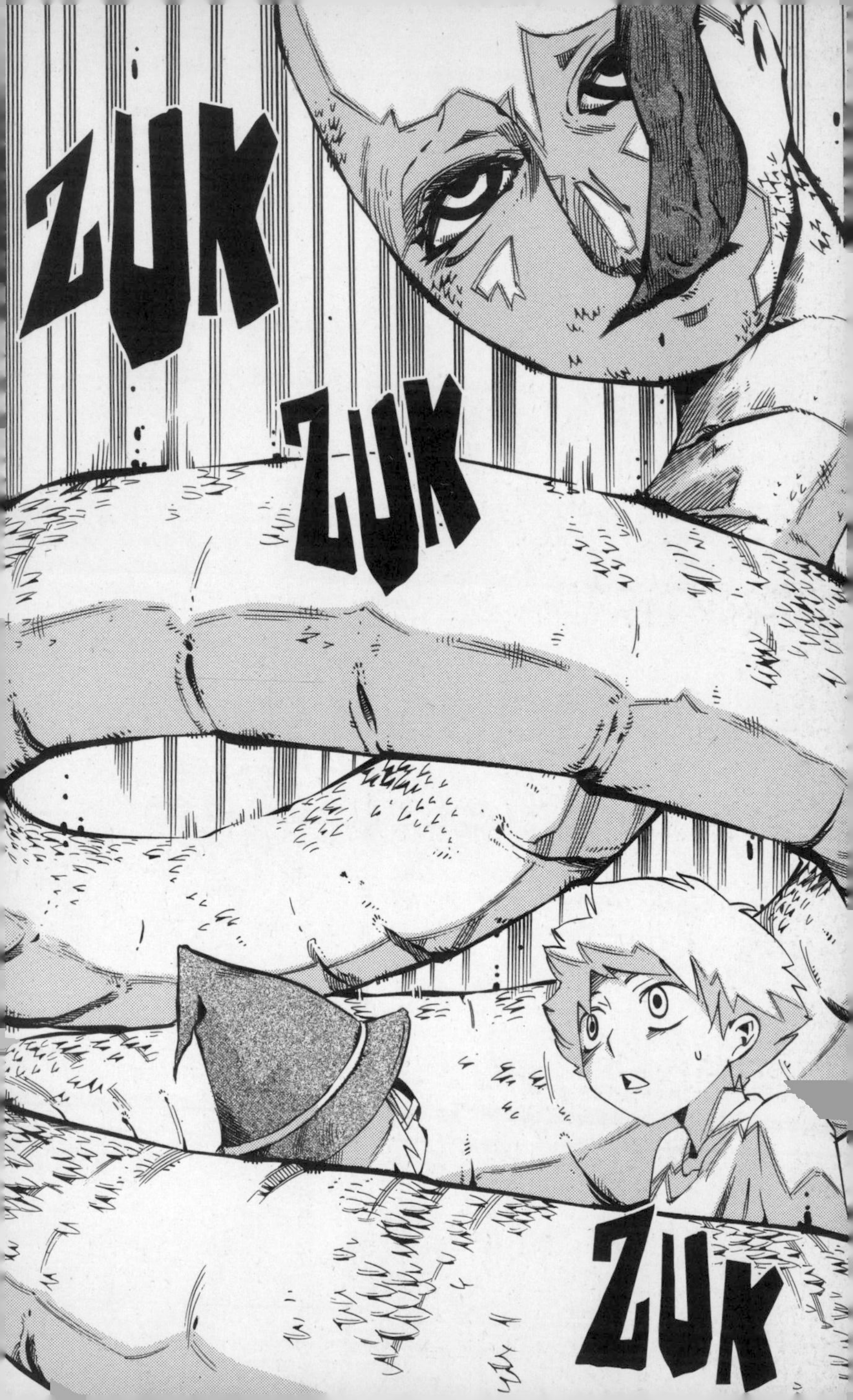
ZUK
ZUK
ZUK

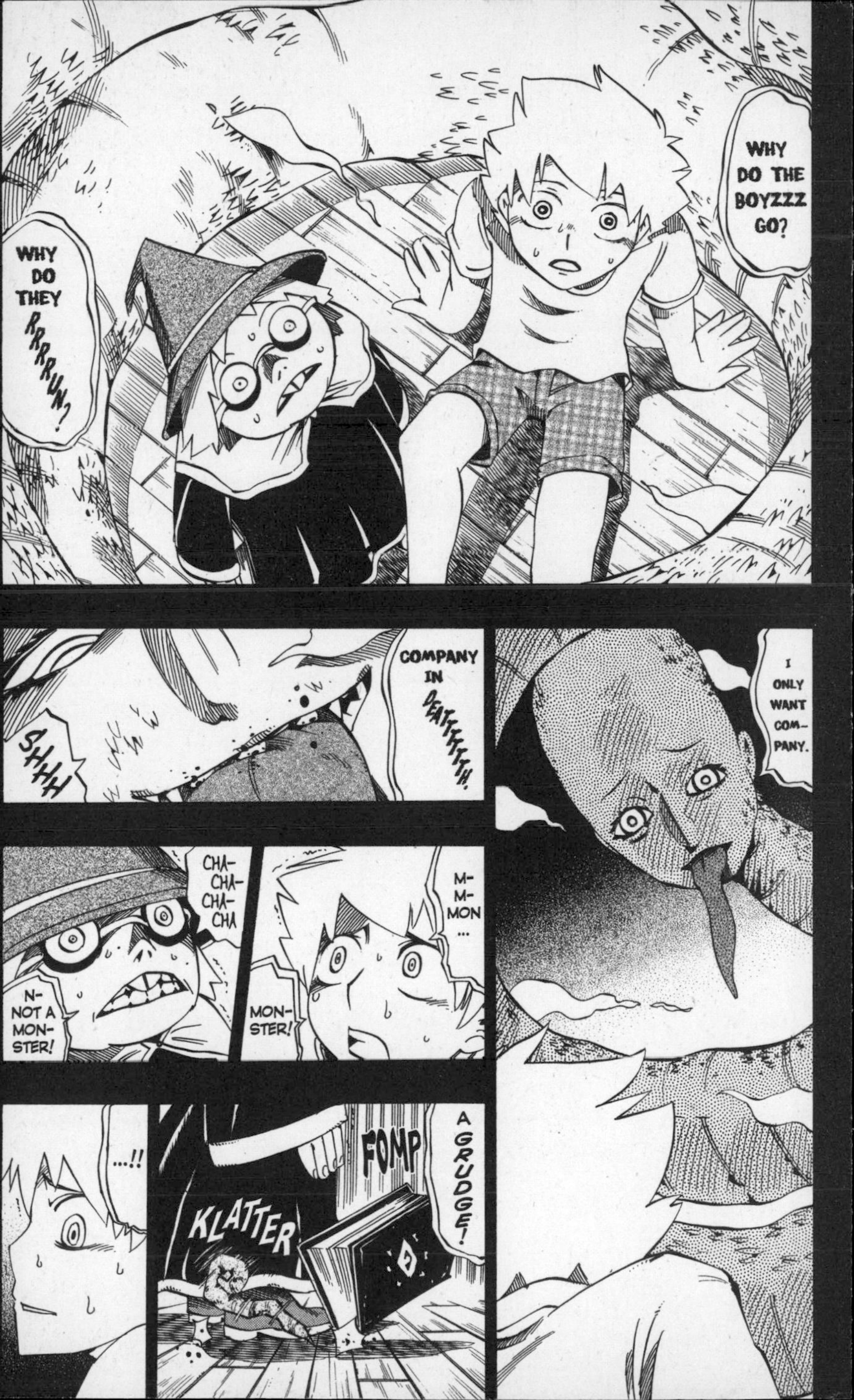
WHY DO THE BOYZZZ GO?
WHY DO THEY RRRRUN?
I ONLY WANT COMPANY.
COMPANY IN DEATTTTTH!
SHHH
M-M-MON...
MON-STER!
CHA-CHA-CHA-CHA
N-NOT A MONSTER!
A GRUDGE!
FOMP
KLATTER
...!!

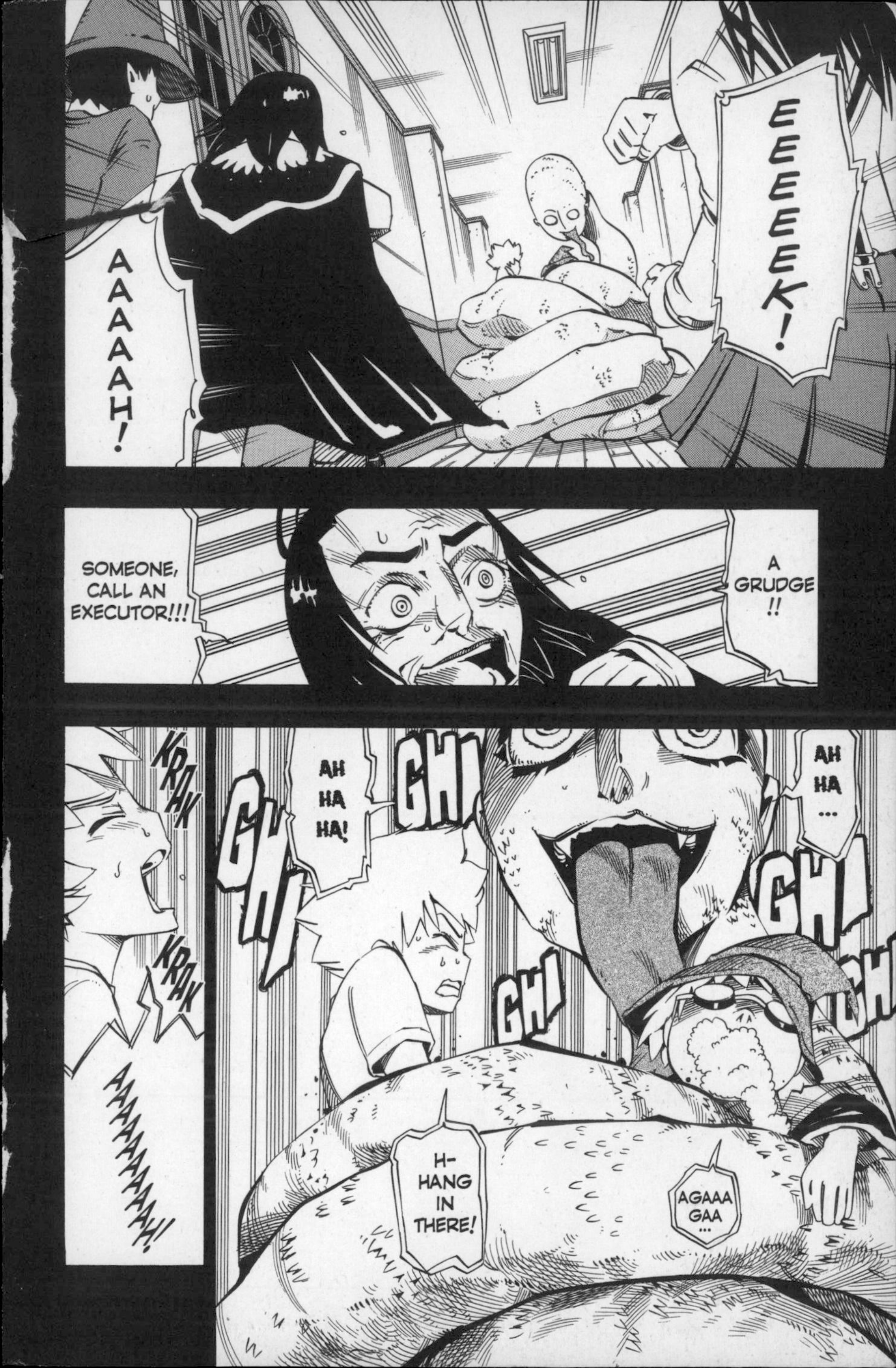
EEEEEK!
AAAAAH!
A GRUDGE !!
SOMEONE, CALL AN EXECUTOR!!!
AH HA ...
GHI
GHI
AH HA HA!
GHI
GHI
AGAAA GAA ...
H- HANG IN THERE!
KRAK
KRAK
AAAAAAAAAAH!

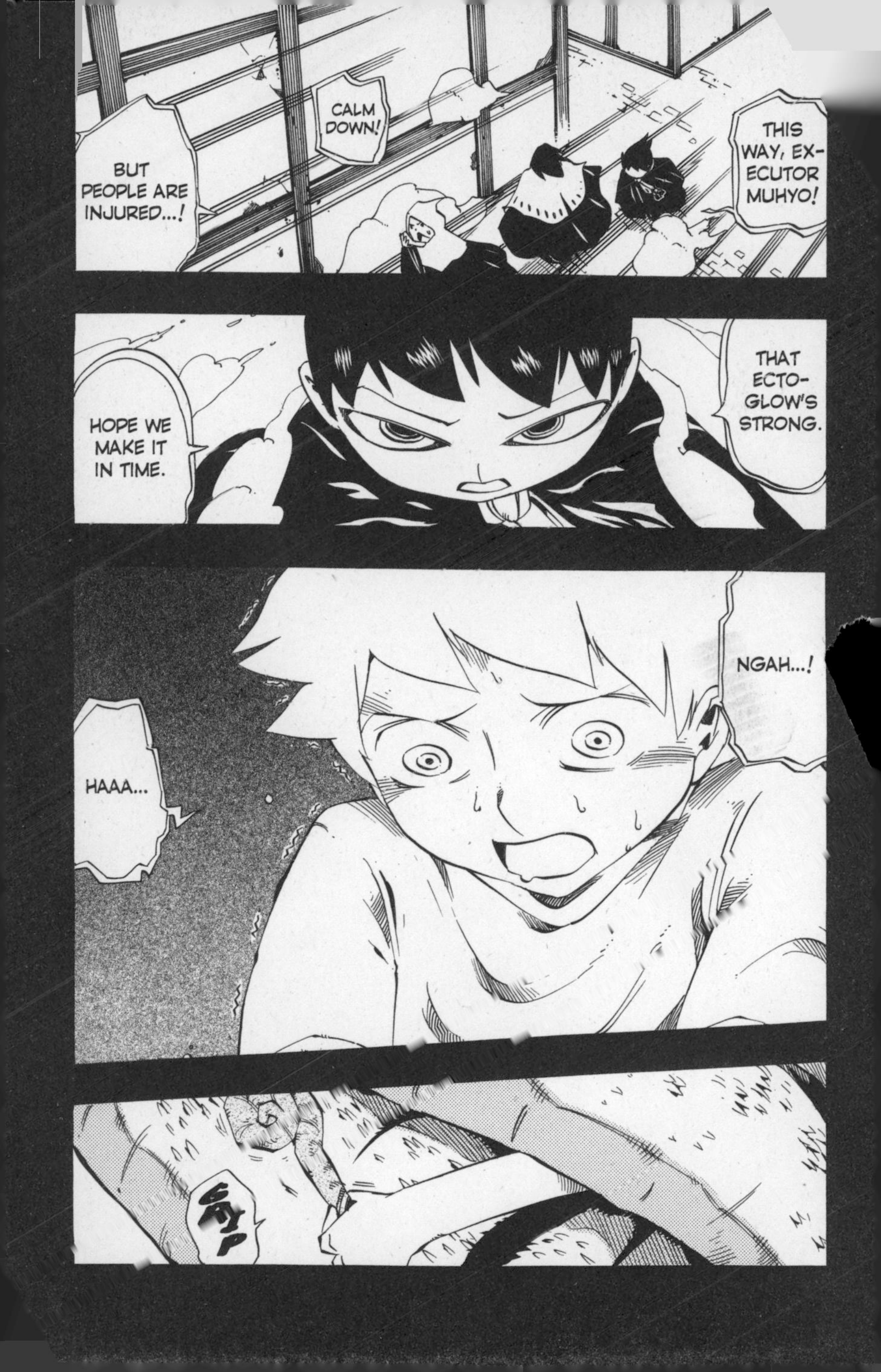
THIS WAY, EXECUTOR MUHYO!
CALM DOWN!
BUT PEOPLE ARE INJURED...!
THAT ECTO-GLOW'S STRONG.
HOPE WE MAKE IT IN TIME.
NGAH...!
HAAA...
GRIP

ONE DAY AT THE ARTIFACTS SHOP

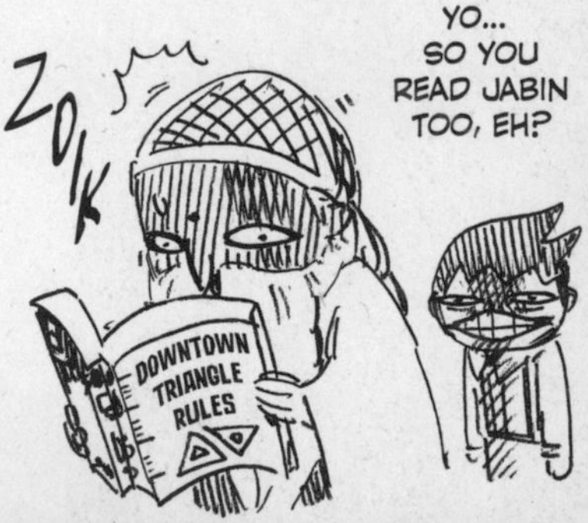
YO... SO YOU READ JABIN TOO, EH?
ZOIK
DOWNTOWN TRIANGLE RULES

ARTICLE 47

MAKING THE GRADE

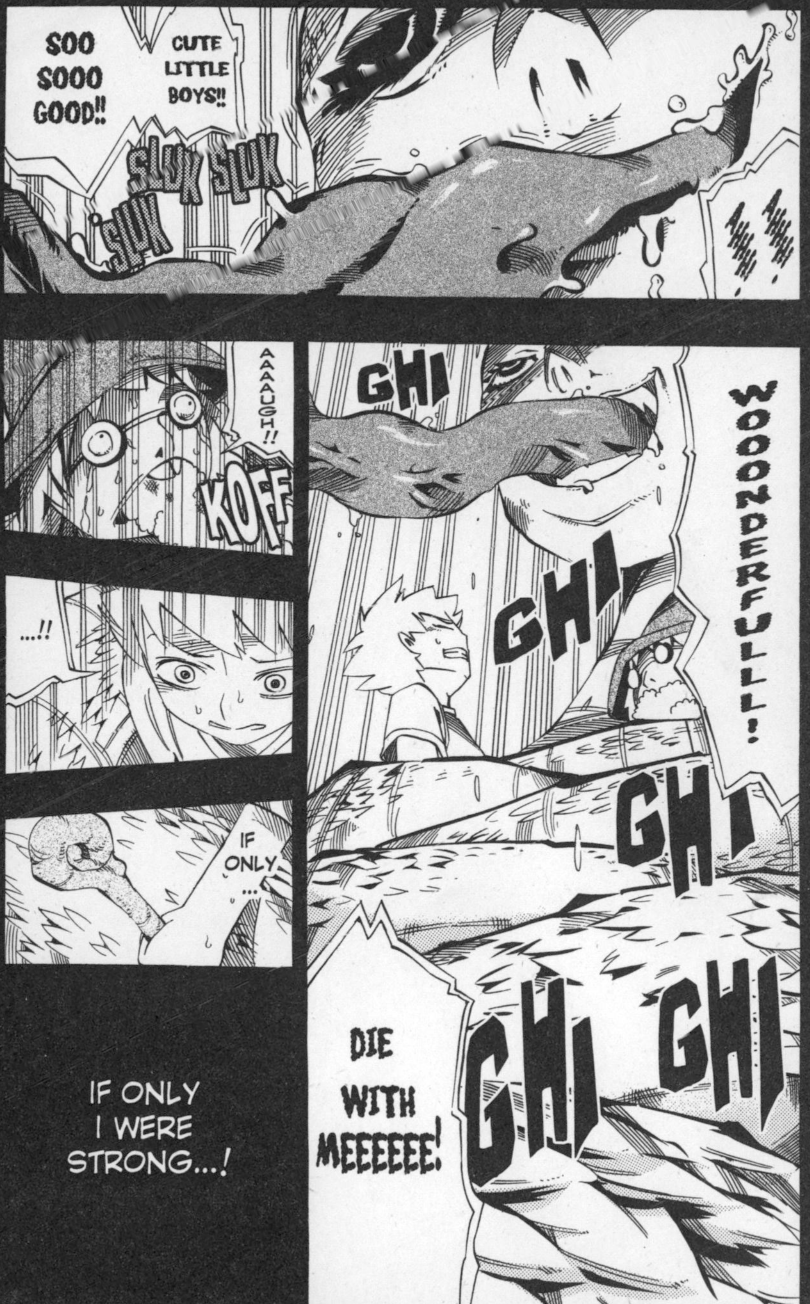
CUTE LITTLE BOYS!!
SOO SOOO GOOD!!
SLUK SLUK SLUK
WOOONDERFULLL!
GHI
GHI
GHI
GHI GHI
DIE WITH MEEEEEE!
AAAAUGH!!
KOFF
...!!
IF ONLY...
IF ONLY I WERE STRONG...!

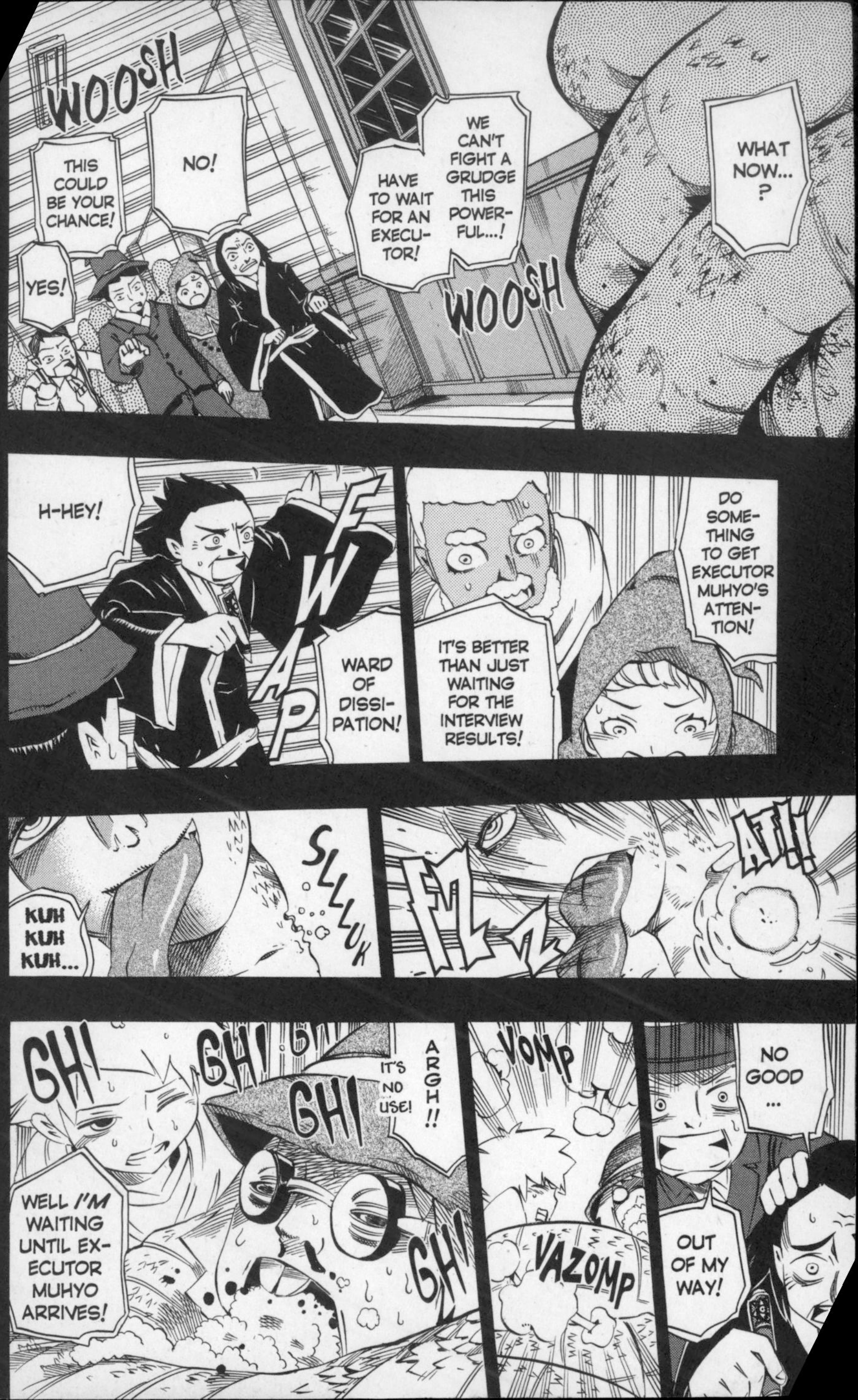
WHAT NOW...?
WOOSH
WE CAN'T FIGHT A GRUDGE THIS POWERFUL...!
HAVE TO WAIT FOR AN EXECUTOR!
NO!
WOOSH
THIS COULD BE YOUR CHANCE!
YES!
DO SOMETHING TO GET EXECUTOR MUHYO'S ATTENTION!
IT'S BETTER THAN JUST WAITING FOR THE INTERVIEW RESULTS!
FWAP
H-HEY!
WARD OF DISSIPATION!
AT!!
FZ
Z
SLLLLUK
KUH KUH KUH...
NO GOOD ...
OUT OF MY WAY!
VOMP
VAZOMP
ARGH!!
IT'S NO USE!
GHI
GHI
GHI
GHI
WELL *I'M* WAITING UNTIL EXECUTOR MUHYO ARRIVES!

IF ONLY...

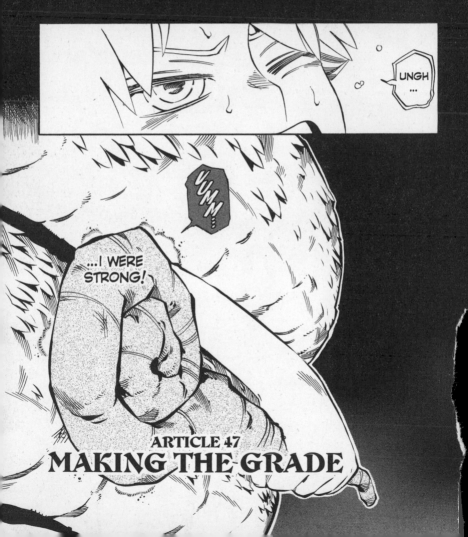

UNGH...

YUMM...

...I WERE STRONG!

ARTICLE 47
MAKING THE GRADE

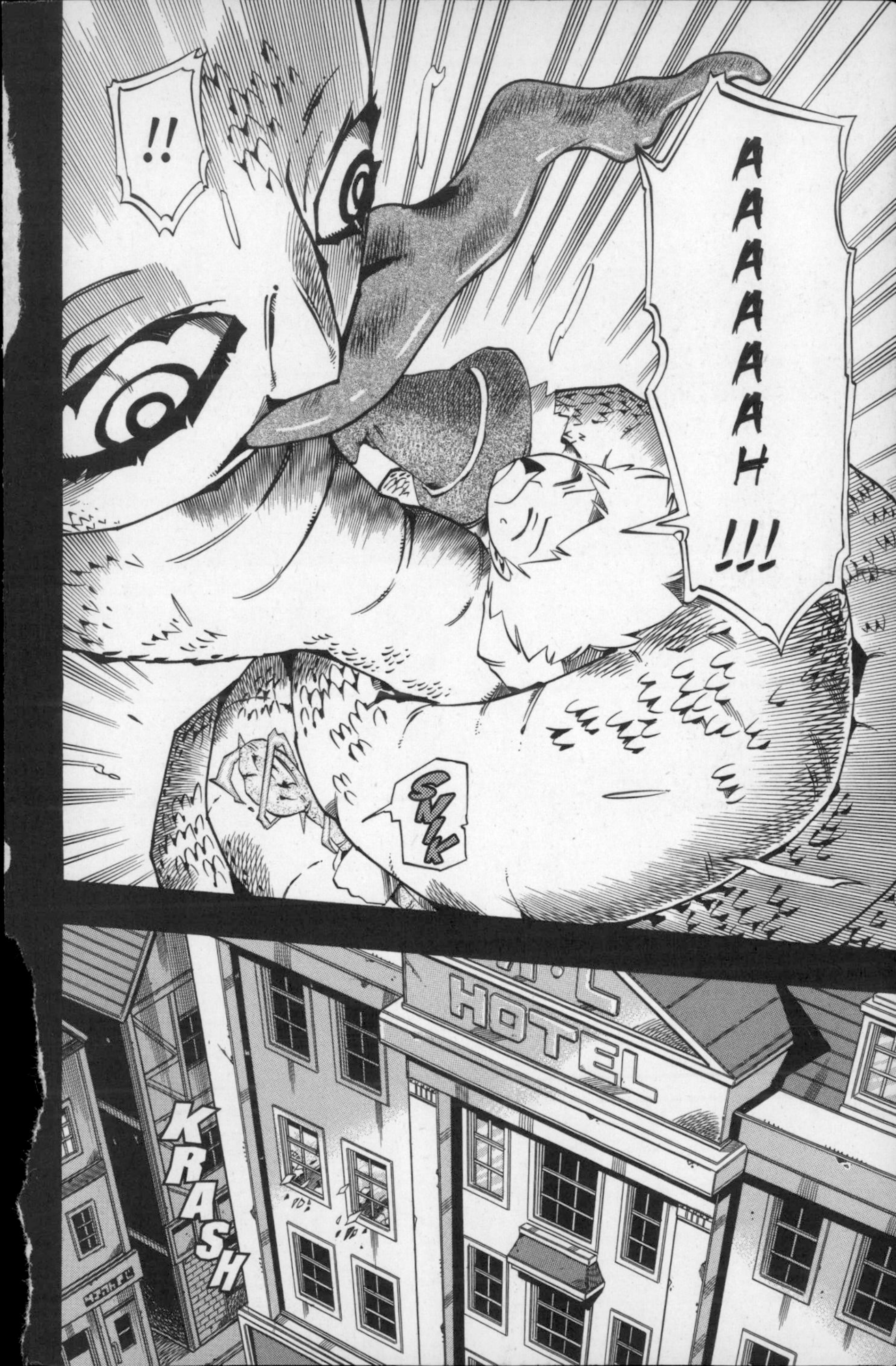
AAAAAAH!!!
!!
SNIK
HOTEL
KRASH

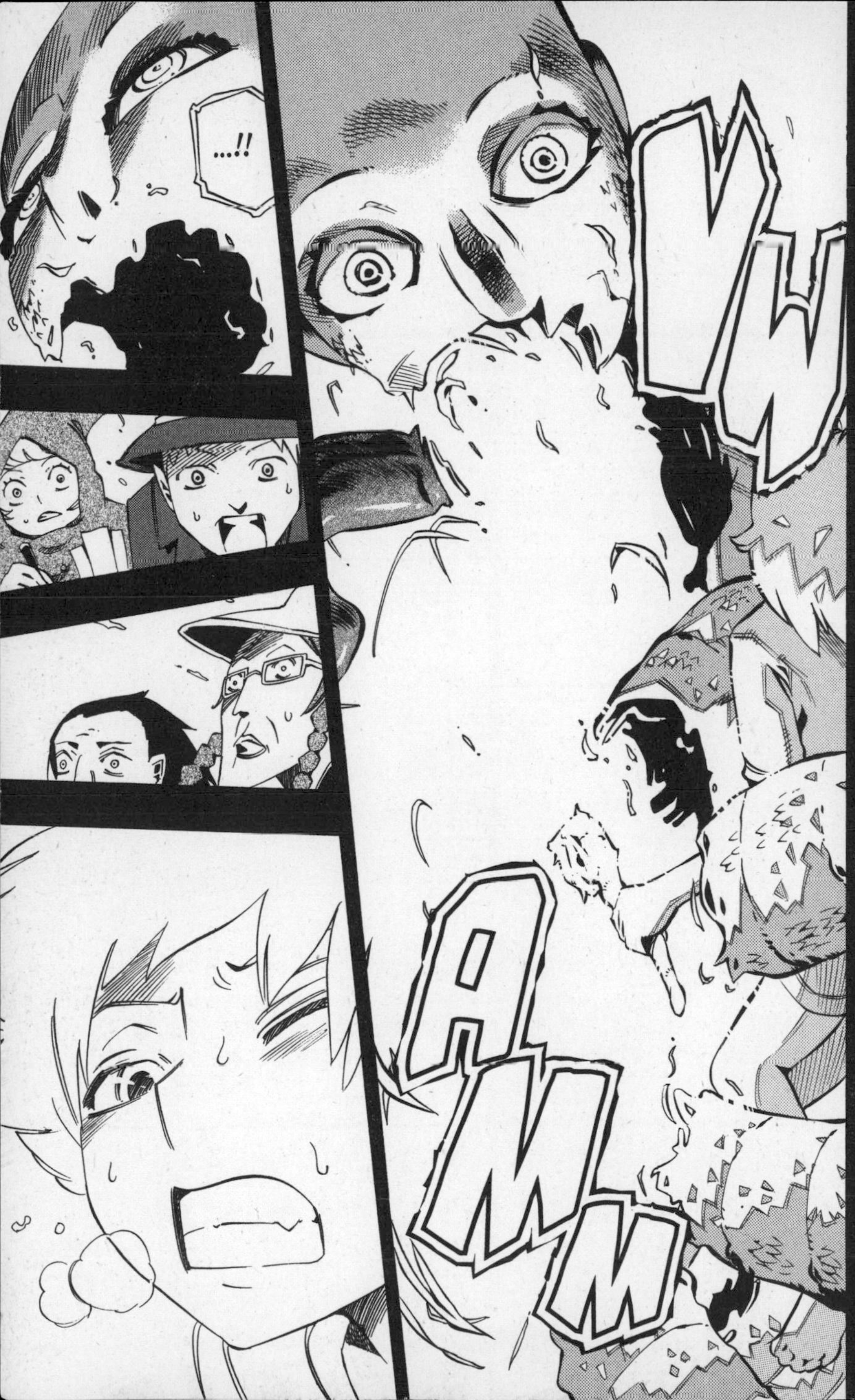
AMM
...!!

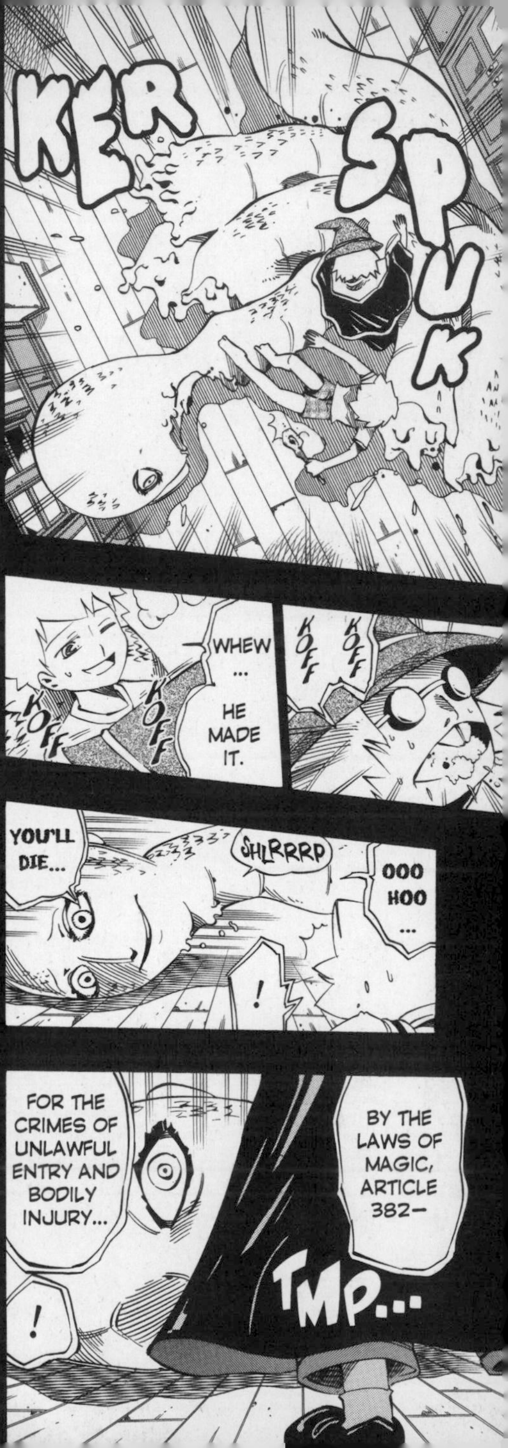
KERSPUK
KOFF KOFF
WHEW... HE MADE IT.
KOFF KOFF
OOO HOO...
SHLRRRP
YOU'LL DIE...
!
BY THE LAWS OF MAGIC, ARTICLE 382—
FOR THE CRIMES OF UNLAWFUL ENTRY AND BODILY INJURY...
TMP...
!
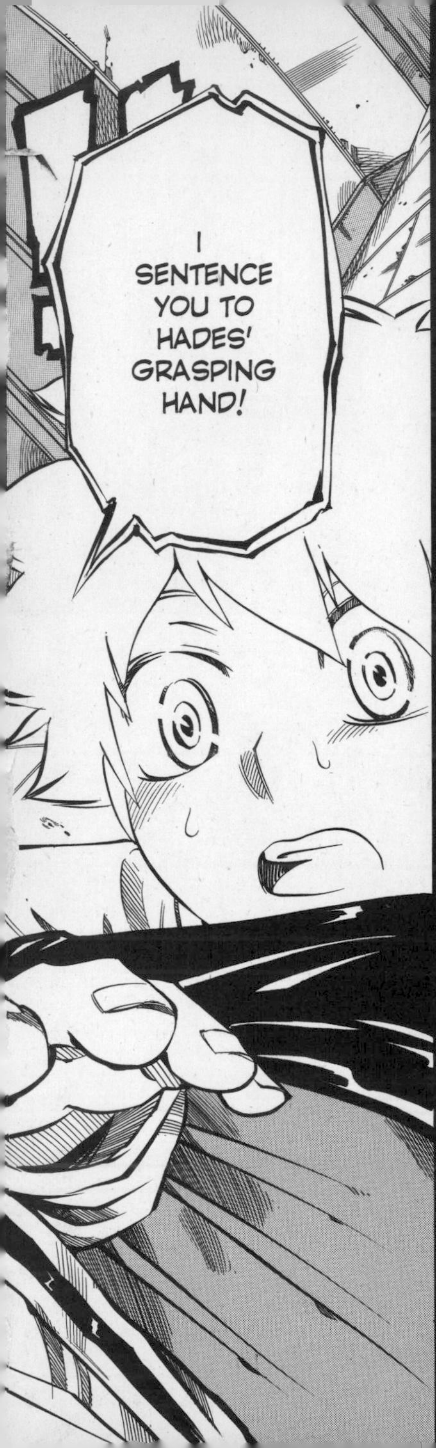
I SENTENCE YOU TO HADES' GRASPING HAND!

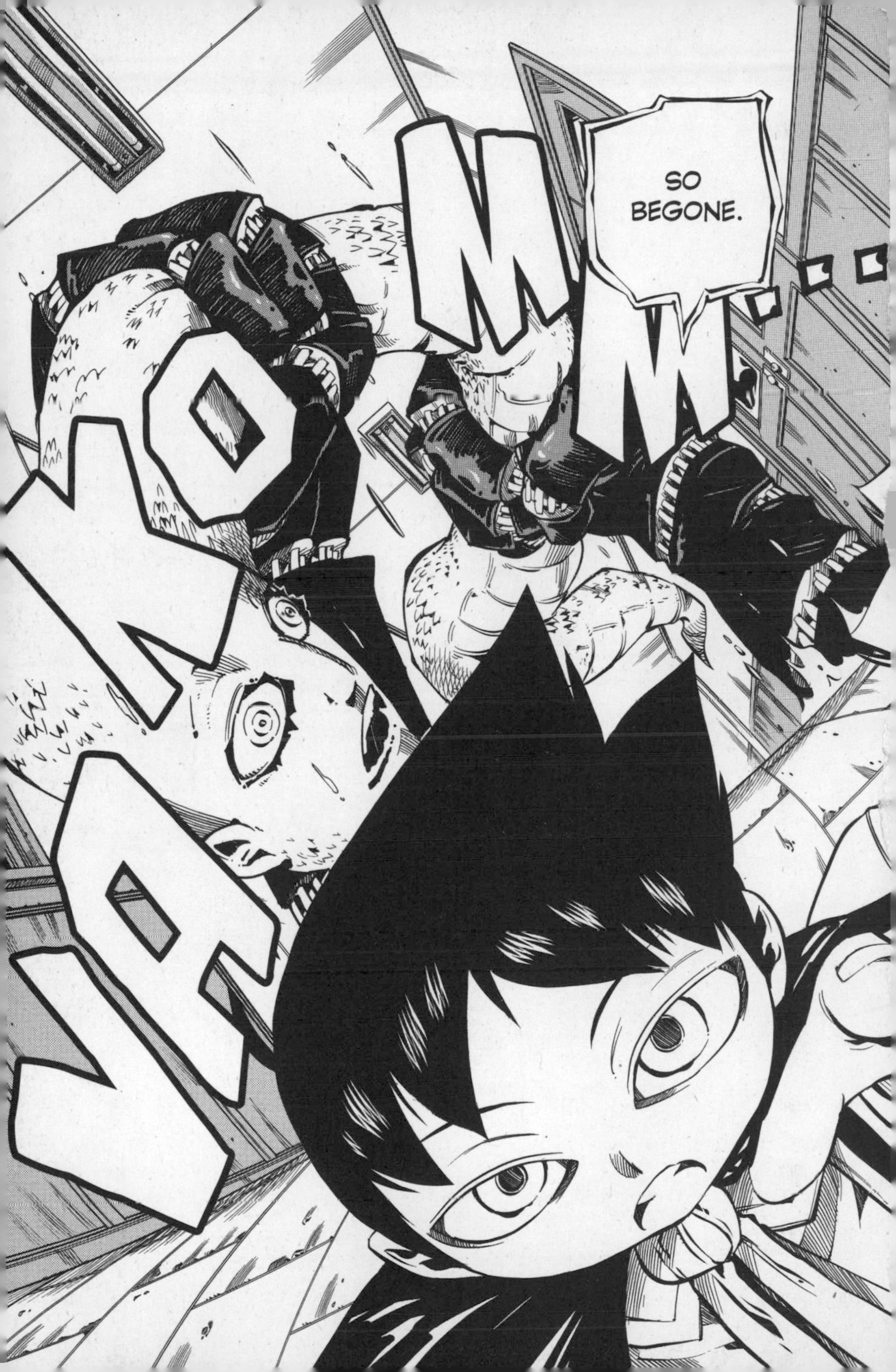
SO BEGONE.

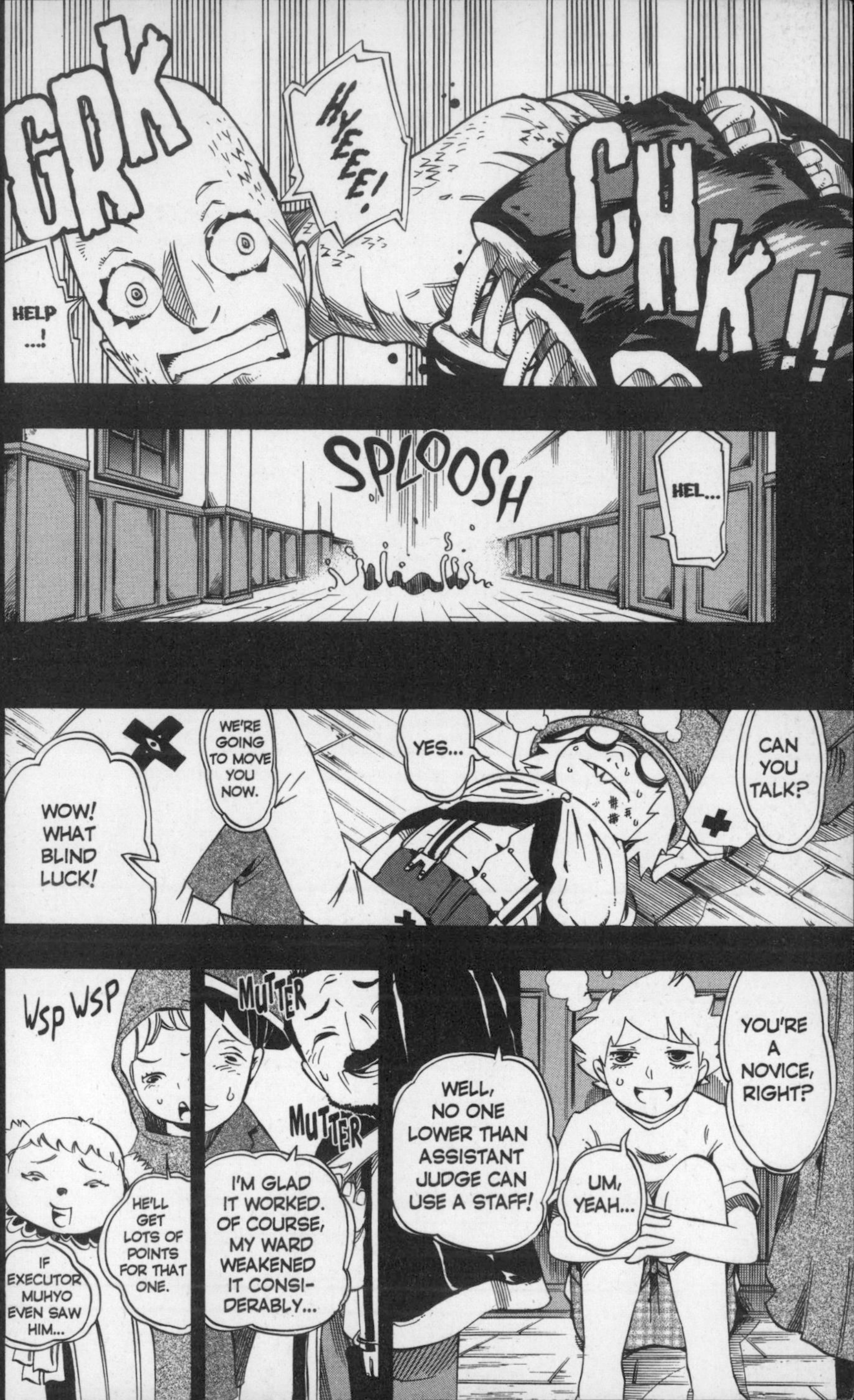

CHK!!
HYEEE!
GRK
HELP ...!
HEL...
SPLOOSH
CAN YOU TALK?
YES...
WE'RE GOING TO MOVE YOU NOW.
WOW! WHAT BLIND LUCK!
YOU'RE A NOVICE, RIGHT?
UM, YEAH...
WELL, NO ONE LOWER THAN ASSISTANT JUDGE CAN USE A STAFF!
MUTTER
MUTTER
I'M GLAD IT WORKED. OF COURSE, MY WARD WEAKENED IT CONSI-DERABLY...
WSP WSP
HE'LL GET LOTS OF POINTS FOR THAT ONE.
IF EXECUTOR MUHYO EVEN SAW HIM...

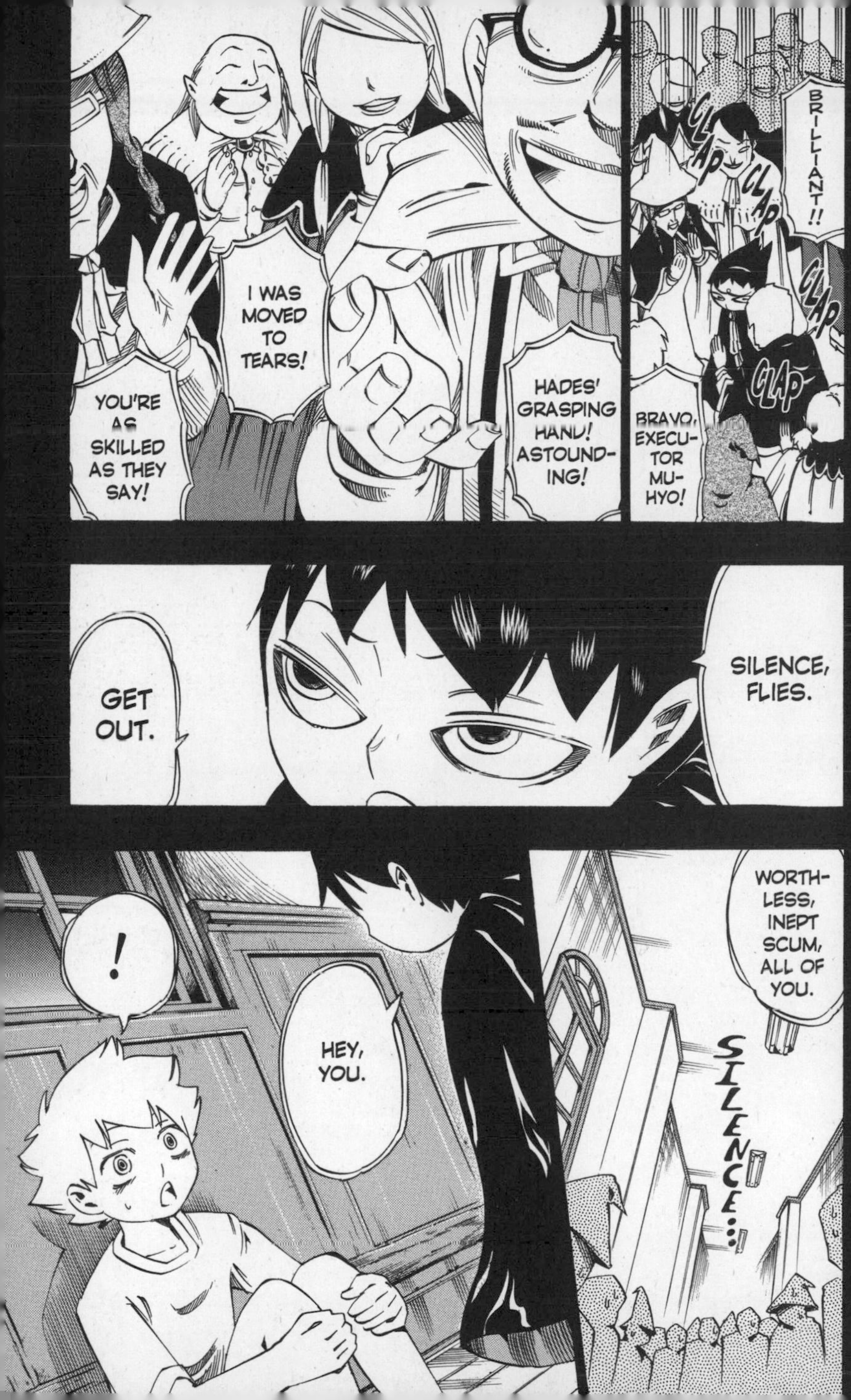
BRILLIANT!!
CLAP CLAP CLAP CLAP
BRAVO, EXECUTOR MUHYO!
HADES' GRASPING HAND! ASTOUNDING!
I WAS MOVED TO TEARS!
YOU'RE AS SKILLED AS THEY SAY!
SILENCE, FLIES.
GET OUT.
WORTHLESS, INEPT SCUM, ALL OF YOU.
SILENCE...
HEY, YOU.
!

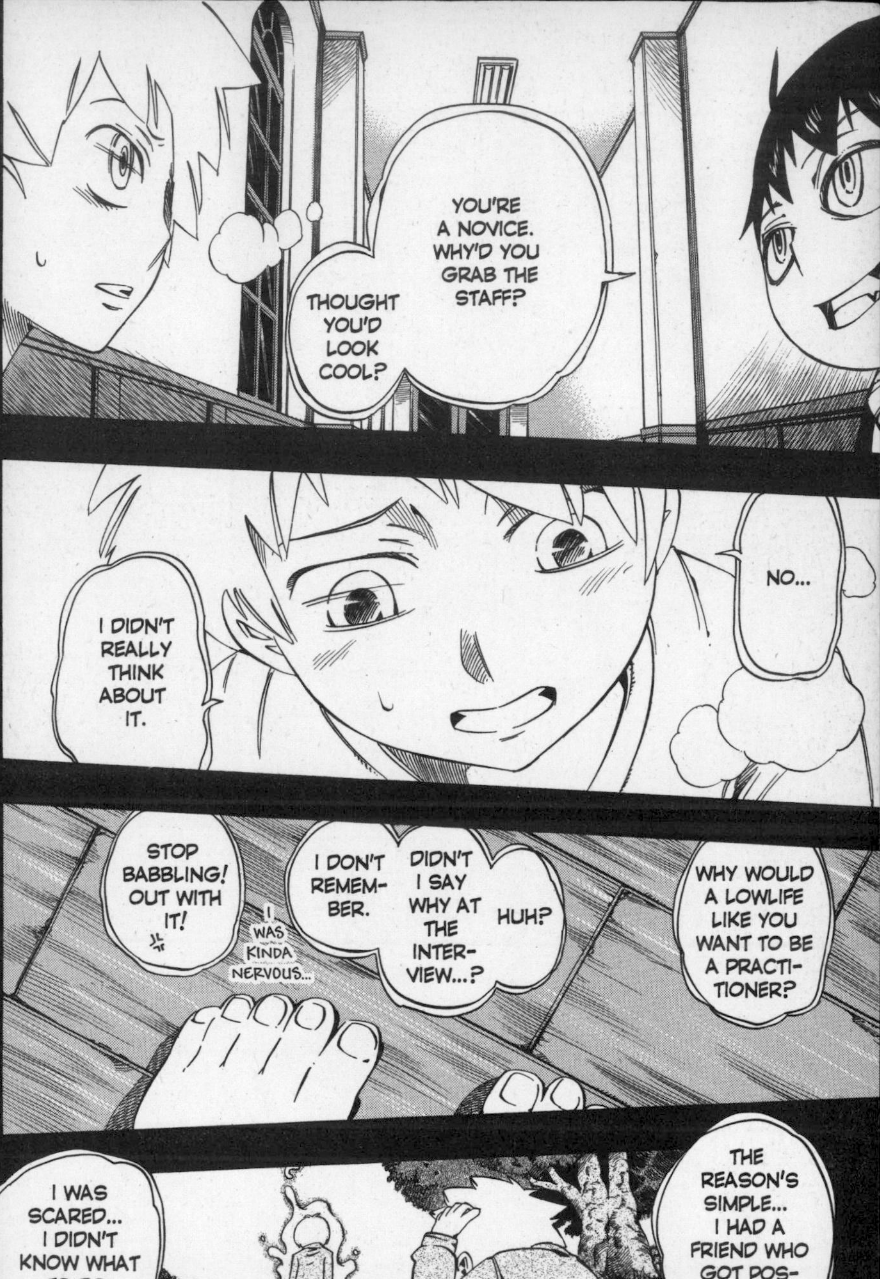
YOU'RE A NOVICE. WHY'D YOU GRAB THE STAFF?
THOUGHT YOU'D LOOK COOL?
NO...
I DIDN'T REALLY THINK ABOUT IT.
WHY WOULD A LOWLIFE LIKE YOU WANT TO BE A PRACTITIONER?
HUH?
DIDN'T I SAY WHY AT THE INTERVIEW...?
I DON'T REMEMBER.
I WAS KINDA NERVOUS...
STOP BABBLING! OUT WITH IT!
THE REASON'S SIMPLE... I HAD A FRIEND WHO GOT POSSESSED.
I WAS SCARED... I DIDN'T KNOW WHAT TO DO.

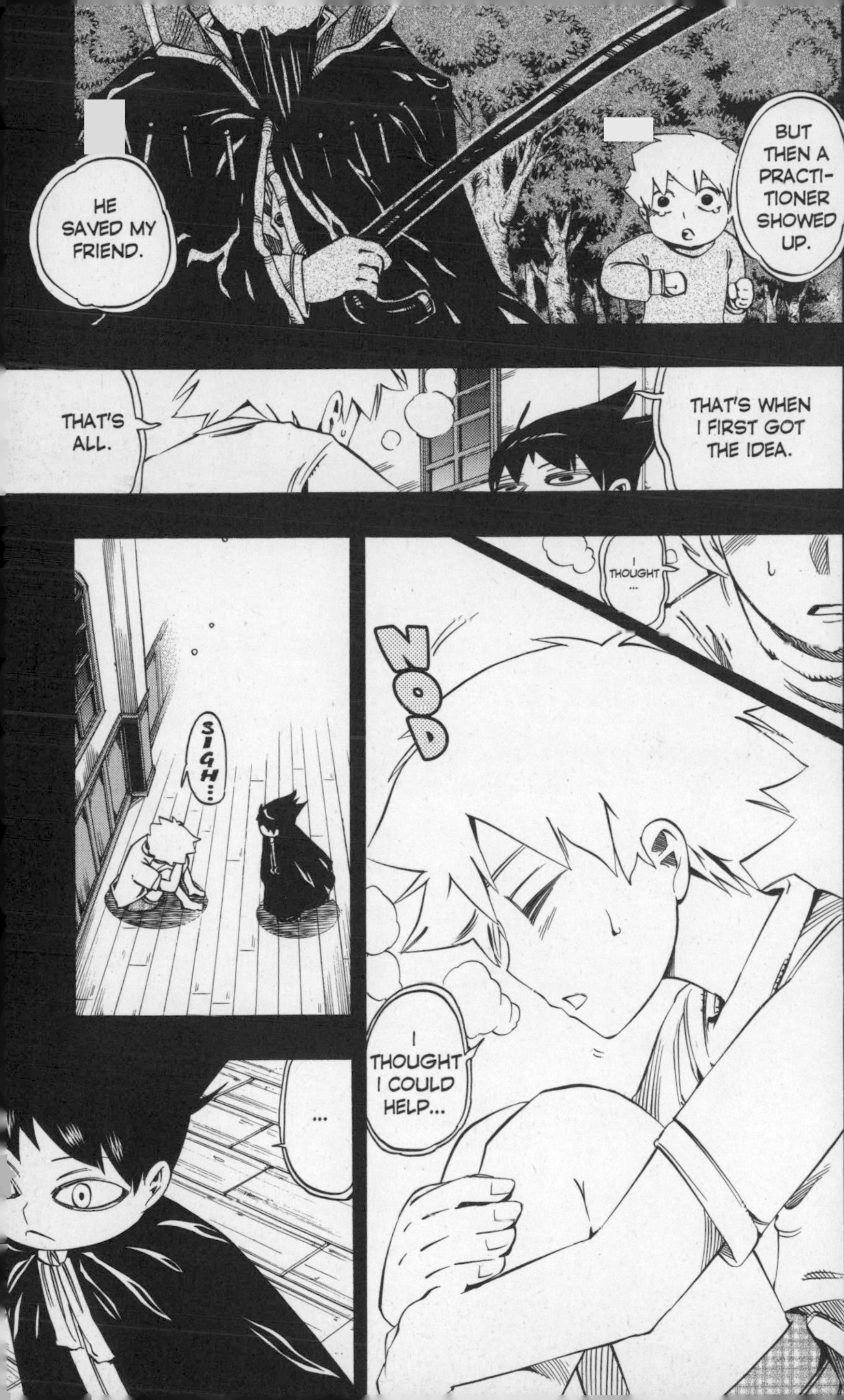
BUT THEN A PRACTITIONER SHOWED UP.
HE SAVED MY FRIEND.
THAT'S WHEN I FIRST GOT THE IDEA.
THAT'S ALL.
I THOUGHT...
NOD
I THOUGHT I COULD HELP...
SIGH...
...

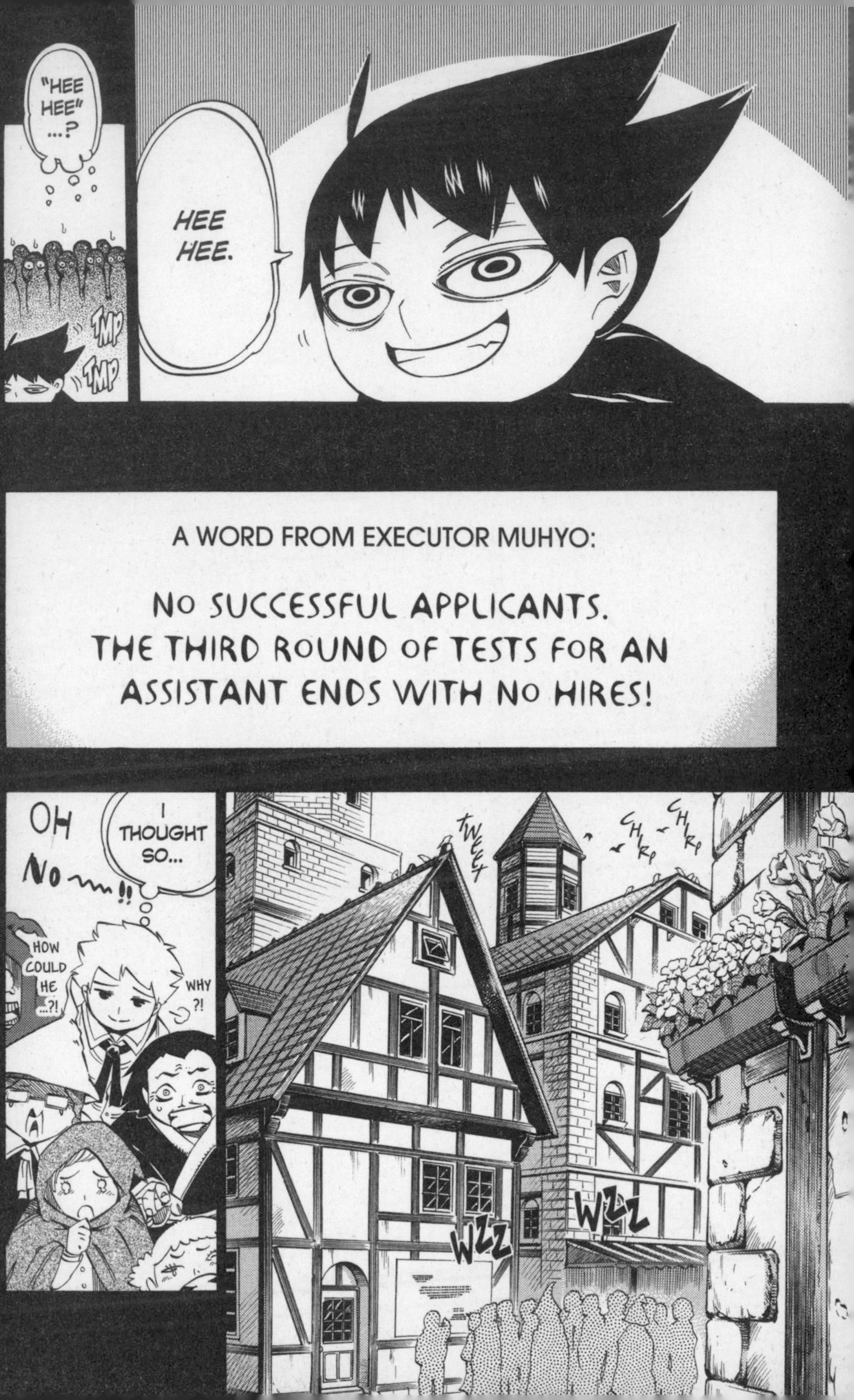
HEE HEE.
"HEE HEE"...?
TMP
TMP
A WORD FROM EXECUTOR MUHYO:
NO SUCCESSFUL APPLICANTS. THE THIRD ROUND OF TESTS FOR AN ASSISTANT ENDS WITH NO HIRES!
TWEET
CHIRP
CHIRP
WZZ
WZZ
OH NO!!
I THOUGHT SO...
HOW COULD HE ...?!
WHY ?!

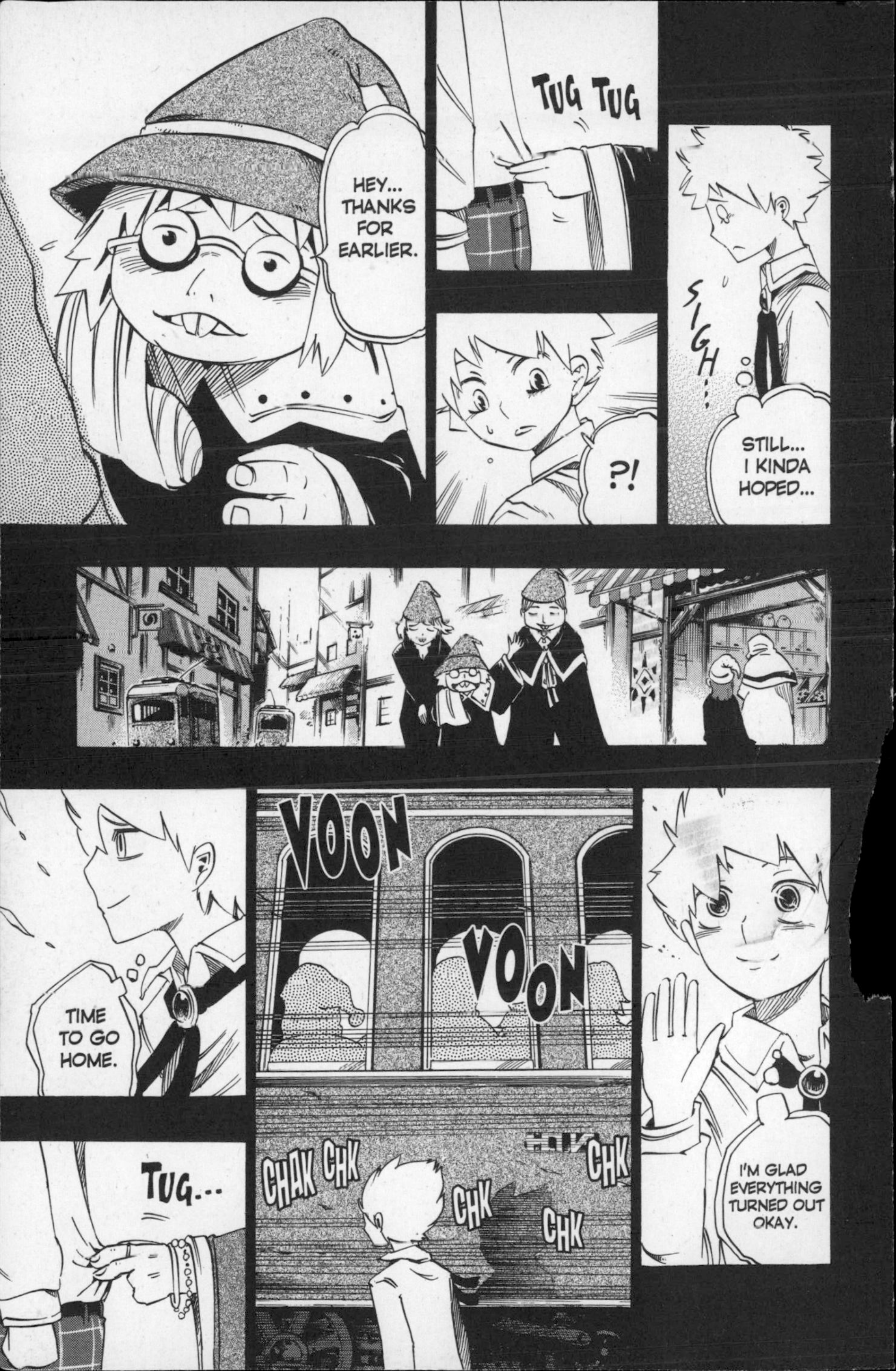
SIGH...
STILL... I KINDA HOPED...
TUG TUG
?!
HEY... THANKS FOR EARLIER.
I'M GLAD EVERYTHING TURNED OUT OKAY.
VOON
VOON
CHK
CHAK CHK
CHK
CHK
TIME TO GO HOME.
TUG...

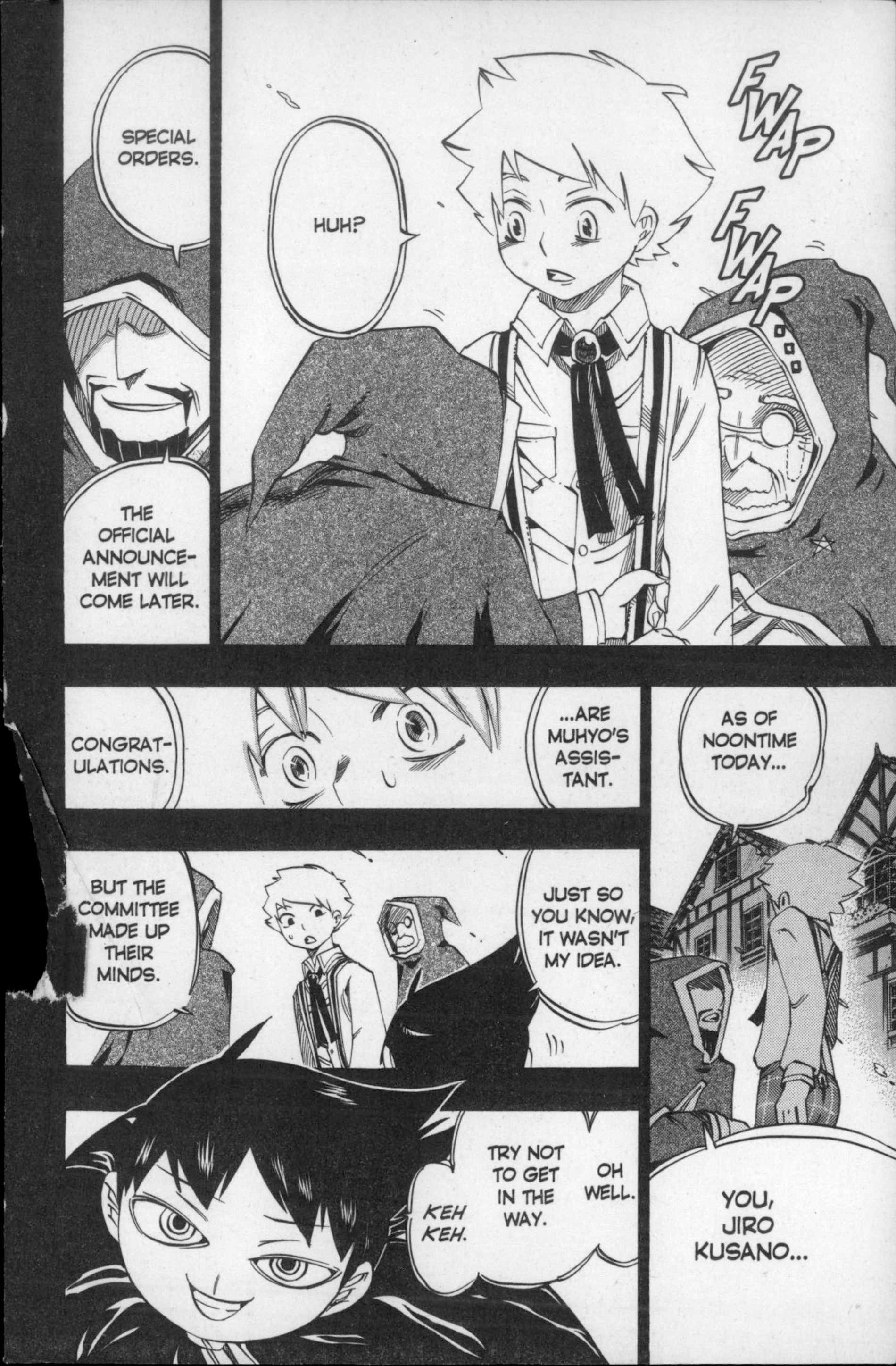
FWAP
FWAP
HUH?
SPECIAL ORDERS.
THE OFFICIAL ANNOUNCEMENT WILL COME LATER.
AS OF NOONTIME TODAY...
YOU, JIRO KUSANO...
...ARE MUHYO'S ASSISTANT.
CONGRATULATIONS.
JUST SO YOU KNOW, IT WASN'T MY IDEA.
BUT THE COMMITTEE MADE UP THEIR MINDS.
OH WELL.
TRY NOT TO GET IN THE WAY.
KEH KEH.

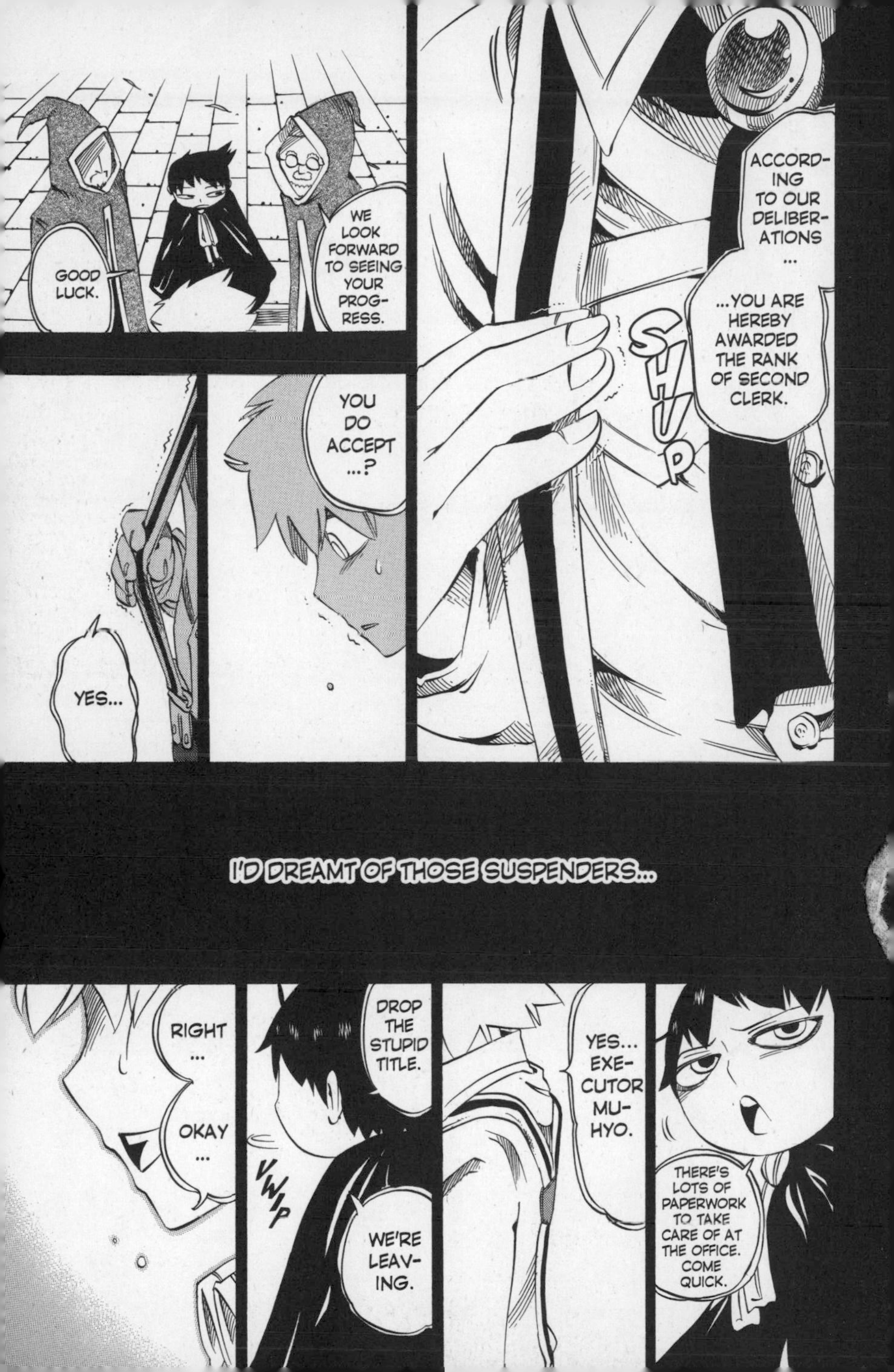
ACCORD-ING TO OUR DELIBER-ATIONS ...
...YOU ARE HEREBY AWARDED THE RANK OF SECOND CLERK.
SHUP
WE LOOK FORWARD TO SEEING YOUR PROG-RESS.
GOOD LUCK.
YOU DO ACCEPT ...?
YES...
I'D DREAMT OF THOSE SUSPENDERS...
THERE'S LOTS OF PAPERWORK TO TAKE CARE OF AT THE OFFICE. COME QUICK.
YES... EXE-CUTOR MU-HYO.
DROP THE STUPID TITLE.
WE'RE LEAV-ING.
VWIP
RIGHT ...
OKAY ...

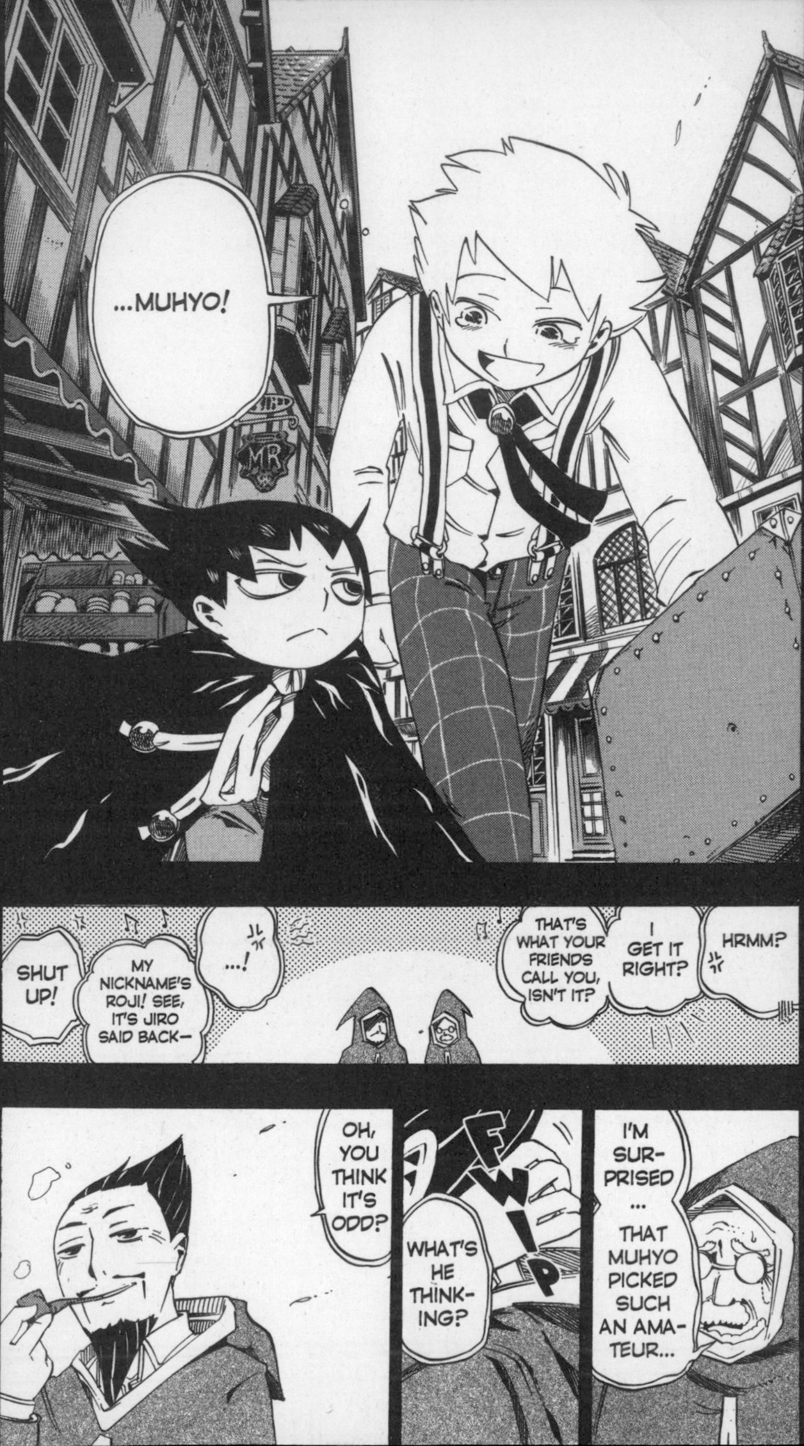
...MUHYO!
HRMM?
I GET IT RIGHT?
THAT'S WHAT YOUR FRIENDS CALL YOU, ISN'T IT?
...!
MY NICKNAME'S ROJI! SEE, IT'S JIRO SAID BACK—
SHUT UP!
I'M SURPRISED ... THAT MUHYO PICKED SUCH AN AMATEUR...
FWIP
WHAT'S HE THINKING?
OH, YOU THINK IT'S ODD?

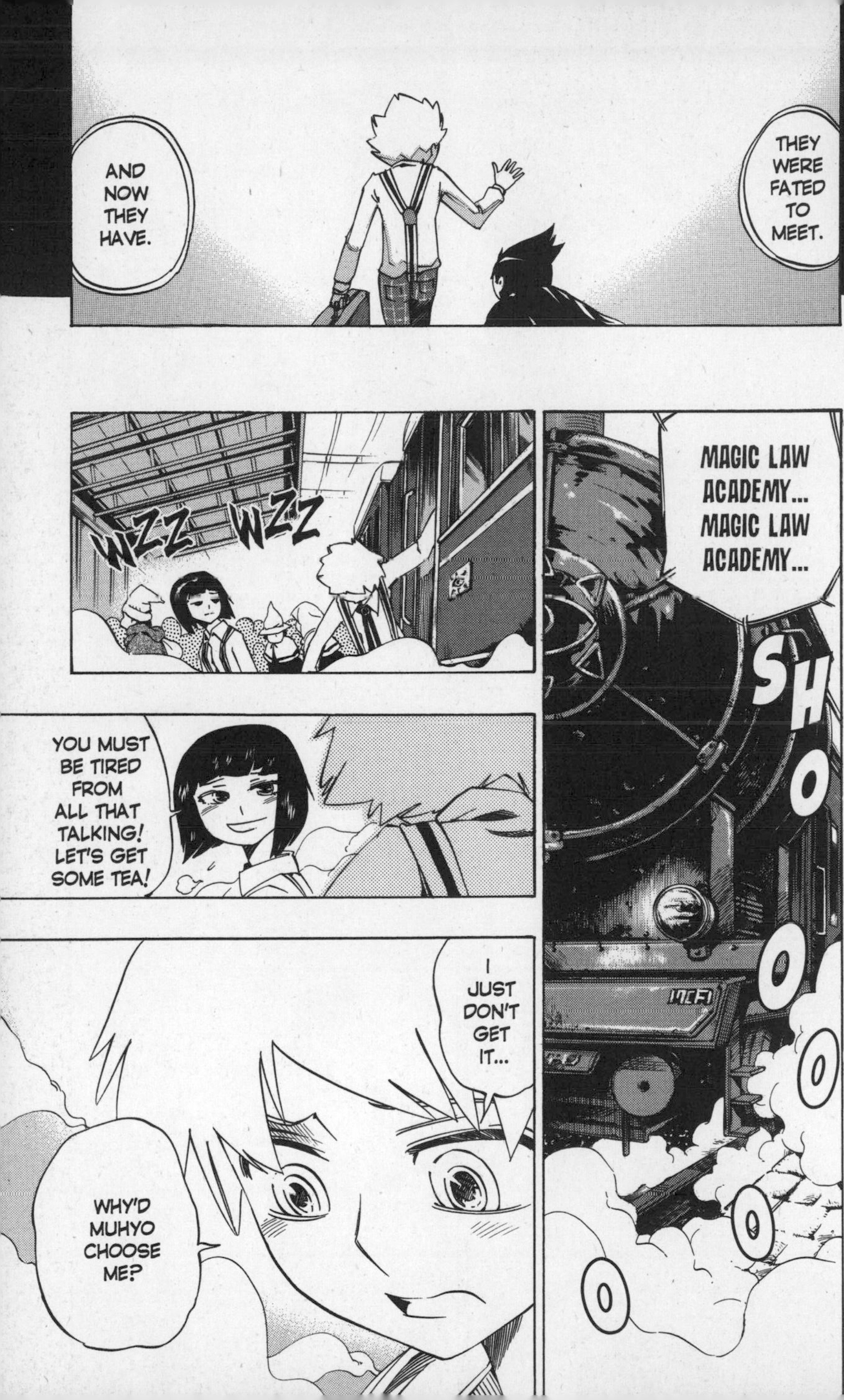
THEY WERE FATED TO MEET.
AND NOW THEY HAVE.
MAGIC LAW ACADEMY... MAGIC LAW ACADEMY...
SHOOOOO
WZZ WZZ
YOU MUST BE TIRED FROM ALL THAT TALKING! LET'S GET SOME TEA!
I JUST DON'T GET IT...
WHY'D MUHYO CHOOSE ME?

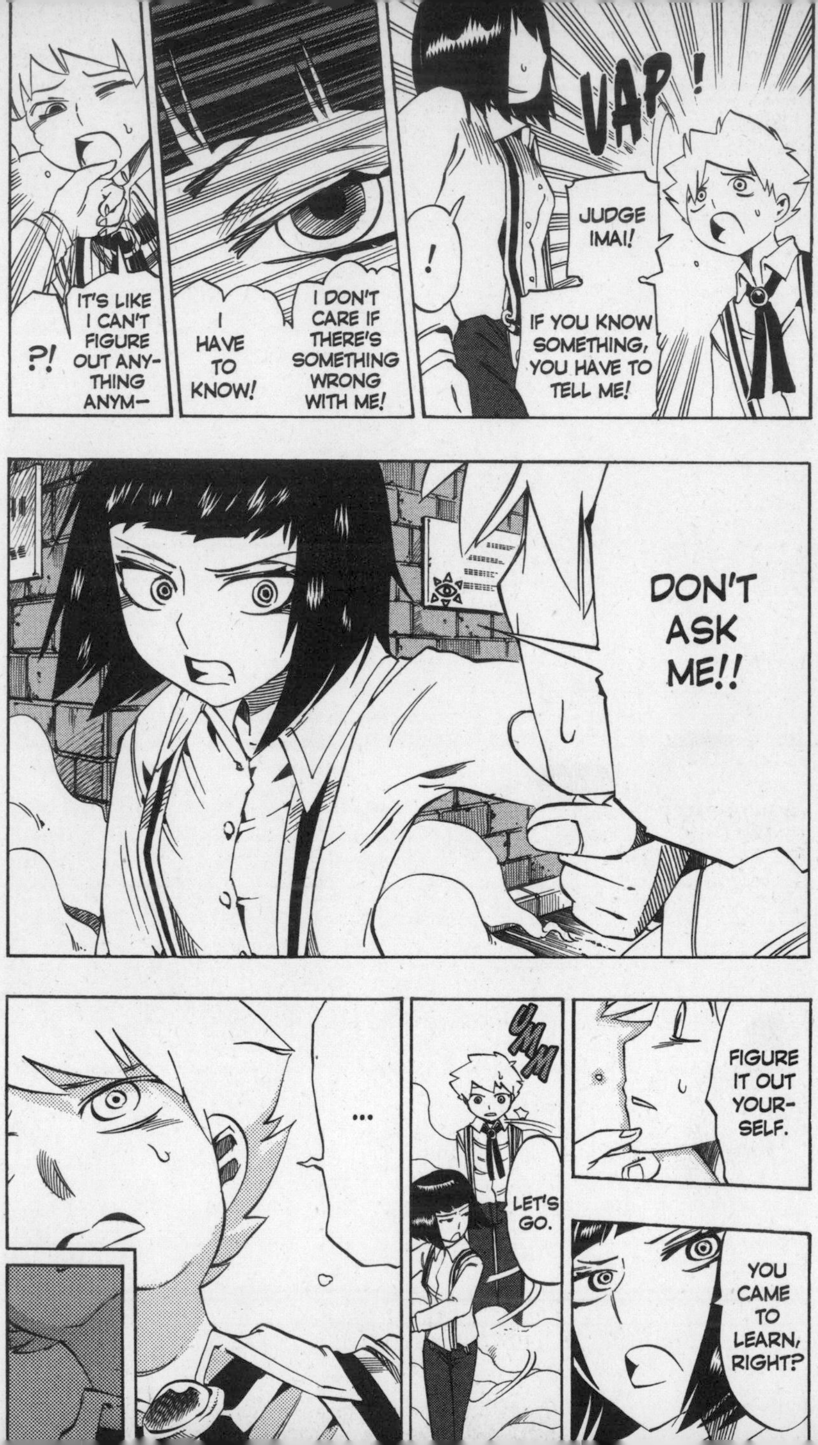
VAP!
JUDGE IMAI!
IF YOU KNOW SOMETHING, YOU HAVE TO TELL ME!
!
I DON'T CARE IF THERE'S SOMETHING WRONG WITH ME!
I HAVE TO KNOW!
IT'S LIKE I CAN'T FIGURE OUT ANYTHING ANYM—
?!
DON'T ASK ME!!
FIGURE IT OUT YOURSELF.
YOU CAME TO LEARN, RIGHT?
UMM
LET'S GO.
...

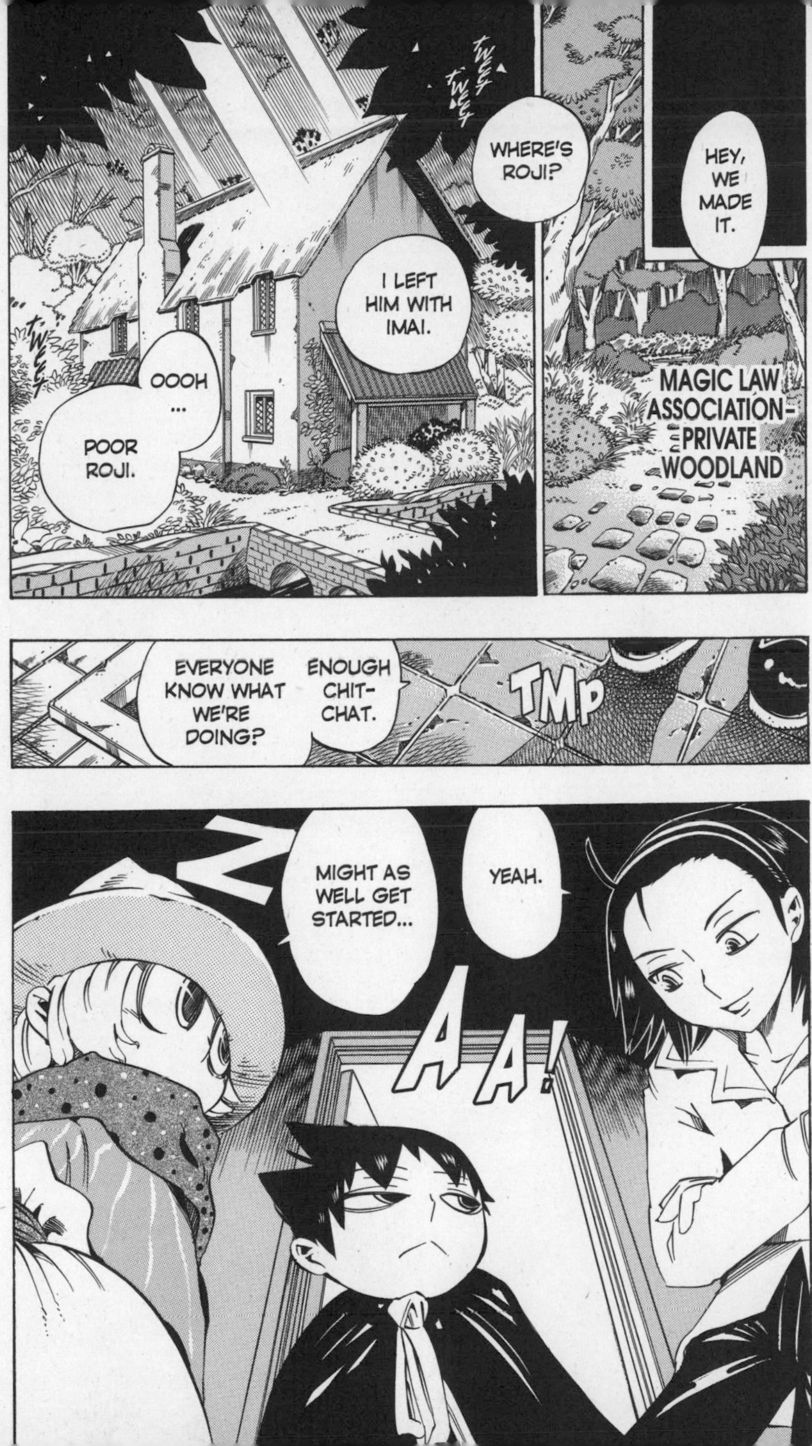
HEY, WE MADE IT.
MAGIC LAW ASSOCIATION—PRIVATE WOODLAND
WHERE'S ROJI?
I LEFT HIM WITH IMAI.
OOOH ...
POOR ROJI.
TMP
ENOUGH CHIT-CHAT.
EVERYONE KNOW WHAT WE'RE DOING?
YEAH.
MIGHT AS WELL GET STARTED...
ZAA!

Q: SO, WHAT DOES MUHYO LIKE FOOD-WISE? IT WASN'T IN HIS PROFILE...

-T.M., HIROSHIMA

A: OH, OOPS. MUST'VE FORGOTTEN. LET'S ASK ROJI, SHALL WE?

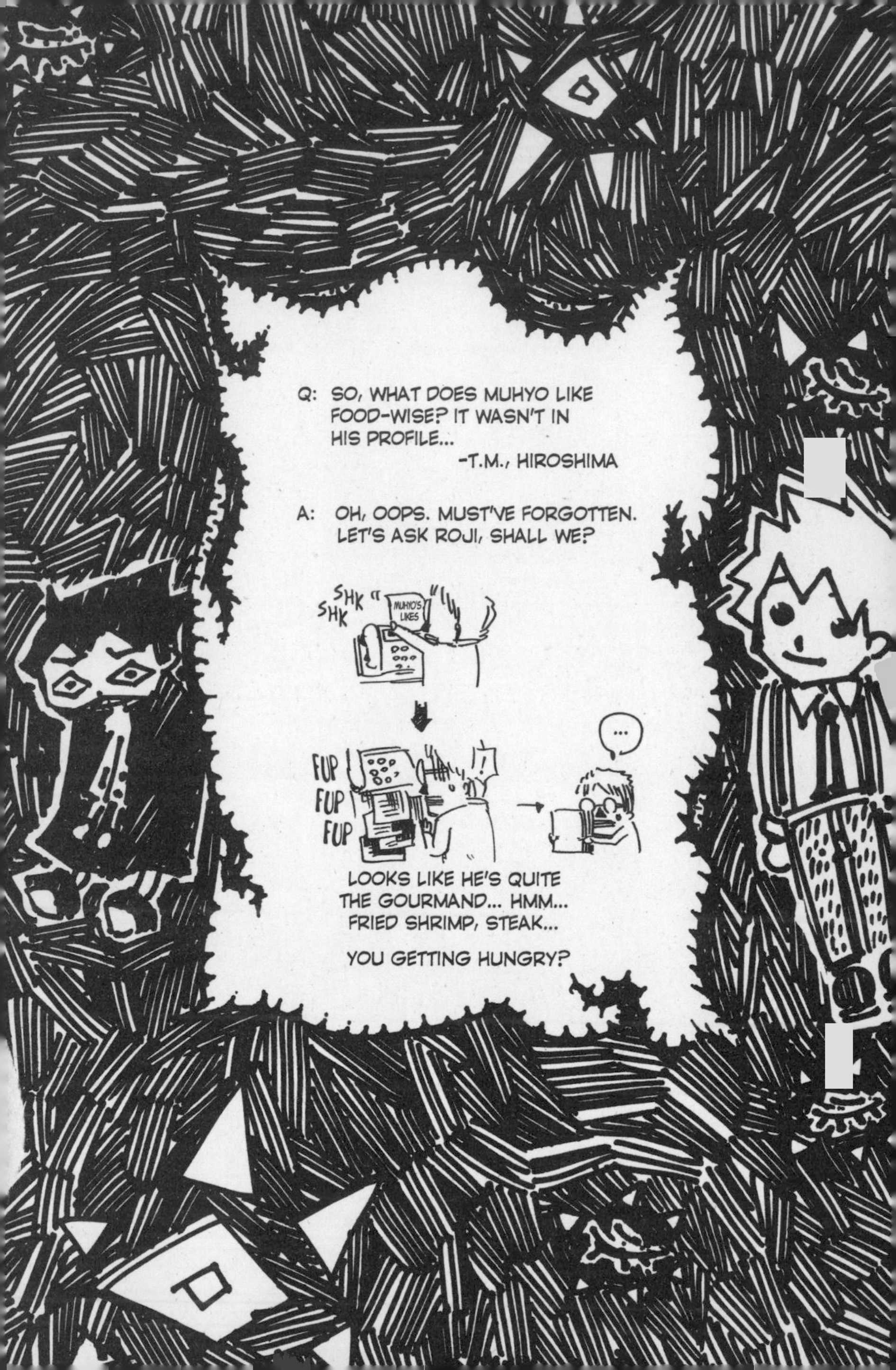
SHHK
SHHK
MUHYO'S LIKES
FUP
FUP
FUP
!
...

LOOKS LIKE HE'S QUITE THE GOURMAND... HMM... FRIED SHRIMP, STEAK...

YOU GETTING HUNGRY?

ARTICLE 48
AWAKENING

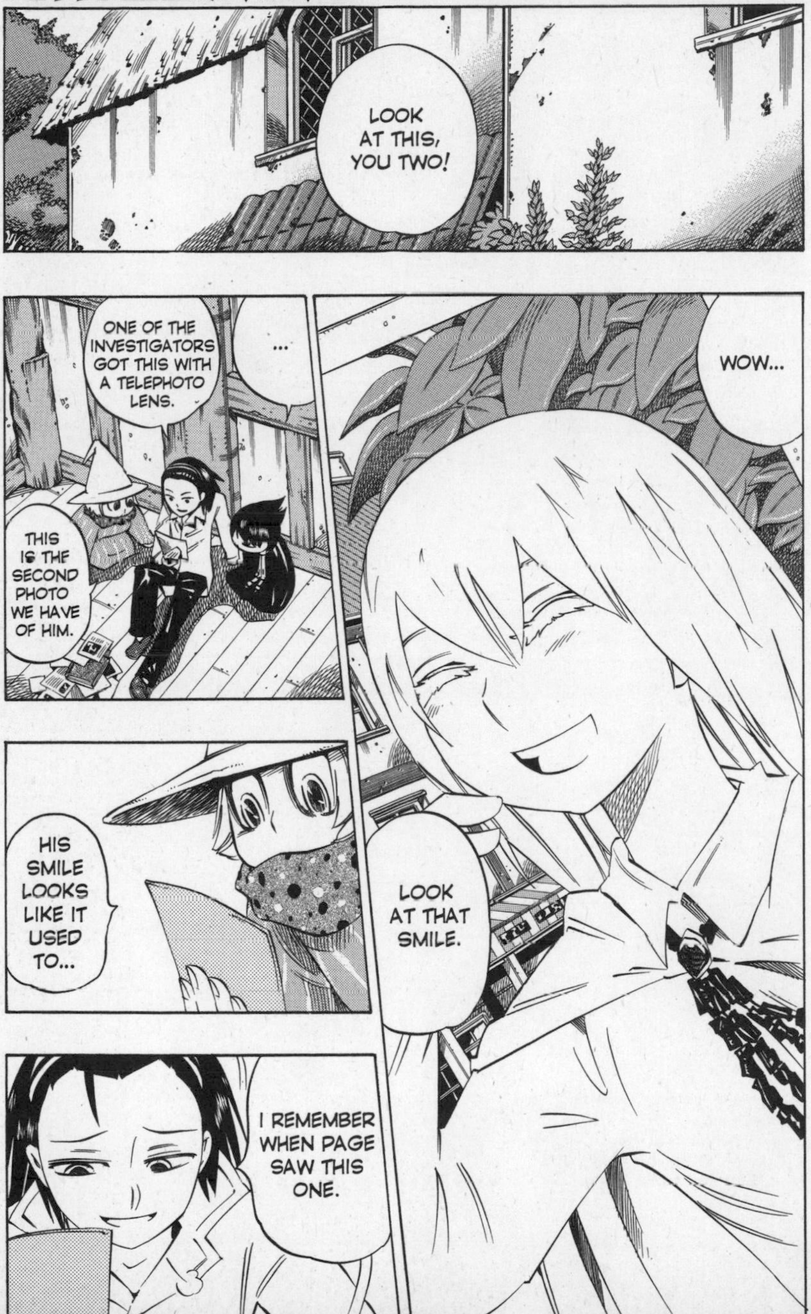

LOOK AT THIS, YOU TWO!
WOW...
LOOK AT THAT SMILE.
...
ONE OF THE INVESTIGATORS GOT THIS WITH A TELEPHOTO LENS.
THIS IS THE SECOND PHOTO WE HAVE OF HIM.
HIS SMILE LOOKS LIKE IT USED TO...
I REMEMBER WHEN PAGE SAW THIS ONE.

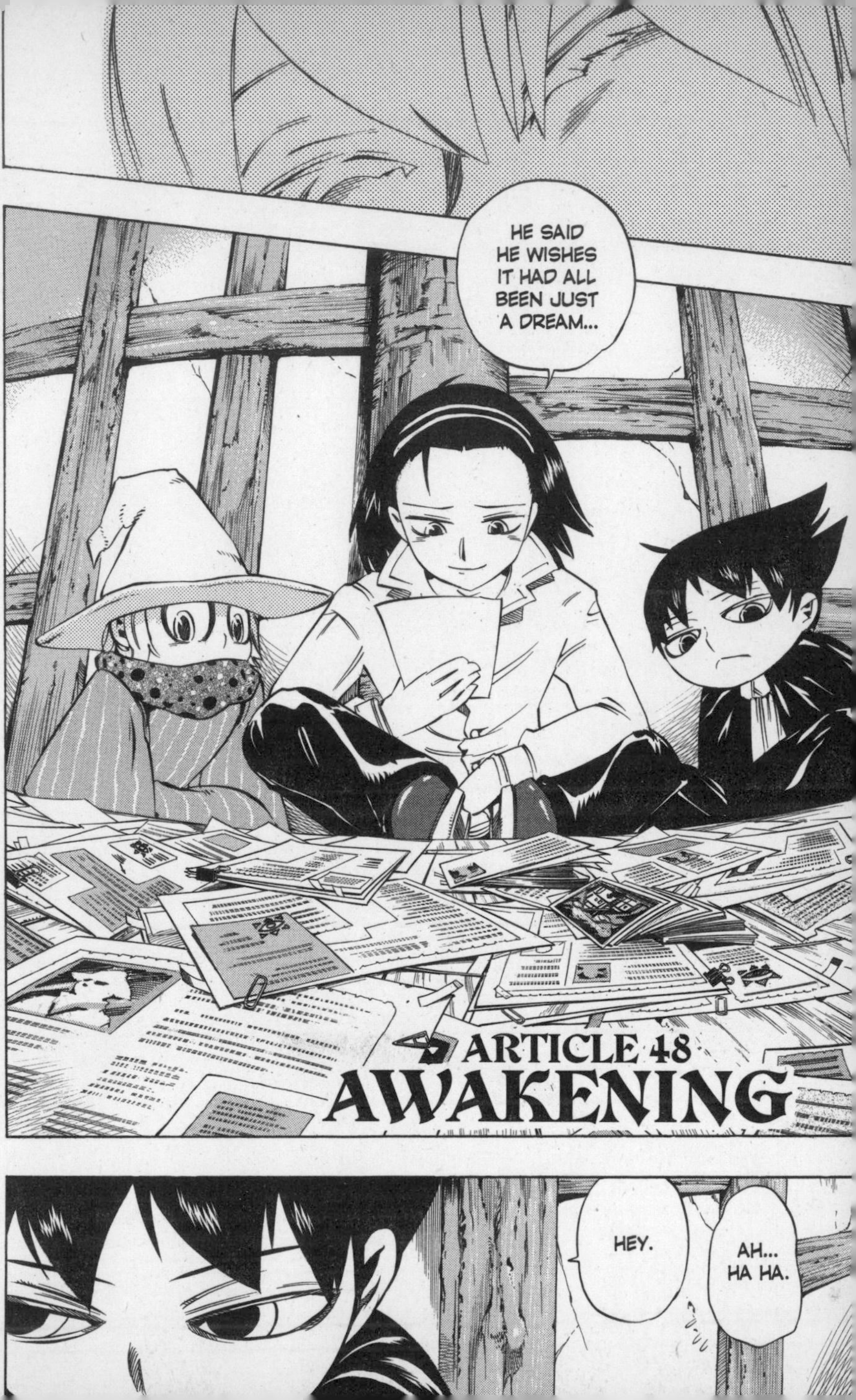
HE SAID HE WISHES IT HAD ALL BEEN JUST A DREAM...
ARTICLE 48
AWAKENING
AH... HA HA.
HEY.

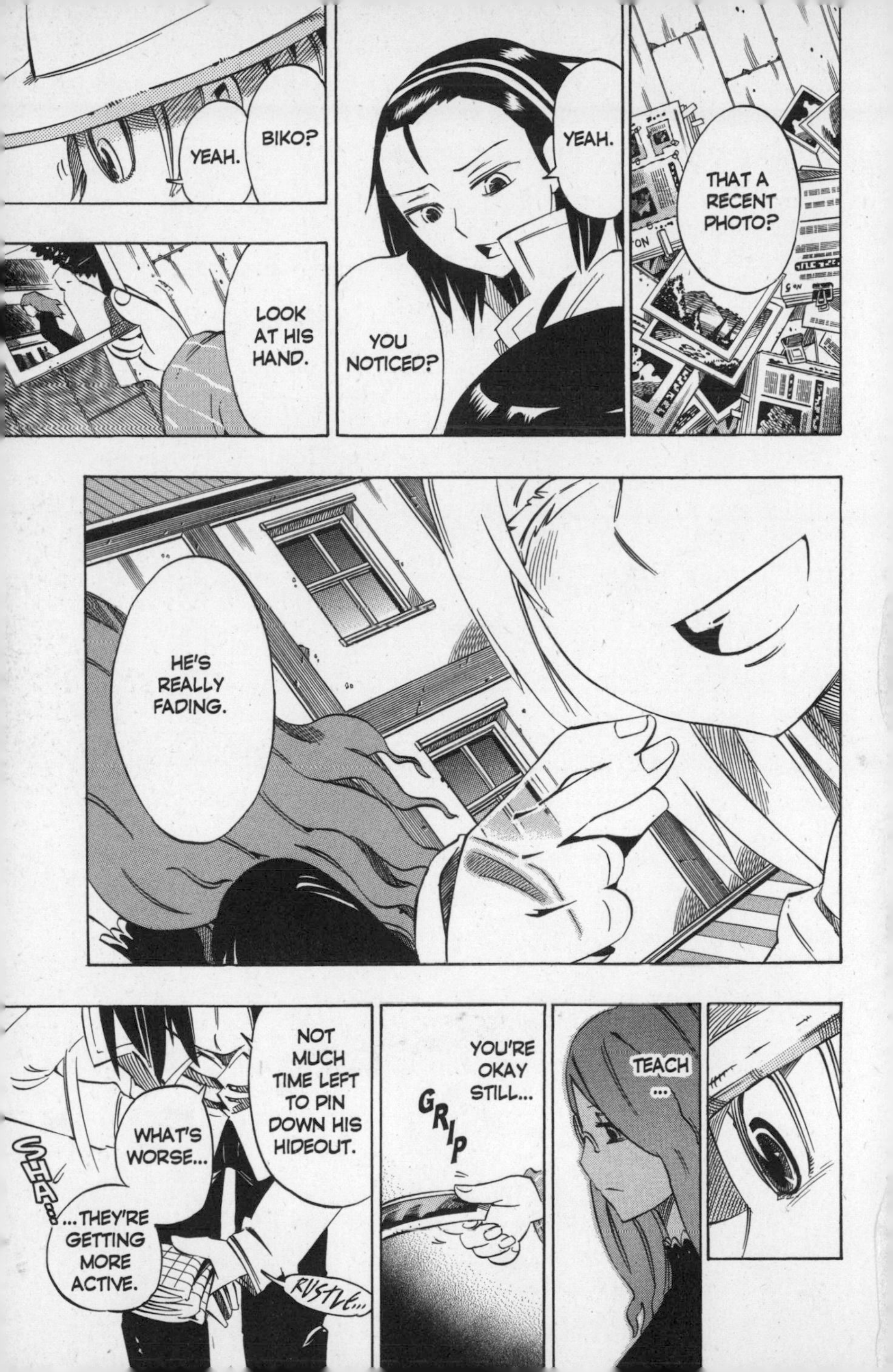
THAT A RECENT PHOTO?
YEAH.
YOU NOTICED?
BIKO?
YEAH.
LOOK AT HIS HAND.
HE'S REALLY FADING.
TEACH ...
YOU'RE OKAY STILL...
GRIP
NOT MUCH TIME LEFT TO PIN DOWN HIS HIDEOUT.
WHAT'S WORSE...
SHHA...
...THEY'RE GETTING MORE ACTIVE.
RUSTLE...

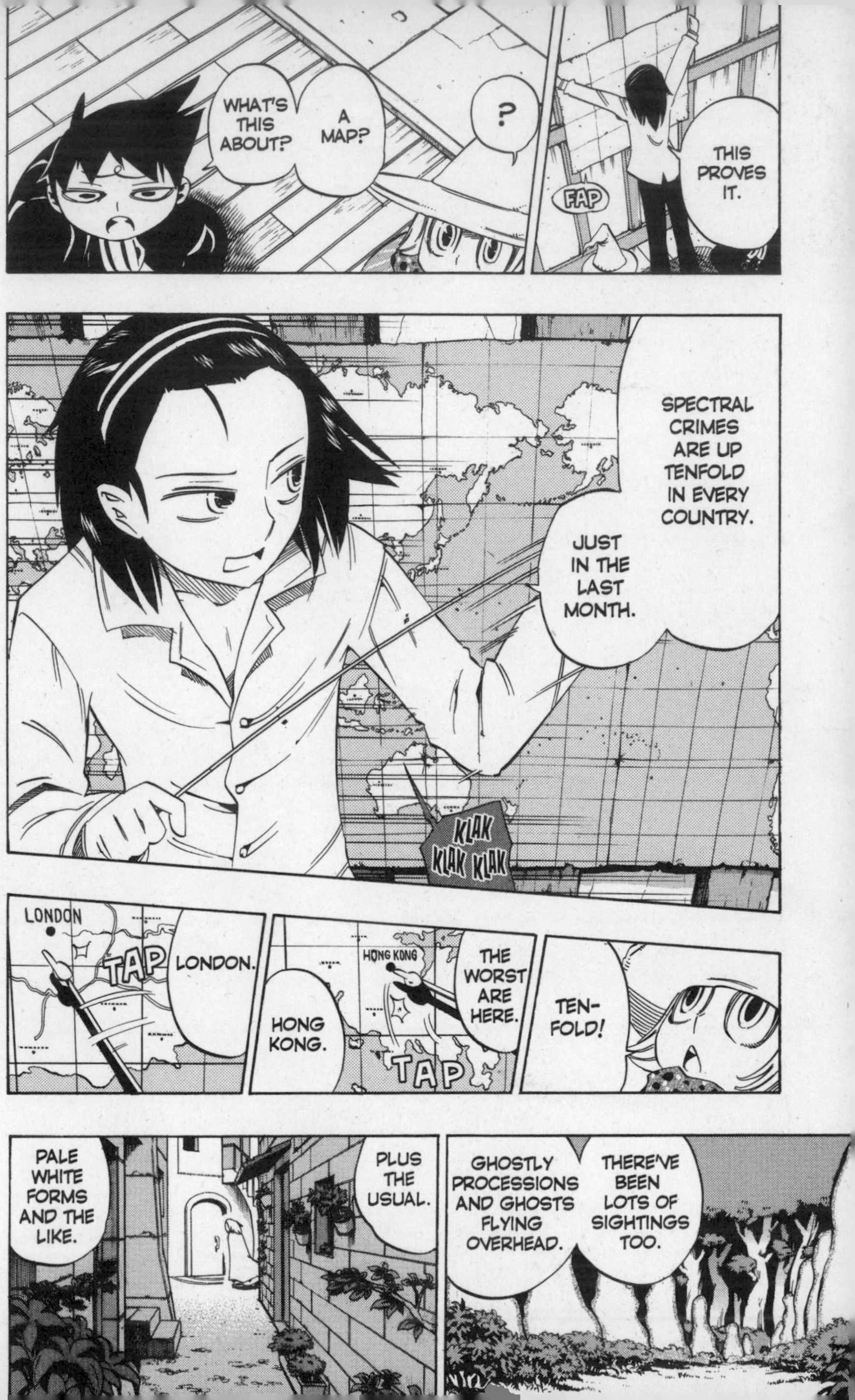
THIS PROVES IT.
FAP
?
A MAP?
WHAT'S THIS ABOUT?
SPECTRAL CRIMES ARE UP TENFOLD IN EVERY COUNTRY.
JUST IN THE LAST MONTH.
KLAK KLAK KLAK
TEN-FOLD!
HONG KONG
THE WORST ARE HERE.
HONG KONG.
TAP
LONDON
LONDON.
TAP
THERE'VE BEEN LOTS OF SIGHTINGS TOO.
GHOSTLY PROCESSIONS AND GHOSTS FLYING OVERHEAD.
PLUS THE USUAL.
PALE WHITE FORMS AND THE LIKE.

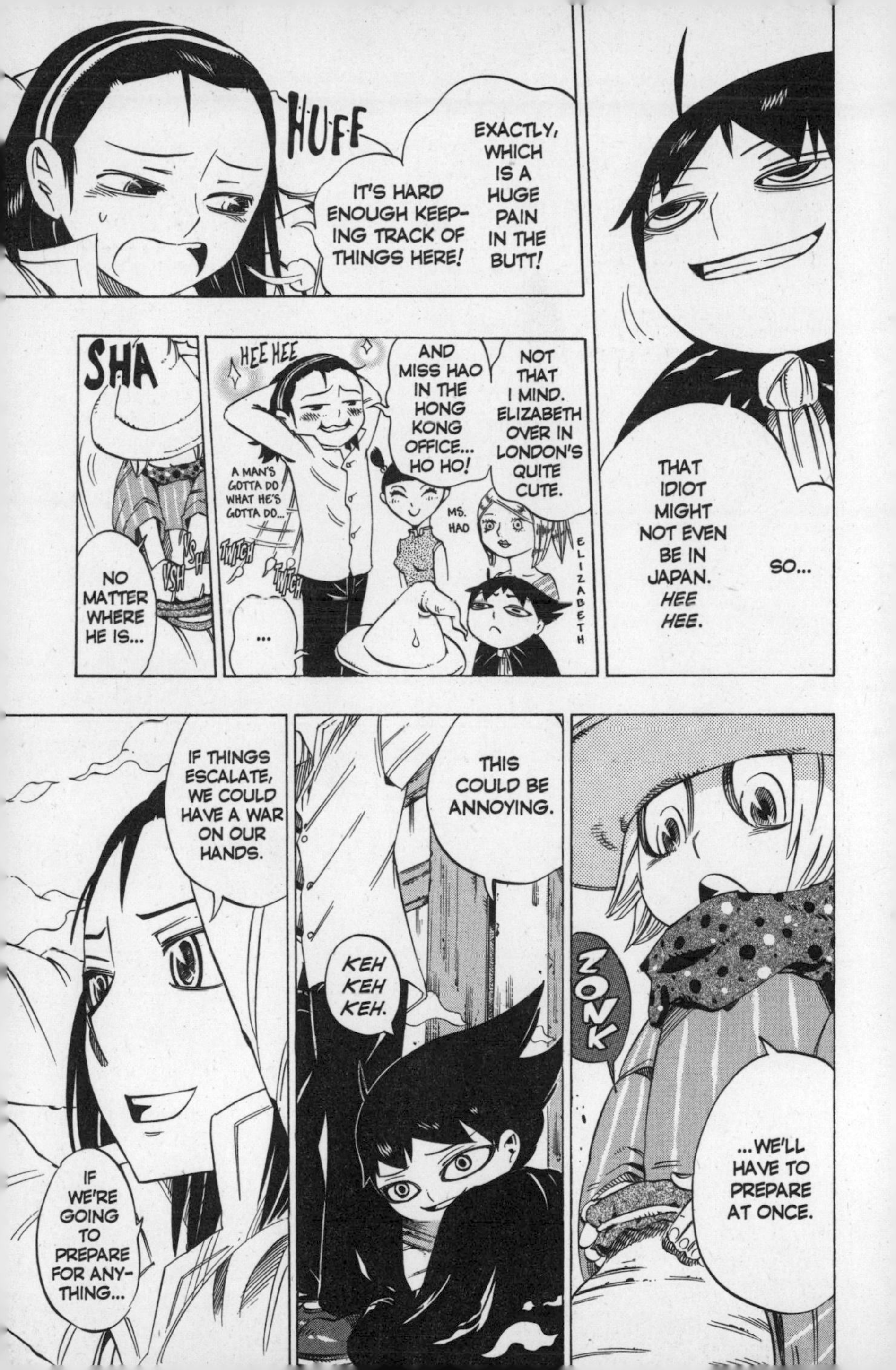
THAT IDIOT MIGHT NOT EVEN BE IN JAPAN. *HEE HEE.*
SO...
EXACTLY, WHICH IS A HUGE PAIN IN THE BUTT!
IT'S HARD ENOUGH KEEPING TRACK OF THINGS HERE!
HUFF
NOT THAT I MIND. ELIZABETH OVER IN LONDON'S QUITE CUTE.
AND MISS HAO IN THE HONG KONG OFFICE... HO HO!
HEE HEE
A MAN'S GOTTA DO WHAT HE'S GOTTA DO...
MS. HAO
ELIZABETH
TWITCH
TWITCH
...
SHA
VSH
VSH
NO MATTER WHERE HE IS...
ZONK
...WE'LL HAVE TO PREPARE AT ONCE.
THIS COULD BE ANNOYING.
KEH KEH KEH.
IF THINGS ESCALATE, WE COULD HAVE A WAR ON OUR HANDS.
IF WE'RE GOING TO PREPARE FOR ANYTHING...

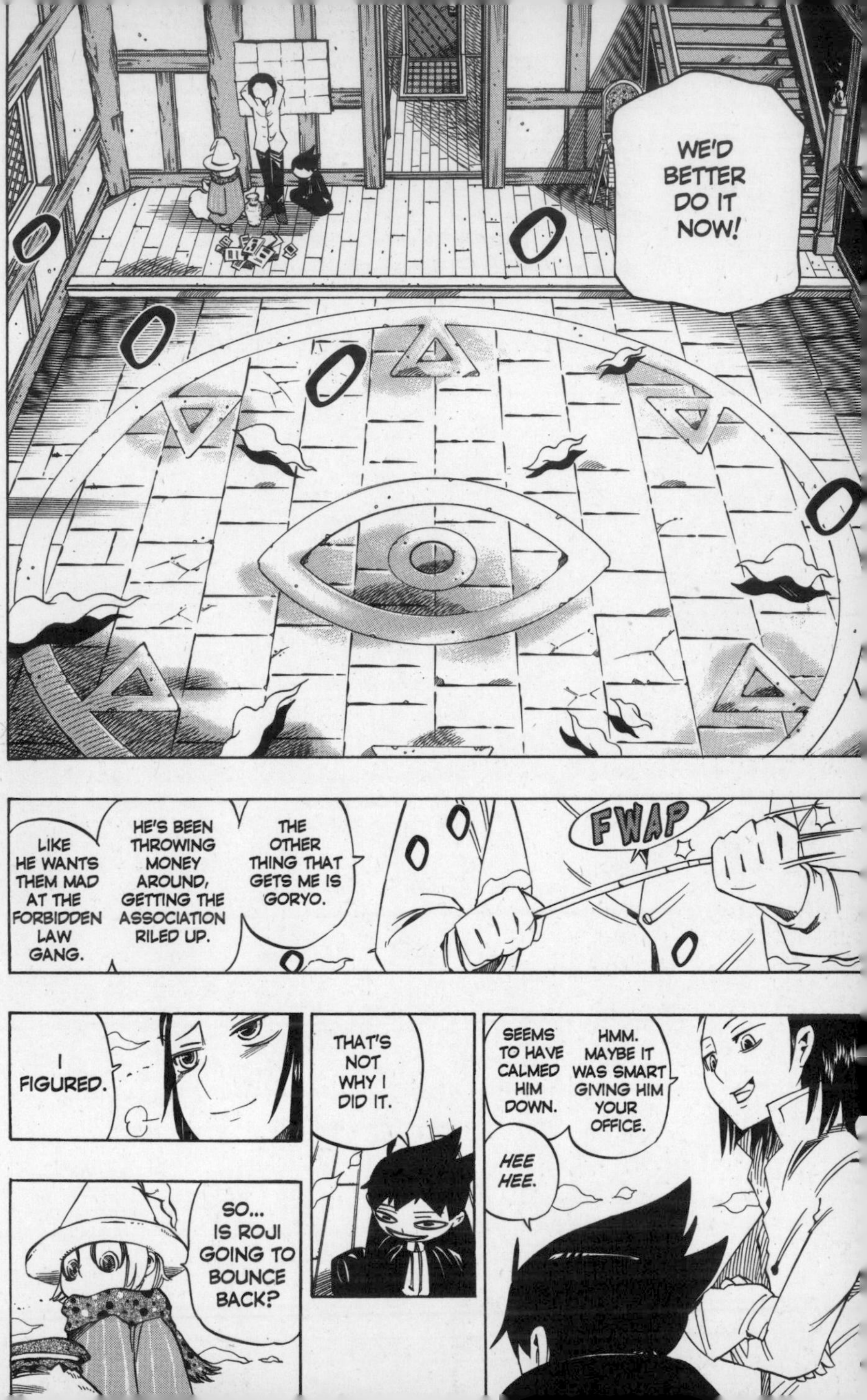
WE'D BETTER DO IT NOW!
FWAP
THE OTHER THING THAT GETS ME IS GORYO.
HE'S BEEN THROWING MONEY AROUND, GETTING THE ASSOCIATION RILED UP.
LIKE HE WANTS THEM MAD AT THE FORBIDDEN LAW GANG.
HMM. MAYBE IT WAS SMART GIVING HIM YOUR OFFICE.
SEEMS TO HAVE CALMED HIM DOWN.
HEE HEE.
THAT'S NOT WHY I DID IT.
I FIGURED.
SO... IS ROJI GOING TO BOUNCE BACK?

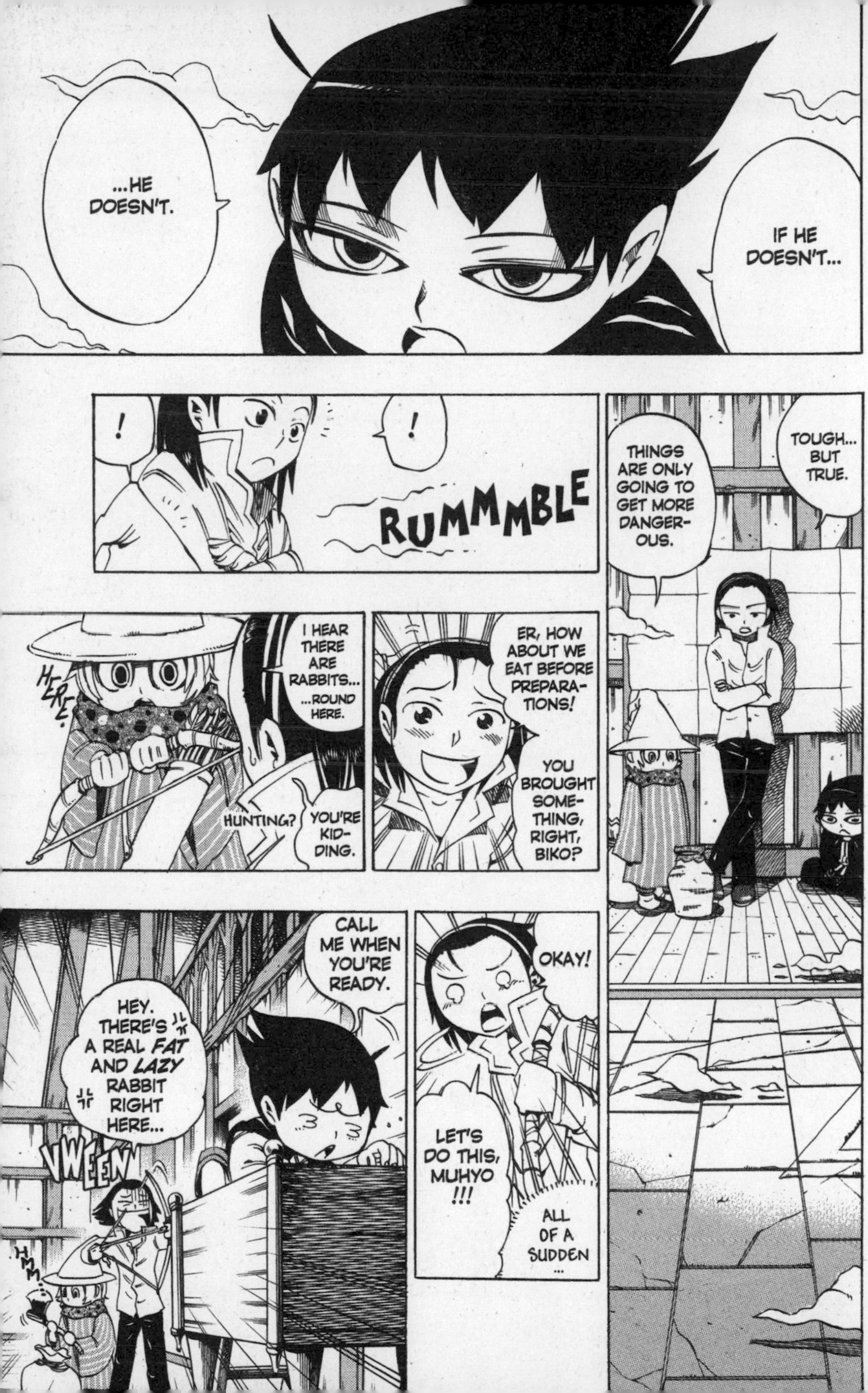
IF HE DOESN'T...
...HE DOESN'T.
TOUGH... BUT TRUE.
THINGS ARE ONLY GOING TO GET MORE DANGER-OUS.
!
!
RUMMMBLE
ER, HOW ABOUT WE EAT BEFORE PREPARA-TIONS!
YOU BROUGHT SOME-THING, RIGHT, BIKO?
YOU'RE KID-DING.
I HEAR THERE ARE RABBITS... ...ROUND HERE.
HERE.
HUNTING?
OKAY!
LET'S DO THIS, MUHYO !!!
ALL OF A SUDDEN ...
CALL ME WHEN YOU'RE READY.
HEY. THERE'S A REAL FAT AND LAZY RABBIT RIGHT HERE...
VWEEN
HMM...

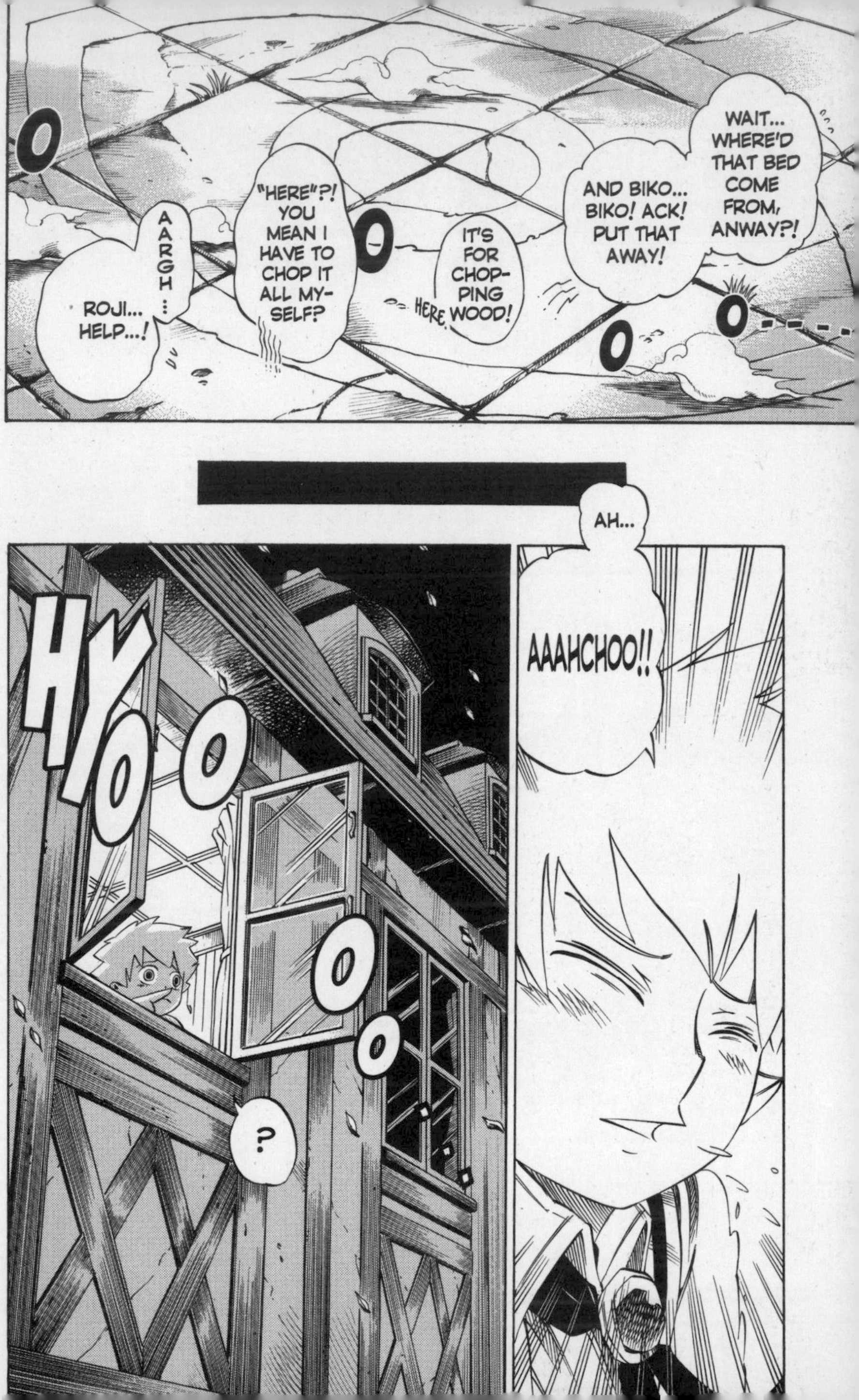
WAIT... WHERE'D THAT BED COME FROM, ANWAY?!
AND BIKO... BIKO! ACK! PUT THAT AWAY!
IT'S FOR CHOP-PING WOOD!
HERE.
"HERE"?! YOU MEAN I HAVE TO CHOP IT ALL MY-SELF?
AARGH...
ROJI... HELP...!
AH...
AAAHCHOO!!
HYOOOOO
?

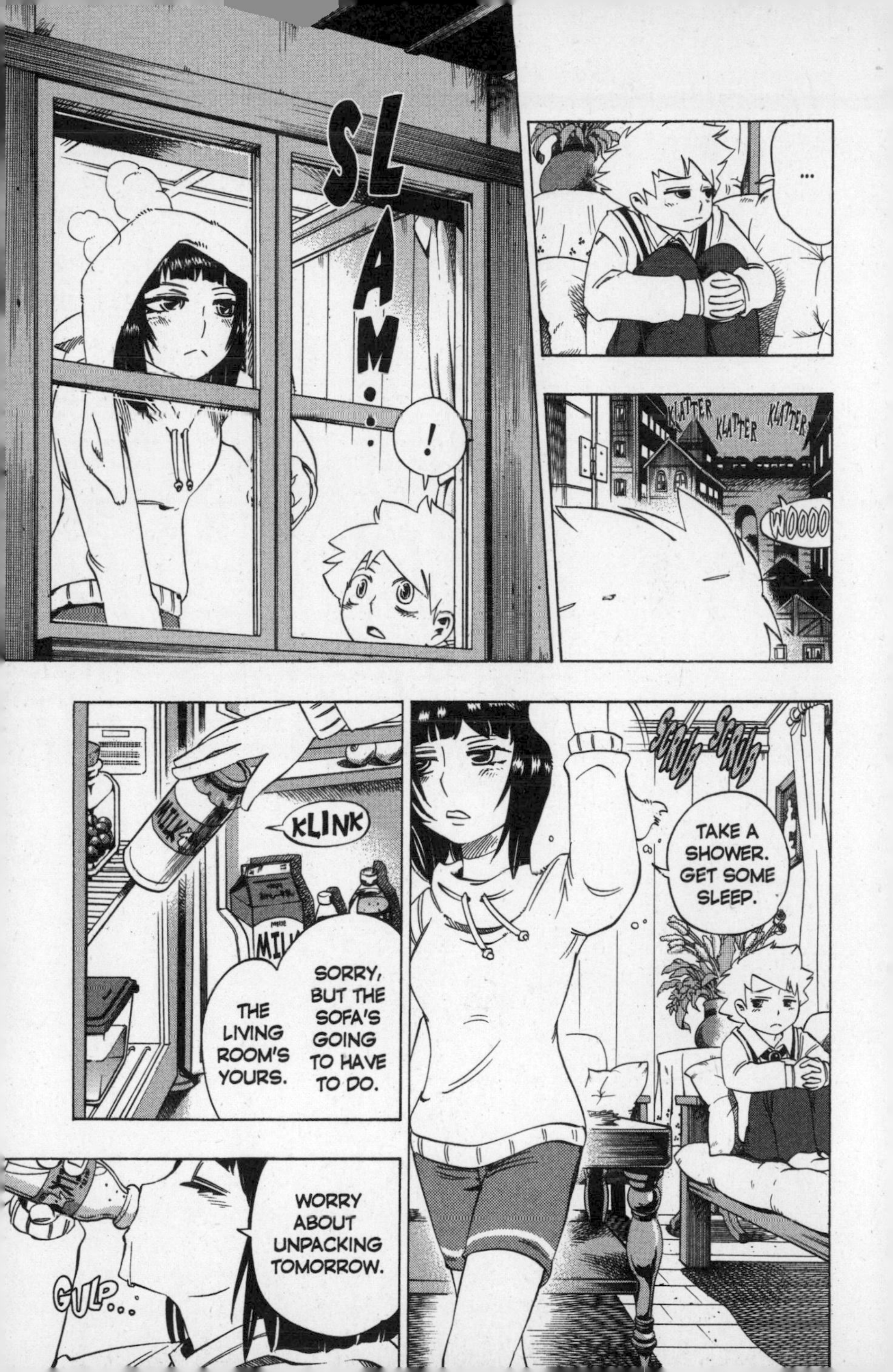
...
KLATTER
KLATTER
KLATTER
WOOOO
SLAM
!
TAKE A SHOWER. GET SOME SLEEP.
KLINK
SORRY, BUT THE SOFA'S GOING TO HAVE TO DO.
THE LIVING ROOM'S YOURS.
WORRY ABOUT UNPACKING TOMORROW.
GULP...

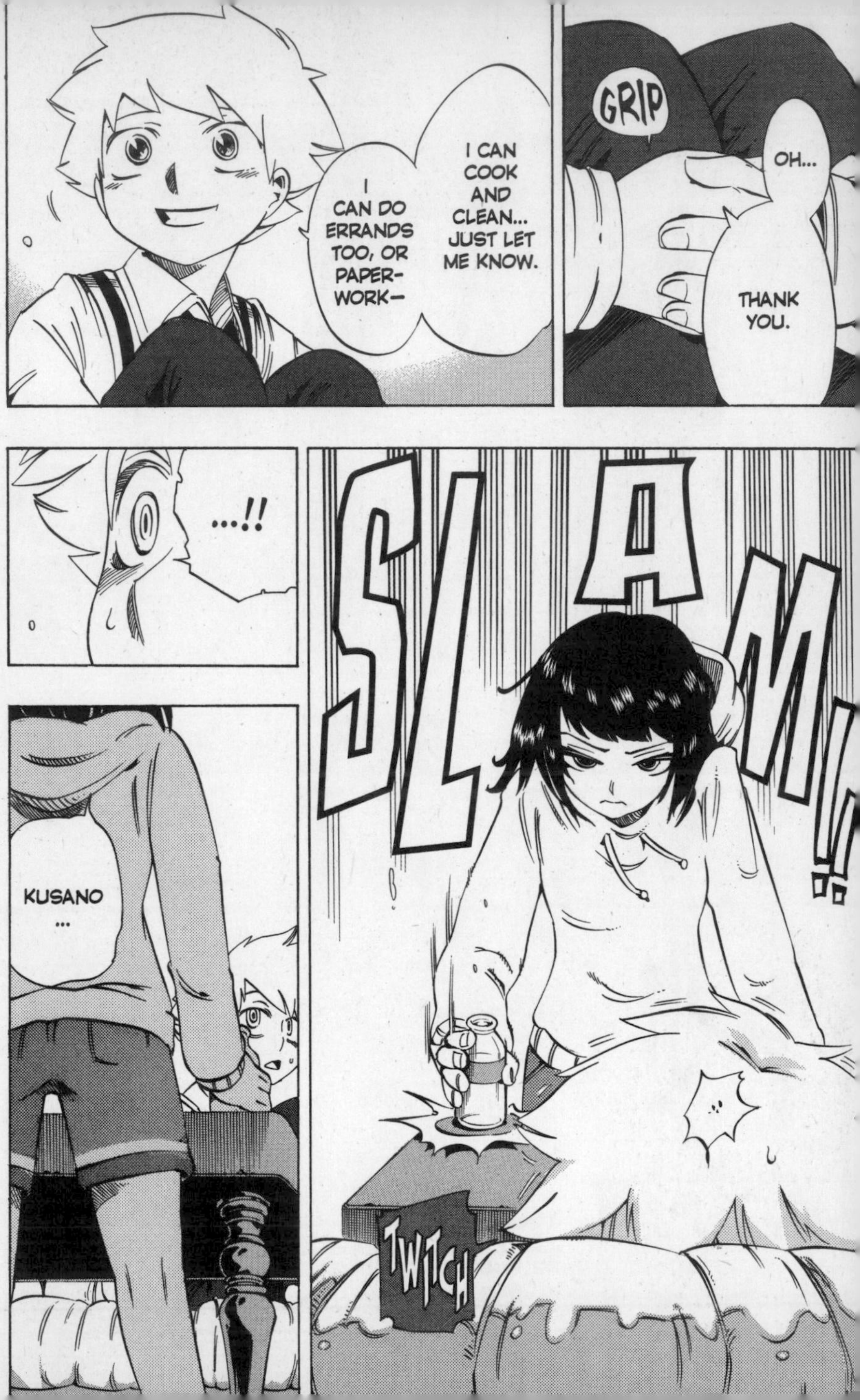
GRIP
OH...
THANK YOU.
I CAN COOK AND CLEAN... JUST LET ME KNOW.
I CAN DO ERRANDS TOO, OR PAPER-WORK—
SLAM!!
TWITCH
...!!
KUSANO ...

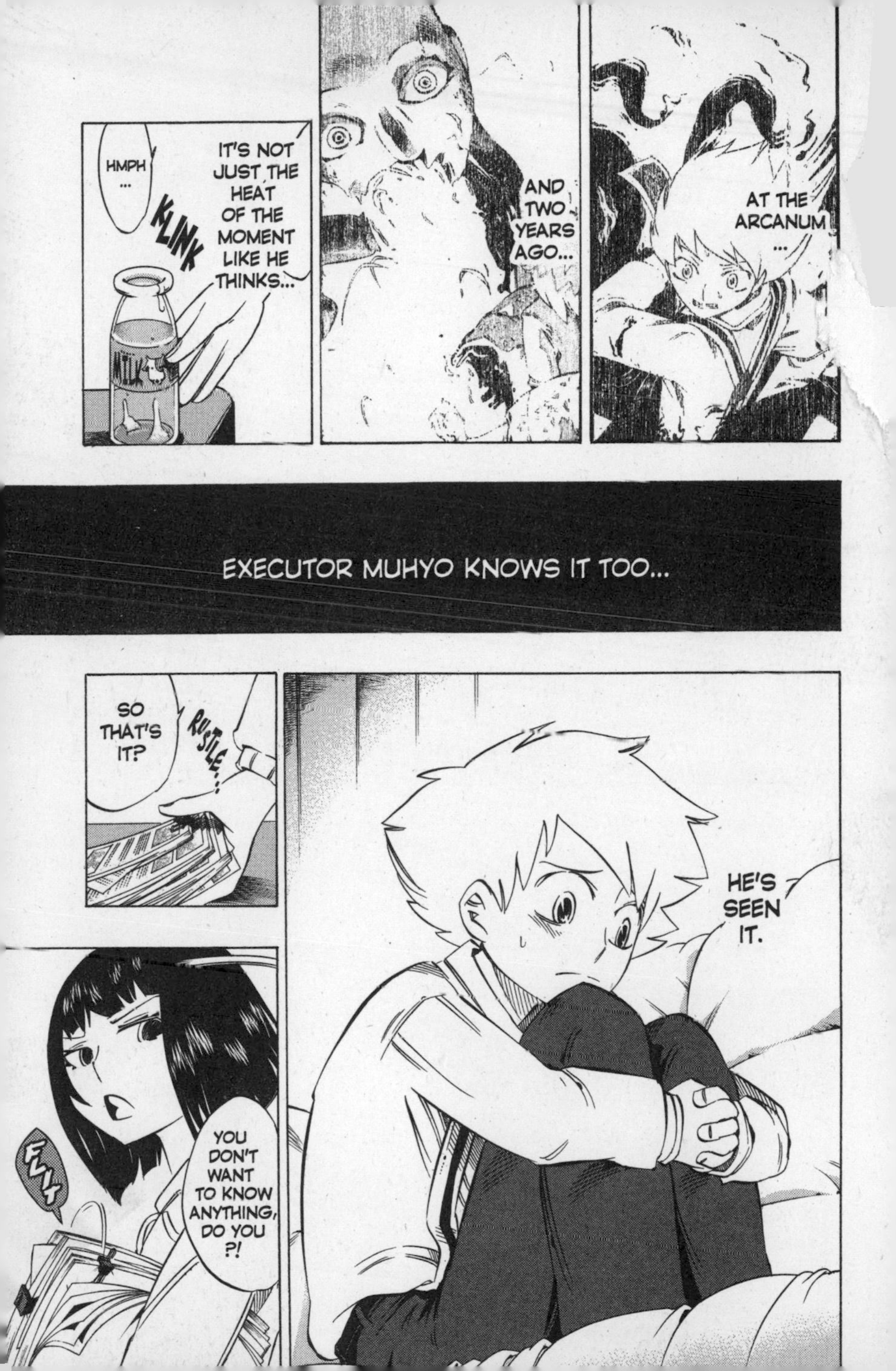
AT THE ARCANUM ...
AND TWO YEARS AGO...
IT'S NOT JUST THE HEAT OF THE MOMENT LIKE HE THINKS...
HMPH ...
KLINK
EXECUTOR MUHYO KNOWS IT TOO...
HE'S SEEN IT.
SO THAT'S IT?
RUSTLE...
YOU DON'T WANT TO KNOW ANYTHING, DO YOU ?!

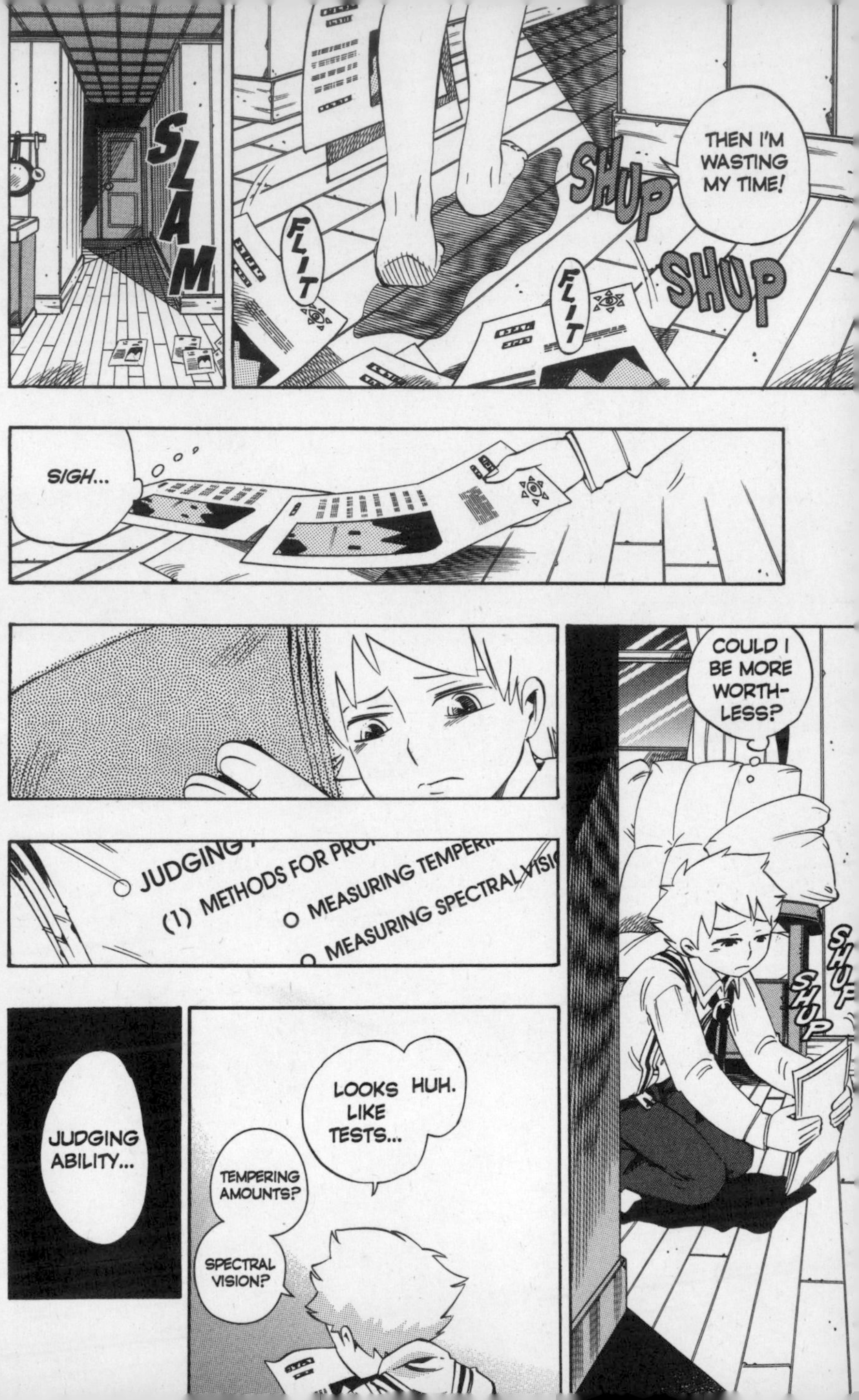
THEN I'M WASTING MY TIME!
SHUP
SHUP
FLIT
FLIT
SLAM
SIGH...
COULD I BE MORE WORTH-LESS?
SHUP
SHUP
JUDGING
(1) METHODS FOR PRO
MEASURING TEMPERI
MEASURING SPECTRAL VISI
MEASURING
HUH.
LOOKS LIKE TESTS...
TEMPERING AMOUNTS?
SPECTRAL VISION?
JUDGING ABILITY...

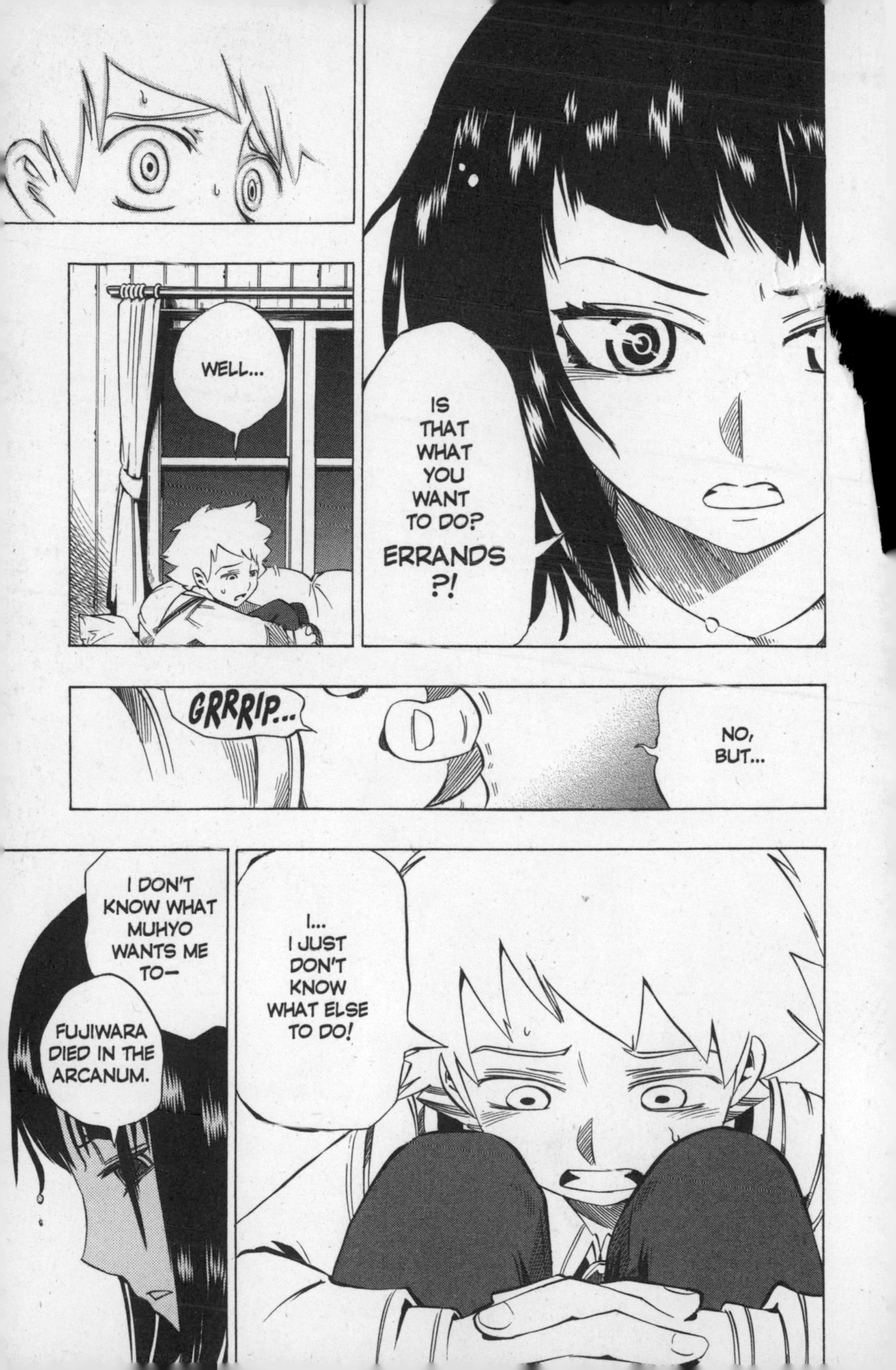
IS THAT WHAT YOU WANT TO DO? ERRANDS?!
WELL...
NO, BUT...
GRRRIP...
I... I JUST DON'T KNOW WHAT ELSE TO DO!
I DON'T KNOW WHAT MUHYO WANTS ME TO—
FUJIWARA DIED IN THE ARCANUM.

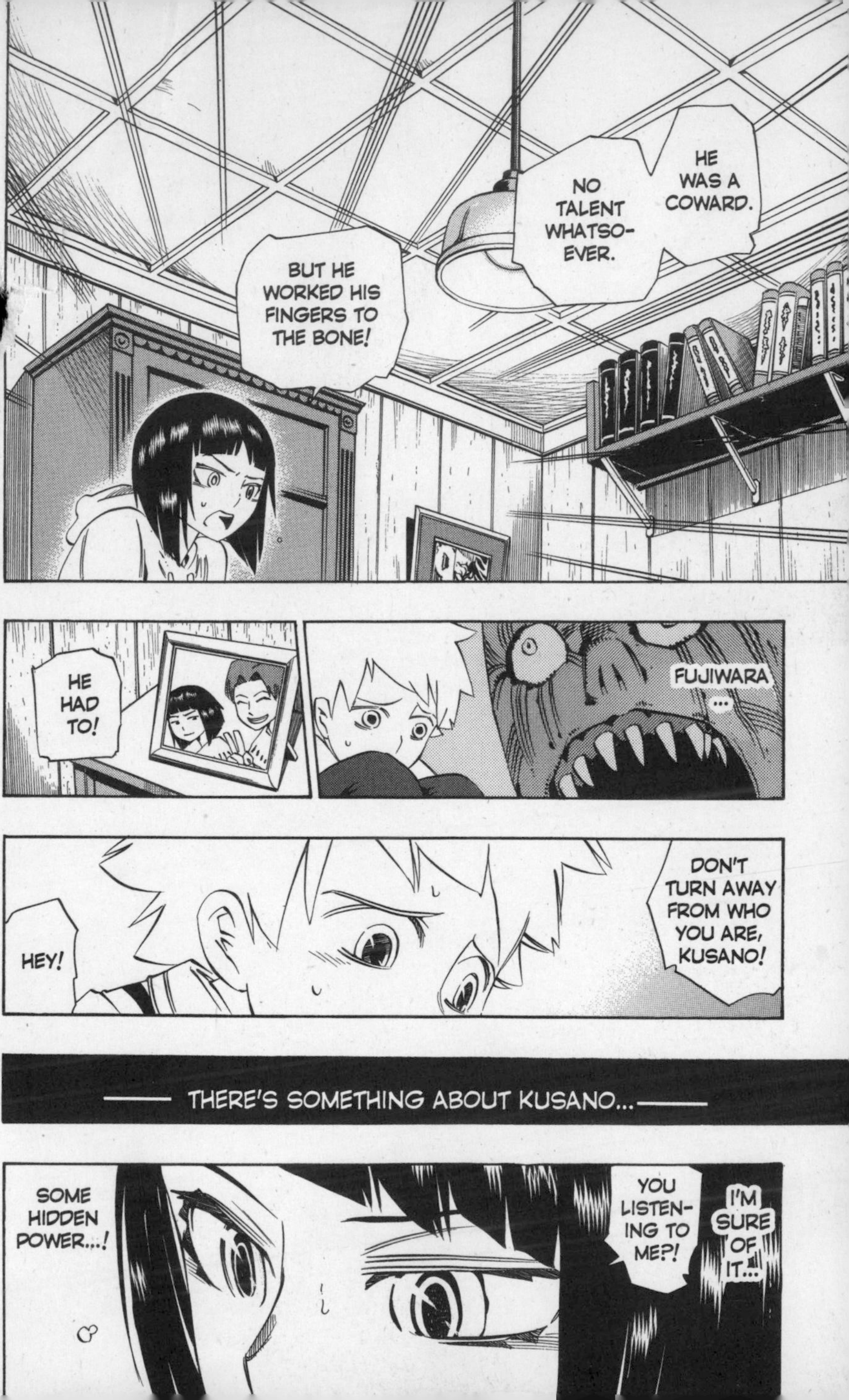
HE WAS A COWARD.
NO TALENT WHATSO-EVER.
BUT HE WORKED HIS FINGERS TO THE BONE!
FUJIWARA ...
HE HAD TO!
DON'T TURN AWAY FROM WHO YOU ARE, KUSANO!
HEY!
THERE'S SOMETHING ABOUT KUSANO...
I'M SURE OF IT...
YOU LISTEN-ING TO ME?!
SOME HIDDEN POWER...!

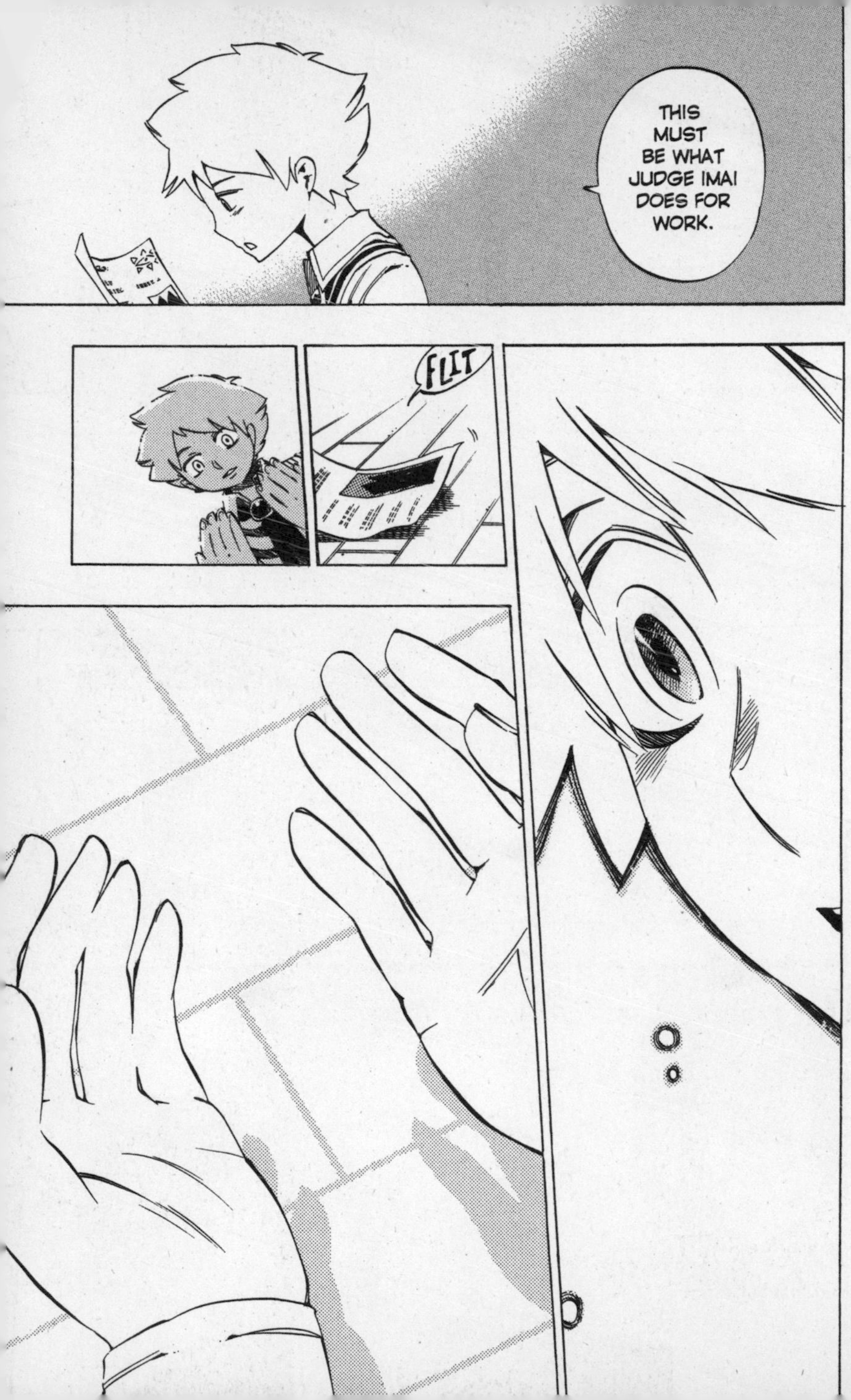
THIS MUST BE WHAT JUDGE IMAI DOES FOR WORK.
FLIT

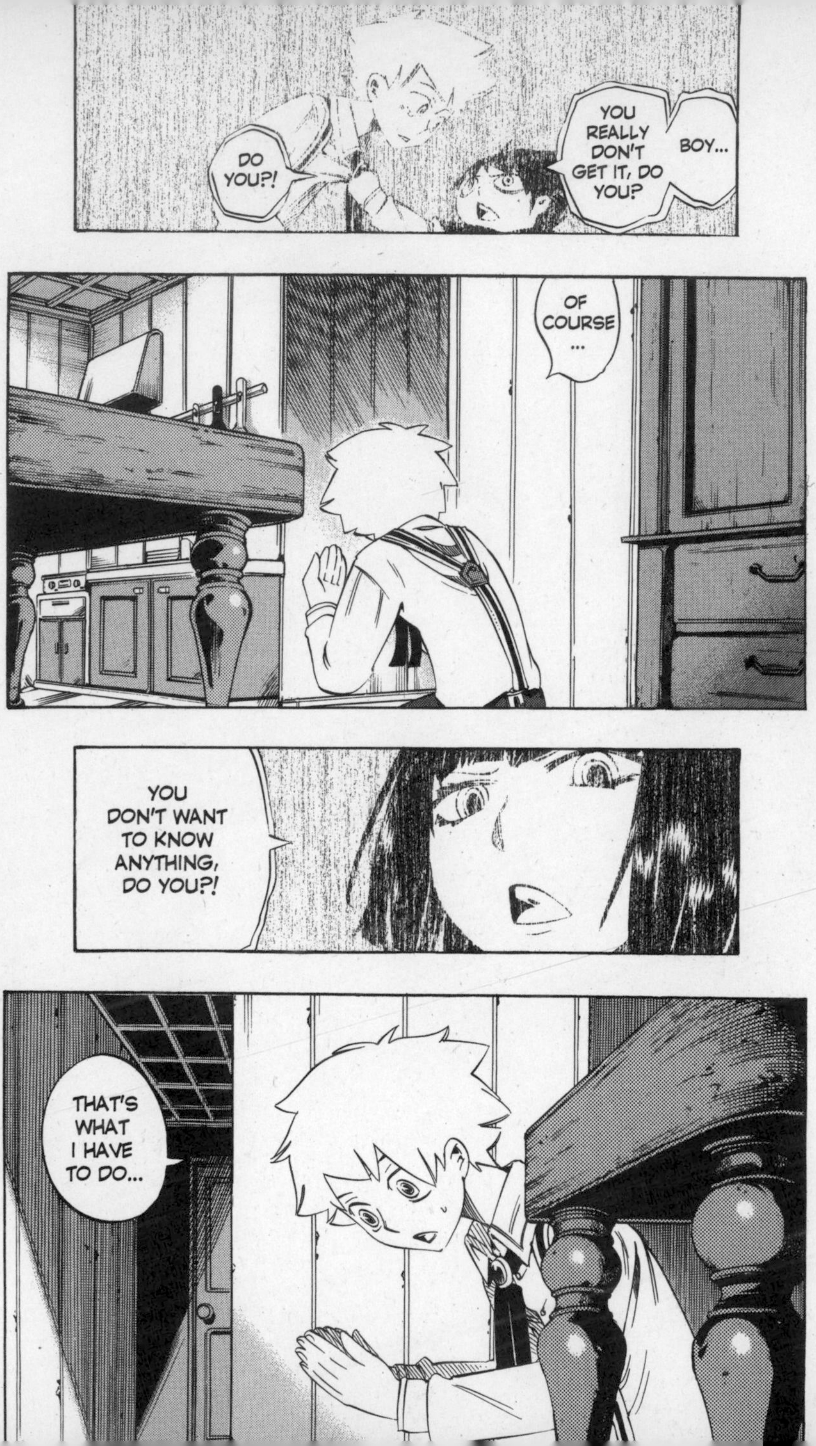
BOY...
YOU REALLY DON'T GET IT, DO YOU?
DO YOU?!
OF COURSE...
YOU DON'T WANT TO KNOW ANYTHING, DO YOU?!
THAT'S WHAT I HAVE TO DO...

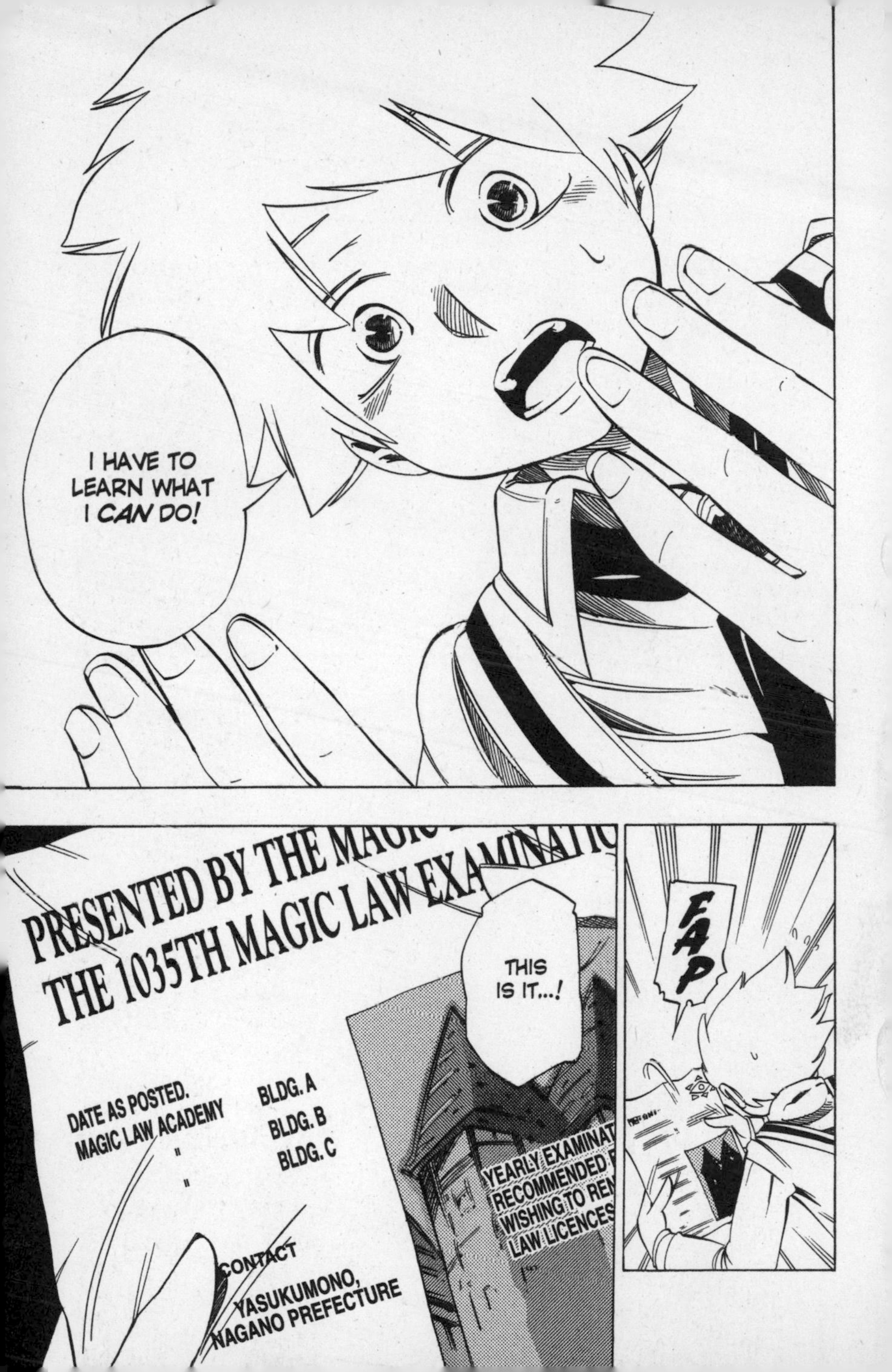
I HAVE TO LEARN WHAT I *CAN* DO!
FAP
YEARLY EXAMINAT
RECOMMENDED
WISHING TO REN
LAW LICENCES
PRESENTED BY THE MAGIC
THE 1035TH MAGIC LAW EXAMINATIO
THIS IS IT...!
DATE AS POSTED.
MAGIC LAW ACADEMY BLDG. A
" BLDG. B
" BLDG. C
CONTACT
YASUKUMONO, NAGANO PREFECTURE

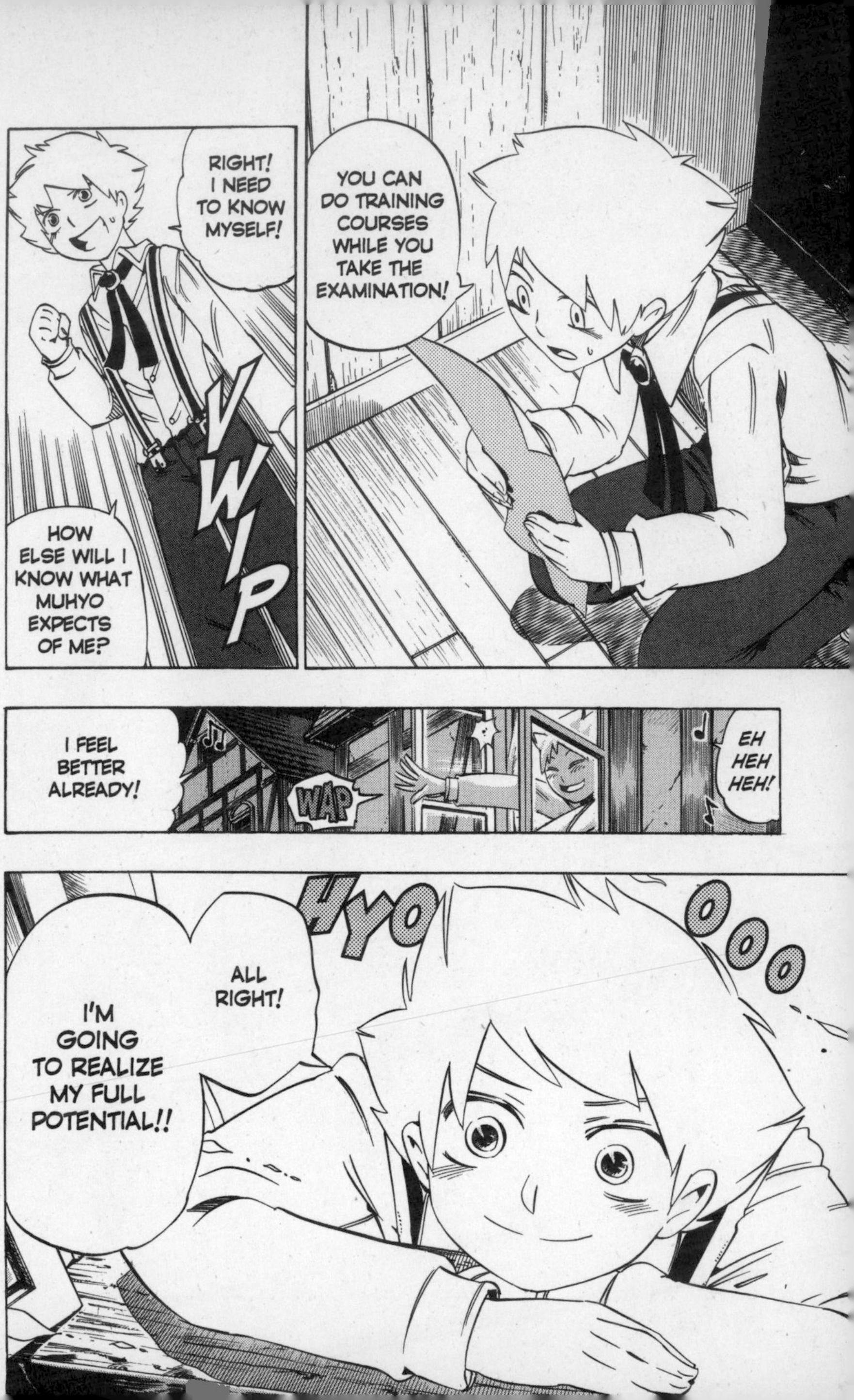
YOU CAN DO TRAINING COURSES WHILE YOU TAKE THE EXAMINATION!
RIGHT! I NEED TO KNOW MYSELF!
VWIP
HOW ELSE WILL I KNOW WHAT MUHYO EXPECTS OF ME?
EH HEH HEH!
WAP
I FEEL BETTER ALREADY!
HYOOOO
ALL RIGHT!
I'M GOING TO REALIZE MY FULL POTENTIAL!!

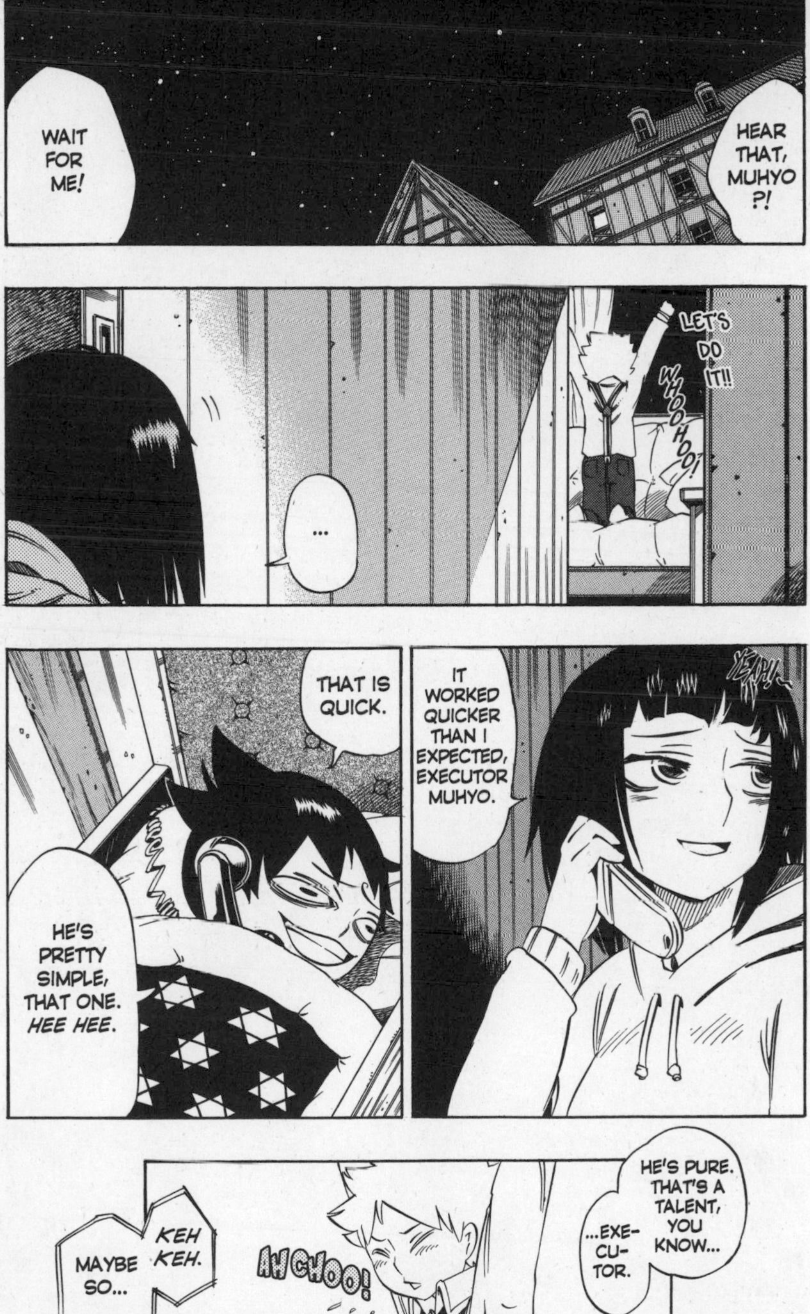
HEAR THAT, MUHYO?!
WAIT FOR ME!
LET'S DO IT!!
WHOOHOO!
...
YEAH!~
IT WORKED QUICKER THAN I EXPECTED, EXECUTOR MUHYO.
THAT IS QUICK.
HE'S PRETTY SIMPLE, THAT ONE. *HEE HEE.*
HE'S PURE. THAT'S A TALENT, YOU KNOW...
...EXE-CU-TOR.
AH CHOO!
KEH KEH.
MAYBE SO...

Q: WHAT INSPIRED YOU TO START
DRAWING MANGA PROFESSIONALLY?
DID YOU HAVE A SPECIFIC INFLUENCE?
WHAT DID YOU DO BEFORE YOU GOT
SERIALIZED?

-A.R., OITA PREFECTURE

A: I GET THIS ONE A LOT TOO. WELL,
I GOTTA SAY I'M GETTING ALONG IN
YEARS, BUT I STILL HAVE THIS LITTLE
GIRL SIDE TO ME, YOU KNOW? IT'S LIKE
THIS AND THAT AND THE OTHER THING
AND WELL, EVERYTHING, REALLY. AND
UM, ER... I KNOW! I'LL USE THE BONUS
SECTION IN MY NEXT MANGA TO
ANSWER THIS QUESTION! (THE STAFF
HERE LOVE MY BONUS SECTIONS,
SO I LIKE TO SAVE THE BEST STUFF
FOR THEM.)

ARTICLE 49
THE ACADEMY

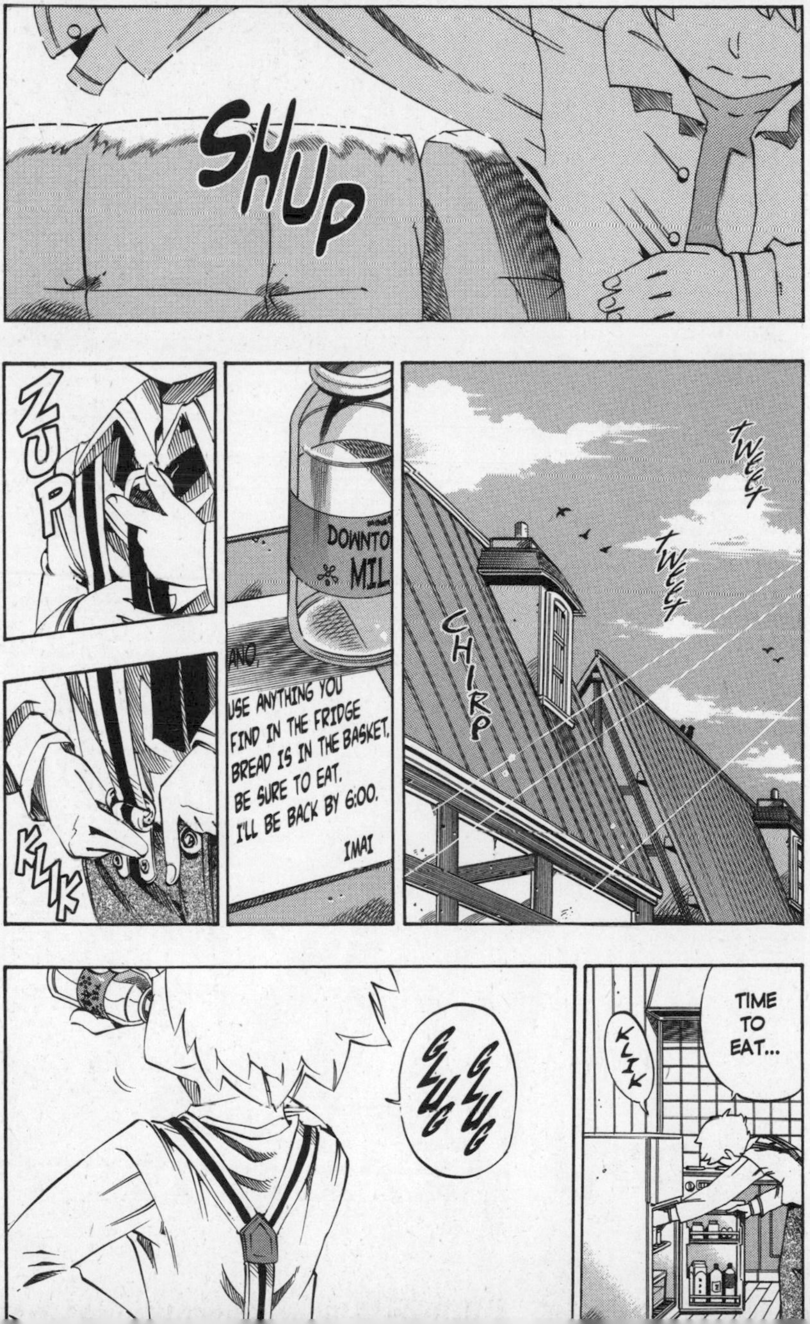

SHUP
TWEET
TWEET
CHIRP
DOWNTO
MIL
ANO,
USE ANYTHING YOU FIND IN THE FRIDGE. BREAD IS IN THE BASKET. BE SURE TO EAT. I'LL BE BACK BY 6:00.
IMAI
ZUP
KLIK
TIME TO EAT...
KLIK
GLUG GLUG

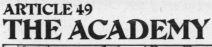

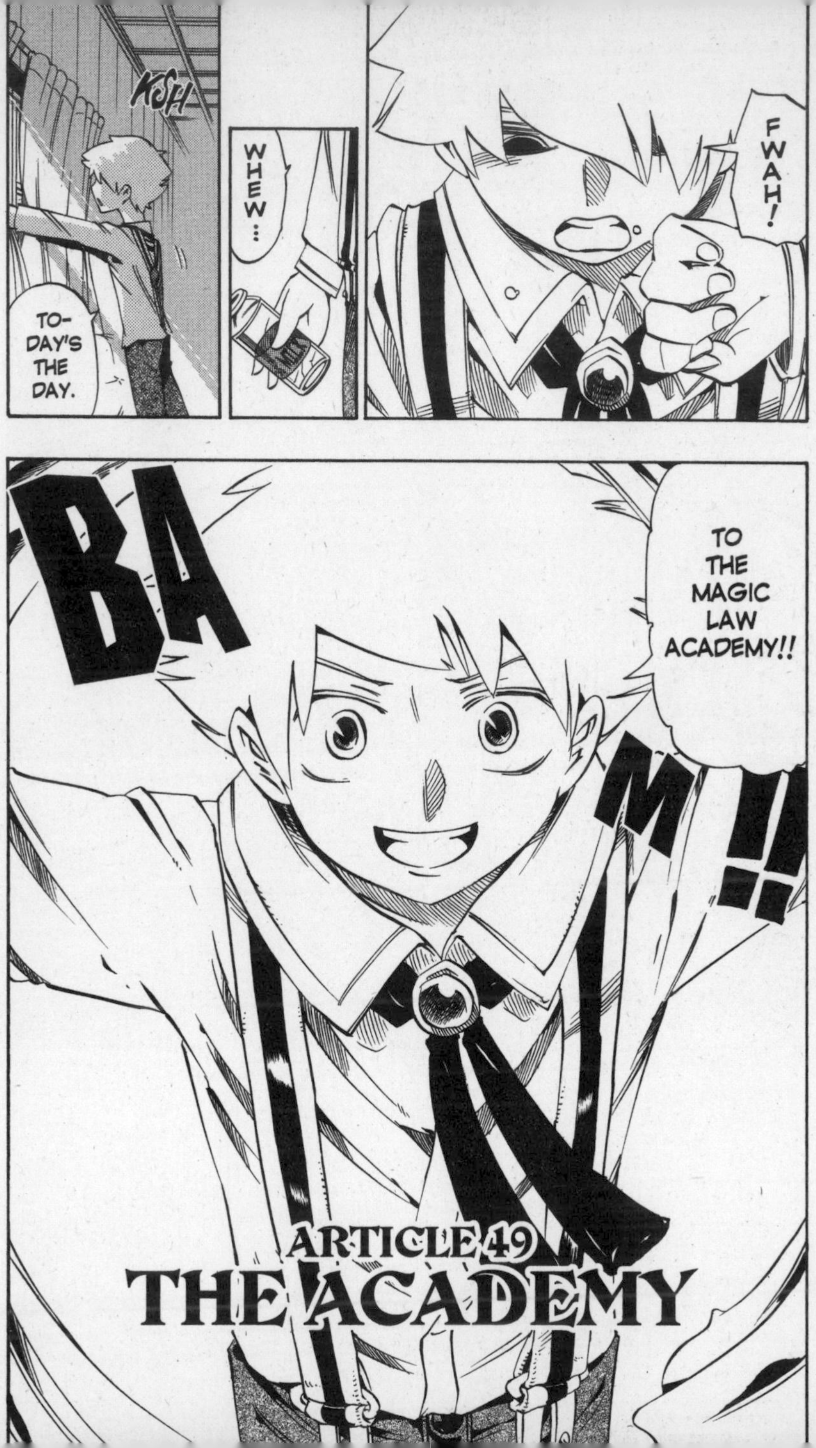
FWAH!
WHEW...
KSH
TO-DAY'S THE DAY.
BAM!!
TO THE MAGIC LAW ACADEMY!!
ARTICLE 49
THE ACADEMY

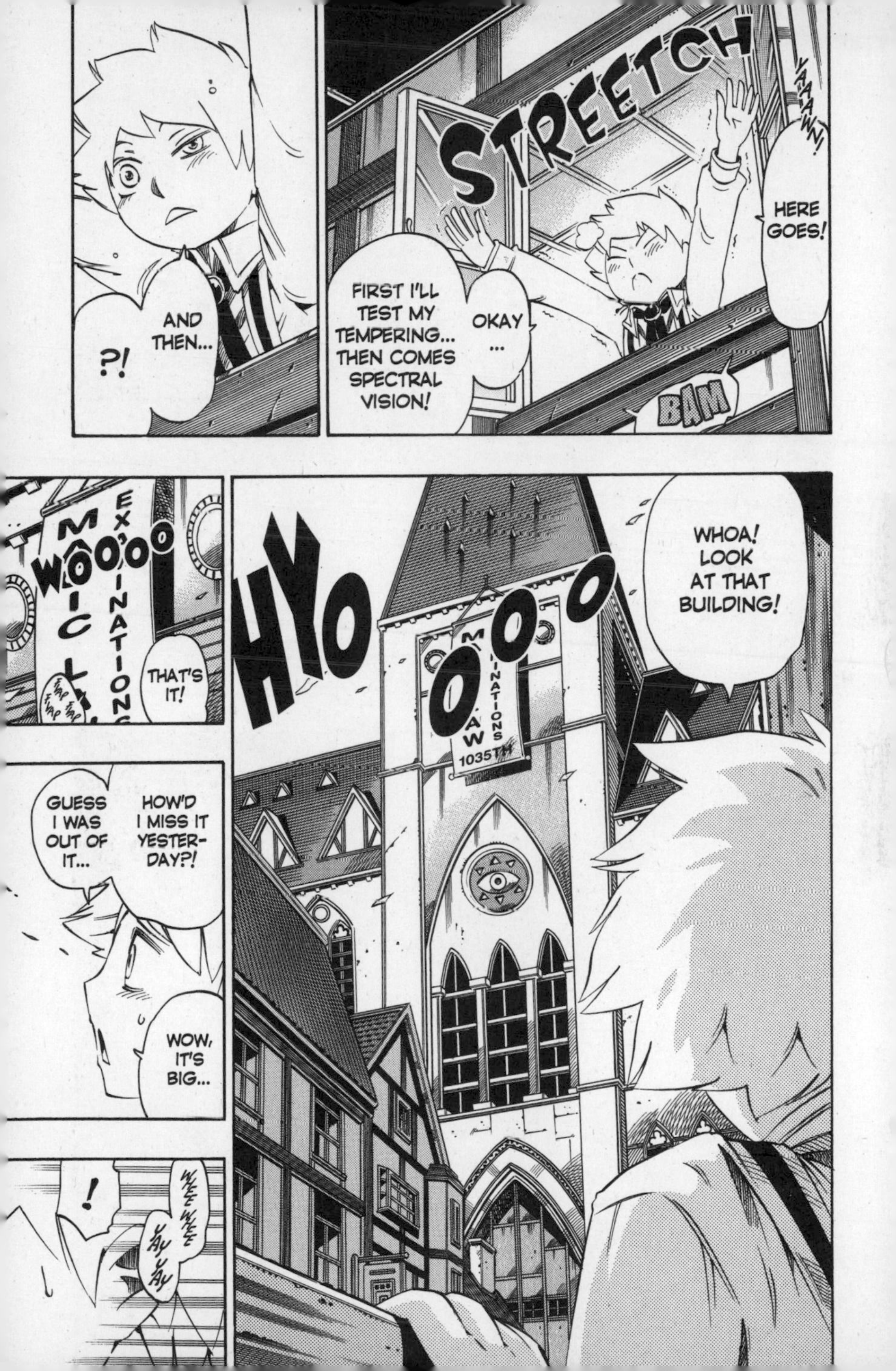
YAAAWN!
HERE GOES!
STREETCH
BAM
OKAY...
FIRST I'LL TEST MY TEMPERING... THEN COMES SPECTRAL VISION!
AND THEN...
?!
WHOA! LOOK AT THAT BUILDING!
HYOOOO
1035TH
WOOOO
THAT'S IT!
FLAP FLAP
FLAP FLAP
HOW'D I MISS IT YESTER-DAY?!
GUESS I WAS OUT OF IT...
WOW, IT'S BIG...
WHEE WHEE
YAY YAY
!

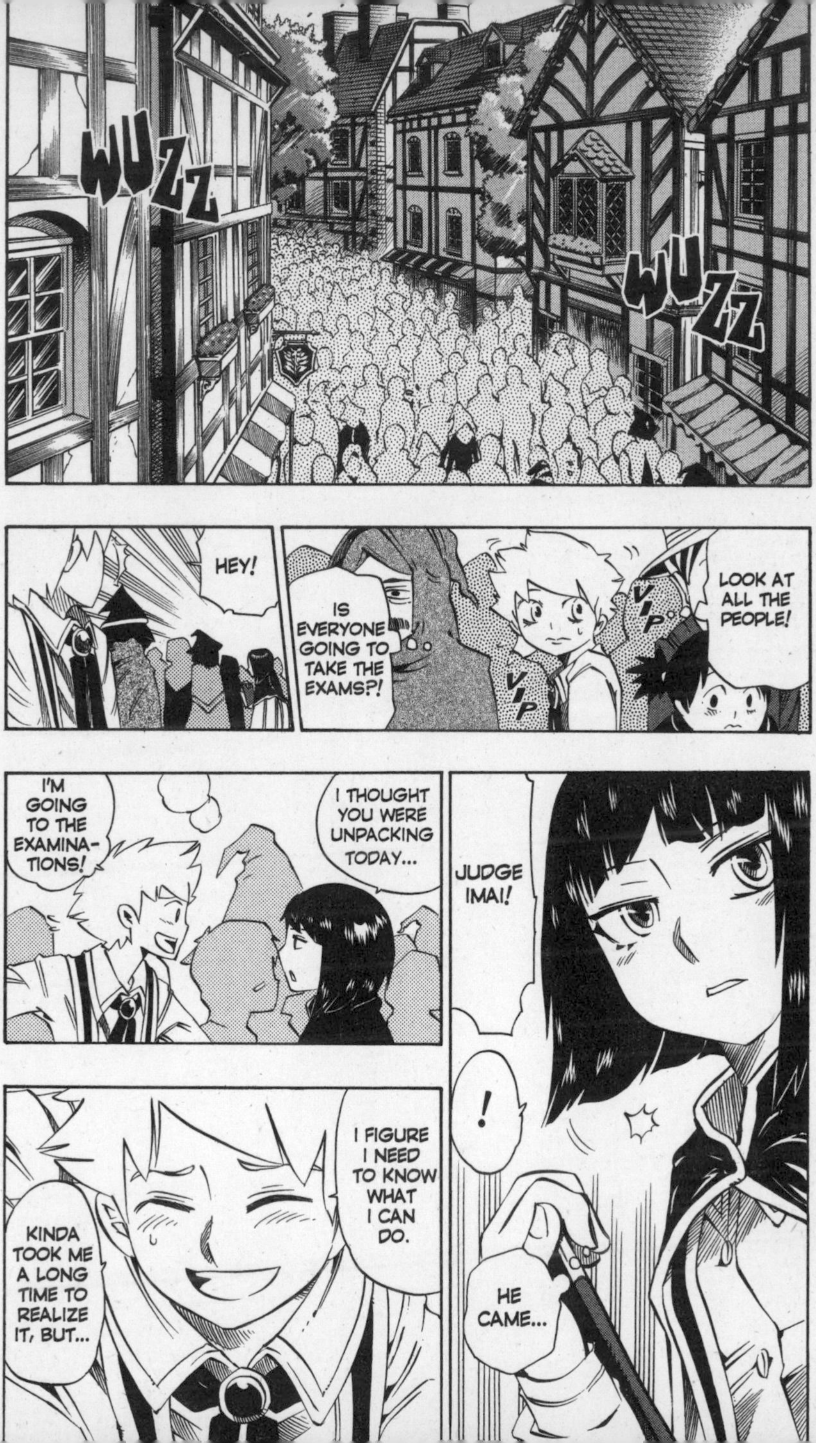
WUZZ
WUZZ
LOOK AT ALL THE PEOPLE!
VIP
VIP
IS EVERYONE GOING TO TAKE THE EXAMS?!
HEY!
JUDGE IMAI!
!
HE CAME...
I THOUGHT YOU WERE UNPACKING TODAY...
I'M GOING TO THE EXAMINATIONS!
I FIGURE I NEED TO KNOW WHAT I CAN DO.
KINDA TOOK ME A LONG TIME TO REALIZE IT, BUT...

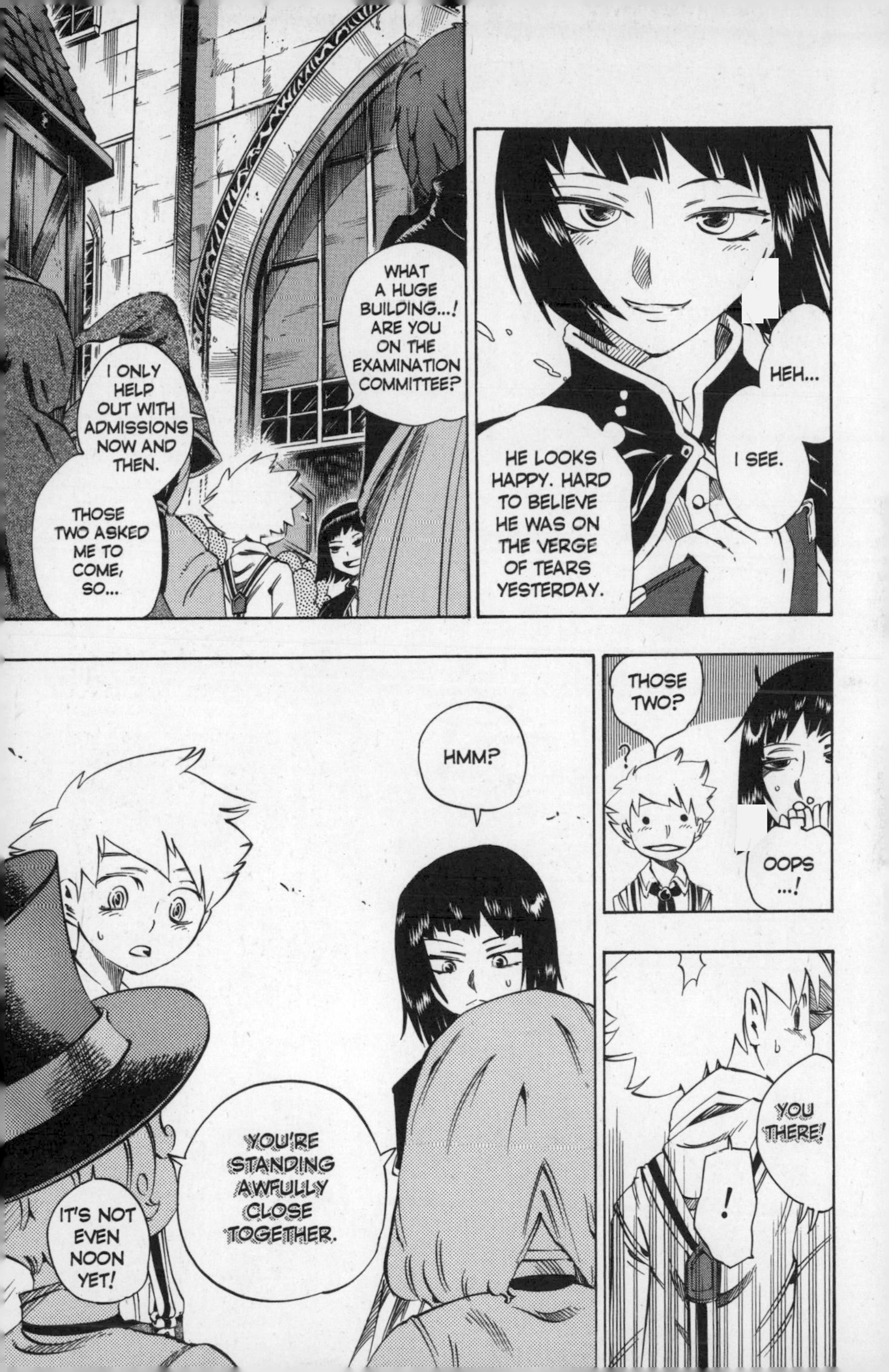
HEH... I SEE.
HE LOOKS HAPPY. HARD TO BELIEVE HE WAS ON THE VERGE OF TEARS YESTERDAY.
WHAT A HUGE BUILDING...! ARE YOU ON THE EXAMINATION COMMITTEE?
I ONLY HELP OUT WITH ADMISSIONS NOW AND THEN.
THOSE TWO ASKED ME TO COME, SO...
THOSE TWO?
OOPS ...!
YOU THERE!
!
HMM?
YOU'RE STANDING AWFULLY CLOSE TOGETHER.
IT'S NOT EVEN NOON YET!

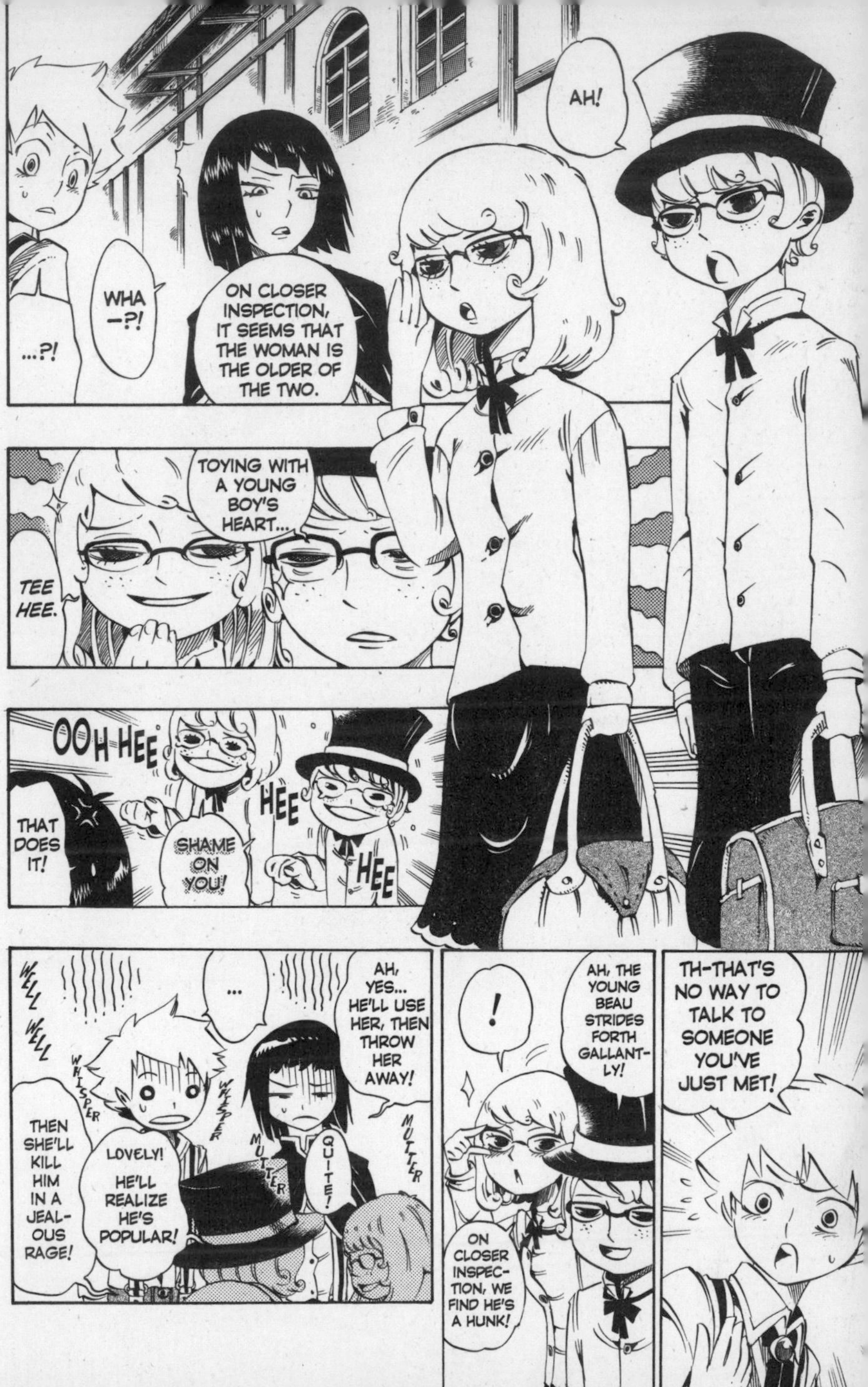
AH!
ON CLOSER INSPECTION, IT SEEMS THAT THE WOMAN IS THE OLDER OF THE TWO.
WHA-?!
...?!
TOYING WITH A YOUNG BOY'S HEART...
TEE HEE.
OOH HEE HEE HEE
SHAME ON YOU!
THAT DOES IT!
TH-THAT'S NO WAY TO TALK TO SOMEONE YOU'VE JUST MET!
AH, THE YOUNG BEAU STRIDES FORTH GALLANT-LY!
!
ON CLOSER INSPEC-TION, WE FIND HE'S A HUNK!
AH, YES... HE'LL USE HER, THEN THROW HER AWAY!
...
WELL WELL
WHISPER WHISPER
MUTTER MUTTER
QUITE!
LOVELY! HE'LL REALIZE HE'S POPULAR!
THEN SHE'LL KILL HIM IN A JEAL-OUS RAGE!

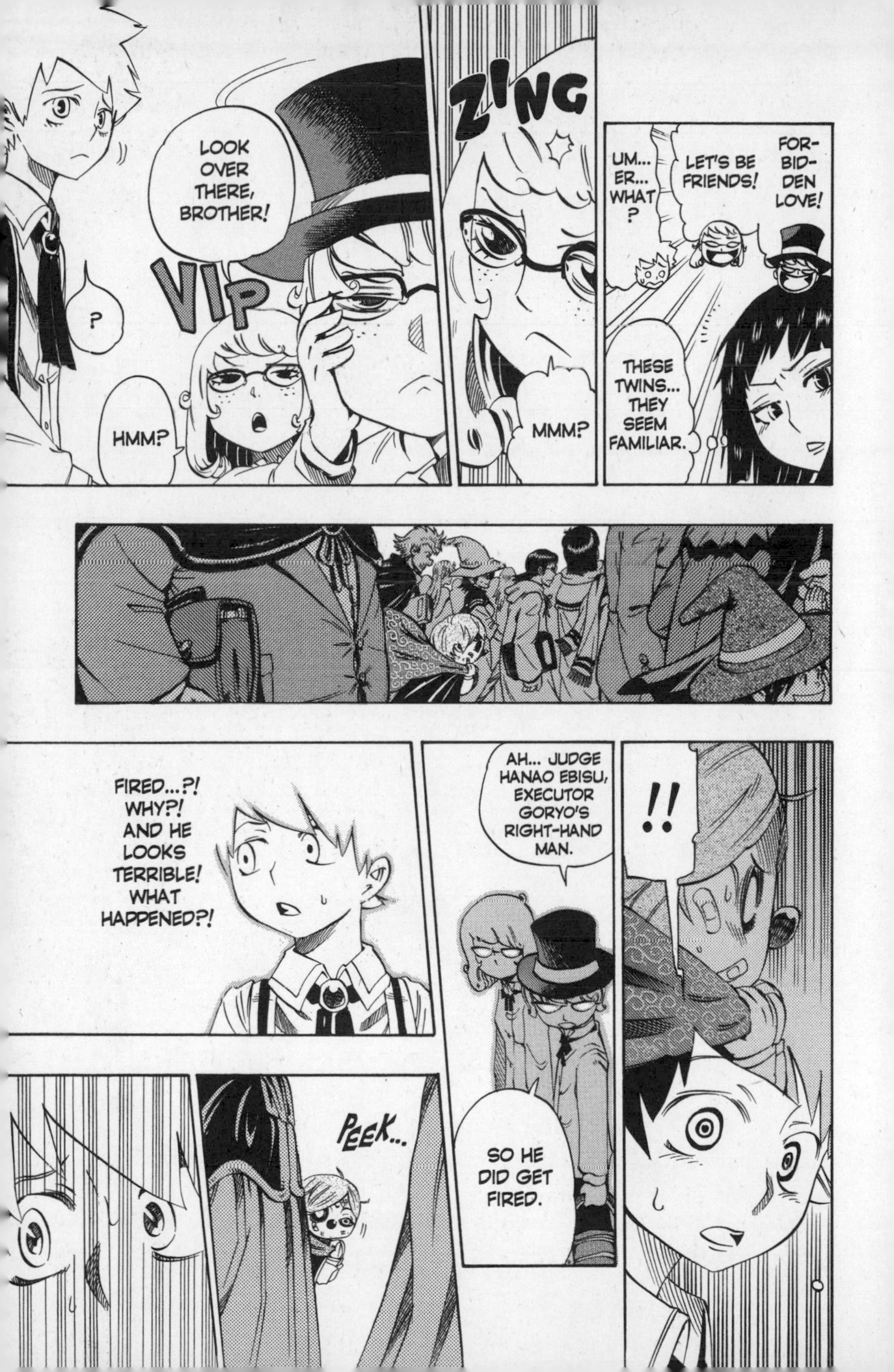
FOR-BID-DEN LOVE!
LET'S BE FRIENDS!
UM... ER... WHAT ?
THESE TWINS... THEY SEEM FAMILIAR.
ZING
MMM?
LOOK OVER THERE, BROTHER!
VIP
?
HMM?
!!
AH... JUDGE HANAO EBISU, EXECUTOR GORYO'S RIGHT-HAND MAN.
SO HE DID GET FIRED.
FIRED...?! WHY?! AND HE LOOKS TERRIBLE! WHAT HAPPENED?!
PEEK...

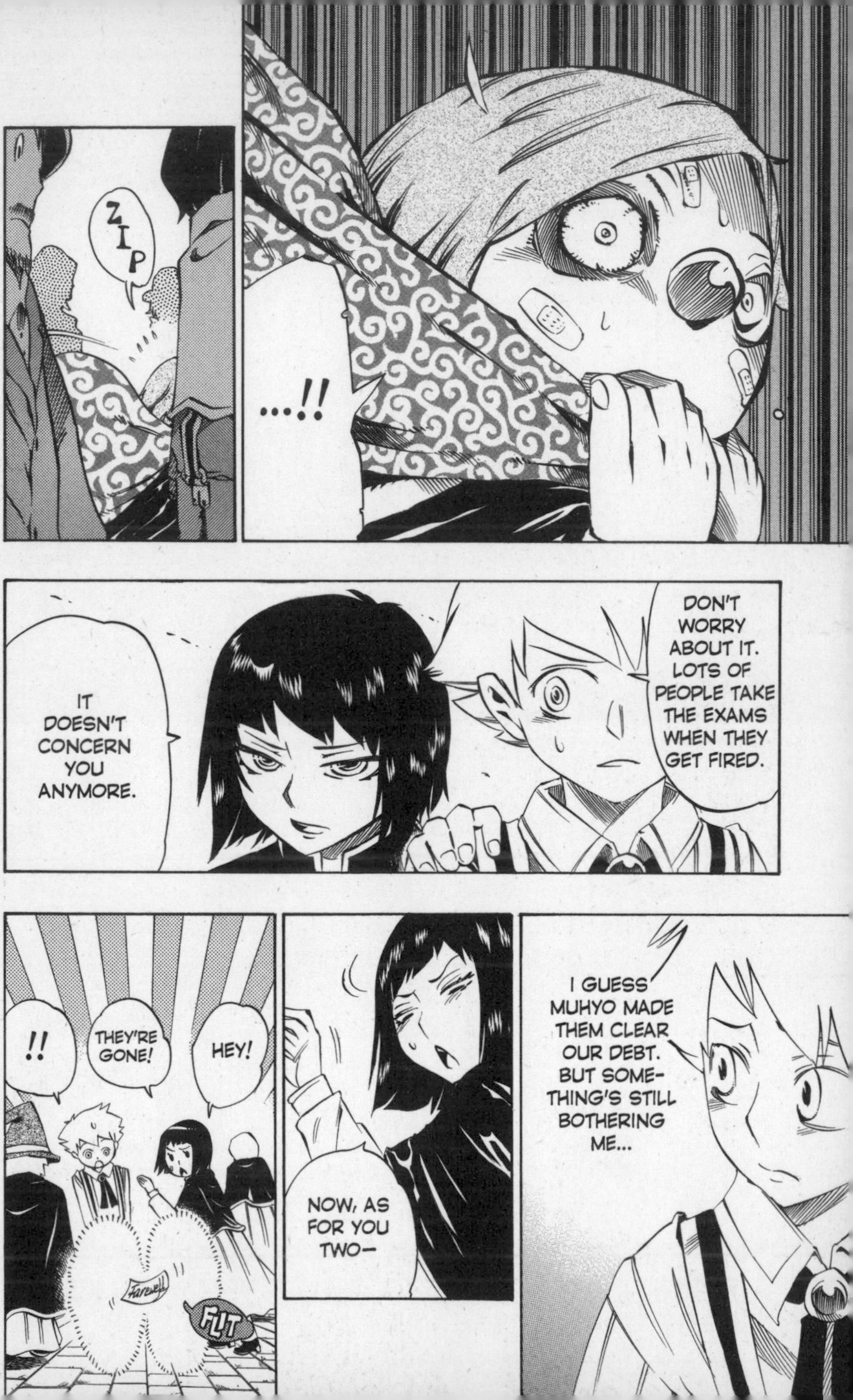
...!!
ZIP
DON'T WORRY ABOUT IT. LOTS OF PEOPLE TAKE THE EXAMS WHEN THEY GET FIRED.
IT DOESN'T CONCERN YOU ANYMORE.
I GUESS MUHYO MADE THEM CLEAR OUR DEBT. BUT SOME-THING'S STILL BOTHERING ME...
NOW, AS FOR YOU TWO—
HEY!
THEY'RE GONE!
!!
Farewell
FLIT

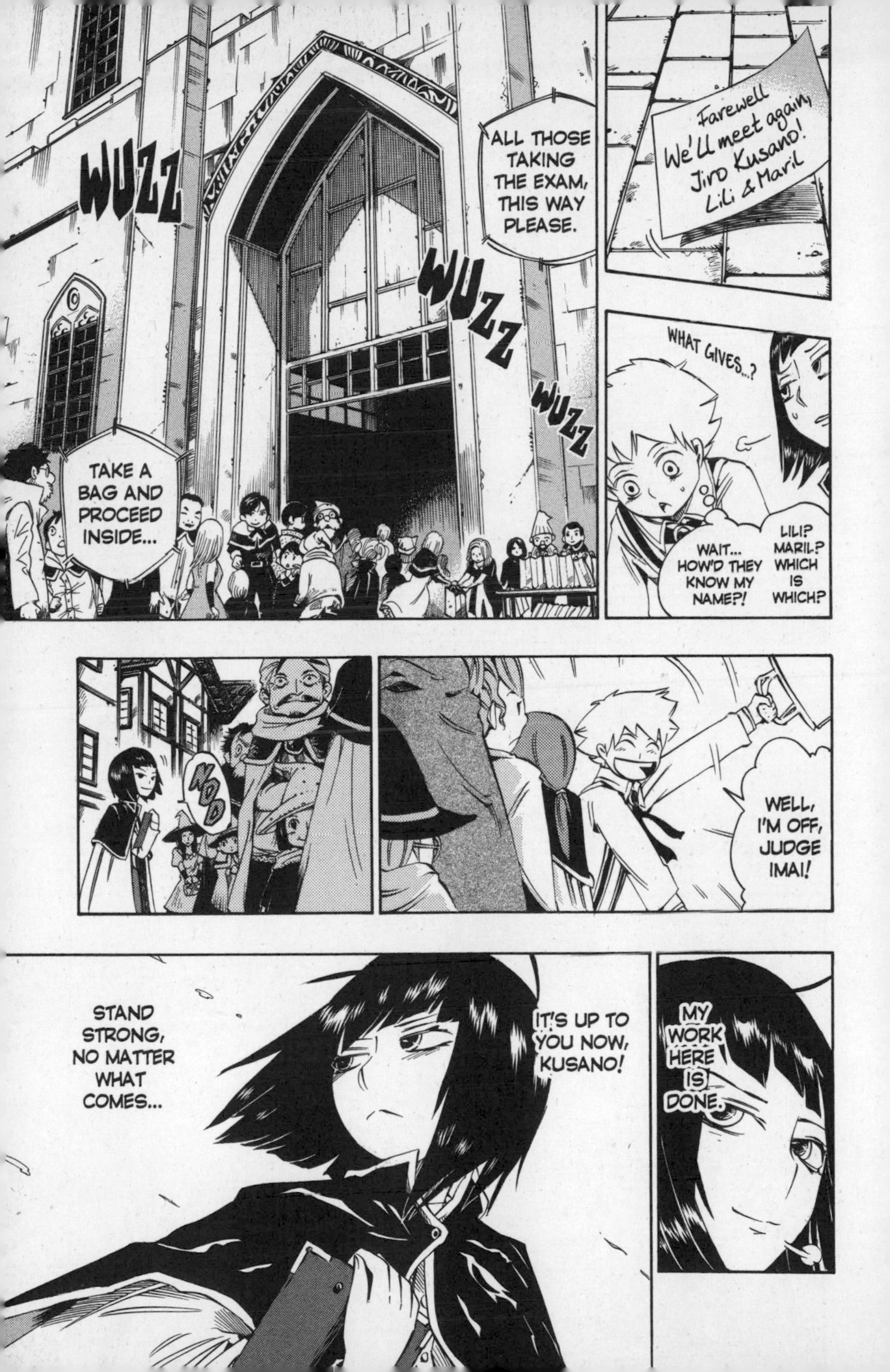
Farewell
We'll meet again,
Jiro Kusano!
Lili & Maril
WHAT GIVES...?
LILI? MARIL? WHICH IS WHICH?
WAIT... HOW'D THEY KNOW MY NAME?!
ALL THOSE TAKING THE EXAM, THIS WAY PLEASE.
WUZZ
WUZZ
WUZZ
TAKE A BAG AND PROCEED INSIDE...
WELL, I'M OFF, JUDGE IMAI!
NOD
MY WORK HERE IS DONE.
IT'S UP TO YOU NOW, KUSANO!
STAND STRONG, NO MATTER WHAT COMES...

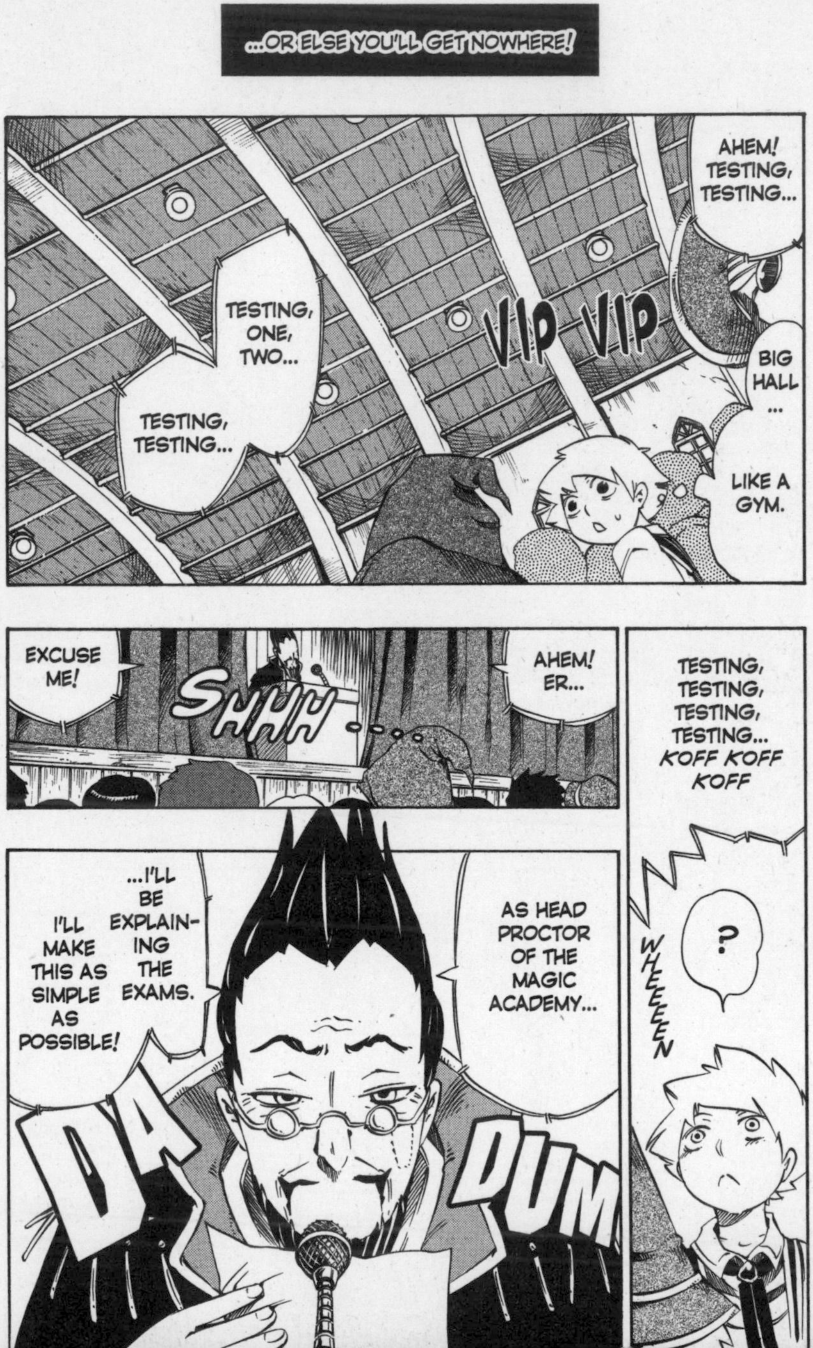
...OR ELSE YOU'LL GET NOWHERE!
AHEM! TESTING, TESTING...
BIG HALL...
LIKE A GYM.
VIP VIP
TESTING, ONE, TWO...
TESTING, TESTING...
TESTING, TESTING, TESTING, TESTING... *KOFF KOFF KOFF*
WHEEEEN
?
AHEM! ER...
SHHH...
EXCUSE ME!
AS HEAD PROCTOR OF THE MAGIC ACADEMY...
...I'LL BE EXPLAINING THE EXAMS.
I'LL MAKE THIS AS SIMPLE AS POSSIBLE!
DA DUM

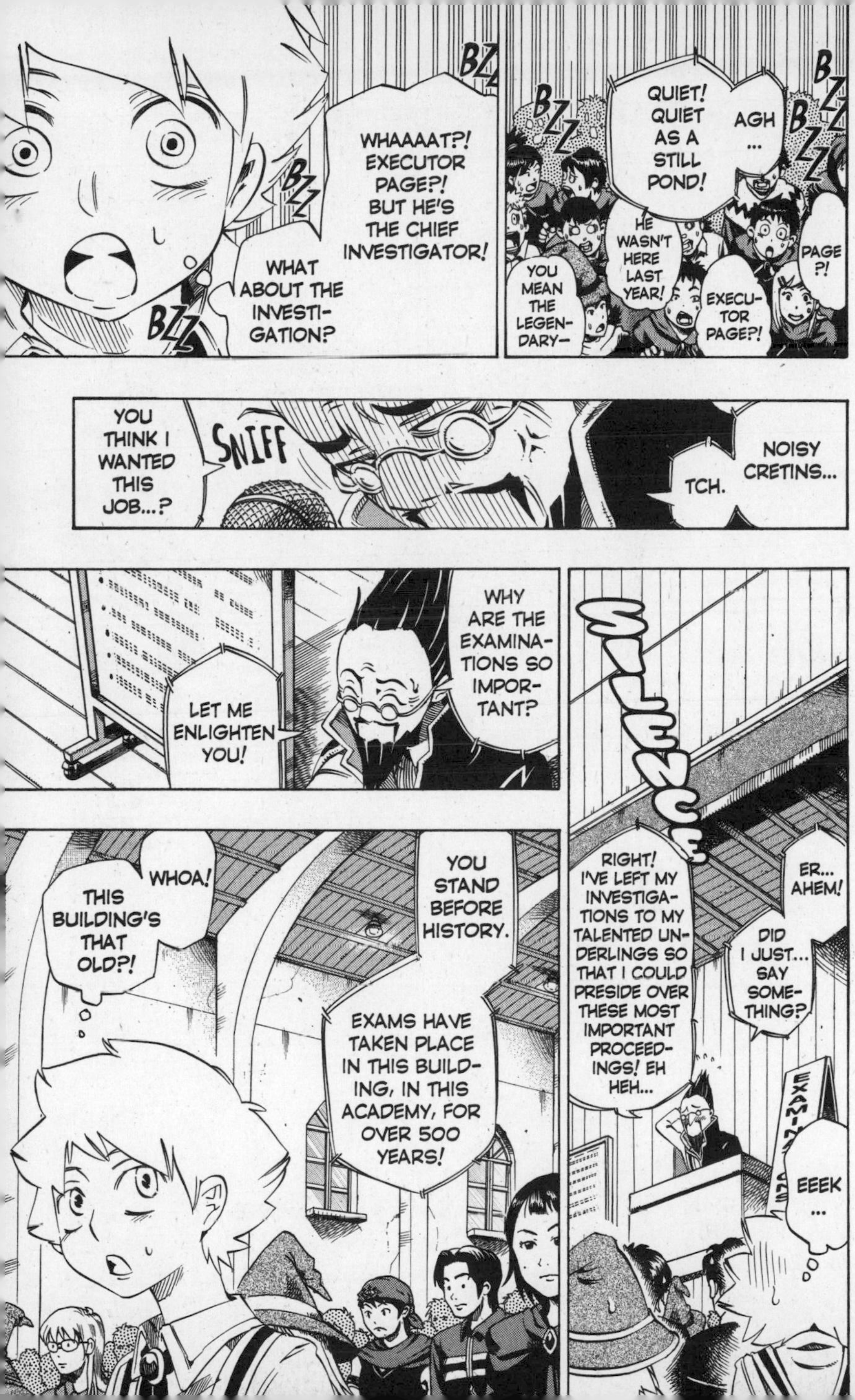
BZZ
QUIET! QUIET AS A STILL POND!
AGH ...
BZZ
PAGE ?!
EXECU-TOR PAGE?!
HE WASN'T HERE LAST YEAR!
YOU MEAN THE LEGEN-DARY—
BZZ
WHAAAAT?! EXECUTOR PAGE?! BUT HE'S THE CHIEF INVESTIGATOR!
BZZ
WHAT ABOUT THE INVESTI-GATION?
BZZ
NOISY CRETINS...
TCH.
SNIFF
YOU THINK I WANTED THIS JOB...?
SILENCE
ER... AHEM!
DID I JUST... SAY SOME-THING?
RIGHT! I'VE LEFT MY INVESTIGA-TIONS TO MY TALENTED UN-DERLINGS SO THAT I COULD PRESIDE OVER THESE MOST IMPORTANT PROCEED-INGS! EH HEH...
EEEK ...
WHY ARE THE EXAMINA-TIONS SO IMPOR-TANT?
LET ME ENLIGHTEN YOU!
YOU STAND BEFORE HISTORY.
EXAMS HAVE TAKEN PLACE IN THIS BUILD-ING, IN THIS ACADEMY, FOR OVER 500 YEARS!
WHOA! THIS BUILDING'S THAT OLD?!

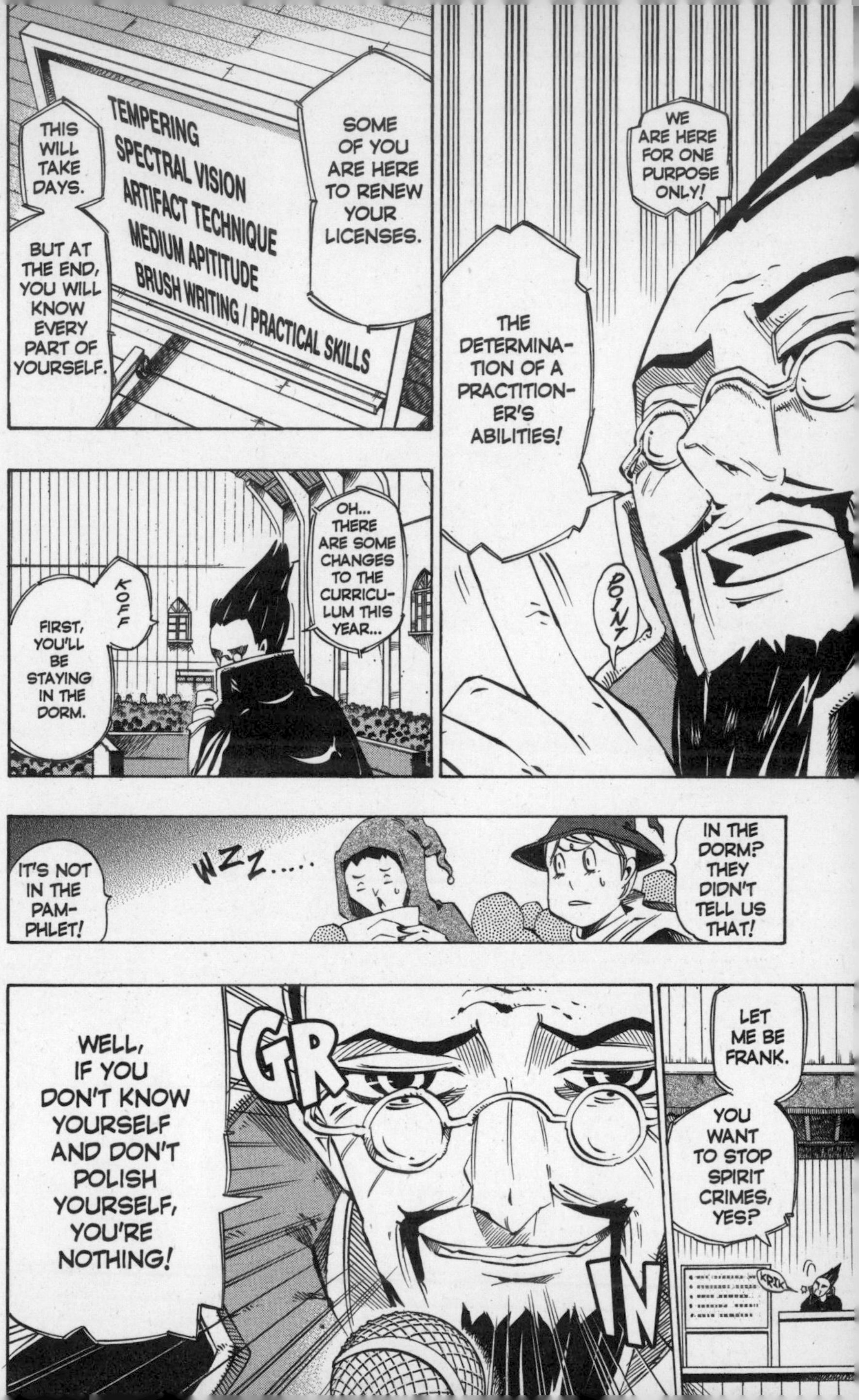
WE ARE HERE FOR ONE PURPOSE ONLY!
THE DETERMINATION OF A PRACTITIONER'S ABILITIES!
POINT
SOME OF YOU ARE HERE TO RENEW YOUR LICENSES.
TEMPERING
SPECTRAL VISION
ARTIFACT TECHNIQUE
MEDIUM APITITUDE
BRUSH WRITING / PRACTICAL SKILLS
THIS WILL TAKE DAYS.
BUT AT THE END, YOU WILL KNOW EVERY PART OF YOURSELF.
OH... THERE ARE SOME CHANGES TO THE CURRICULUM THIS YEAR...
KOFF
FIRST, YOU'LL BE STAYING IN THE DORM.
IN THE DORM? THEY DIDN'T TELL US THAT!
WZZ.....
IT'S NOT IN THE PAMPHLET!
LET ME BE FRANK.
YOU WANT TO STOP SPIRIT CRIMES, YES?
KRIK
GRIN
WELL, IF YOU DON'T KNOW YOURSELF AND DON'T POLISH YOURSELF, YOU'RE NOTHING!

READ THIS WAY

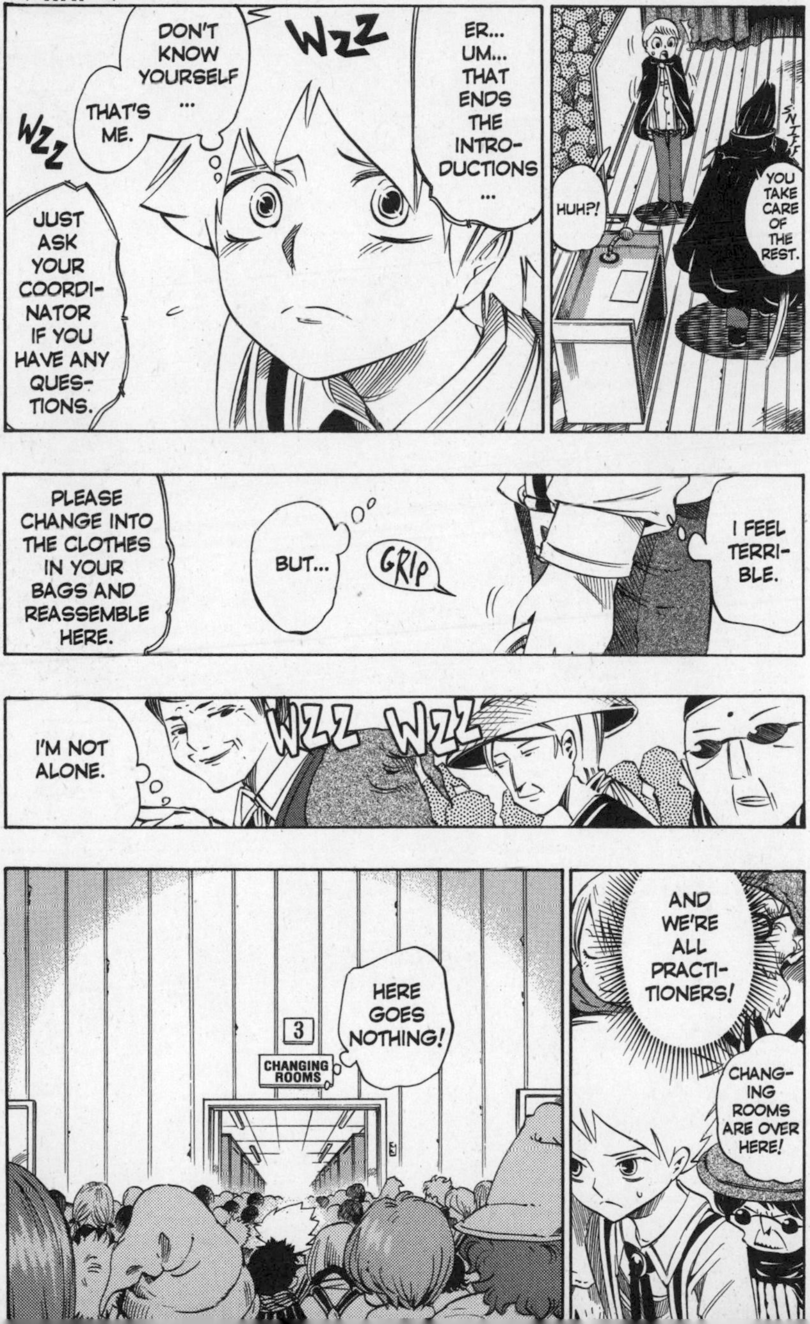
SNIFF
YOU TAKE CARE OF THE REST.
HUH?!
ER... UM... THAT ENDS THE INTRODUCTIONS ...
WZZ
DON'T KNOW YOURSELF ...
THAT'S ME.
WZZ
JUST ASK YOUR COORDINATOR IF YOU HAVE ANY QUESTIONS.
I FEEL TERRIBLE.
GRIP
BUT...
PLEASE CHANGE INTO THE CLOTHES IN YOUR BAGS AND REASSEMBLE HERE.
WZZ WZZ
I'M NOT ALONE.
AND WE'RE ALL PRACTITIONERS!
CHANGING ROOMS ARE OVER HERE!
HERE GOES NOTHING!
3
CHANGING ROOMS

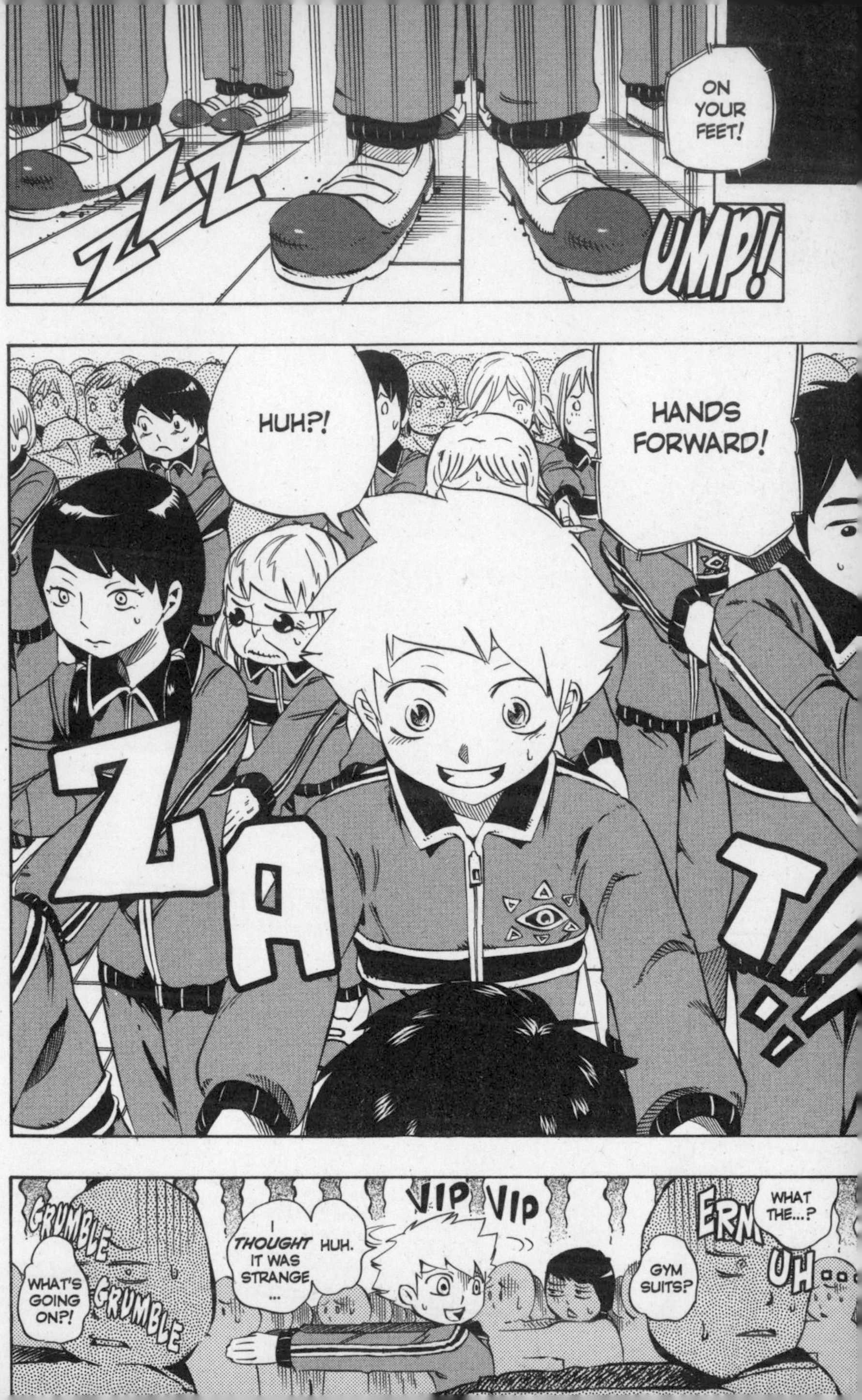
ON YOUR FEET!
UMP!
ZZZ
HANDS FORWARD!
HUH?!
ZAT!!
WHAT THE...?
ERM
UH...
GYM SUITS?
VIP VIP
HUH.
I *THOUGHT* IT WAS STRANGE...
GRUMBLE
WHAT'S GOING ON?!
GRUMBLE

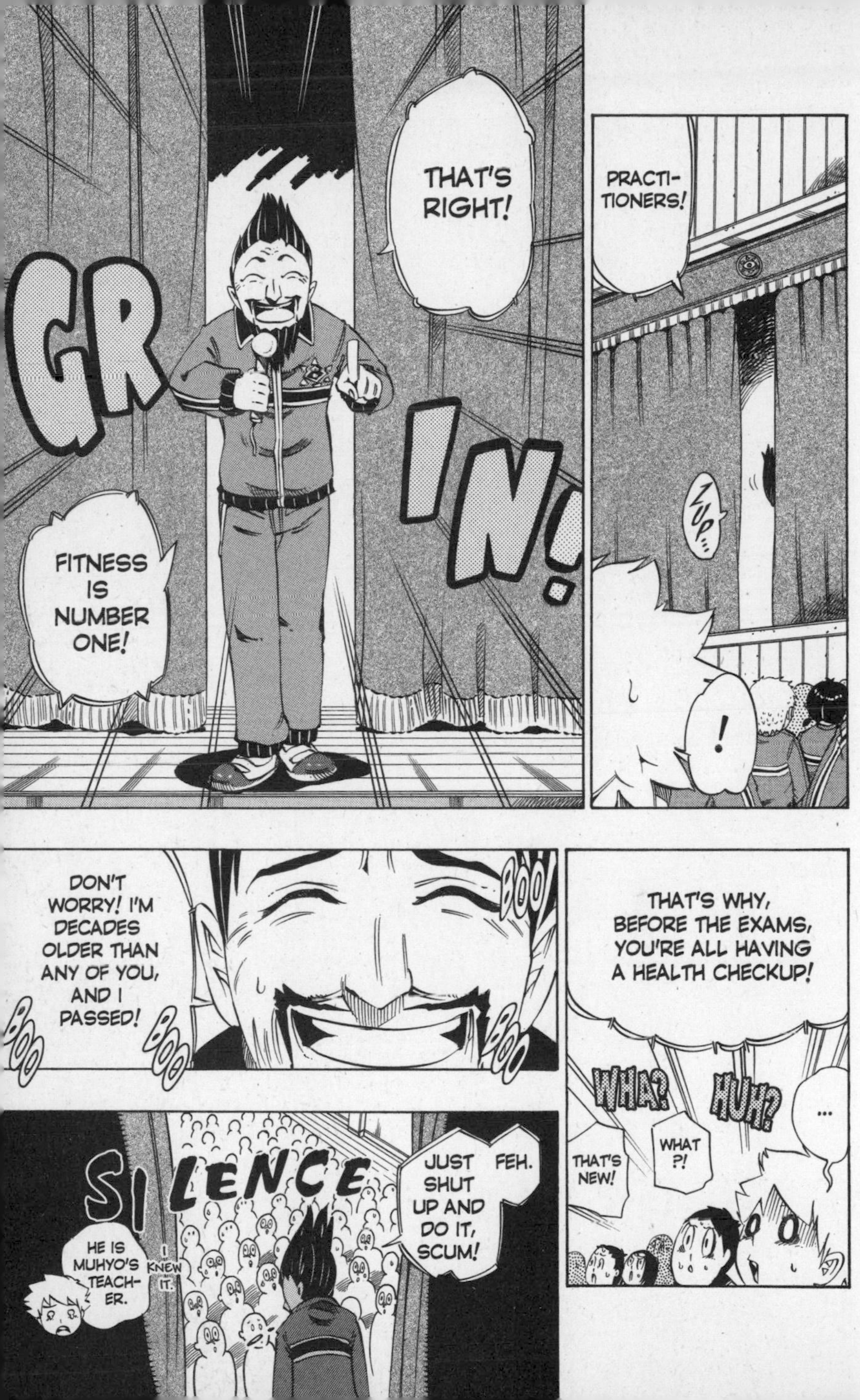
PRACTI-TIONERS!
ZUP...
!
THAT'S RIGHT!
GR
IN!
FITNESS IS NUMBER ONE!
THAT'S WHY, BEFORE THE EXAMS, YOU'RE ALL HAVING A HEALTH CHECKUP!
...
HUH?
WHAT?!
WHA?
THAT'S NEW!
BOO
BOO
DON'T WORRY! I'M DECADES OLDER THAN ANY OF YOU, AND I PASSED!
BOO
BOO
FEH.
JUST SHUT UP AND DO IT, SCUM!
SILENCE
I KNEW IT.
HE IS MUHYO'S TEACH-ER.

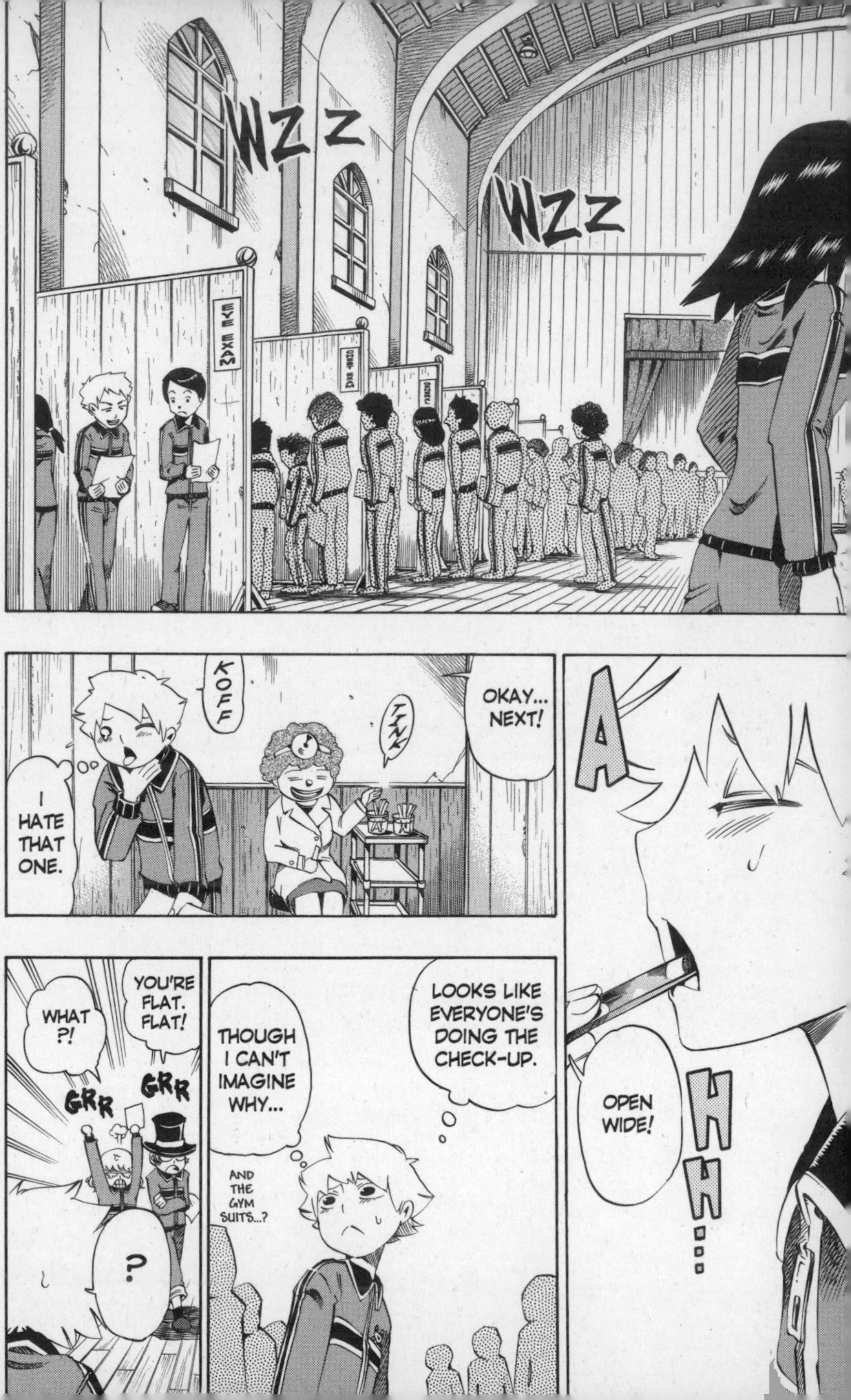
WZZ
WZZ
EYE EXAM
AHHH...
OPEN WIDE!
OKAY... NEXT!
TINK
KOFF
I HATE THAT ONE.
LOOKS LIKE EVERYONE'S DOING THE CHECK-UP.
THOUGH I CAN'T IMAGINE WHY...
AND THE GYM SUITS...?
YOU'RE FLAT. FLAT!
WHAT?!
GRR
GRR
?

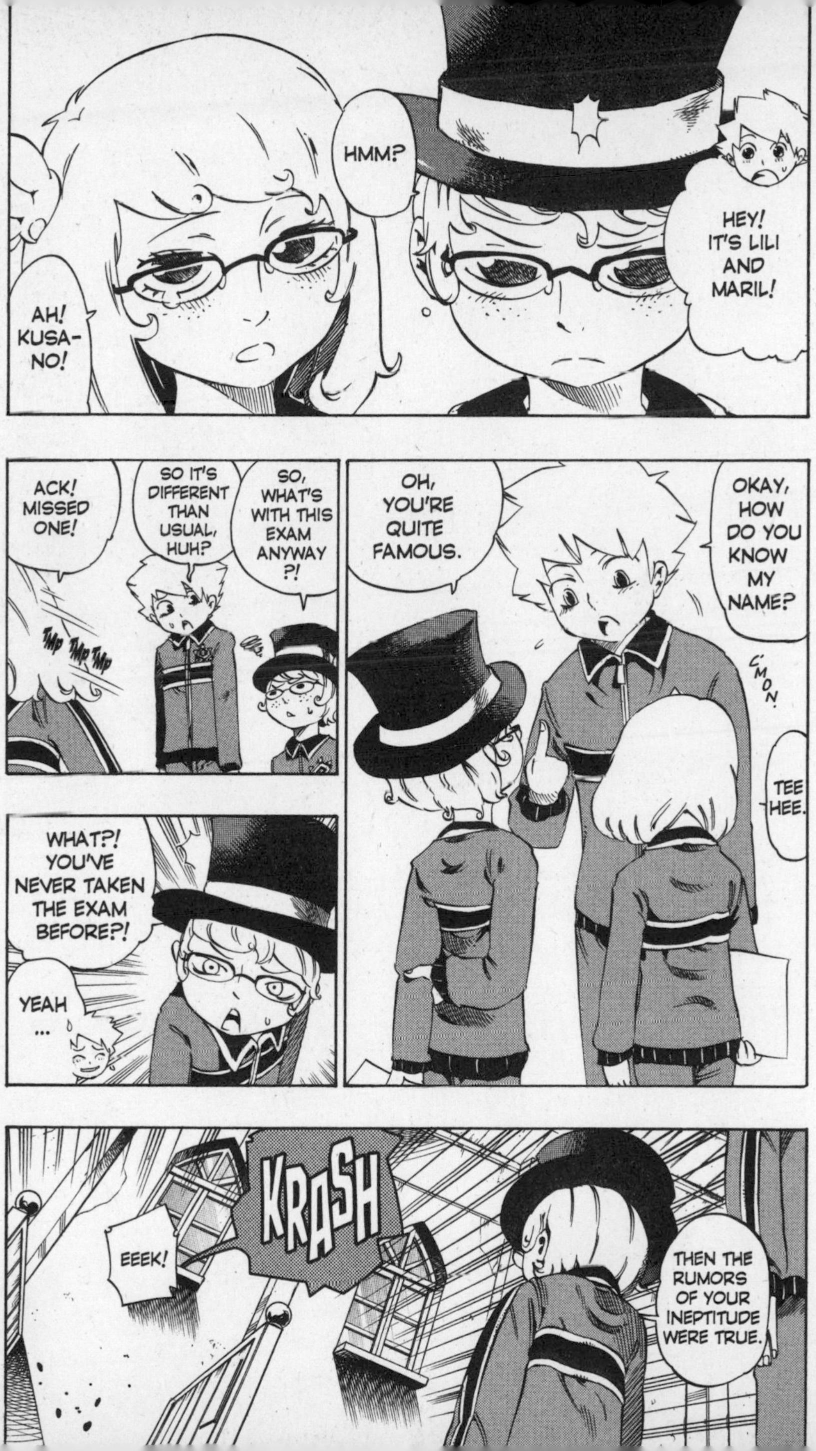
HEY! IT'S LILI AND MARIL!
HMM?
AH! KUSANO!
OKAY, HOW DO YOU KNOW MY NAME?
OH, YOU'RE QUITE FAMOUS.
C'MON
TEE HEE.
SO, WHAT'S WITH THIS EXAM ANYWAY?!
SO IT'S DIFFERENT THAN USUAL, HUH?
ACK! MISSED ONE!
TMP TMP TMP
WHAT?! YOU'VE NEVER TAKEN THE EXAM BEFORE?!
YEAH ...
THEN THE RUMORS OF YOUR INEPTITUDE WERE TRUE.
KRASH
EEEK!

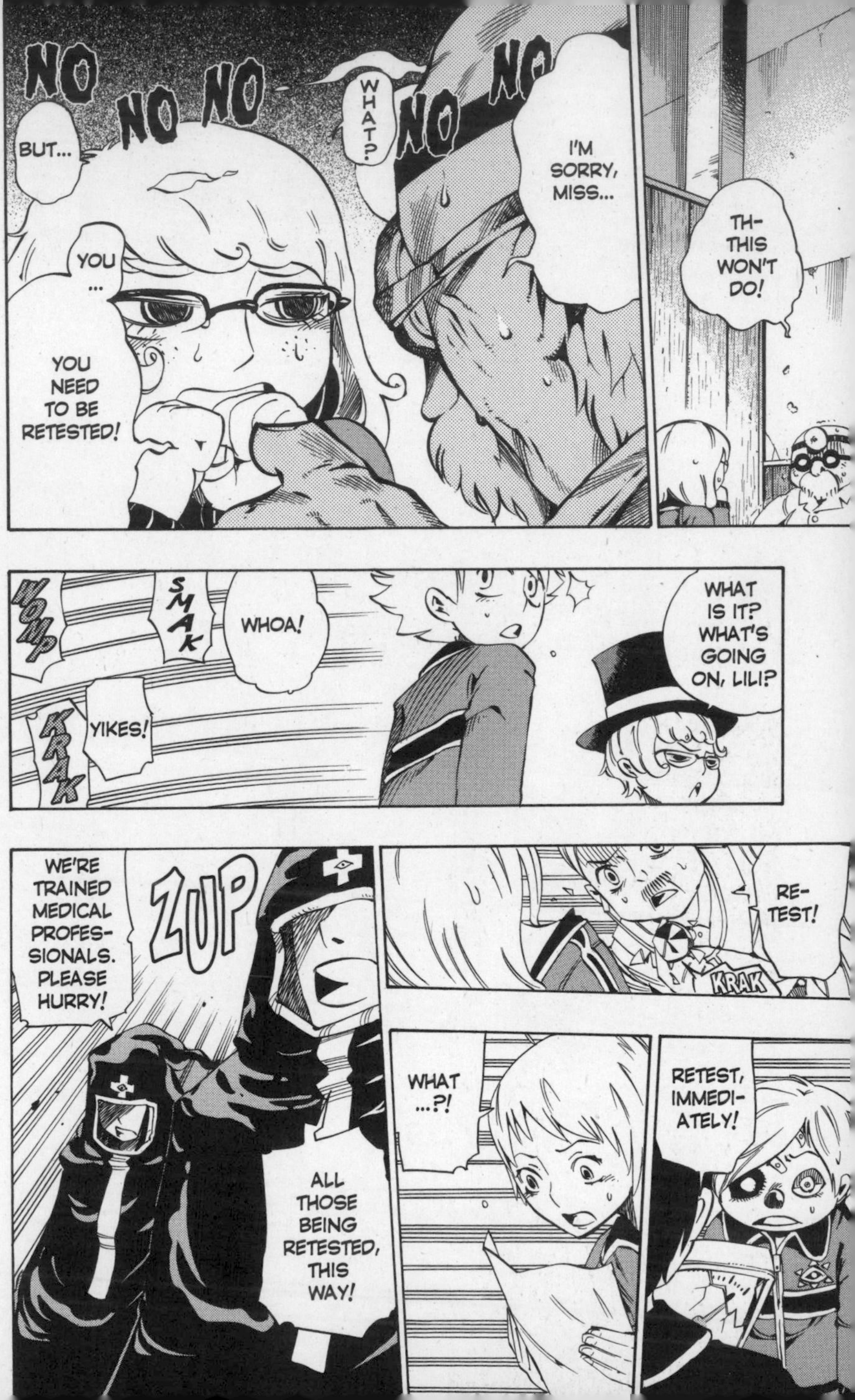
TH-THIS WON'T DO!
I'M SORRY, MISS...
NO
NO
WHAT?
NO NO
NO
BUT...
YOU ...
YOU NEED TO BE RETESTED!
WHAT IS IT? WHAT'S GOING ON, LILI?
WHOA!
SMAK
WOMP
YIKES!
KRAK
RE-TEST!
KRAK
RETEST, IMMEDIATELY!
WHAT ...?!
ZUP
WE'RE TRAINED MEDICAL PROFESSIONALS. PLEASE HURRY!
ALL THOSE BEING RETESTED, THIS WAY!

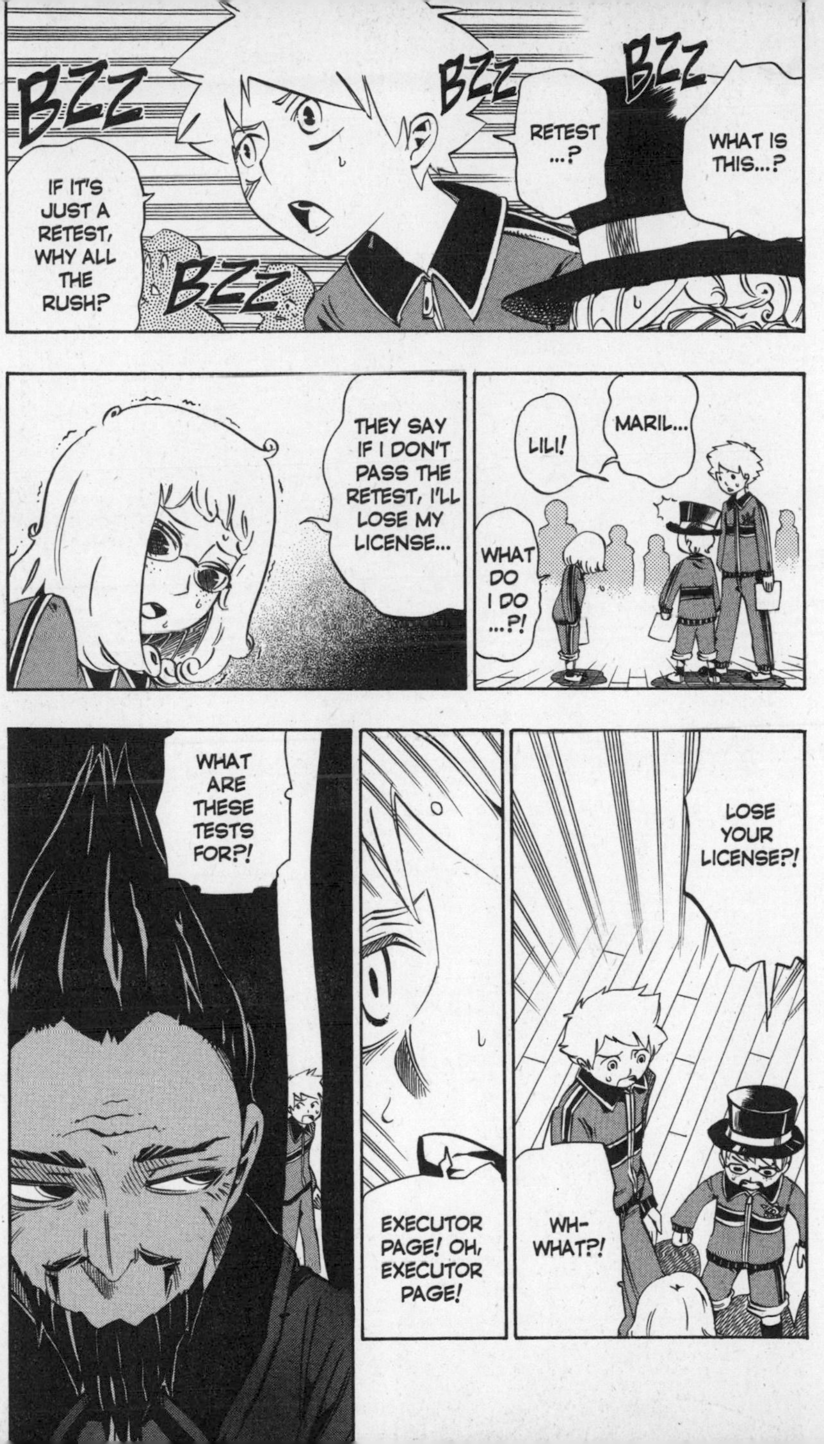
BZZ
WHAT IS THIS...?
BZZ
RETEST ...?
BZZ
BZZ
IF IT'S JUST A RETEST, WHY ALL THE RUSH?
MARIL...
LILI!
WHAT DO I DO ...?!
THEY SAY IF I DON'T PASS THE RETEST, I'LL LOSE MY LICENSE...
LOSE YOUR LICENSE?!
WH- WHAT?!
EXECUTOR PAGE! OH, EXECUTOR PAGE!
WHAT ARE THESE TESTS FOR?!

LILI MATHIAS   MARIL MATHIAS
BIRTHDAY: OCTOBER 13

LIKES:
PEN AND PAPER
INFORMATION
(LIKE MARIL)
CAKE

TALENTS:
HYPERACTIVE
IMAGINATION
ANALYSIS
RESEARCH

NOT GOOD WITH:
SPICY FOODS
STUBBORN MARIL

LIKES:
BOOKS
INFORMATION (GOSSIP,
HAPPENINGS, ETC.)
CAKE

TALENTS:
HYPERACTIVE
IMAGINATION
ANALYSIS
RESEARCH

NOT GOOD WITH:
SPICY FOODS
MEAN LILI

ARTICLE 50
THE TESTS BEGIN

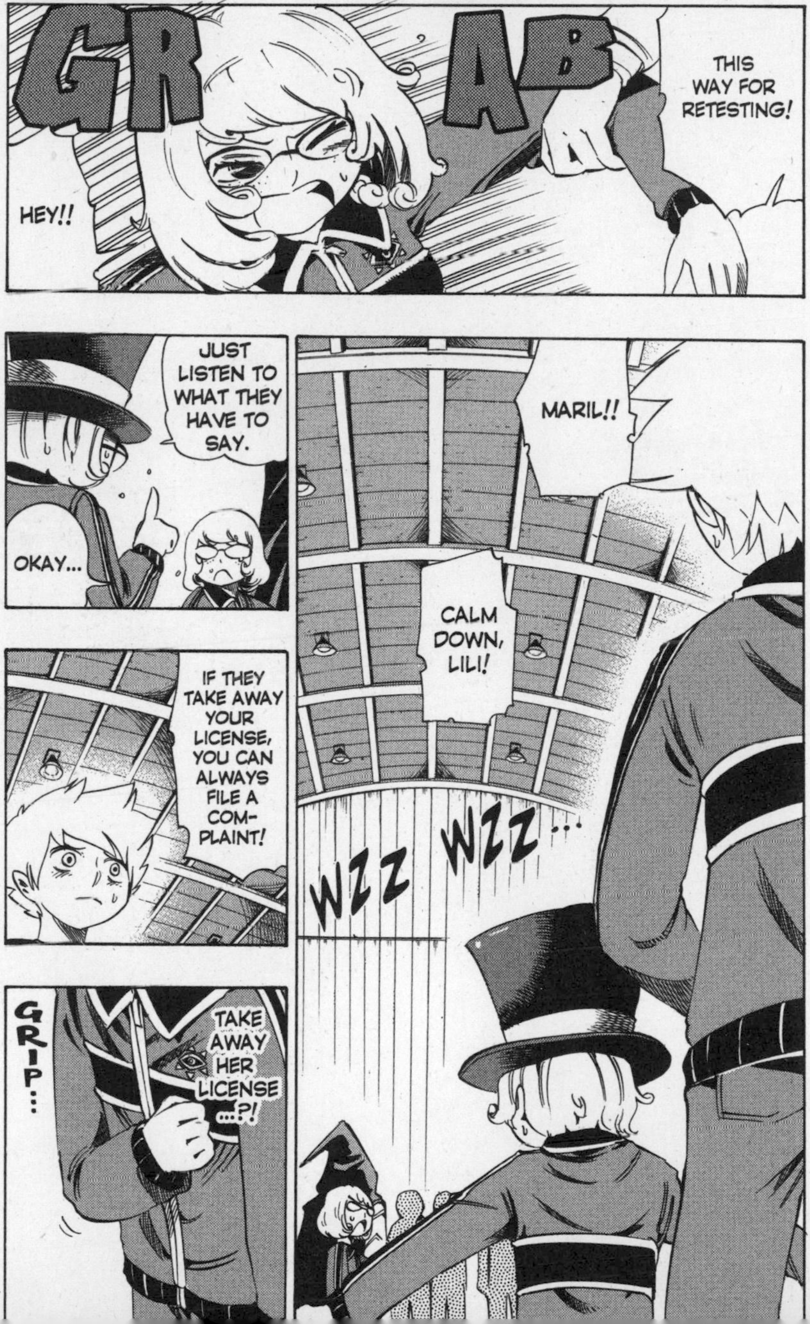
GRAB
THIS WAY FOR RETESTING!
HEY!!
MARIL!!
CALM DOWN, LILI!
WZZ WZZ...
JUST LISTEN TO WHAT THEY HAVE TO SAY.
OKAY...
IF THEY TAKE AWAY YOUR LICENSE, YOU CAN ALWAYS FILE A COM-PLAINT!
GRIP...
TAKE AWAY HER LICENSE ...?!

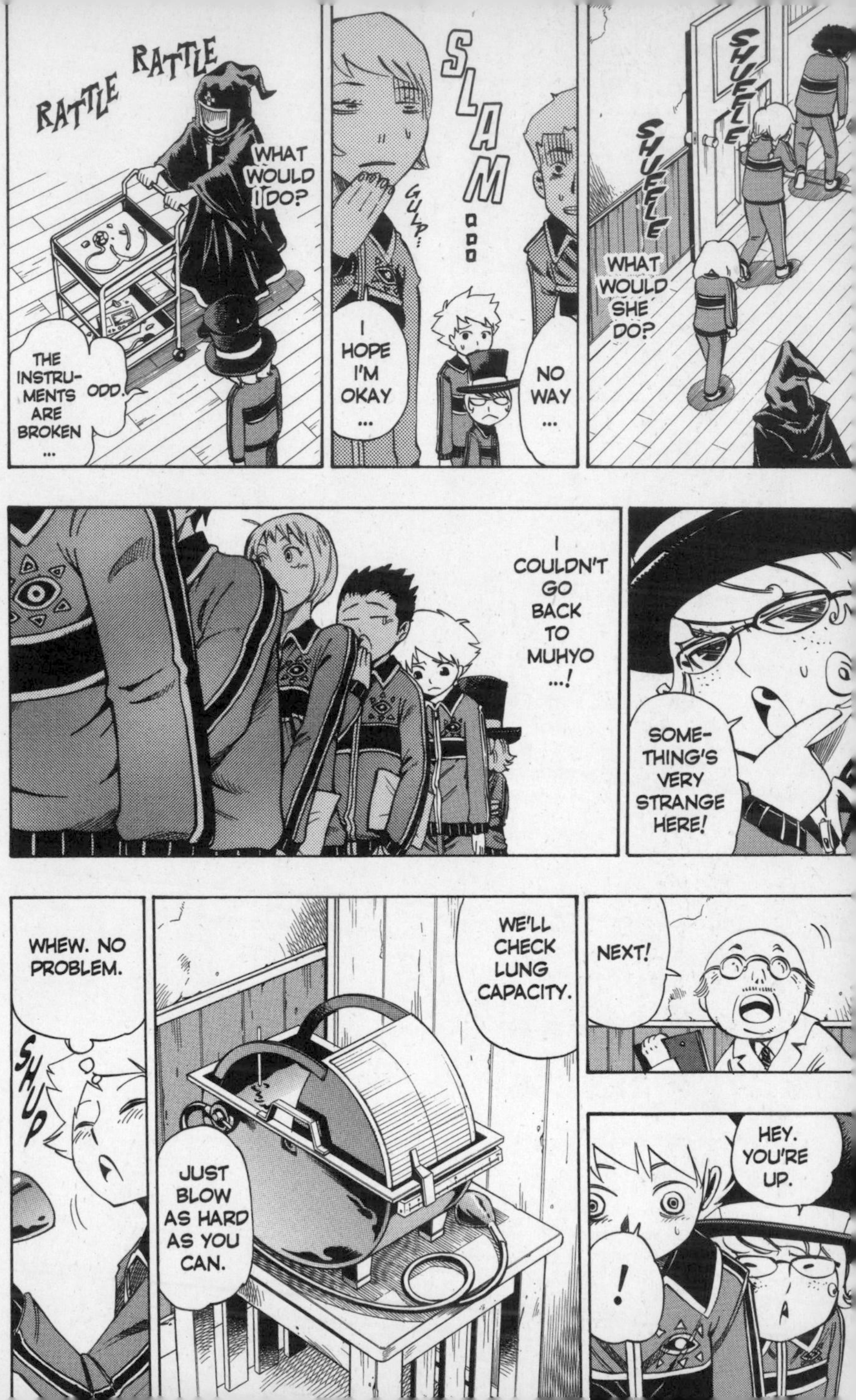
SHUFFLE
SHUFFLE
WHAT WOULD SHE DO?
SLAM
GULP...
NO WAY...
I HOPE I'M OKAY...
RATTLE RATTLE
WHAT WOULD I DO?
THE INSTRU-MENTS ARE BROKEN...
ODD.
SOME-THING'S VERY STRANGE HERE!
I COULDN'T GO BACK TO MUHYO...!
NEXT!
HEY. YOU'RE UP.
!
WE'LL CHECK LUNG CAPACITY.
JUST BLOW AS HARD AS YOU CAN.
WHEW. NO PROBLEM.
SHUP

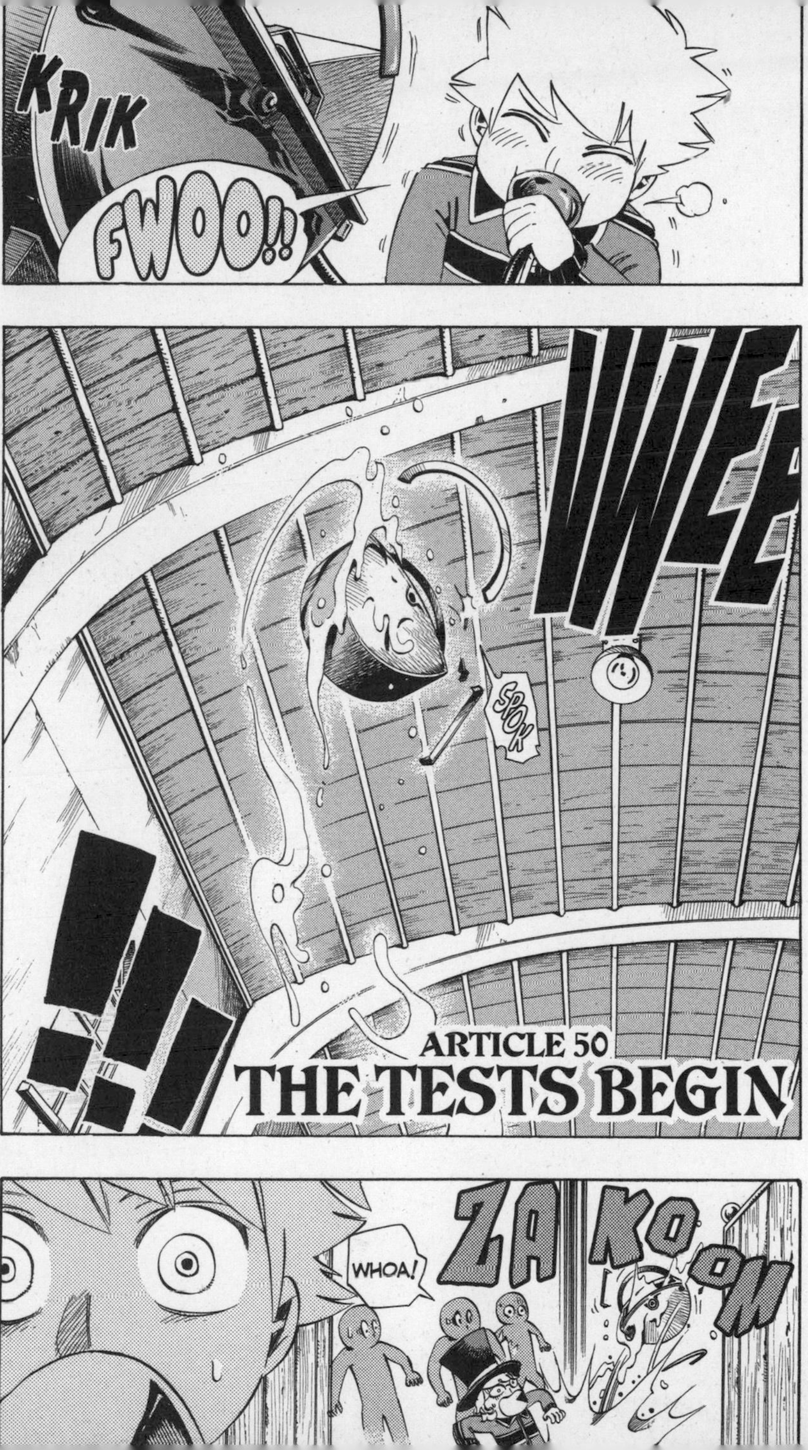
KRIK
FWOO!!
WHEE!
SPOK
!!
ARTICLE 50
THE TESTS BEGIN
ZAKOOON
WHOA!

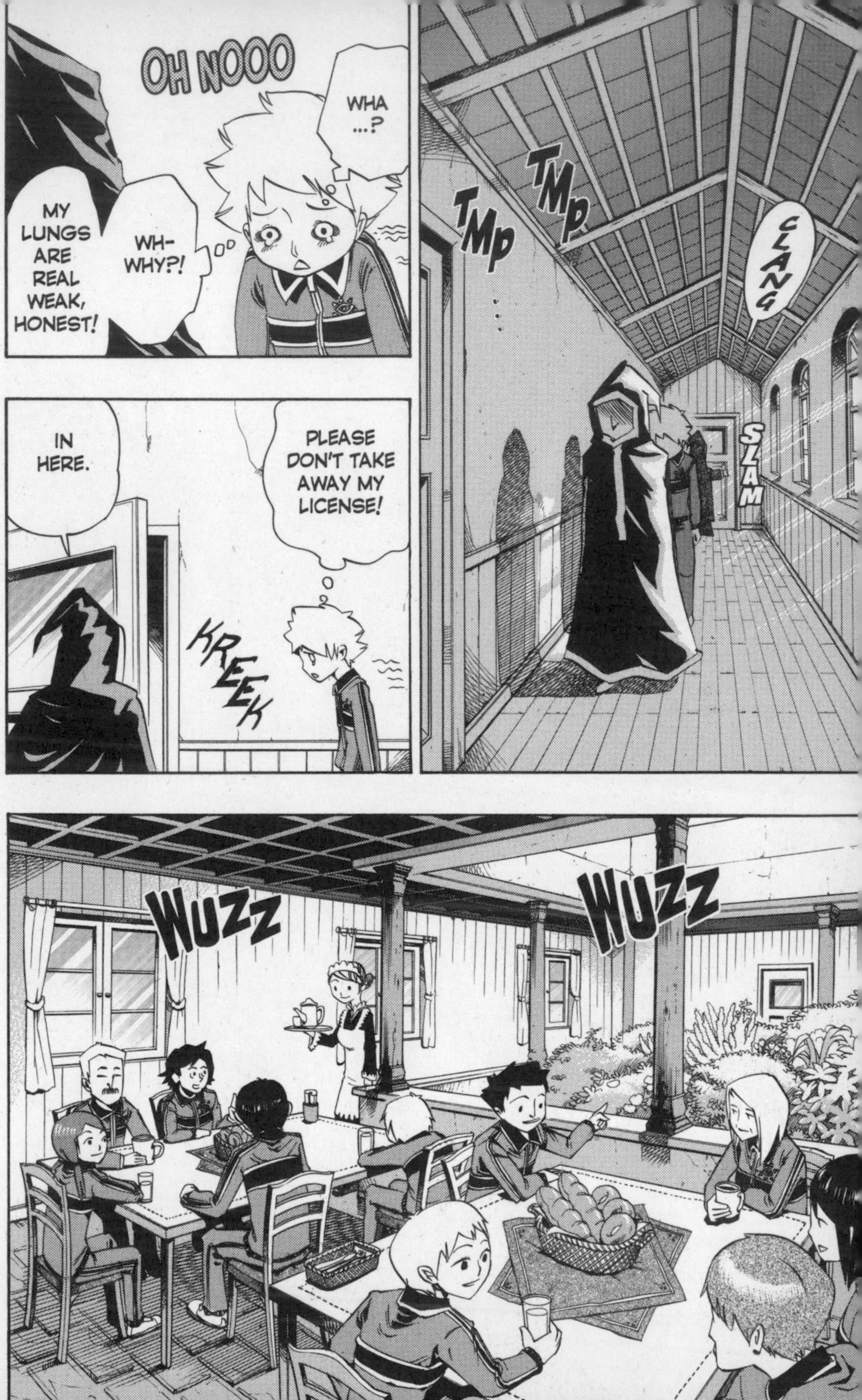
TMP
TMP
CLANG
SLAM
WHA ...?
OH NOOO
WH-WHY?!
MY LUNGS ARE REAL WEAK, HONEST!
PLEASE DON'T TAKE AWAY MY LICENSE!
IN HERE.
KREEK
WUZZ
WUZZ

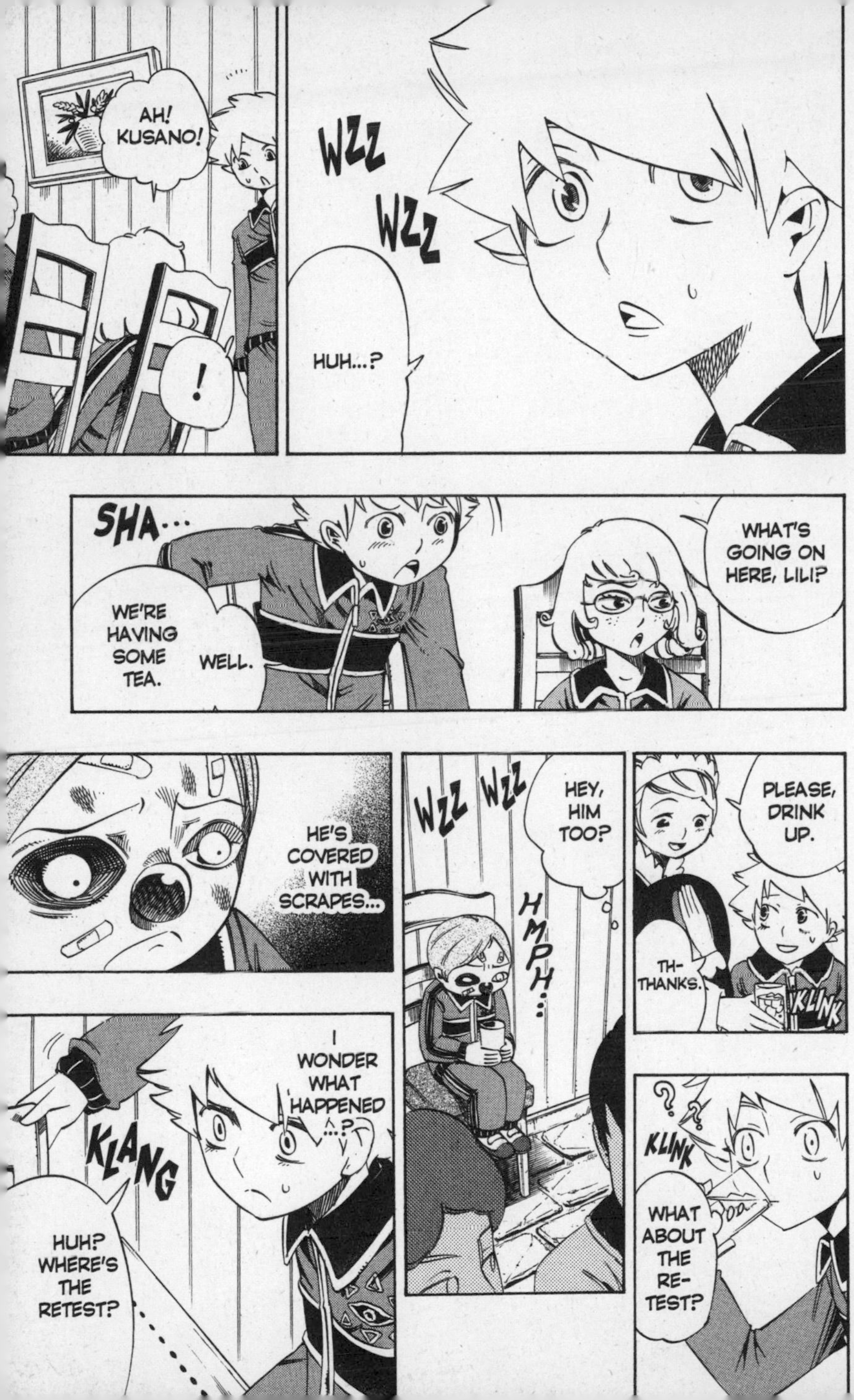

WZZ
WZZ
HUH...?
AH! KUSANO!
!
WHAT'S GOING ON HERE, LILI?
SHA...
WE'RE HAVING SOME TEA.
WELL.
PLEASE, DRINK UP.
TH- THANKS.
KLINK
KLINK
WHAT ABOUT THE RE-TEST?
WZZ WZZ
HEY, HIM TOO?
HMPH...
HE'S COVERED WITH SCRAPES...
I WONDER WHAT HAPPENED ...?
KLANG
HUH? WHERE'S THE RETEST?

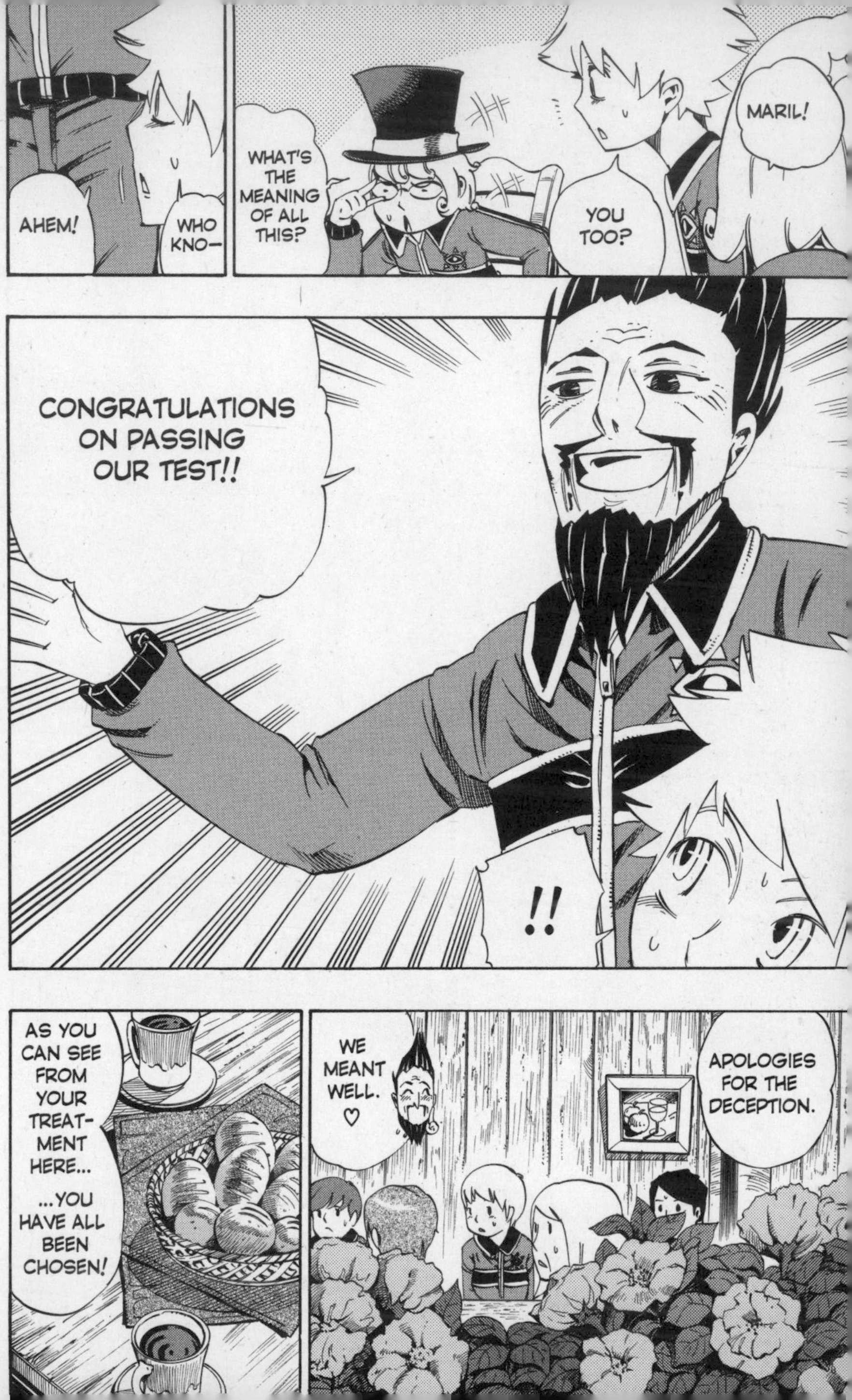
MARIL!
YOU TOO?
WHAT'S THE MEANING OF ALL THIS?
WHO KNO—
AHEM!
CONGRATULATIONS ON PASSING OUR TEST!!
!!
APOLOGIES FOR THE DECEPTION.
WE MEANT WELL. ♡
AS YOU CAN SEE FROM YOUR TREATMENT HERE...
...YOU HAVE ALL BEEN CHOSEN!

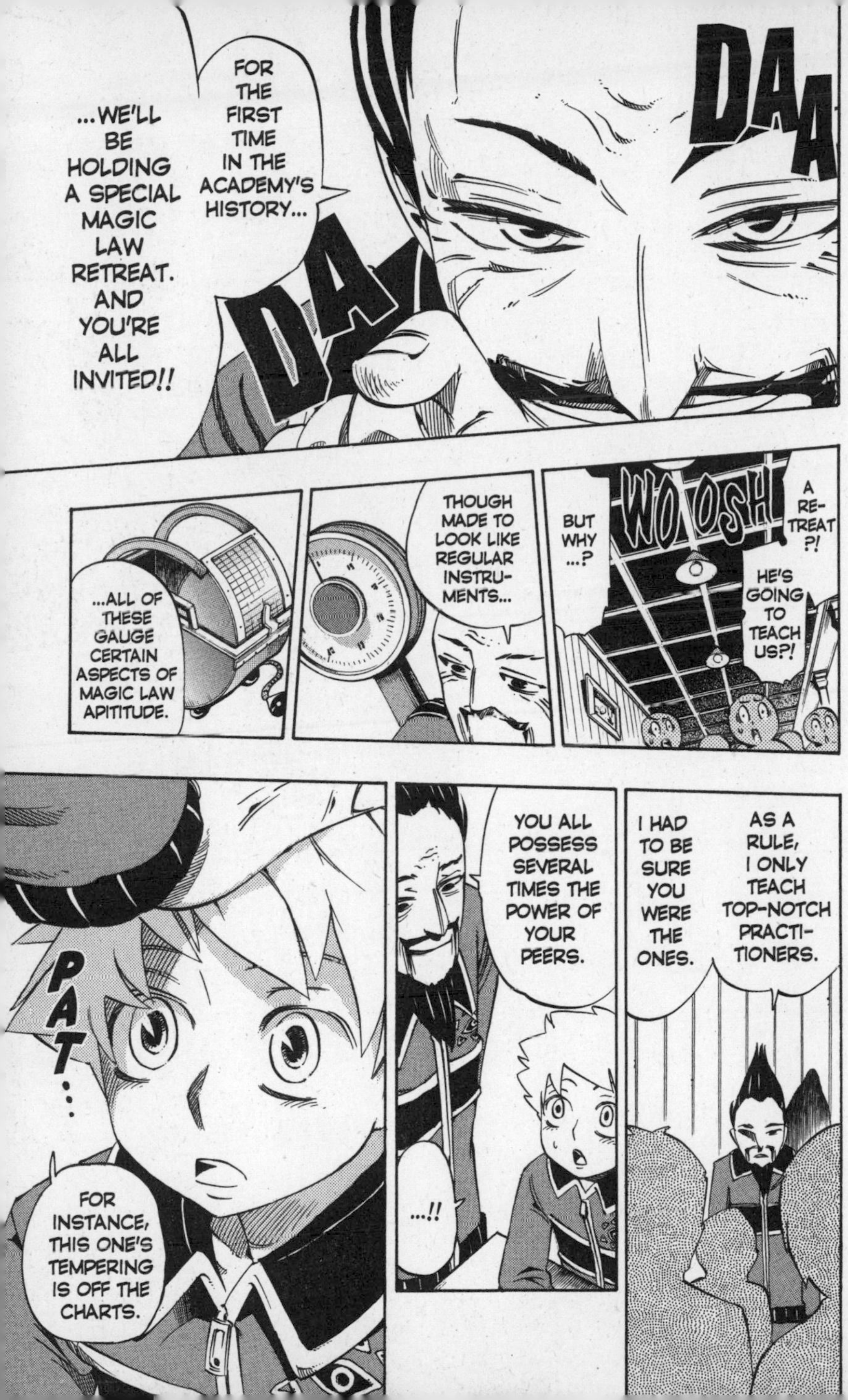
DAA
FOR THE FIRST TIME IN THE ACADEMY'S HISTORY...
...WE'LL BE HOLDING A SPECIAL MAGIC LAW RETREAT. AND YOU'RE ALL INVITED!!
DA
WOOSH
A RE-TREAT?!
HE'S GOING TO TEACH US?!
BUT WHY ...?
THOUGH MADE TO LOOK LIKE REGULAR INSTRU-MENTS...
...ALL OF THESE GAUGE CERTAIN ASPECTS OF MAGIC LAW APITITUDE.
AS A RULE, I ONLY TEACH TOP-NOTCH PRACTI-TIONERS.
I HAD TO BE SURE YOU WERE THE ONES.
YOU ALL POSSESS SEVERAL TIMES THE POWER OF YOUR PEERS.
...!!
PAT...
FOR INSTANCE, THIS ONE'S TEMPERING IS OFF THE CHARTS.

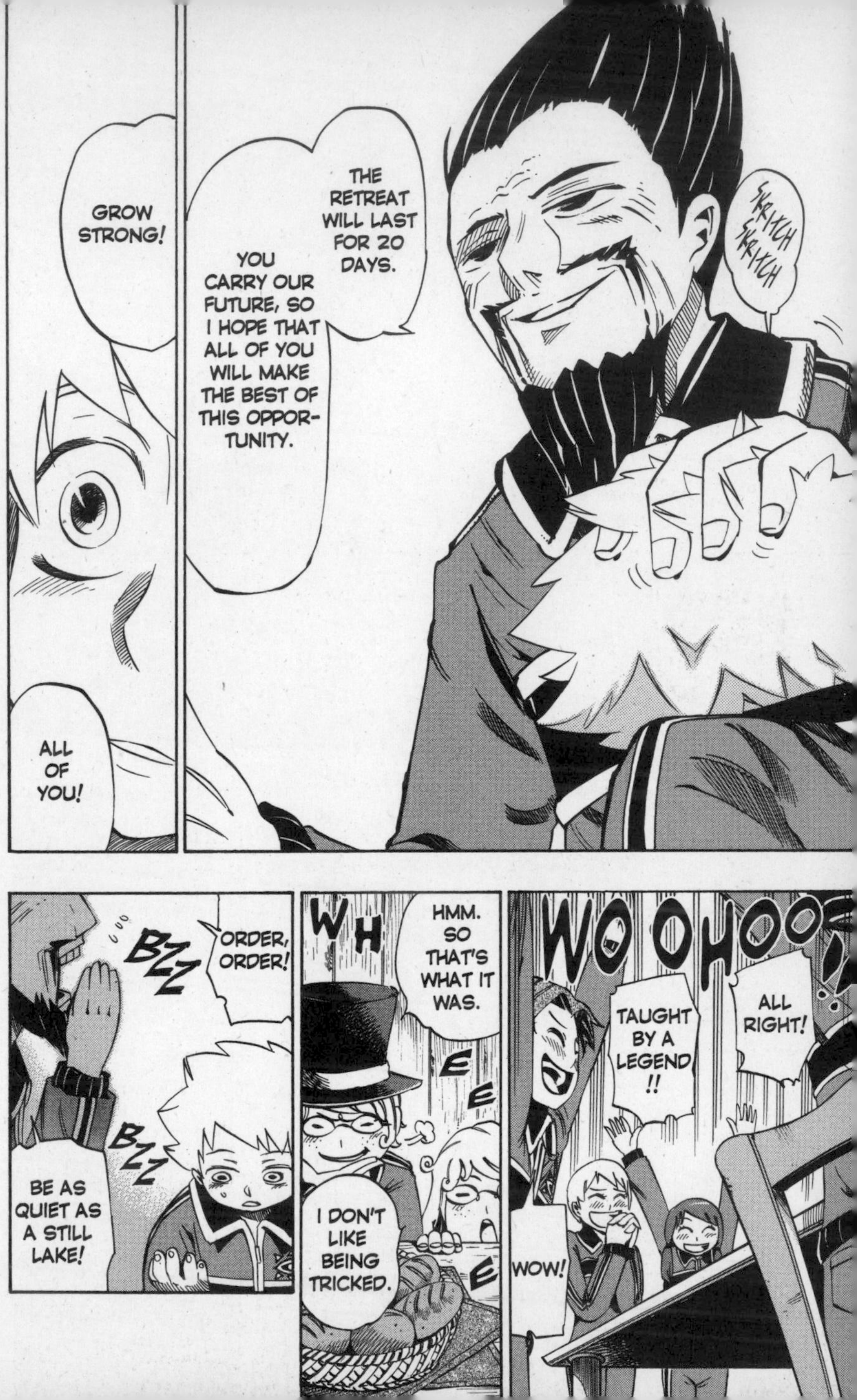
SKRITCH SKRITCH
THE RETREAT WILL LAST FOR 20 DAYS.
YOU CARRY OUR FUTURE, SO I HOPE THAT ALL OF YOU WILL MAKE THE BEST OF THIS OPPORTUNITY.
GROW STRONG!
ALL OF YOU!
WOOHOO
ALL RIGHT!
TAUGHT BY A LEGEND!!
WOW!
WHEEE
HMM. SO THAT'S WHAT IT WAS.
I DON'T LIKE BEING TRICKED.
ORDER, ORDER!
BZZ
BZZ
BE AS QUIET AS A STILL LAKE!

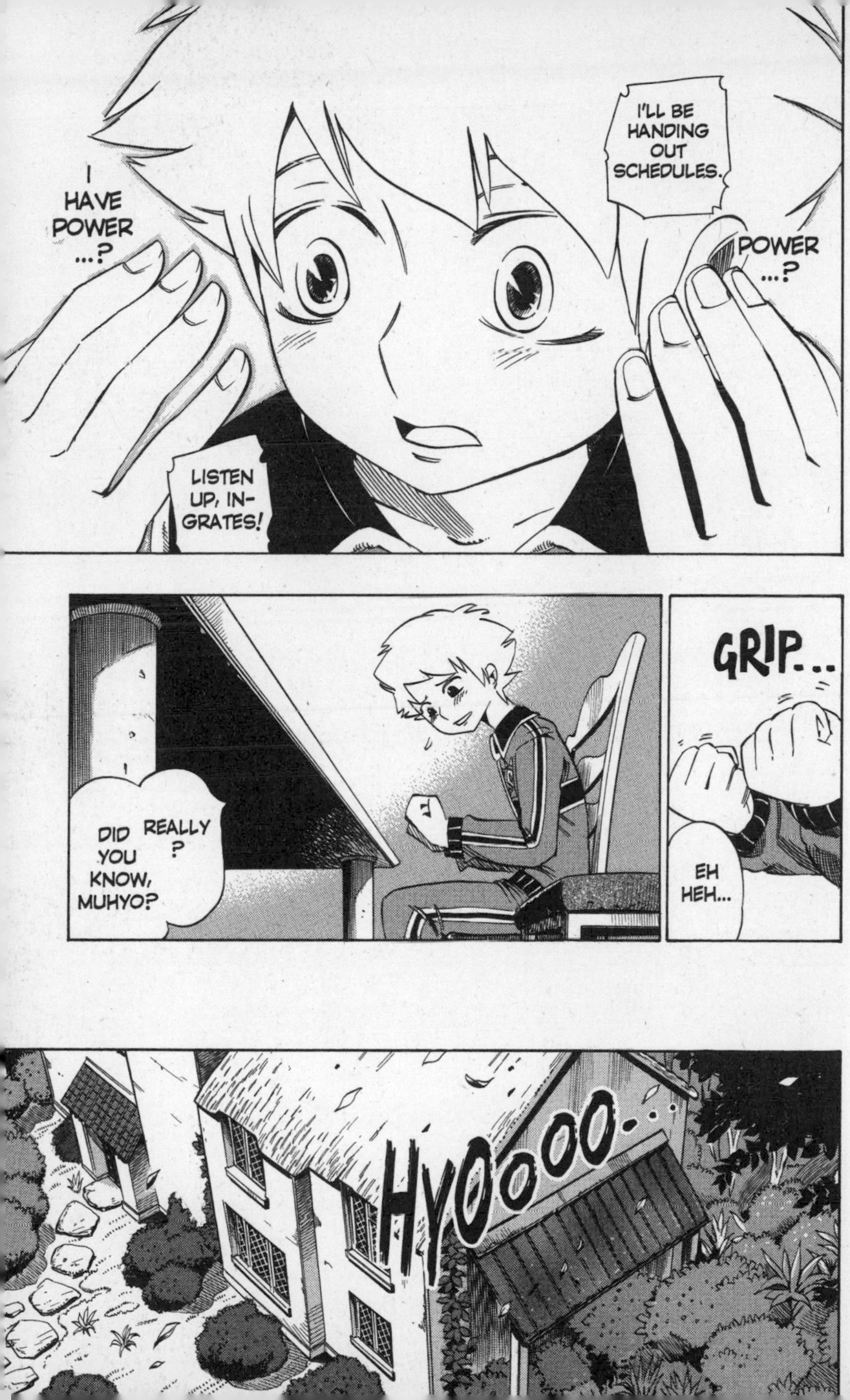
I'LL BE HANDING OUT SCHEDULES.
POWER ...?
I HAVE POWER ...?
LISTEN UP, IN-GRATES!
GRIP...
EH HEH...
REALLY?
DID YOU KNOW, MUHYO?
HYOOOO...

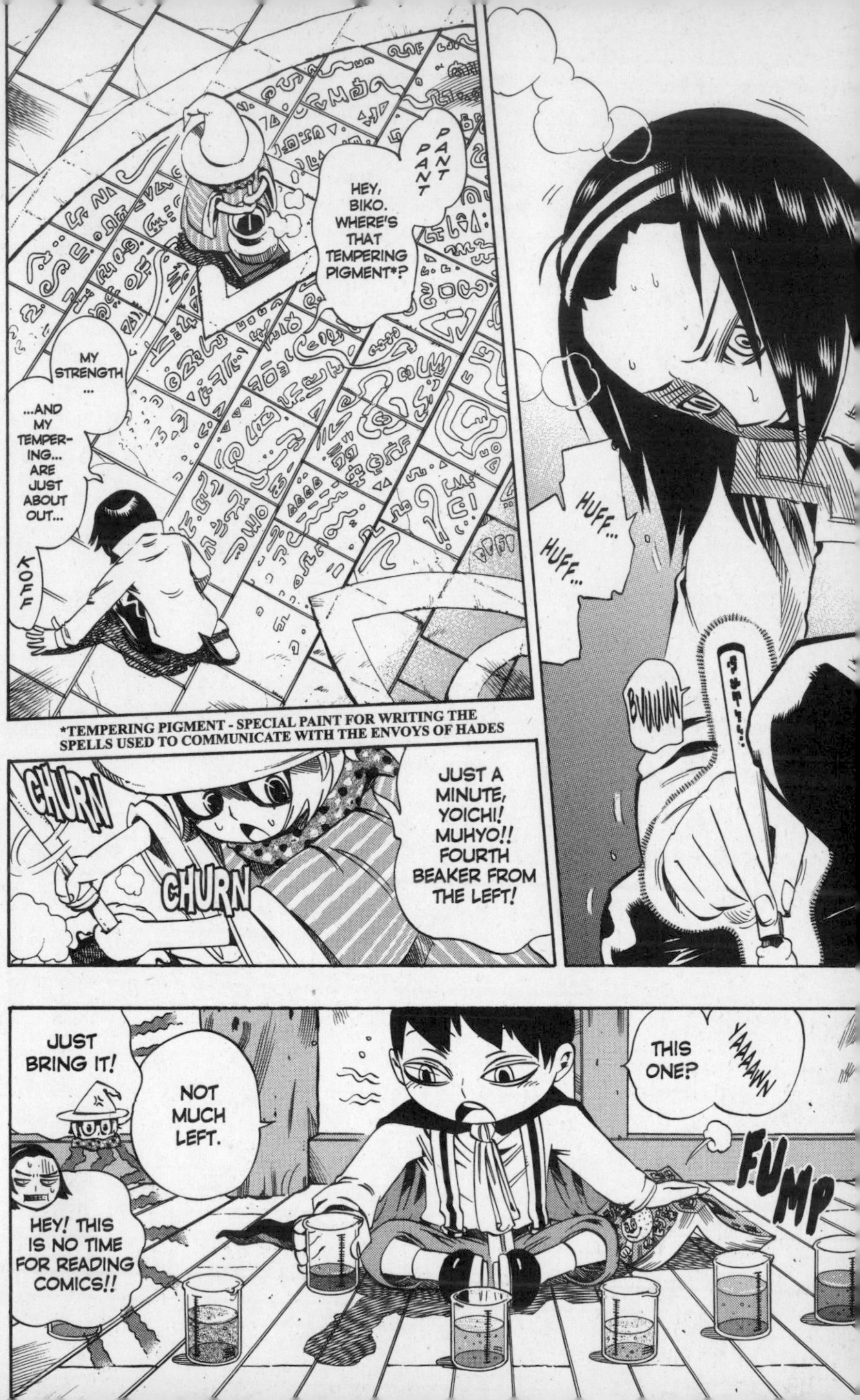
HUFF...
HUFF...
BUUUUN
PANT PANT PANT
HEY, BIKO. WHERE'S THAT TEMPERING PIGMENT*?
MY STRENGTH...
...AND MY TEMPERING... ARE JUST ABOUT OUT...
KOFF
*TEMPERING PIGMENT - SPECIAL PAINT FOR WRITING THE SPELLS USED TO COMMUNICATE WITH THE ENVOYS OF HADES
JUST A MINUTE, YOICHI! MUHYO!! FOURTH BEAKER FROM THE LEFT!
CHURN
CHURN
THIS ONE?
YAAAAWN
FUMP
NOT MUCH LEFT.
JUST BRING IT!
HEY! THIS IS NO TIME FOR READING COMICS!!

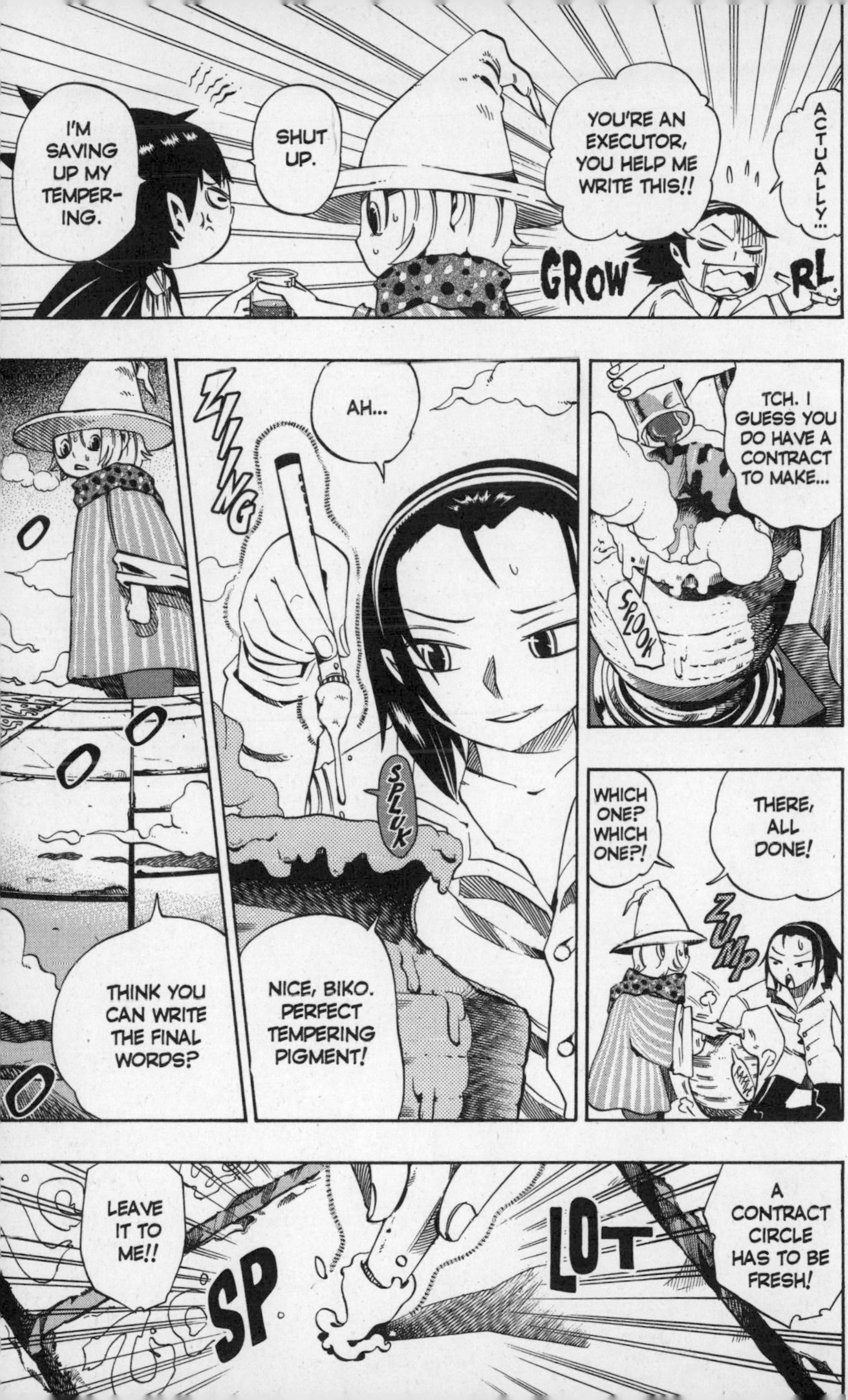
ACTUALLY...
YOU'RE AN EXECUTOR, YOU HELP ME WRITE THIS!!
GROWRL
SHUT UP.
I'M SAVING UP MY TEMPER-ING.
TCH. I GUESS YOU DO HAVE A CONTRACT TO MAKE...
SPLOOK
THERE, ALL DONE!
WHICH ONE? WHICH ONE?!
ZUMP
ZIIING
AH...
SPLUK
NICE, BIKO. PERFECT TEMPERING PIGMENT!
THINK YOU CAN WRITE THE FINAL WORDS?
A CONTRACT CIRCLE HAS TO BE FRESH!
SPLOT
LEAVE IT TO ME!!

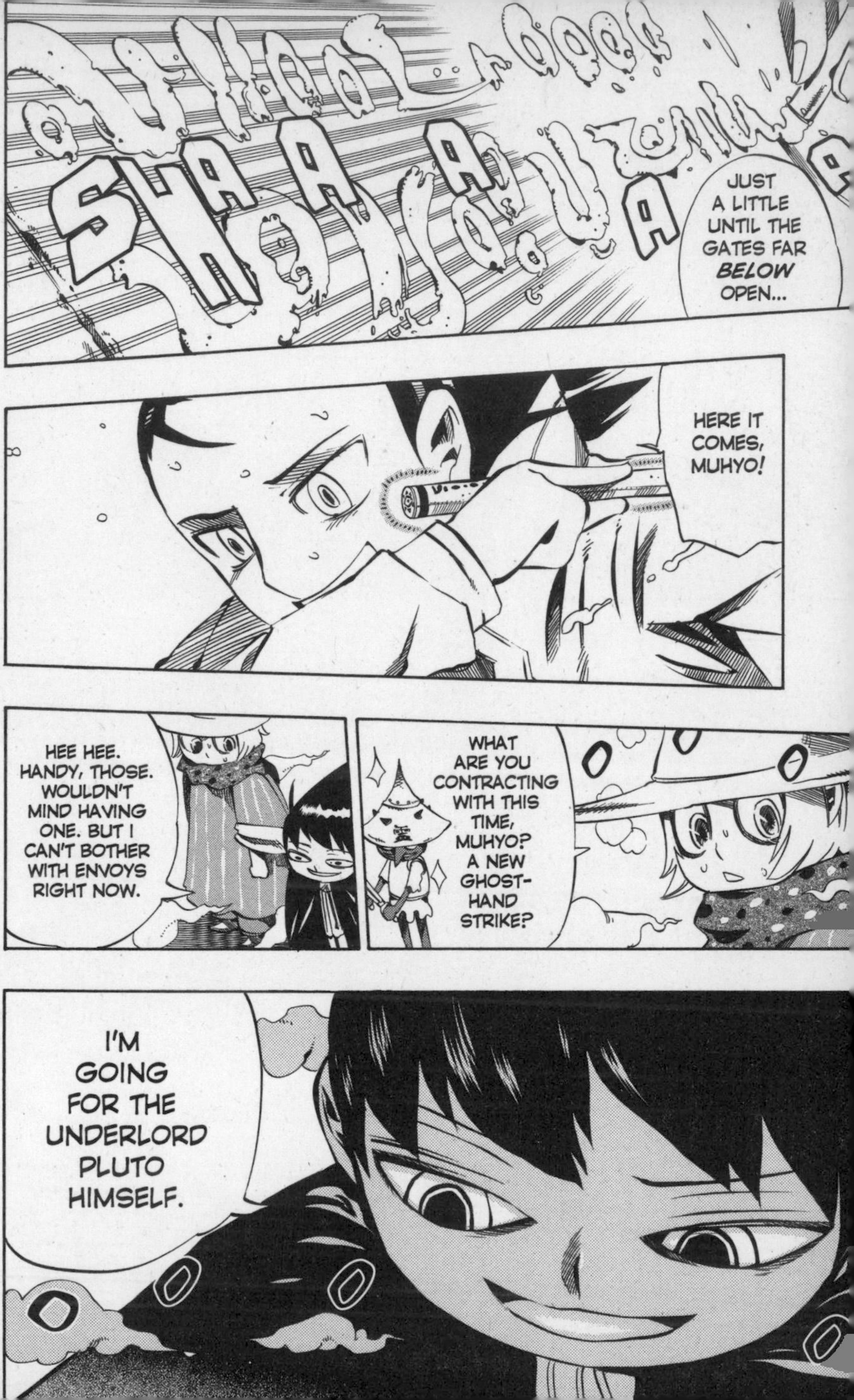
SHAAA
JUST A LITTLE UNTIL THE GATES FAR *BELOW* OPEN...
HERE IT COMES, MUHYO!
WHAT ARE YOU CONTRACTING WITH THIS TIME, MUHYO? A NEW GHOST-HAND STRIKE?
HEE HEE. HANDY, THOSE. WOULDN'T MIND HAVING ONE. BUT I CAN'T BOTHER WITH ENVOYS RIGHT NOW.
I'M GOING FOR THE UNDERLORD PLUTO HIMSELF.

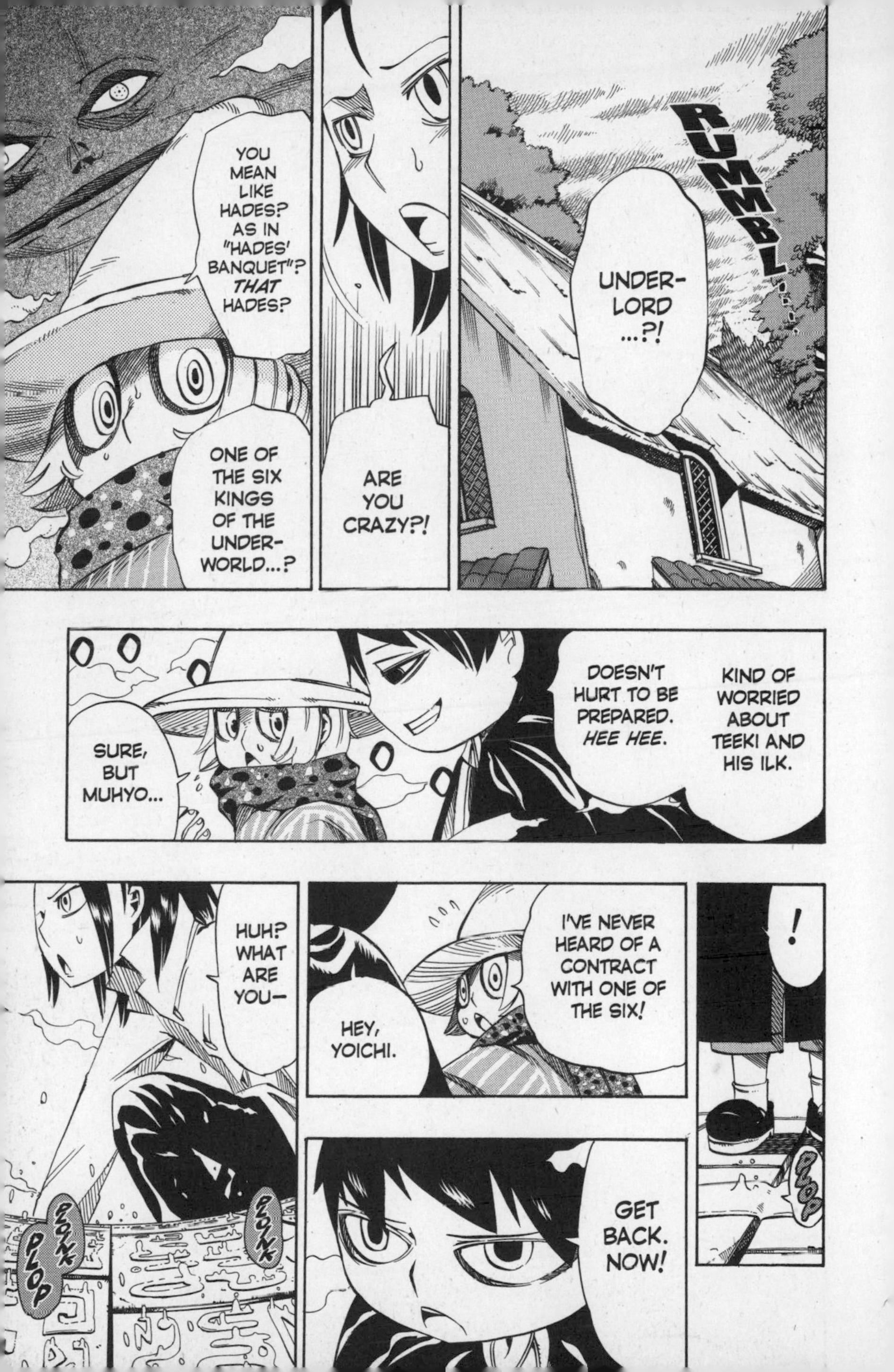
RUMBL...
UNDER-LORD ...?!
ARE YOU CRAZY?!
YOU MEAN LIKE HADES? AS IN "HADES' BANQUET"? *THAT* HADES?
ONE OF THE SIX KINGS OF THE UNDER-WORLD...?
KIND OF WORRIED ABOUT TEEKI AND HIS ILK.
DOESN'T HURT TO BE PREPARED. *HEE HEE.*
SURE, BUT MUHYO...
!
PLOP
I'VE NEVER HEARD OF A CONTRACT WITH ONE OF THE SIX!
HEY, YOICHI.
GET BACK. NOW!
HUH? WHAT ARE YOU—
PLONK
PLONK
PLOP

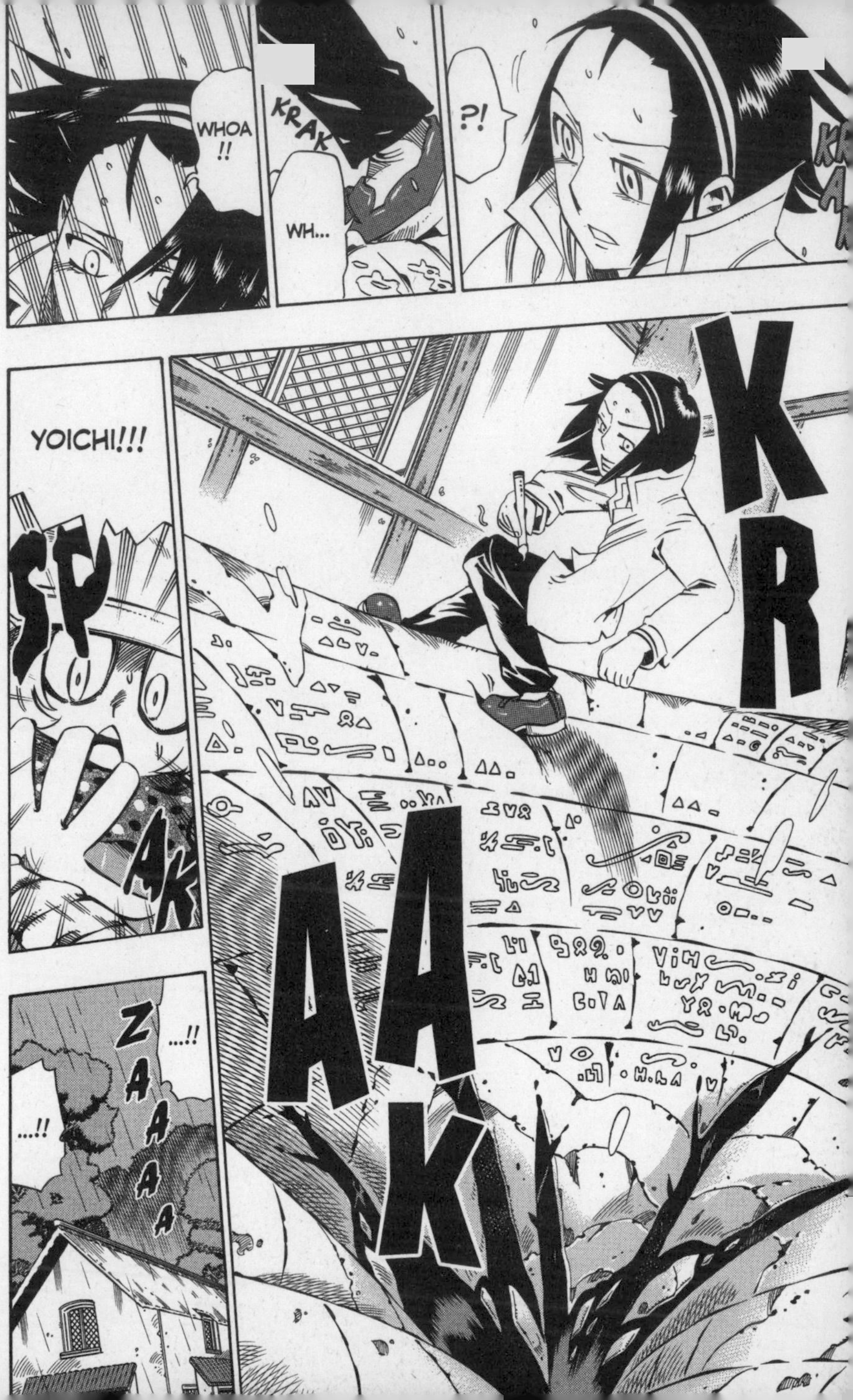
?!
KRAK
WH...
WHOA !!
KRAAK
YOICHI!!!
ZAAAAA
...!!
...!!

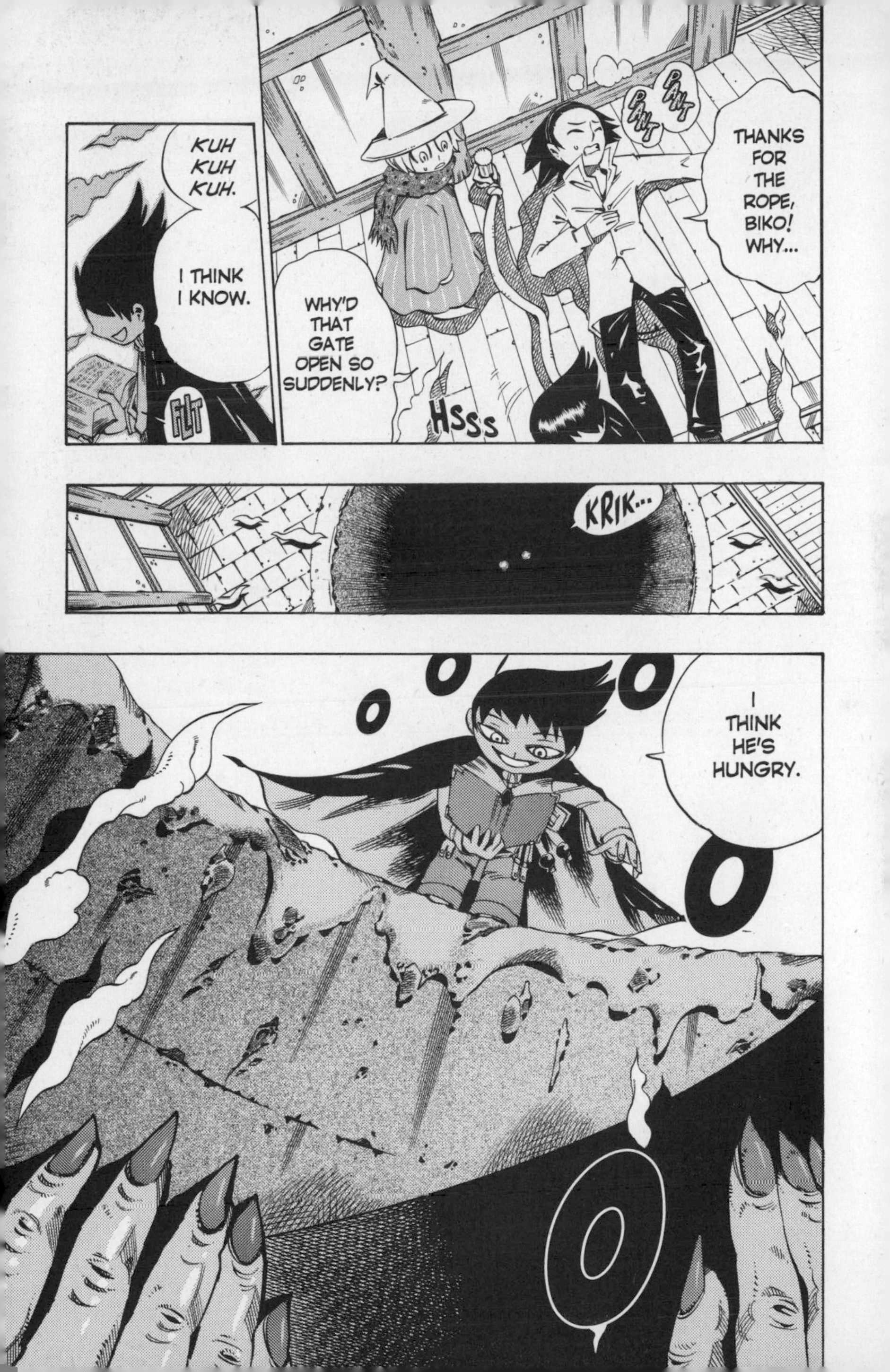
PANT PANT
THANKS FOR THE ROPE, BIKO! WHY...
WHY'D THAT GATE OPEN SO SUDDENLY?
HSSS
KUH KUH KUH.
I THINK I KNOW.
FLIT
KRIK...
I THINK HE'S HUNGRY.

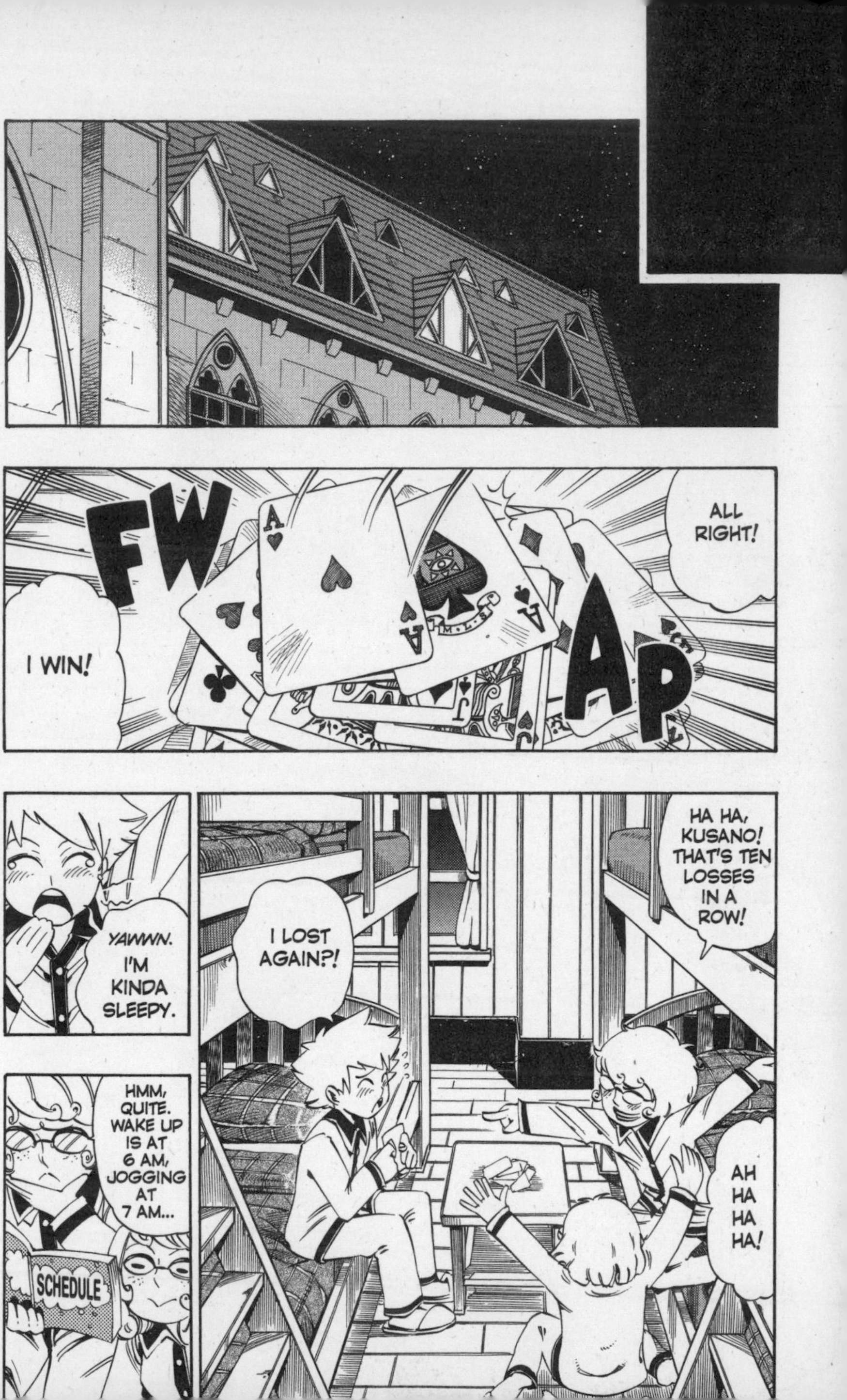
ALL RIGHT!
FWAP
I WIN!
HA HA, KUSANO! THAT'S TEN LOSSES IN A ROW!
I LOST AGAIN?!
AH HA HA HA!
YAWWN. I'M KINDA SLEEPY.
HMM, QUITE. WAKE UP IS AT 6 AM, JOGGING AT 7 AM...
SCHEDULE

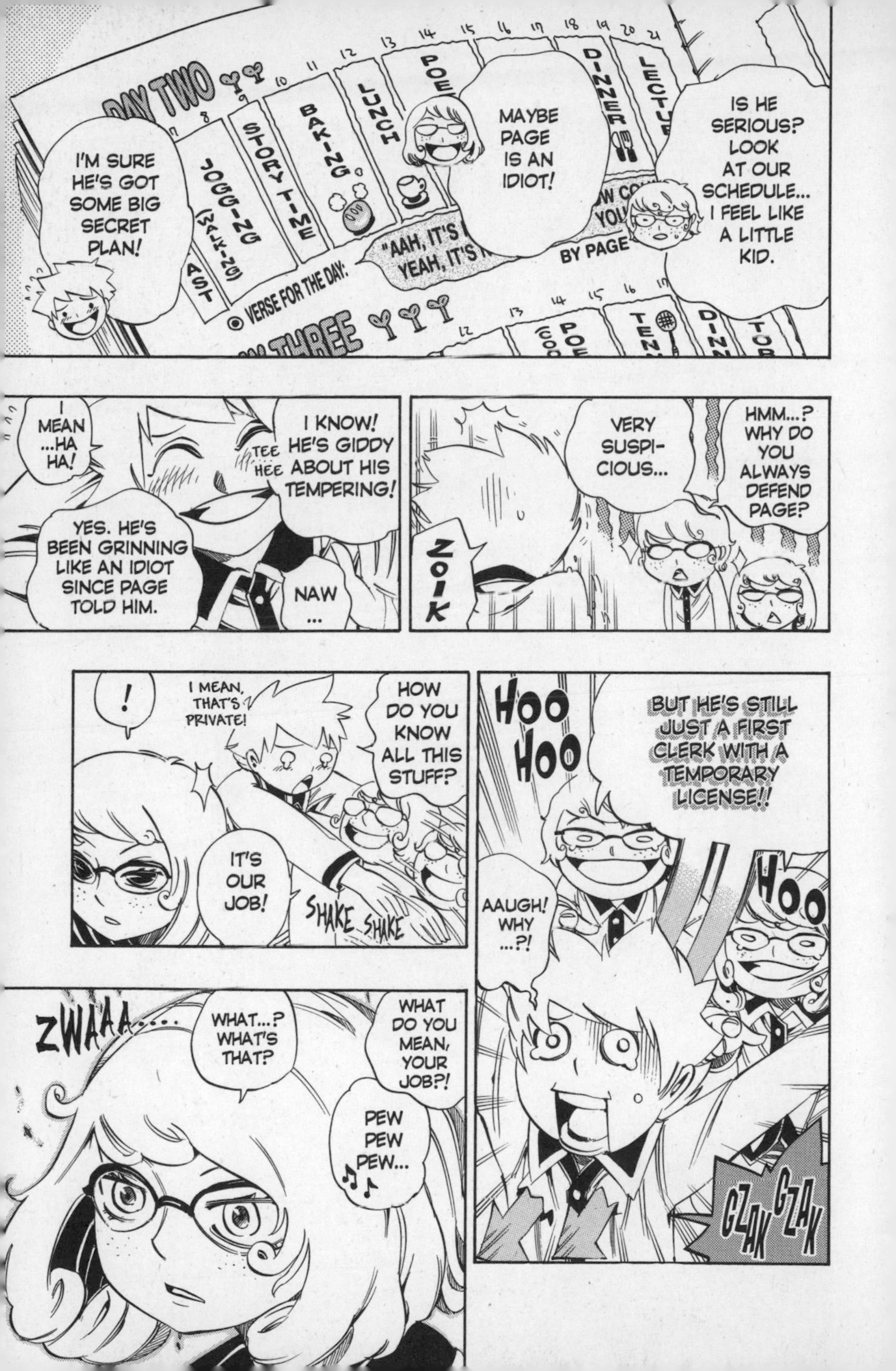
IS HE SERIOUS? LOOK AT OUR SCHEDULE... I FEEL LIKE A LITTLE KID.
DINNER
BY PAGE
MAYBE PAGE IS AN IDIOT!
LUNCH
BAKING
STORY TIME
JOGGING (WALKING)
DAY TWO
VERSE FOR THE DAY:
I'M SURE HE'S GOT SOME BIG SECRET PLAN!
HMM...? WHY DO YOU ALWAYS DEFEND PAGE?
VERY SUSPICIOUS...
ZOIK
I KNOW! HE'S GIDDY ABOUT HIS TEMPERING!
TEE HEE
I MEAN ...HA HA!
YES. HE'S BEEN GRINNING LIKE AN IDIOT SINCE PAGE TOLD HIM.
NAW ...
BUT HE'S STILL JUST A FIRST CLERK WITH A TEMPORARY LICENSE!!
HOO HOO
HOO
AAUGH! WHY ...?!
GZAK GZAK
HOW DO YOU KNOW ALL THIS STUFF?
I MEAN, THAT'S PRIVATE!
!
IT'S OUR JOB!
SHAKE SHAKE
WHAT DO YOU MEAN, YOUR JOB?!
WHAT...? WHAT'S THAT?
PEW PEW PEW...
ZWAAA....

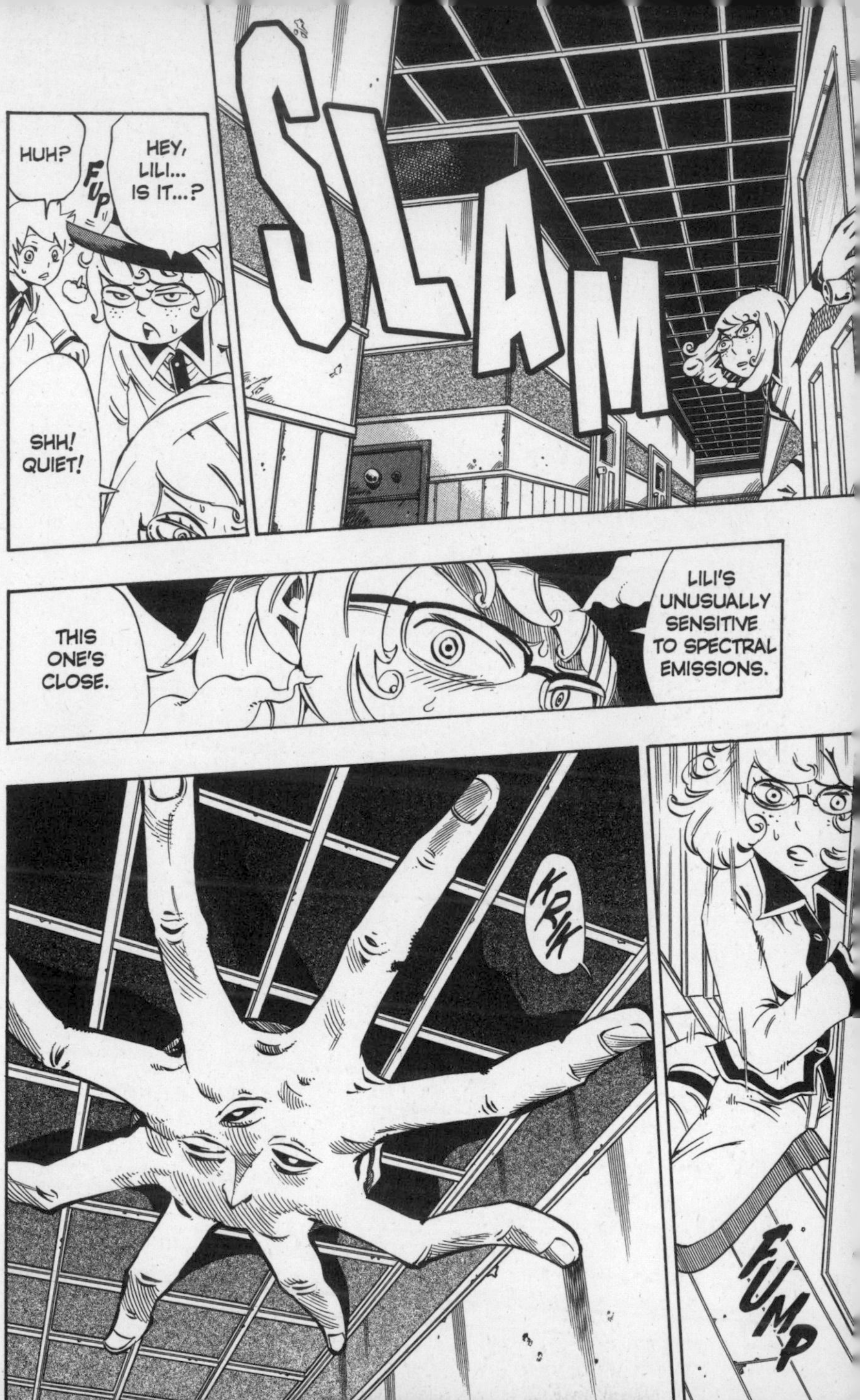
SLAM
HEY, LILI... IS IT...?
FUP
HUH?
SHH! QUIET!
LILI'S UNUSUALLY SENSITIVE TO SPECTRAL EMISSIONS.
THIS ONE'S CLOSE.
FUMP
KRIK

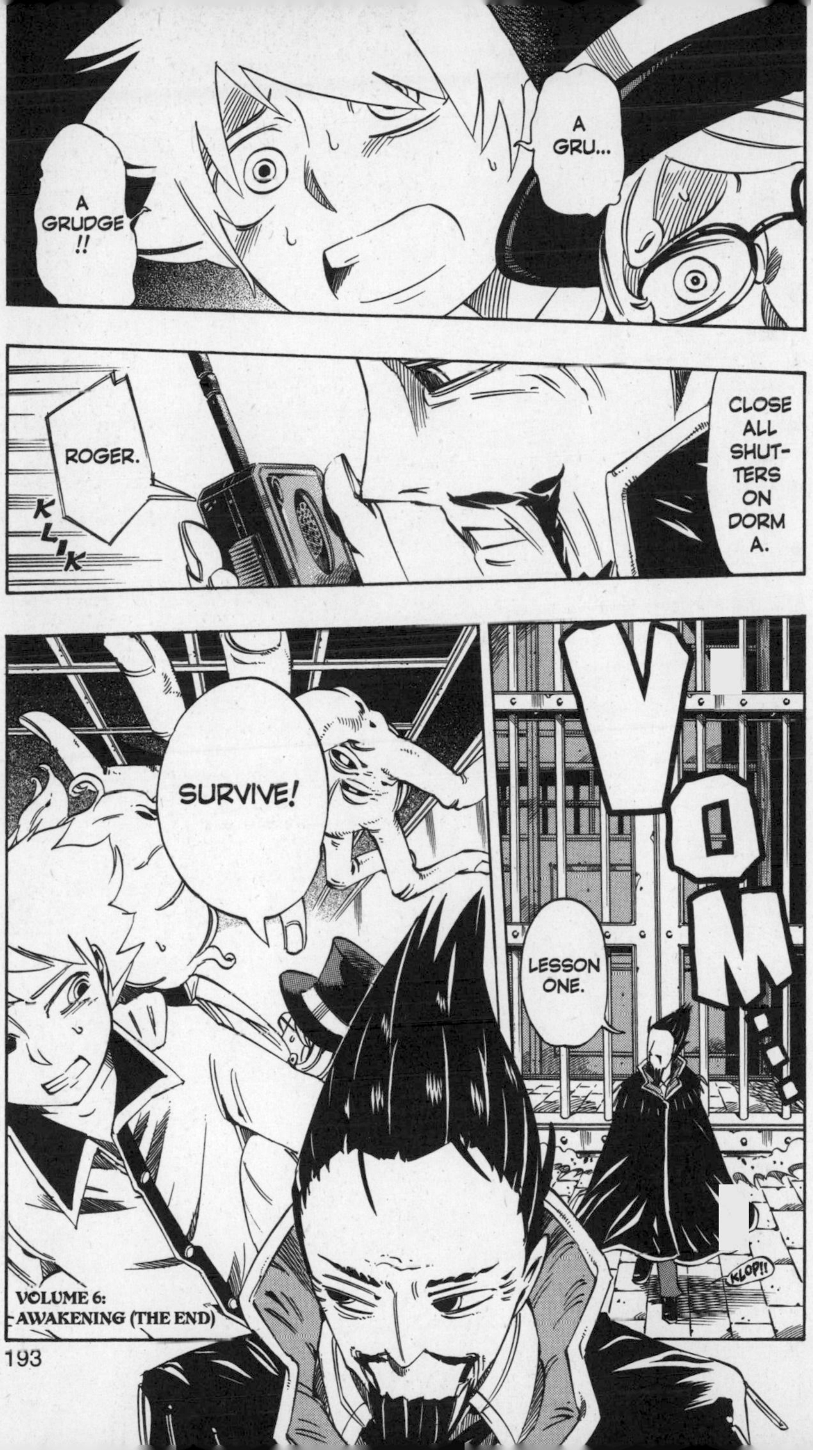
A GRU...
A GRUDGE !!
CLOSE ALL SHUTTERS ON DORM A.
ROGER.
KLIK
VOM...
LESSON ONE.
KLOP!!
SURVIVE!
VOLUME 6: AWAKENING (THE END)

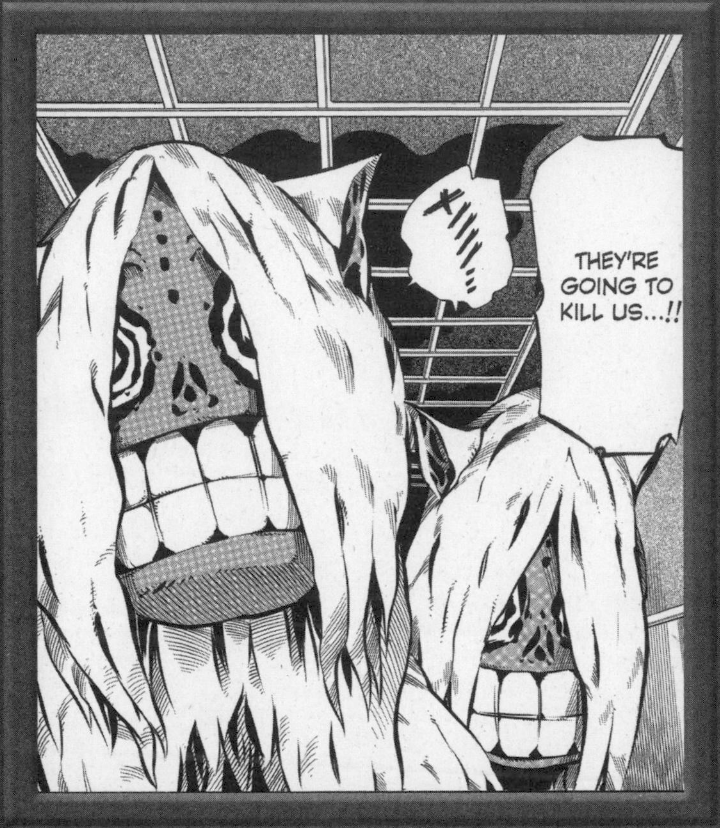
THEY'RE GOING TO KILL US...!!

In The Next Volume...

Roji and his classmates face all kinds of challenges at Page's testing camp...but it looks like some of the horrors are real!

Available August 2008!

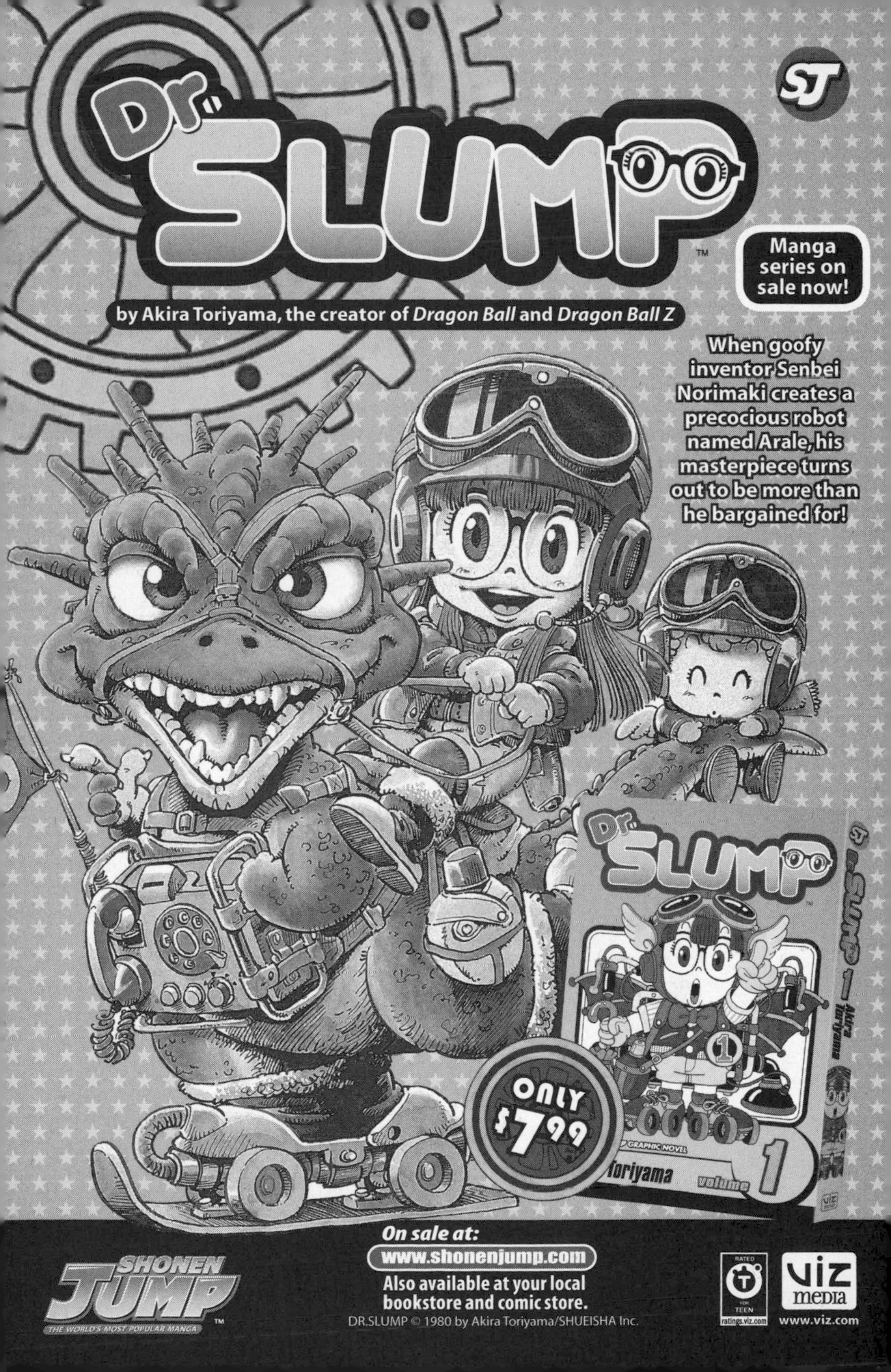
SJ
Dr. SLUMP™
Manga series on sale now!
by Akira Toriyama, the creator of *Dragon Ball* and *Dragon Ball Z*
When goofy inventor Senbei Norimaki creates a precocious robot named Arale, his masterpiece turns out to be more than he bargained for!
Dr. SLUMP
GRAPHIC NOVEL
Toriyama
volume 1
ONLY $7.99
On sale at:
www.shonenjump.com
Also available at your local bookstore and comic store.
DR.SLUMP © 1980 by Akira Toriyama/SHUEISHA Inc.
SHONEN JUMP™
THE WORLD'S MOST POPULAR MANGA
RATED T FOR TEEN
ratings.viz.com
VIZ media
www.viz.com

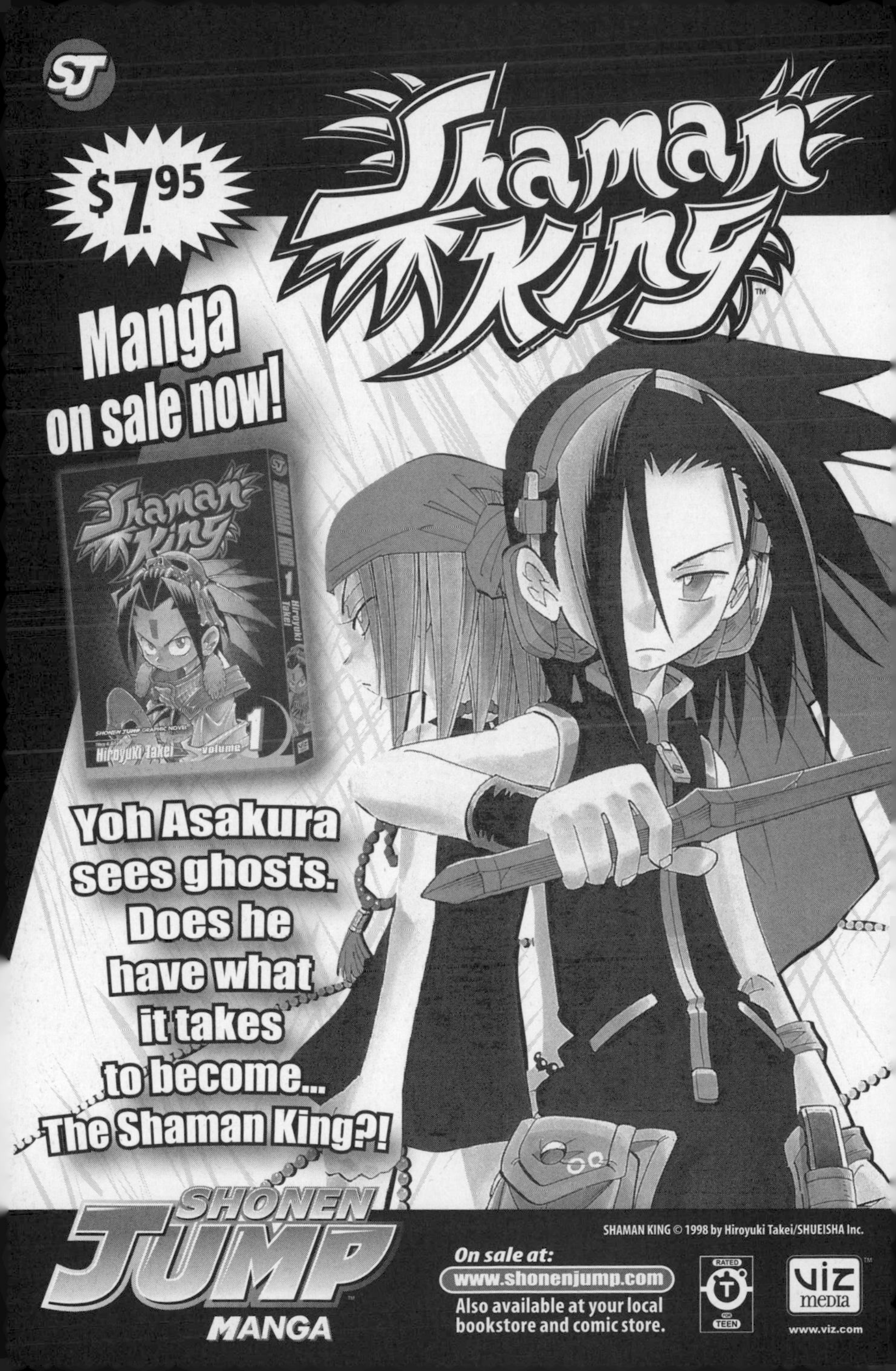
SJ
$7.95
Shaman King™
Manga on sale now!
Shaman King
SHONEN JUMP GRAPHIC NOVEL
Hiroyuki Takei
volume 1
Yoh Asakura sees ghosts. Does he have what it takes to become... The Shaman King?!
SHONEN JUMP MANGA
SHAMAN KING © 1998 by Hiroyuki Takei/SHUEISHA Inc.
On sale at:
www.shonenjump.com
Also available at your local bookstore and comic store.
RATED T FOR TEEN
VIZ media
www.viz.com

Tell us what you think about SHONEN JUMP manga!

Our survey is now available online.
Go to: www.SHONENJUMP.com/mangasurvey

Help us make our product offering better!